PRAISE FOR *THE WORLD TURNED UPSIDE DOWN*

"With ferocious courage, Melanie Phillips challenges a series of myths and irrationalities that have achieved canonical status in the contemporary world. If civilization depends on the ability to give dissenting voices a hearing, then *The World Turned Upside Down* may well be one of the most important tests of Western civilization in our time."

—Chief Rabbi Lord Sacks

"Melanie Phillips has written a fascinating book that is both urgent and important, provocative and deep. It's almost a guide of the perplexed for our time."

—William Kristol, Editor, *The Weekly Standard*

"One is disturbed each day by verifiably untrue statements touted as incontrovertible facts about hot-button issues. With cold, perceptive, exhaustive and persistent passion, Melanie Phillips dissects the phenomenon among disparate movements, to reach disturbing but compelling conclusions about the erosion of modern liberal society by ideologies whose surprising interconnections are meticulously identified. One can only hope that her book will penetrate the information cocoon into which many of our intelligentsia have sealed themselves."

—Richard S. Lindzen, Alfred P. Sloan Professor of
 Meteorology, MIT

"A trenchant sequel to George Orwell's *Politics and the English Language*. Melanie Phillips courageously flushes out today's equivalents of Orwell's targets—those who with indignant self-righteousness suppress free debate and liberty itself."

—R. James Woolsey, former Director of Central Intelligence
 (1993–1995)

"Her book is an immensely accomplished piece of writing. How the West can be got out of the hole she has described it as being in will, one hopes, form the subject of its sequel."

—David Conway, The Jewish Chronicle Online

"*The World Turned Upside Down* is a courageous exposé of many of the myths and fallacies which are being imposed on us and which our society has absorbed....This cri de coeur is a stunning and thought-provoking book that should be read by all who seek to understand the sources of the malaise of this generation in Western society."

—Isi Leibler, The Jerusalem Post Online

"Ms. Phillips lives up to her reputation for tackling political and social issues in this attempt to create an overarching thesis for why we have seen such absurdities as climate change fraud, political correctness run amok, unbalanced portrayals bordering on propaganda regarding Islam and Israel, and the war in Iraq. This is a challenge that Phillips meets head-on and masters."

—Ed Lasky, *American Thinker*

"Phillips has done her part in sounding the alarm, detailing the war we are in, and highlighting the many battlefronts this war is waging on. She has done her service admirably. It is hoped that readers of this important book will now do theirs."

—Bill Muehlenberg, CultureWatch

"As far as any writer can be, she is at the forefront of the battle for good, and in writing this book she has made a powerful contribution to that battle. By helping make sense of where things have gone wrong, she takes the reader a significant step closer to helping us back to the correct path."

—Chas Newkey-Burden, OyVaGoy.com

"Agree or disagree, Ms. Phillips argues her case in strong, vital prose with intensity and high intelligence. She deserves a wide and respectful hearing."

—John R. Coyne Jr., *The Washington Times*

"... Phillips's book shines with her intellectual integrity."

—Mark Silinksy, *Middle East Quarterly*

"Phillips is the inheritor of an identifiable and admirable tradition of robust writing on the broad right of politics—both her approach and her conclusions would be embraced, by example, by William F. Buckley Jr., who said (using "liberals" in the American sense) that 'liberals claim to want to give a hearing to other views, but then are shocked and offended to discover that there are other views.' That is precisely the problem with Britain's cultural discourse today, and it is precisely what Phillips skewers so gratifyingly and so well."

—Alex Deane, CityAM.com

"*The World Turned Upside Down: The Global Battle Over God, Truth, and Power* will appeal both to religious and political science libraries, offering keys to understanding conspiracy theories, cults, and the loss of religious belief in the West. Ideology and prejudice have replaced spirituality—and this book ties political trends and world encounters with the falsehoods and propaganda that cause instability in the West."

—Midwest Book Review

THE WORLD TURNED UPSIDE DOWN

THE GLOBAL BATTLE OVER GOD, TRUTH, AND POWER

MELANIE PHILLIPS

ENCOUNTER BOOKS
NEW YORK · LONDON

First American edition published in 2010 by Encounter Books,
an activity of Encounter for Culture and Education, Inc.,
a nonprofit, tax exempt corporation.

Encounter Books website address: www.encounterbooks.com

Manufactured in the United States and printed on
acid-free paper. The paper used in this publication meets
the minimum requirements of ANSI/NISO Z39.48-1992
(R 1997) (*Permanence of Paper*).

PAPERBACK EDITION ISBN 978-1-59403-574-6

THE LIBRARY OF CONGRESS HAS CATALOGUED THE
HARDCOVER EDITION AS FOLLOWS:

Phillips, Melanie, 1951–
The world turned upside down : the global battle over god, truth, and power /
by Melanie Phillips.
     p.   cm.
Includes bibliographical references and index.
ISBN-13: 978-1-59403-375-9 (hc : alk. paper)
ISBN-10: 1-59403-375-7 (hc : alk. paper)
1. Religion and state. 2. Religion and politics. I. Title.
BL65.S8P45   2010
201.72—dc22
2009040614

10 9 8 7 6 5 4 3 2 1

For Maya Mabel and Libby Sarah,
in the hope that they inherit a more rational world.

CONTENTS

FOREWORD
DAVID MAMET

Almost all Victorian novels feature the stock Jew. But what do the British know of the Jews? Shylock was written when Britain was *Judenrein*, and Shakespeare no more met a Venetian Jew than he had met a Moor. But the prejudice was there, and the stock Jew was as expected a set piece in their literature (then and now) as the amusing "colored" man or woman was in American cinema up to and through the 1960s. See Dickens's Fagin and Trollope's Mr. Kneefit, Melmotte, et cetera. Even the noted Jews of George Eliot's *Daniel Deronda* are cut-and-paste figures drawn, if in good will, in stunning ignorance. The stock Jew exists still today not only in British drama and popular fiction, but in the journalism proffered daily as "news."

***

The British, historically, find the Arabs just wonderful. See *The Talisman*, Sir Walter Scott's novel of King Richard and Saladin, and more recently, *Seven Pillars of Wisdom*, by T. E. Lawrence, which is a paean (indeed a convincing and moving one) to the Bedouin—and, coincidentally, to sadomasochism.

An astute observer might detect this love of self-flagellation in Britain's postwar cultural suicide. Their Archbishop of Canterbury, for instance, proclaimed in 2008 that it was probably inevitable that Britain would one day accept for all its citizens some measure of Sharia law. So much for the Magna Carta.

In a fit of absentmindedness, our British cousins helped create the Jewish State. They thought, no doubt, that it would serve as a good counterbalance to the French in Syria after the League of Nations finished carving the roast.

xi

But, lo, the Jewish State wanted not vassaldom but self-determination and accepted at face value President Wilson's insistence at Versailles on universal self-determination. The continued exercise of this self-determination by the sovereign State of Israel has of late been an irritation to those in Britain and throughout the West who are piqued, as usual, at the necessity of moral choice.

The choice here is between defending Western civilization and defaulting into some inchoate one-worldism that a more honest if less pleasant assessment would name "Islamic theocracy." The existence of Israel makes the choice clear, so the affronted liberal West turns against Israel and, so, against the Jews, returning us to our handy and historic function as Designated Criminal.

* * *

Much has been made in the supposedly neutral Western press of the disproportionate representation of Jews among the neoconservatives. The media, with this critique, are firing off a "preemptive challenge" to the neocons. Unfortunately, this is par for the course: the Jews, now as in the past, and always, are liable to be accused of split allegiance, that is, of treason.

It is not only in John 8 or in the *Protocols of the Elders of Zion* that Jews are indicted per se, but also in forums and publications worldwide and constantly, the "Israel Lobby" handily replacing the "worldwide Jewish conspiracy" as the purportedly more rational term.

But it is not more rational. And the fools who boycotted the Toronto Film Festival for showing Israeli films are no more sane and no less vicious (although they are, at this writing, less physical) than were the thugs of Simon de Montfort who expelled the Jews from Leicester in 1231, or those of Klaus Barbie in 1944.

Islamic fascists have both invited and accepted the aid rendered them in the West by seemingly fair-minded rationalists, whose acquiescent, suggestible, and intellectually lazy approach the Islamists have put to good use—as support (passive if not active) for an indictment of their most vulnerable neighbors. The Obama administration insists upon its right not to know that various acts of terror have been perpetrated by Islamic Fascists in the name of Jihad. The Western press refuses to notice the omission.

This is called codependence. It seduces passive participants into rejecting reason and commits them to continuation of the farce. A dedication to irrationality grows more difficult to renounce with each reiteration of unreason, for the deluded must increasingly face the shame not only of his folly but of the misery it begets. As the tally grows, the likelihood of self-correction diminishes; and the committed one-worlder, now chained to his oars, must insulate himself against both reality and countervailing opinion. He does so handily by demonizing those trying to restore him to sanity.

Who is speaking up?

Melanie Phillips in her book *The World Turned Upside Down.*

The title comes from a seventeenth-century British ballad: "… if Summer were Spring and the other way round, then all the World would be upside down."

Ms. Phillips points out that the world *is* upside down.

The West indicts the archfiend Israel (population six million) for terrorizing a billion Arabs, and condemns Big Brother America for somehow being (magically) the root cause all "global unrest" (unrest previously known as "the human condition"). Capitalism is reviled generally, in the so-called news as well as in a vast amount of entertainment; and the Bible, the West's guidebook through two thousand years of increasing prosperity, is derided as irrelevant, ludicrous, exploitative, or "noninclusive" (as if every society in history has not either inherited or manufactured its own religion, however it named this new thing).

Well, the New Religion, as Ms. Phillips teaches, is "Secular Humanism," which, although it lacks logically consistent precepts, does contain innumerable sanctions and taboos. Of these latter, the most observed is loud and clear: do not tell the truth.

Ms. Phillips has broken the rules and is doubtless experiencing the sanctions. We can support her by buying, and ourselves by reading, her book.

PREFACE

This book arose from a sense of perplexity and cultural disorientation. It appears to me that much of public discourse has departed sharply from reality. Self-evident common sense appears to have been turned on its head. Reality seems to have been recast, with fantasies recalibrated as facts while demonstrable truths are dismissed as a matter of opinion at best, or as evidence of some sinister "right-wing" plot. This isn't just a question of disagreement over issues or policies. Those who dissent are vilified as beyond the pale, and many fear speaking up. The phenomenon has affected not just the political sphere, where ideology often crowds out facts, for even parts of the scientific domain have given in to irrationality. Over a diverse range of issues, such as the war in Iraq, Israel and the Palestinians, manmade global warming and Darwinism—not to mention all the "phobias" and "isms" such as homophobia, racism and sexism—no debate is possible because there is to be no dissent from positions that are indisputably true and right.

Except that they are not. The planet is supposedly about to fry or drown and succumb to epidemic famine and disease because of manmade global warming—but all the evidence suggests that there is nothing untoward about the climate at all, let alone that mankind is responsible for an imminent catastrophe. We are told repeatedly that we were "taken to war in Iraq on a lie"—but a glance at what was actually said at the time by President George W. Bush and Prime Minister Tony Blair shows that this was not so. As for Israel, its representation as the regional aggressor is both historically and currently false, while the obsessive campaign of demonization mounted against it looks positively unhinged. Nearer to home, self-designated "victim groups" have turned right and wrong, victim and aggressor inside out. Their "right" not to be insulted or discriminated against in any way has become the basis for discrimination and injustice against the representatives of majority values.

It is as if one has wandered onto the set of a Bunuel movie scripted by Kafka. Nothing is really as it is said to be. Society seems to be in the grip of a mass derangement. The sense that the world has slipped off the axis of reason has been greatly exacerbated by the fact that so many prominent people—professors of this and research directors of that, chief scientists and Nobel Peace Prize winners and fellows of the Royal Society, judges and diplomats, intelligence agents who suddenly materialized from the shadows and started firing off in public—have been saying all these strange and disturbing things. How could they all be wrong? Am I perhaps wrong? How is anyone to work out who is right in such a babble of "experts" and with so much conflicting information?

But if I have been perplexed, so it seems are many others who feel exactly the same way on some if not all of these issues. Indeed, it has become apparent that there is deep division on these matters— not on conventional "left-wing" versus "right-wing" lines, but between ordinary people on the one hand and the intelligentsia on the other. And the striking thing is that, while the ordinary people appear to be connected to reality and able to tell fact from fantasy and right from wrong, it is the intelligentsia—supposedly the custodians of reason—who seem to be taking the most irrational, prejudiced and intolerant positions, clothed nevertheless in the most high-minded concerns of "progressive" politics. Yet it has also become clear that within the intelligentsia there are people who are bucking the loudly proclaimed "consensus" on some if not all of these issues, but whose voices have been all but stifled.

I am a journalist, not a scientist or a military strategist. So in trying to work my way through these minefields, I merely did what I was always taught to do: go where the evidence leads. As the perplexing claims mounted, I looked again at what was already known, at the internal logic of each assertion, at all the available supporting facts, at the robustness and intellectual rigor of the arguments on both sides. And to me it seemed that all the evidence pointed to a widespread dislocation between certain commonly accepted positions and reality. So then I started to look more carefully at whether these were all random issues or connected in some way, and how this apparent mass departure from rationality might have come about. The explanations I arrived at were startling, and they led to this book.

But am I right? I readily accept that I may be mistaken, and I am always open to reasoned evidence that challenges what I think. All I can do is offer my own take on what is knowable and invite readers to form their own conclusions. For those who may think I must have a prior agenda, however, let me attempt to disabuse them. I am not a supporter of any political party, movement or ideology. I am not a covert creationist, a secret Mossad agent or in the pay of Big Oil. I am an agnostic although traditionally minded Jew. I have a deep concern for the security and survival of the Jewish people and for the security and survival of Western civilization, which I happen to believe are symbiotically connected. Beyond that, I am a journalist who believes in telling truth to power and following the evidence. What I have concluded is that power has now hijacked truth and made it subservient to its own ends. The result is a world turned upside down.

This book should be read as a developing argument, in which I try to explain how I think we have arrived at such a pass. In the first few chapters, I look at the evidence of mass irrationality over a wide range of issues. Let me stress that I am not trying to persuade people to agree with the personal view I take on each of these matters—although it would be nice if they did. My aim is to make the case that there has been a departure from reason and logic because objectivity has been replaced in large measure by ideology.

The book sets out the extraordinary similarities between the attempt by the Western intelligentsia to impose secular ideologies such as materialism, environmentalism or scientism and the attempt to impose Islam upon the free world. Not only do all these ideologies display zero tolerance of dissent, but in enforcing what amounts to a secular Inquisition the Western world displays a modernized version of the medieval millenarian and apocalyptic movements—replicated also in the present-day Islamic jihad—which not only repudiated reason in the name of religion but led to tyranny, oppression, persecution and war.

A word in passing about secularism. To reassure those with overexcitable imaginations, let me emphasize that I am *not* suggesting that secular democracy should be replaced as a preferred form of governance by some kind of Judeo-Christian theocracy. Nor am I suggesting that those who have no religious faith are necessarily amoral social wreckers or mini Stalins in the making. But one does not have to be a religious believer to grasp that the core values of Western civilization are grounded in religion, and to be concerned that the erosion of religious observance therefore undermines those values and the "secular ideals" they reflect.

A word also about my treatment of the subject of Islam. I have used the word "Islamist" to denote those who wish to impose Islam upon unbelievers and to extinguish individual freedom and human rights among Muslims. There are, however, scholars who hold that Islam is an inherently coercive ideology and that therefore "Islamist" is a meaningless word that creates a false distinction. It is not my purpose here to enter that particular argument. I use the term "Islamist" not to make a theological point but to allow for the acknowledgment of those Muslims who support freedom and human rights and who threaten no one—and who are themselves principal victims of the jihad. I believe it is very important to acknowledge the existence of such Muslims who have a peaceable interpretation of their religion, just as it is very important not to sanitize and thus misrepresent the doctrines and history of Islam as a religion of conquest.

The book explores the remarkable links and correspondences between left-wing "progressives" and Islamists, environmentalists and fascists, militant atheists and fanatical religious believers. All are united by the common desire to bring about through human agency the perfection of the world, an agenda which history teaches us leads invariably—and paradoxically—to tyranny, terror and crimes against humanity. Remarkably, all happen to be united also by a common and fundamental hostility to the central precepts of Jewish religious belief or peoplehood, the deep animosity against which is a phenomenon demanding explanation on its own account. While I do not believe this common thread constitutes any kind of conspiracy, the fact that it is common to such a range of apparently disparate issues suggests it is around this startling cultural replicator that we should be looking for the deepest clues to the global retreat from reason.

I examine the historical ideas that have led us to where we are today, and attempt to explain how some of the most enlightened people living in the most enlightened era in the history of mankind have managed to depart so comprehensively from reality. In particular, I look very hard at today's governing assumption that religion and reason are on opposite sides, and reach some paradoxical conclusions about what "enlightenment" actually means.

I have consulted many people in the course of writing this book and am indebted to all of them for their time, patience and erudition. In particular I would like to thank Rabbi Harvey Belovski, Dr. David Berlinski, Professor David Conway, Canon Dr. Giles Fraser, Professor John Haldane, Professor Raphael Israeli, Professor Richard Landes, Professor John Lennox, Professor Paul Merkley, the Reverend Peter Mullen, Professor Robert Pinker, Professor David-Hillel Ruben, the Chief Rabbi Lord Sacks, Dr. Patrick Sookhdeo, Dr. Anne Stott and Professor Philip Stott for all their insights. Any mistakes are entirely my own. My thanks also to my son and daughter, Gabriel and Abigail, for their unflagging attempts to protect their mother from herself; and above all to my husband, Joshua, who is himself the epitome of rationality and for whose forbearance and support I remain deeply grateful.

London, December 2009

1

CULTS AND CONSPIRACIES
FROM DIANA TO OBAMA

The rock star Madonna is an icon of Western modernity. She is also the world's most famous proponent of "Kabbalah," a modern perversion of a branch of Jewish mysticism bearing that name. This pseudo-Kabbalah has been denounced by rabbinic authorities as a brainwashing cult that has absolutely nothing to do with Judaism and, indeed, stands in direct opposition to it, accused as it is of engaging in acts of extortion by threatening people with curses if they refuse to give it money and making ludicrous promises of physical health and wealth if they buy its publications.

Like punk rock, says Madonna, "Kabbalah" is a way of "thinking outside the box." But in fact, "thinking" is hardly the word to express any activity associated with it. Devotees wear a red thread around the wrist as protection against the evil eye; by meditating on "stem cells" or drinking "holy water," they are promised immortality of the body on the basis of a doctrine that teaches "Not to accept things as is" [sic].[1]

Accepting things that are demonstrably *not*, however, is by no means confined to rock stars. Both the late Princess Diana and Cherie Blair, the wife of the former British prime minister Tony Blair, reportedly believed in the transcendent properties of stones; Mrs. Blair commonly sported a crystal pendant around her neck to ward off harmful rays from computers and mobile phones.[2] Mrs.

Blair also reportedly consulted an octogenarian former market gardener named Jack Temple who ran a "healing center" from a barn next to his home in West Byfleet, Surrey. Temple told her that he was able to read her DNA by consulting rocks he kept in a room at the center and by swinging a pendulum over her body.

Shortly after the 1997 election, Mrs. Blair reportedly gave Mr. Temple a selection of small jars, each containing hair and toenail clippings obtained from both herself and the prime minister. Temple claimed that by "dowsing" the jars with his pendulum he was able to detect any signs of "poisons and blockages" in the first couple. The media reported: "It was not uncommon for her to fax several A4 pages of questions at a time to Temple so he could advise her which decisions should be taken immediately and which should be put off until the 'vibes' he was receiving from their hair and nail clippings were more positive."[3]

If anything defines the modern age in the West, it is surely the worship of reason. To be modern, we tell ourselves, is to be rational. Anything that doesn't carry the imprimatur of reason is deemed to be no more than dogma and mumbo-jumbo belonging to the unenlightened past. It is on this basis that science is held to have delivered a lethal blow to religion and given rise to a supposedly secular Western culture, which will have no truck with claims such as religious miracles or the existence of God. These are dismissed as the superstitious beliefs of a bygone primitive age of myth and bigotry.

Yet this central claim of the modern world is not borne out by its own behavior. Far from basking in an age of reason, Western society is characterized by a profound and widespread irrationality. While organized religion in many parts of the West is on the wane, with dwindling church attendance and a systematic erosion of Judeo-Christian principles by an intelligentsia for whom belief in God is evidence of deep stupidity or even insanity, Western society has filled the gap with a range of bizarre, irrational and premodern beliefs and behavior.

Madonna, Cherie Blair and Princess Diana represent the rise of what Chris Partridge has termed "occulture."[4] While most people remain rooted in solid reality, a growing number of supposedly super-rational twenty-first-century men and women now subscribe to a range of New Age cults, paganism, witchcraft and belief in psychic phenomena such as reincarnation, astrology and parapsychology.

What previously belonged to the province of the quack and the charlatan have become mainstream treatments and therapies, including faith healers, psychic mediums, astrologers, "angel thera-pists" and "aura photographers." "Wicca"—or witchcraft—and paganism constitute the fastest-growing religious category in Amer-ica, with between 500,000 and 5 million adherents. If "New Age spirituality" is included, the number reaches 20 million and growing.

In 1990 there were five thousand practicing British pagans; nearly a decade later, the number had risen to a hundred thousand.[5] Whereas paganism would once have been seen as inimical to religion, it is now viewed in Britain's multicultural nirvana as just another faith. So hospital authorities in Tayside, Scotland, for example, have agreed to allow pagans to practice meditation, healing rituals and spe-cial prayers in health service hospitals, with patients permitted to keep a small model of a pagan "healing goddess" on their bedside tables.[6] Britain's prison authorities are equally hospitable to the occult: under instructions issued to every prison governor, pagan "priests" are allowed to use wine and wands during ceremonies in jails. Inmates practicing paganism are allowed a hoodless robe, incense and a piece of religious jewelry among their personal posses-sions.[7] And a Pagan Police Association has been set up to represent officers who "worship nature and believe in many gods," with the Hertfordshire police force allowing officers eight days' pagan holidays per year, including Halloween and the summer solstice.[8]

Along with such beliefs has grown the use of mediums, psychics, séances, telepathy and other aspects of the paranormal. Undoubt-edly, for many people these practices amount to little more than playful whims or amusements rather than serious beliefs. Neverthe-less, thousands of cults combine irrational beliefs with sinister pro-grams to control people's minds and behavior, which have made inroads into the religious and medical worlds and the prison system. In America, there are an estimated 2,500 cults involving between 3 and 10 million people. Their techniques of mind control are many and various. They include food and sleep deprivation; trance induc-tion through hypnosis or prolonged rhythmical chanting; and "love bombing," where cult members are bombarded with conditional love, which is removed whenever there is a deviation from the dic-tates of the leader.

Such cults often promote bizarre theories about conspiracies by agents of the modern world or by extraterrestrial forces. These the-ories cross political divides, linking neofascist, New Age, Islamist and green groups. Millions of people—including many who wouldn't have anything to do with any cult—now appear only too eager to believe that the world is controlled by dark conspiracies of covert forces for which there is not one shred of evidence. Once, such theories would have been seen as indications of extreme eccen-tricity. Now, growing numbers of people treat them as legitimate subjects for debate, creating an infectious kind of public hysteria.

Examples of these conspiracy theories include the notion that AIDS was created in a CIA laboratory, that Princess Diana was mur-dered to prevent her from marrying a Muslim, and that the 9/11 attack on New York was orchestrated by the Bush administration, in some versions (particularly popular in the Muslim world) aided and abetted by the Israeli Mossad. These notions are all advanced in press articles or in television documentaries as hypotheses to be seriously entertained. The ninety-minute documentary *Loose Change*, which posits the 9/11 conspiracy theory, was shown on television in the United States and the UK, and was discussed as if it presented a rea-sonable hypothesis. Although the film was denounced in some quar-ters as risible, its thesis is believed by a significant number of people and has generated what is known as the "Truther" movement. According to opinion polls, more than a third of Americans suspect that federal officials either facilitated the 9/11 attacks or knew they were imminent but did nothing to stop them, so the government would have a pretext for going to war in the Middle East.[9]

Similarly, thousands of people apparently believe that Princess Diana was murdered at the hands of a conspiracy involving the Duke of Edinburgh, Prince Charles and MI5. The overwhelming evidence that she died because she was not wearing a seat belt when her drunken chauffeur crashed while speeding through a Paris tunnel did not prevent British public opinion from forcing a three-year investigation followed by a long-drawn-out inquest at enormous public expense—all to test out a conspiracy theory that belongs to the realm of fantasy.

On a steadily enlarging fringe, fevered discussions of UFOs, aliens and mind control veer into allegations of conspiracies by hidden elites in the Bilderberg Group of foreign affairs specialists or the Rothschild banking firm, heavily laden with antisemitic paranoia about the alleged sinister power of the Jews.

Books by David Icke, the former soccer player and TV sports presenter who has announced that he is "the son of God," are bestsellers advancing a mixture of New Age philosophy and apocalyptic conspiracy theory. In these, he argues that Britain will be devastated by tidal waves and earthquakes, and that the world is ruled by a secret group called the "Global Elite" or "Illuminati," which was responsible for the Holocaust, the Oklahoma City bombing and 9/11, and which he has linked to the iconic text of Jewish conspiracy theory, *The Protocols of the Elders of Zion*—despite the fact that this was a hoax fabricated by the tsarist secret police at the turn of the twentieth century. Icke has said he is guided by beings on "higher levels" to make such information available to the public.[10]

Meanwhile the forces in the U.S. citizens' militia movement that were indeed responsible for the Oklahoma City bombing are themselves fueled by similar paranoid conspiracy theories involving hidden elites, secret societies and international organizations and plots featuring everything from UFOs to gun control, Freemasonry to AIDS.

SUSPENSION OF POLITICAL JUDGMENT

The postreligious Western world is struggling to adjust to a profound loss of moral and philosophical moorings. A consequence of this radical discombobulation is widespread moral, emotional and intellectual chaos, resulting in shattered and lonely lives, emotional incontinence and gullibility to fraud and charlatanry. There is an increasing tendency to live in a fantasy world where irrational beliefs in myths are thought to restore order to chaotic lives, and where psychological projection creates the comforting illusion of control.

In the Western world, there have been two notable instances of this mythmaking in recent years. The first was the fantasy woven around the personality of the late Princess Diana, and the extraordinary passions unleashed by her untimely demise in the Alma tunnel in Paris. It was only with the death of the "People's Princess" that the extent of Britain's transformation—from a country of reason, intelligence, stoicism, self-restraint and responsibility into a land of credulousness, sentimentality, emotional excess, irresponsibility and self-obsession—became shatteringly apparent.

Princess Diana was an icon of the new Britain because she embodied the latter characteristics. In a country where epidemic family breakdown and mass fatherlessness testified to a society oblivious to the lethal downside of its culture of instant gratification, Princess Diana—herself the product of a family broken by divorce, a pattern she then replicated in her own marriage breakdown—became a symbol of dysfunctionality redeemed. Her bulimia and the story of her apparent unhappiness with a purportedly cold and unfaithful husband and an unfeeling and callous royal family confirmed her as the national emblem of victimhood. But she was also beautiful and rich, a fashion icon and a future Queen of England. And in her reported stand against the supposedly remote, rigid and repressed royals, she stood for "real" values such as love and kindness. So she became a mythic personality onto whom the public projected the fantasy that she was just like them in the chaos of her personal life but had transcended it all to become a near-sainted figure, laying her hands upon AIDS sufferers or campaigning emotionally against land mines.

It was all rubbish, of course. No one actually *knew* what she was really like; people just thought they did. Only later did her deeply disturbed, manipulative and selfish behavior become apparent. But since people were unable to distinguish between the true and the ersatz, her death unleashed an orgy of sentimentality. People sobbed in the streets and buried the gates of Kensington Palace, where the Princess had lived, under mountains of cellophane-wrapped bouquets. Indeed, reaction to the death took an explicitly religious form: the shrines of flowers, the praying, the hushed and reverent atmosphere.

This was all vicarious feeling, however. In postreligious Britain, it was devotion at a distance by people who no longer possessed what they still deeply longed for—belief in something beyond themselves, and emotional health and support. It was kitsch emotion over someone they had never known; grief for the death of an imagined personality, which sanctified the elevation of feeling, image and spontaneity over reason, reality and restraint.

Feelings were associated with being a nice and good person, while restraint was seen as evidence of callousness. But feelings were deemed to exist only if they were visible. Tears were good; stiff upper lips were bad. Accordingly, people carried their mourning bouquets like badges of moral worth. The Queen and the Prince of Wales, by contrast, were judged to be cold and heartless because they weren't weeping or emoting. The scene threatened to become ugly when the public turned savagely against the Queen for failing to fly the Union Flag at half-mast over Buckingham Palace and were mollified only when the monarch, alerted to the dangerous public mood, allowed the people to see how deeply the family had been affected by the tragedy.

This "Dianafication" of the culture is essentially empty, amoral, untruthful and manipulative; eventually people see through it and realize they have been played for suckers. But while the mood lasts—and it can last long enough to create presidents and prime ministers—reason doesn't have a chance. Warm, fuzzy feelings win hands down because they anaesthetize us to reality and blank out those issues that require difficult decisions. This disorder raises up political icons who achieve instantaneous and unshakeable mass followings of adoring acolytes because they permit the public to suspend judgment and avoid making any hard choices, indulging instead in fantasies of turning swords into ploughshares.

The second conspicuous example of postreligious mythology was the election of Barack Obama to the presidency of the United States—although buyers' remorse and disillusionment appeared to set in within a few months of his inauguration and soon threatened to swamp his period of office altogether. Obama came to power as a mythic figure, like Princess Diana, who seemed to sublimate and transcend the public's various cultural traumas. By virtue of the fact that he was half black, he allowed people to fantasize that he would both redeem America's shameful history of slavery and racial prejudice *and* bring peace to the world. After all, did he not embody in his own history a fusion of black and white, Muslim and Christian?

Brushed aside were highly troubling details of his personal history: his ambivalence about his fractured identity, his efforts to conceal or misrepresent crucial details about his background, and a pattern of unsavory or radical associations. The fact that his preelection statements were intellectually and politically incoherent, frighteningly naive or patently contradictory was of no consequence.

In his personal story and troubled family background, people imagined they could see someone who had overcome adversity by force of
character. Like Princess Diana, he appeared to have emerged from
this troubled past committed to spreading peace, love and reconciliation. Instead of waging war, he would bring harmony simply
through his personality, charisma and will.

Reason was suspended for the duration; emotion and sentimentality took over. People didn't want to hear about the anti-white,
anti-Western church to which he had belonged for twenty years, nor
about his questionable associations with people in Chicago's corrupt
political machine, nor about his friendships with and tutelage by
anti-Western radicals. The appeal of the myth he embodied, with its
capacity to redeem America, was simply too strong.

After all, the American public had just endured the global
ignominy of a president—the embodiment of their nation—who
was reviled as a cretinous, bigoted, warmongering, inarticulate,
gauche and incompetent cowboy. In Barack Obama, by contrast,
they had a political rock star, a global icon and the epitome of cool by
virtue of his handsomeness, elegance, laid-back thoughtfulness,
apparent intelligence, blessed articulacy (they ignored the
teleprompters) and charisma. *And* he was black to boot. And so by
electing him to the presidency they were redeeming both America
and themselves, upon whom his reflected glory would shine, illumi-
nating the virtue of those who had the moral clarity and insight to
vote for him. Aghast at the murderous and apparently hopeless com-
plexities of defending America against the Islamic jihad, they were
seduced by his promise that the exercise of reason would bring an
end to conflict. He made them feel good about themselves; he stood
for hope, love, reconciliation, youthfulness and fairies at the bottom
of the garden.

Obama himself did nothing to dispel this impression. He suggested that he would win the wars in Iraq and Afghanistan. He was
going to break the deadlock in the Middle East. He would change

the climate (literally). When he won the Democratic Party nomination, he declared that this would be seen as "the moment when the rise of the oceans began to slow and our planet began to heal."[11]

Presented with this absurd display of hubris and narcissism, Americans reacted by junking rationality altogether and elevating Obama not just to the presidency but to divinity. Early in the election campaign, Oprah Winfrey proclaimed Obama to be "the one. He is the one!"[12] She herself was likened to "John the Baptist, leading the way for Obama to win."[13] A poll taken in January 2009 just before his inauguration found that his popularity was greater than that of Jesus Christ, Martin Luther King and Mother Teresa.[14] According to Susan Sarandon, "He is a community organizer like Jesus was, and now we're a community and he can organize us."[15] A Chicago art student, David Cordero, made a papier-mâché figure of Obama as Jesus, complete with blue neon halo, titled "Blessing." Cordero explained: "All of this is a response to what I've been witnessing and hearing, this idea that Barack is sort of a potential savior that might come and absolve the country of all its sins."[16] And after Obama's speech in Cairo in June 2009 reaching out to Muslims, *Newsweek* editor Evan Thomas declared on MSNBC: "I mean in a way Obama's standing above the country, above—above the world, he's sort of God."[17] The Norwegian Nobel Committee appeared to agree. In October 2009, it caused almost universal astonishment and derision by awarding the Nobel Peace Prize to President Obama for having "created a new climate in international politics," even though he had not achieved any perceptible advance towards peace anywhere in the world.[18]

The urge to impose some artificial order through myth and fantasy is not confined to the "Princess Obama" syndrome. The climate of unreason has also profoundly affected attitudes on the big issues of the day. Obviously, there are always differences of opinion and interpretation in which one side of an argument will think the beliefs of the other side are false. What is notable about some of today's debates is the extent to which it has become all but impossible for factual evidence to make any contribution, with pre-existing assumptions framing the discussion and permitting no deviation. Facts are simply ignored as if they didn't exist, or denied on the grounds that those who bring them forward are either evil or deranged. What follows is a brief examination of four deeply controversial issues from which evidence, reason and logic have been exiled in favor of irrationality, ideology and prejudice—issues on which much of the Western mind has been closed tightly shut.

2

THE MYTH OF ENVIRONMENTAL ARMAGEDDON

I n November 2009, a scandal erupted at a British research center that was to have far-reaching implications for one of the most sedulously contrived beliefs of the post–Cold War age. Thousands of emails that surfaced from the Climatic Research Unit at the University of East Anglia revealed that some of the most influential scientists behind the theory of manmade or anthropogenic global warming (AGW) had apparently been trying to manipulate and distort the scientific data.[1] This was done, it appeared, to fit the evidence to their prior agenda of catastrophic climate change, and to conceal the fact that their theory didn't stand up.

What these emails exposed was far more than a localized scandal involving a few rogue scientists. The CRU was one of the principal sources of temperature data behind the AGW analysis and the forecasts of imminent environmental apocalypse being put forward by the Intergovernmental Panel on Climate Change—resulting in pressure on the world's governments to make painful adjustments to their economies in order to avert disaster. The apparent fraud revealed by the emails threatened not just the reputation of the CRU but the very foundations of AGW theory.[2] And yet the reaction by the media and political class was largely to ignore, downplay or dismiss the scandal. It was left to scientists skeptical of AGW theory, such as Steve McIntyre and Anthony Watts, to extract the devastating implications for the idea of catastrophic manmade global warming.[3] Even so, AGW proponents such as the British government's former chief scientific adviser Sir David King and its climate change minister Ed Miliband continued to insist that the significance of the emails had been totally overblown and that the science behind AGW theory was "settled."[4]

This was because ever since the late 1980s, scarcely a day has passed without an ever more hair-raising prediction of environmental apocalypse as a result of manmade global warming. Despite a counter-movement that is rapidly gaining ground, the belief within the political and intellectual classes that carbon dioxide emissions are heating up the earth's atmosphere to an unprecedented and catastrophic degree has been afforded the status of unchallengeable fact. It is taught as such in geography lessons in schools, which have received bulk supplies of Al Gore's movie *An Inconvenient Truth*, deemed to be an authoritative study aid on the topic (even though the fact that he won the Nobel Prize for peace rather than for science might have prompted a measure of caution).

Britain and Australia have appointed government ministers for "climate change," suggesting absurdly that politicians can influence the composition of the atmosphere in the same way that they can affect, say, public sector housing or the country's defenses. At the same time, AGW alarmists state repeatedly that catastrophic global warming is now unstoppable. But then, an absence of logic can hardly be acknowledged when a theory achieves unchallengeable status.

Sir David King is one of several who have claimed that AGW poses a more serious threat to the world than terrorism.[5] He also said that climate change had the potential to destabilize the political and economic basis of the entire global system.[6] At the Copenhagen climate change summit in December 2009, Prince Charles warned that the survival of mankind itself was in peril and that a mere seven years remained "before we lose the levers of control" over the climate.[7] When the summit ended inconclusively, the green activist George Monbiot wrote the planet's obituary: "Goodbye Africa, goodbye south Asia; goodbye glaciers and sea ice, coral reefs and rainforest. It was nice knowing you."[8] In 2008, the Harvard physicist John Holdren, newly appointed director of the White House Office of Science and Technology Policy, warned: "There is already wide-spread harm ... occurring from climate change. This is not just a problem for our children and our grandchildren."[9] The former British environment secretary David Miliband said in 2006 that people "should be scared" about global warming. "The truth is staring us in the face," he said. "Climate change is here, in our country; it is an issue for our generation as well as future generations; and those who deny it are the flat-earthers of the 21st century."[10]

By the time his brother Ed Miliband succeeded him in the same job, its title had been altered to "secretary for energy and climate change." In 2009 he introduced the Climate Change Bill, which obliged Britain to reduce its "carbon emissions" by 2050 to 20 percent of what they were in 1990—a target that was achievable, wrote the journalist Christopher Booker, only by shutting down most of the economy. The government estimated this would cost the country £404 billion, or £760 per household every year for four decades. Similarly in the United States, the cost of President Obama's "cap and trade" bill to curb "carbon emissions" was put at $1.9 trillion, a yearly cost of $4,500 to each American family.[11] These sums are vast. But any progressive politician has to demonstrate commitment to tackling global warming. The issue has changed the face of Western politics.

Yet the astonishing fact is that, despite this unprecedented degree of terrifying global alarmism and crippling government spending to curb "carbon emissions," the claimed evidence for the belief that is fueling all this panic simply doesn't stack up. The theory of anthropogenic global warming is perhaps the single most dramatic example of scientific rationality being turned on its head.

People who have absorbed the never-ending barrage of media head-lines about environmental Armageddon emanating from folks sporting impressive scientific qualifications—along with the scorn and vituperation heaped upon anyone who dares question any of it—may find this hard to believe, but it is difficult to find *any* credible evidence to back up global warming alarmism.

THEORY SAYS ONE THING, EVIDENCE SUGGESTS ANOTHER

First of all, the theory of manmade global warming contradicts what we know historically to be the case. There is precious little to support the idea that something out of the ordinary is happening to the climate. The world has always warmed and cooled; the climate changes continually and, at times, quite rapidly. According to Professor R. Timothy Patterson, director of the Ottawa-Carleton Geoscience Centre at Carleton University, "As recently as 6,000 years ago, it was about 3°C warmer than now. Ten thousand years ago, while the world was coming out of the thousand-year-long 'Younger Dryas' cold episode, temperatures rose as much as 6°C in a decade—100 times faster than the past century's 0.6°C warming that has so upset environmentalists."[12]

So nothing new there. Moreover, there is no straightforward link between CO_2 and temperature. From 1860 to 1875 temperatures rose, then decreased from 1875 to 1890, rose until 1903, fell until 1918, rose dramatically until 1941, then cooled until 1976. As the geologist Ian Plimer suggests, AGW proponents have to explain why the rate and amount of warming at the beginning of the twentieth century was greater than now, despite *lower* CO_2 emissions; or why Greenland has cooled since the 1940s, when emissions were higher; or why the Arctic was warmer in the 1920s and 1930s than now.[13]

Global warming theory rests on the belief that rising CO_2 levels drive up the temperature of the atmosphere. But historically, temperature increases have often *preceded* high CO_2 levels, destroying this theory of cause and effect. Moreover, there have been periods when atmospheric CO_2 levels were as much as sixteen times what they are now, periods characterized not by warming but by glaciation.[14]

Proponents of AGW theory also have to explain how carbon dioxide can have a cataclysmic effect on the climate given that it forms only a minute proportion of the atmosphere. According to Roy Spencer, a research scientist in meteorology at the University of Alabama and co-developer of the original method of monitoring global temperatures from earth-orbiting satellites, if the preindustrial atmospheric CO_2 concentration were to double by late in the century, the earth's natural greenhouse gas effect would be enhanced merely by about 1 percent.[15] Yet even less than this tiny amount is supposed to cause climate catastrophe and the end of the world.

We are constantly told that the temperature is increasing, the seas are rising, the ice is shrinking and the polar bears are vanishing. Not one of these claims is supported by the evidence; indeed, the *opposite* is the case.

On the subject of sea level, the world's foremost expert is probably Nils-Axel Mörner, a former IPCC expert reviewer, former head of the Department of Paleogeophysics and Geodynamics at Stockholm University in Sweden, past president of the INQUA Commission on Sea Level Changes and Coastal Evolution, and leader of the Maldives Sea Level Project. In 2007, Professor Mörner said there was no evidence of an unusual rise in sea level anywhere. None. Not around Tuvalu, where Al Gore told the world that the islands' inhabitants faced an imminent choice between evacuation and inundation; nor around any of the Pacific Islands north of New Zealand and Fiji, also said to be in danger of disappearing into the ocean; nor around the South Pole or the North Pole or Greenland. Sea-level rise was a myth.[16]

As for the polar bears, they were allegedly being left stranded on shrinking icebergs as the Arctic ice sheets melted and fell into the sea. Their fate aroused a global furor. One article quoted a visitor to the Arctic who claimed he saw two such distressed animals, noting that one of them "looked to be dead and the other one looked to be exhausted."[17] Global warming, we were told, was even turning polar bears into cannibals as they were forced to start eating each other due to "nutritional stress" from their disappearing habitat.[18] In January 2007, the U.S. interior secretary, Dirk Kempthorne, was moved to recommend that the polar bear be listed as "threatened" under the Endangered Species Act. "We are concerned," said Mr. Kempthorne, that "the polar bears' habitat may literally be melting."[19]

Yet in fact there are four to five times *more* polar bears in the world now than there were forty years ago. Dr. Mitchell Taylor, a biologist from the Arctic government of Nunavut, Canada, noted: "Of the 13 populations of polar bears in Canada, 11 are stable or increasing in number. They are not going extinct, or even appear to be affected at present."[20]

Contrary to the repeated claims that both the Arctic and Antarctica are melting, the evidence shows nothing of the kind. Global ice cover always expands and contracts; nothing new here, and there are many reasons for these movements that have nothing to do with carbon dioxide. It is a highly complex and fluctuating picture; to take one small area where ice is melting and announce on that basis that all sea ice is disappearing through global warming is simply mendacious.

In fact, temperatures in the Arctic were lower at the end of the twentieth century than they had been between 1920 and 1940.[21] Between 1966 and 2000, Antarctica cooled.[22] Between 1992 and 2003, the Antarctic ice sheet was growing at the rate of 5 mm per year.[23] By 2009, global sea ice levels equaled those seen twenty-nine years earlier, according to data derived from satellite observations of the northern and southern polar regions.[24]

Most devastating of all to the AGW camp, the global temperature has been falling. The dogma of manmade global warming states that as CO_2 rises so too will atmospheric temperature. CO_2 has been rising, yet there has been no significant warming since 1995, and temperatures have not increased at all since 1998. The NASA Goddard Institute for Space Studies, the University of Alabama and the UK's Hadley Centre for Forecasting have observed a firm *downtrend* in global temperature since late 2001.[25] According to Dr. Richard Keen, a climatologist with the Department of Atmospheric and Oceanic Sciences at the University of Colorado, in defiance of the predictions by the Intergovernmental Panel on Climate Change (IPCC) "the global temperature for 2007 was the coldest in a decade."[26]

Let's remind ourselves: AGW theory has no ifs or buts. If CO_2 levels go up, so does the temperature. Yet AGW proponents, faced with the fact that the IPCC in 1990 predicted a 0.3°C global average temperature rise per decade, claimed that the earth's recent failure to get warmer was merely a pause and that the prediction always allowed for pauses. Nowhere had such a pause actually been predicted, yet they now claimed to expect a "lull" for up to a decade while natural variations in climate cancelled out the increases caused by manmade greenhouse gas emissions—but apparently just until 2015, when it would all start up again.[27] There was no evidence whatever for this assertion. They simply made it up.

So, the theory goes, more carbon dioxide inevitably means more global warming, except when "natural variations in climate" get in the way of this immutable process. With predictive skills that would have caused medieval sorcerers to junk their crystal balls, climate scientists claimed they could foretell precisely when these "natural climate variations" would subside—even though, at the very same time, Richard Wood of the Hadley Centre confided that "climate predictions for a decade ahead would always be to some extent uncertain."[28]

FALLING TEMPERATURES, RISING HYSTERIA

As the evidence continued to roll in that AGW theory was as dead as Monty Python's famous parrot, the claims of imminent environmental doom became ever more outlandish, hysterical and absurd.

In January 2009, Dr. James Hansen, head of the Goddard Institute for Space Studies, adviser to Al Gore and guru of global warming theory, said that President-elect Obama had "only four years" to save the world from "imminent peril," that ice melt is accelerating and that most estimates of expected sea-level rise are far too conservative.[29] This was the same James Hansen who had predicted that 2007 would be the hottest year on record.

In May 2009, Steven Chu, the Nobel Prize-winning physicist appointed by President Obama as energy secretary, told the Nobel Laureate Symposium convened by Prince Charles that the world should be painted white to combat global warming. Whitewashing roofs, roads and pavements so that they reflected more sunlight and heat, he solemnly announced, would cut CO_2 emissions by as much as taking all the world's cars off the roads for eleven years.[30]

Also in May 2009, the Massachusetts Institute of Technology published a study predicting "a 90 percent probability" that worldwide surface temperatures will rise between 2 and 9 degrees by 2100[31] and that this increase will kill billions of people.[32] This was more than twice the increase that MIT had predicted six years earlier, even though the evidence pointed in the opposite direction: plummeting temperatures and increasing ice.

The same year, scientists warned that sea levels would rise twice as fast as was forecast by the United Nations only two years previously, threatening hundreds of millions of people with catastrophe. Rapidly melting ice sheets in Greenland and Antarctica were likely to push levels up by a meter or more by 2100, swamping coastal cities and obliterating the living space of 600 million people in deltas, low-lying areas and small island countries. The Greenland ice sheet, in particular, was said to be collapsing in places as meltwater seeped down through crevices and speeded up its disintegration.[33] Yet only a few months previously an article in *Science*, drawing upon a meeting of the American Geophysical Union, had said that the speed of Greenland's ice melt appeared to have slowed down.[34]

Also in 2009, an IPCC member, Chris Field, told the American Association for the Advancement of Science meeting in Chicago that "the actual trajectory of climate change is more serious" than any of the climate predictions in the IPCC's Fourth Assessment Report. He said recent climate studies suggested that the continued warming of the planet could touch off large, destructive wildfires in tropical rainforests and melt permafrost in the Arctic tundra, releasing billions of tons of greenhouse gases that could raise global temperatures even more.[35]

But like all the predictions, this rested on an assessment of still higher increases in global CO_2 emissions. Similarly, the international climate change conference in Copenhagen in March 2009 soared into the hyperbolic stratosphere by predicting that the seas might rise by as much as a meter by 2100;[36] that they would turn into acid and return the earth to conditions not seen since the time of the dinosaurs;[37] and that up to 85 percent of the rainforests would be felled not by the loggers' chainsaws but by the seemingly greatest pollutant in the history of the universe, carbon dioxide.[38]

Read these reports carefully and you can see the scam at work. All these predictions revolve around a massive "if." They are all based on the assumption that rising CO_2 levels produce runaway global warming and inevitable ecological catastrophe. Ignoring the self-evident fact that this theory has already been proved false, they then apply this bogus premise to topics not previously covered—the acidity of seas, rainforests—and presto, a fresh range of even greater catastrophes is conjured up from their computer models.

But ludicrous as all this is, there are yet more profound ways in which anthropogenic global warming theory is unscientific. Most fundamental, the very idea that climate is at all predictable flies in the face of the complexity of climate change. The assumption that highly complex natural systems can be predicted at all is absurd.

And climate is arguably the most complex system there is: coupled, nonlinear, chaotic. The number of feedback mechanisms involved is vast. The idea that a predictable outcome can be achieved by changing just one factor—and a minute factor at that—is scarcely more believable than the extraction of sunbeams from cucumbers on Jonathan Swift's satirical island of Laputa.

Moreover, the idea that climate change can be predicted through computer modeling is even more ridiculous. As John McLean has written, "modeling a chaotic object whose initial state and evolutionary processes are not known to a sufficient precision has a validation skill not significantly different from zero."[39] Computer modeling is beset by notorious flaws. First, the integrity of the forecasts that computers produce depends on what is fed into them in the first place. And second, computers are simply unable to deal with all the compound feedback mechanisms that climate change entails.

The temptation to manipulate the source data in order to produce a result that will keep the grant money flowing in is enormous. As Roy Spencer has observed, the results are dependent on the modeler's assumptions being correct—but some assumptions are fed in opportunistically to achieve a desired outcome. "Climate models are purposely simplified so they can run to completion on today's computers and provide results before scientists reach retirement age," Spencer writes.[40] Ian Plimer, who has likened computer modeling to playing sophisticated computer games, says that it proves nothing except its own limitations—as demonstrated by the fact that it suggested constant warming until the end of time but failed to predict either post-1998 cooling or El Niño events (global ocean/atmosphere fluctuations). "Data collection in science is derived from observation, measurement and experimentation, not from modeling," he writes. "... If computer models torture the data enough, the data will confess to anything."[41]

It is ironic that the philosophical granddaddy of green thinking, James Lovelock, should understand this point very well. In his latest book, *The Vanishing Face of Gaia*, he warns about the perils of scientific modeling:

> Gradually the world of science has evolved to the dangerous point where model-building has precedence over observation and measurement, especially in Earth and life sciences. In certain ways, modeling by scientists has become a threat to the foundation on which science has stood: the acceptance that nature is always the final arbiter and that a hypothesis must always be tested by experiment and observation in the real world.[42]

THE "CONSENSUS" MELTS FASTER THAN ARCTIC ICE

It is quite comical that a movement of thought that is all about rescuing the natural world from the perceived predations and dehumanizing effects of technology should itself be abandoning human observation of the natural world and using technology instead to falsify the truths of nature. And as Lovelock and Plimer both observe, this betrays the principles of science. One of the most fundamental of these principles is that science can never be a closed book. Scientific minds must always be open, all theories are contestable, and all science is an arena of argument and debate. If a scientific argument is said to be "over," settled through a "consensus" of unchallengeable conclusions, it stops being science and turns instead into dogma.

That, however, is exactly how anthropogenic global warming theory is couched. Lord May, president of Britain's premier scientific academy, the Royal Society, declared that there was "a clear scientific consensus on the facts" of manmade global warming and thus the argument was over.[43]

In April 2001, Robert Watson, chairman of the IPCC, dismissed suggestions that there was a 50–50 split in the scientific community over climate change or humanity's role in producing it. "It's not even 80–20 or 90–10 (in percentage terms). I personally believe it's something like 98–2 or 99–1," he said. And Sir John Houghton, the former head of Britain's Meteorological Office, said that worldwide there were no more than ten scientists active in the field and well versed in the arguments who disagreed with the notion of human-induced climate change.[44]

The *Washington Post* asserted that there were only "a handful of skeptics" of manmade global warming theory.[45] The ABC News reporter Bill Blakemore—who declared, "I don't like the word 'balance' much at all" in global warming coverage—reported that "after extensive searches, ABC News has found no such [scientific] debate" on global warming.[46]

Well, they can't have been looking very hard. For not only is the idea of a global warming consensus antiscientific, it is not remotely true. On April 6, 2006, sixty scientists wrote a letter to the Canadian prime minister criticizing AGW theory. "Observational evidence does not support today's computer climate models, so there is little reason to trust model predictions of the future," they said.[47] In 2007, some 450 scientists from more than two dozen countries, several of them current and former participants in the IPCC, voiced significant objections to the claims made by the IPCC and Al Gore. By 2009, that number had risen to 700 scientists.[48]

In his book *The Deniers*, Lawrence Solomon observes that the skeptics tend to be far more accomplished and distinguished scientists than those pushing the theory as a settled and incontrovertible truth. A number of them are so eminent they were used as experts by the IPCC, but then came to realize that they were involved in an innately corrupted process and that some of their own work was being abused and distorted in order to promulgate the false doctrine of anthropogenic global warming.

The skeptical scientists include, for example, Dr. Christopher Landsea, a former chairman of the American Meteorological Society's Committee on Tropical Meteorology and Tropical

Cyclones and an IPCC author, who discovered that the IPCC was falsifying the relationship between climate change and hurricanes.

There is Dr. Richard Lindzen, a much-garlanded professor of meteorology at MIT and another IPCC author, who says that the IPCC's politicized summary of its defining 2001 report created the false impression that climate models were reliable when the report itself indicated precisely the opposite, with numerous problems in the models including those arising from the effects of clouds and water vapor.

There is Zbigniew Jaworowski, former chairman of the UN Scientific Committee on the Effects of Atomic Radiation, who says the IPCC's ice-core research is wrong and that therefore it has "based its global warming hypothesis on arbitrary assumptions and these assumptions, it is now clear, are false."

Or Dr. Tom Segalstad, head of the Geological Museum at the University of Oslo and another IPCC reviewer, who says that "most leading geologists throughout the world know that the IPCC's view of Earth processes are implausible if not impossible," and that climate change scientists have launched "a search for a mythical CO_2 sink to explain an immeasurable CO_2 lifetime to fit a hypothetical CO_2 computer model that purports to show that an impossible amount of fossil-fuel burning is heating the atmosphere. It is all a fiction."[49]

There are many other distinguished scientists who have said that anthropogenic global warming is unscientific, untrue and even fraudulent. In 2007, Gerhard Gerlich of the Institute of Mathematical Physics at the Technical University Carolo-Wilhelmina in Braunschweig, Germany, and Dr. Ralf D. Tscheuschner co-authored a devastating paper titled "Falsification of the Atmospheric CO_2 Greenhouse Effects Within the Frame of Physics." This paper stated that there was no scientific basis to anthropogenic global warming theory whatsoever. The authors concluded:

The horror visions of a risen sea level, melting Pole caps and developing deserts in North America and in Europe are fictitious consequences of fictitious physical mechanisms, as they cannot be seen even in the climate model computations. The emergence of hurricanes and tornados cannot be predicted by climate models, because all of these deviations are ruled out. The main strategy of modern CO_2-greenhouse gas defenders seems to hide themselves [*sic*] behind more and more pseudo-explanations, which are not part of the academic education or even of the physics training. . . . The derivation of statements on the CO_2 induced anthropogenic global warming out of the computer simulations lies outside any science.[50]

THE FLAWS, AND WORSE, IN THE RESEARCH

Far from being grounded in rigorous scientific studies, the theory of manmade global warming has been sustained on the back of research that has been shown to be sloppy and badly flawed. NASA, for example, had claimed that 1998 was the warmest year on record in the continental United States. After the National Center for Policy Analysis showed that this claim resulted from a serious mathematical error, NASA corrected itself and said instead that 1934 was now the warmest year on record. Moreover, NASA also had to admit that three of the five warmest years on record had occurred before 1940, contrary to its previous claim that all five occurred after 1980. And perhaps most devastating of all to the manmade global warming backers, it is now admitted that six of the ten hottest years on record occurred when only 10 percent of the amount of greenhouse gases that have been emitted in the last century were in the atmosphere. And why did NASA get all this so wrong? Because—and this is hard to credit—it had been calculating atmospheric temperatures through mechanisms that measured the ground.[51]

The biggest scandal, however, concerned what is known as the "hockey-stick" graph created by the climatologist Michael Mann.

His research appearing to show that the earth's climate was very stable from 1000 to 1900 CE, then suddenly began to rise dramatically—thus creating the hockey-stick shape—was central to the IPCC's 2001 Third Assessment Report. It was this graph which led to the claim that the 1990s ranked as the warmest decade of the millennium and 1998 as the warmest year.[52] And this appeared to pin global warming firmly on industrialization, thus enabling activists to blame the Western world for the imminent frying of the planet.

The hockey-stick graph served to solve a difficulty in blaming industrialization for global warming, and that was the Medieval Warm Period, from about 1000 to 1300 CE. This preindustrial warm interval had been succeeded by a cold period called the Little Ice Age, which lasted until the latter part of the nineteenth century. So twentieth-century warming would appear to be simply a recovery from those cold years. In other words, it was nothing out of the ordinary.

So why is industrialization nevertheless widely seen as the cause of global warming? In 1995, David Deming made a startling revelation. As a geoscientist at the University of Oklahoma, he had gained significant credibility in the community of scientists working on climate change. "They thought I was one of them, someone who would pervert science in the service of social and political causes," Deming wrote. "So one of them let his guard down. A major person working in the area of climate change and global warming sent me an astonishing email that said 'We have to get rid of the Medieval Warm Period.'"[53]

The hockey stick did just that. Its vertiginous rise in global temperature following nine hundred years of stasis was achieved by eradicating some seven centuries of history, excising the Medieval Warm Period and subsequent Little Ice Age altogether. Remarkable detective work by the Canadian researchers Steve McIntyre and Ross McKitrick showed that an algorithm had been built into the computer program so that a hockey-stick curve would have been created whatever data were fed into it.

A subsequent titanic battle over these findings ended with a devastating report in 2006 by a panel of three independent statisticians headed by an eminent statistics professor, Edward Wegman, former chairman of the U.S. National Academy of Sciences Committee on Theoretical and Applied Statistics. This panel resoundingly upheld the finding that the hockey-stick curve was bogus and said that Dr. Mann's "de-centered methodology is simply incorrect mathematics." Wegman said, "I am baffled by the claim that the incorrect method doesn't matter because the answer is correct anyway. Method Wrong, Answer Correct = Bad Science."[54]

In October 2009, McIntyre cast serious doubt on another set of research papers that had been used to underpin AGW theory. These were based on tree-ring records from the Yamal Peninsula in Siberia. On the basis of this evidence, studies by Keith Briffa and others claimed that the Medieval Warm Period had in fact been cool, and so current temperatures were unusually hot by historical standards. When McIntyre finally extracted the raw data, however, he discovered that a larger and more recent set of tree-ring data from the same area told a very different story: that the medieval era was actually quite warm and the late twentieth century was unexceptional.[55]

One tiresome difficulty for AGW proponents is that Antarctica has been not warming but cooling, with ice reaching record levels. In January 2009, Professor Eric Steig and others—including Michael Mann—caused some excitement by claiming that West Antarctica was warming so much that it more than made up for the cooling in East Antarctica.[56] Various other scientists immediately spotted the flaw in Steig's methodology of combining satellite evidence since 1979 with temperature readings from surface weather stations. Because Antarctica has so few weather stations, the computer that Steig used was programmed to *guess* what data would have been produced by more stations had they existed.[57] So the findings that caused such excitement were based on data that had been made up.

A number of expert reviewers for the IPCC have discovered to their horror that some of the research on which it bases its global warming predictions is actively fraudulent. The sea-level expert Nils-Axel Mörner was one such IPCC reviewer. This is what he said about the process that led the IPCC to make its predictions of alarming (if subsequently reduced) sea-level rise:

> Then, in 2003, the same data set, which in their [IPCC's] publications, in their website, was a straight line—suddenly it changed, and showed a very strong line of uplift, 2.3 mm per year, the same as from the tide gauge. And that didn't look so nice. It looked as though they had recorded something; but they *hadn't* recorded anything. It was the original one which they had suddenly twisted up, because they entered a "correction factor," which they took from the tide gauge. So it was not a measured thing, but a figure introduced from outside.
>
> I accused them of this at the Academy of Sciences in Moscow—I said you have introduced factors from outside; it's not a measurement. It looks like it is measured from the satellite, but you don't say what really happened. And they answered, that we had to do it, because otherwise we would not have gotten any trend! That is terrible! As a matter of fact, it is a falsification of the data set. Why? Because they know the answer. And there you come to the point: They "know" the answer; the rest of us, we are *searching* for the answer. Because we are field geologists; they are computer scientists. So all this talk that sea level is rising, this stems from the computer modeling, not from observations. The observations don't find it!
>
> …I have been the expert reviewer for the IPCC, both in 2000 and last year. The first time I read it, I was exceptionally surprised. First of all, it had 22 authors, but none of them—*none*—were sea-level specialists. They were given this mission, because they promised to answer the right thing.[58]

And then there was Al Gore's movie *An Inconvenient Truth*, that classroom resource now used in so many school geography lessons, even though it contains dozens of falsehoods and errors. In October 2007, in a court case relating to this movie, the High Court in London identified nine such "errors"—but in fact there are many more. As Christopher Booker has catalogued, the movie misrepresents the scientific literature, states there are threats where there are none and exaggerates them where they may exist. For example, Gore claimed that sea levels would rise by a massive 20 feet—as opposed to the IPCC, which had forecast the likely rise at between 4 and 17 inches over the next century. Gore said that low-lying inhabited Pacific coral atolls were already being inundated because of anthropogenic global warming, leading to the evacuation of several island populations to New Zealand. However, the atolls are not being inundated; in a large area of the central Pacific, between 1955 and 1996 sea levels had gone down by an average of 2 mm per year. Gore says that global warming dried up Lake Chad in Africa. It did not. Overextraction of water and changing agricultural patterns dried up the lake, which was also dry in 8500 BCE, 5500 BCE, 1000 BCE and 100 BCE. And so on.[59]

SCIENCE IS REPLACED BY THE MANUFACTURE OF MYTHS

The egregious catalogue of error and worse that passes for "science" in anthropogenic global warming theory is not merely evidence of a lot of careless and sloppy scientists, or superannuated politicians seeking the limelight. Undoubtedly, much evidence associated with climate change is contradictory or lends itself to numerous different interpretations. And equally undoubtedly, many scientists promoting this theory are consumed by a genuine fear that the climate is spinning out of control and mankind is to blame. But some have made remarks that appear to suggest the subordination of facts to an ideology that distorts the truth in the supposed interests of a higher cause.

In 1989, Stephen Schneider, a professor of "environmental biology and global change" at Stanford University, said candidly that scientists wanted to see the world become a better place, which meant working out the risk of potentially disastrous climate change.

> To do that we need to get some broad-based support, to capture the public's imagination. That, of course, entails getting loads of media coverage. So we have to offer up scary scenarios, make simplified, dramatic statements, and make little mention of any doubts we might have. This "double ethical bind" we frequently find ourselves in cannot be solved by any formula. Each of us has to decide what the right balance is between being effective and being honest. I hope that means being both.[60]

Well, it is hard to see how it can do so. Paul Watson, one of the founders of Greenpeace, was rather more blunt: "It doesn't matter what is true; it only matters what people believe is true.... You are what the media define you to be. [Greenpeace] became a myth and a myth-generating machine."[61]

This was not about submitting theories or hypotheses or evidence for public debate. This was about using "science" to stifle public debate and alter people's behavior.

So in a report on global warming titled *Warm Words: How Are We Telling the Climate Story and Can We Tell It Better?* the Institute for Public Policy Research, a British think tank, argued that

> the task of climate change agencies is not to persuade by rational argument but in effect to develop and nurture a new "common sense".... [We] need to work in a more shrewd and contemporary way, using subtle techniques of engagement.... The "facts" need to be treated as being so taken-for-granted that they need not be spoken.... It amounts to treating climate-friendly activity as a brand that can be sold. This is, we believe, the route to mass behaviour changes.[62]

The outcome of sidelining rational argument in favor of advertising strategy, as the geologist Ian Plimer observed, is that actual evidence about climate change is dismissed in a mass act of cognitive dissonance. Support goes instead to a theory that is "contrary to validated knowledge from solar physics, astronomy, history, archaeology and geology," flying in the face of science and defeating reason. Scientific facts are now deemed to be extraneous to the issue. Professor Plimer writes:

> When science was born, the consensus at that time was driven by religion, politics, prejudice, mysticism and self-interested power. From Galileo to Newton and through the centuries, science debunked the consensus by experiment, calculation, observation, measurement, repeated validation, falsification and reason.... Scientific fact now no longer seems to be necessary. Human-induced global warming is one such example, where one camp attempts to demolish the basic principles of science and install a new order based on political and sociological collectivism.... There has been an uncritical, unthinking acceptance by the community of the media barrage about catastrophic climate change. For many, critical thinking is an anathema.[63]

But then, as the former astronaut Walter Cunningham astutely observed, "true believers" in the dogma of global warming "are beyond being interested in evidence; it is impossible to reason [people] out of positions they have not been reasoned into."[64]

Manmade global warming theory lies in shreds, and yet this fact is denied and ruthless attempts are made to suppress it, even as the counterargument has gained ground and exposed the hollowness of its claims. That is because the theory is not science. As will be discussed later in the book, it is rather a quasi-religious belief system; and the only reason it was sustained for so long was through the abuse of authority and intimidation of dissent.

3

THE IRAQ WAR

L ike the global warming issue, the war in Iraq changed the course of Western politics. Against the backdrop of Islamist terrorism, the ousting of Saddam Hussein crystallized a fundamental disagreement: was the West involved in a war of civilizations—which might be better termed a war *over* civilization—against an "axis of evil," or did it face merely a localized terrorist problem. And behind that argument lay a much more profound set of disagreements over the role of America and Israel in world affairs; whether these countries were the front line of the West's defenses or the cause of its problems; and whether the right way to safeguard peace and freedom was to topple tyrants through war or deal with them instead through law and diplomacy. The Iraq war became a lightning rod for all these passions, the strength and ferocity of which helped force Tony Blair out of the British prime minister's office early, crippled the presidency of George W. Bush, and paved the way for the election of Barack Obama to the White House.

It is not the purpose here to argue whether toppling Saddam Hussein was the right judgment call or not (my view, for what it's worth, is that it was, even though the prosecution of the war was deeply flawed). The case that war in Iraq was the wrong course to take was an entirely legitimate argument, and to that extent the controversy was a perfectly proper example of democratic discourse.

The point at issue here is a different one. It is that the debate about Iraq stopped being a legitimate conflict of views, and instead gave rise to a wholesale denial of evidence and reason. What started as a valid argument about whether war was the right way of dealing with the threat posed by Saddam Hussein mutated into a rewriting of history, a distortion of the facts and a descent into mass irrationality and even hysteria.

REWRITING THE CAUSE OF THE WAR

A belief took hold widely, particularly in Britain but also in America, that the Western allies were "taken to war on a lie" by President George W. Bush and Prime Minister Tony Blair, who had claimed that Saddam possessed weapons of mass destruction (WMD) when he did not, and that he was a threat to the West, which he was not. Sir Max Hastings expressed this view in the *Guardian*: "Yet it bears stating again and again that we went to war, launching thousands of British soldiers into Iraq, on a pretext now conclusively exposed as false."[1] Similarly, the former director of public prosecutions for England and Wales, Sir Ken Macdonald, wrote in 2009:

> Our Government's decision to go to war in Iraq was based upon an assertion that turned out to be completely untrue. Everybody knows this. In the face of a million protesters on the streets of London, Tony Blair assured us that Saddam Hussein had weapons of mass destruction that he would happily use to threaten our way of life. That's why the dictator had to be stopped, even at the cost of a military invasion. Whether Mr Blair really believed this is not the point. If he did, he was dreadfully wrong—and the result of this misjudgment was a lengthy conflict with many British dead joining the tens of thousands of innocent Iraqi victims.[2]

This belief has changed the face of politics in Britain and America. But it is very far from the truth. It is based on a set of assumptions that built on a false premise and compounded it many times over, refracting everything that happened in connection with Iraq and the "war on terror" through a distorting prism until it became impossible to seek recourse to facts or logic, proportion or fairness. The distortion had become fixed in the public mind as unquestionable reality.

The initial false premise was the misrepresentation of the reason for war in Iraq as the maintenance by Saddam Hussein of illegal stockpiles of WMD. But from the actual speeches and written statements by President Bush and Prime Minister Blair, it is clear that the stockpiles were not the main point at all.[3] The overwhelming emphasis was instead on Saddam's refusal to obey binding United Nations resolutions and the need to enforce the authority of the UN; on Saddam's concomitant failure to prove that he had destroyed his stocks of WMD and to renounce his intention to continue developing such weapons; and on the unconscionable danger posed by the "triple lock" of his attachment to such weapons and past record of using them, his regional ambitions and hostility towards the West, and his connections to terrorism.

Certainly, the existence of the stockpiles was inferred from the fact that the UN weapons inspectors had repeatedly itemized all the WMD that Saddam was known to have had and were still unaccounted for. But those stockpiles were not in themselves the reason for war. They were the supposed backup evidence. The reason was rather that, in the wake of the 9/11 attacks upon America, the threat posed by Saddam's "triple lock" could no longer safely be brushed aside. It was all about a fundamental recalibration of risk.

Nevertheless, the belief took hold that Bush and Blair had lied about Saddam's purported retention of WMD capability. Yet at every level, this claim was itself demonstrably untrue. First, *every* Western government and intelligence agency had said they believed that Saddam was retaining stocks of these illegal weapons and was intent on continuing to develop them. As the former CIA director

George Tenet said in February 2004, they had good reason for thinking this. It was known that Saddam had had chemical and biological weapons during the 1980s and 1990s. He had used chemical weapons on his own people on at least ten different occasions. He had launched missiles against Iran, Saudi Arabia and Israel. In the early 1990s, Iraq was just a few years away from a nuclear weapon on which the intelligence services of the world had significantly underestimated his progress. And Iraq had lied repeatedly about its unconventional weapons.[4]

The United Nations could not—and Saddam would not—account for all the weapons the Iraqis had undoubtedly possessed: tons of chemical weapons precursors, hundreds of artillery shells and bombs filled with chemical or biological agents. In intercepts of conversations and other transactions, intelligence officials heard Iraqis trying to hide prohibited items, worrying about their cover stories, and seeking to procure items that Iraq was not permitted to have. Satellite photos showed a pattern of activity designed to conceal the movement of material from places where chemical weapons had been stored in the past. There was also reconstruction of dual-purpose facilities previously used to make biological agents or chemical precursors. And human sources told intelligence agents of efforts to acquire and hide materials used in the production of such weapons.[5] The issue was not whether Saddam possessed WMD stockpiles but whether he had retained the capacity to use WMD if he so decided. In March 2002, British intelligence officials advised:

> Iraq continues to develop weapons of mass destruction, although our intelligence is poor. . . . Iraq continues with its BW [biological warfare] and CW [chemical warfare] programmes and, if it has not already done so, could produce significant quantities of BW agents within days and CW agents within weeks of a decision to do so. We believe it could deliver CBW by a variety of means, including in ballistic missile warheads. There are also some indications of a continuing nuclear

programme. Saddam has used WMD in the past and could do so again if his regime were threatened.[6]

IGNORING THE EVIDENCE THAT WAS FOUND

Subsequently, some of the claims made by clandestine sources about Saddam's activities turned out to be flaky or untrue. This is a common hazard of intelligence gathering. But to say, as so many have done, that therefore *all* such claims were false and even amounted to a deliberate and collective lie is not sustainable. Obviously, calibrating a risk involves assessing all the evidence in the round. What's more, evidence that exists to support such claims has simply been airbrushed out of the picture. For although the weapons stockpiles were never found, evidence of Saddam's continuing illegal weapons activity certainly was. In his 2003 interim report as head of the Iraq Survey Group, Dr. David Kay reported that he had discovered "dozens of WMD-related program activities" that had been successfully concealed from the UN inspectors. These included a clandestine network of laboratories containing equipment suitable for chemical and biological weapons research, and new research on the biological agents *Brucella* and Congo-Crimean hemorrhagic fever. The ISG found a network of laboratories and safe houses controlled by Iraqi intelligence and security services that contained equipment for chemical and biological research as well as a prison laboratory complex possibly used in human testing for biological weapons agents, none of which had been declared to the UN.[7]

Yet virtually none of this was reported by the media, which merely trumpeted Kay's blasts against the faulty intelligence over weapons stockpiles to give the false impression that Kay was against the war and that he thought Saddam had posed no threat from WMD. Their headlines told a misleading story: "No Illicit Arms Found in Iraq, US Inspector Tells Congress" (*New York Times*);[8] "Search in Iraq Finds No Banned Weapons" (*Washington Post*);[9]

"Inspectors Find Aims Not Arms" (*Los Angeles Times*).[10] So sharp was the dislocation between what Kay had found and the way it was reported that Kay said he was "amazed" that "powerful information about both their intent and their actual activities that were not known and were hidden from UN inspectors seems not to have made it to the press." This information pointed to "prohibited activities they've carried on. And this continued right up to 2003 in these four cases, unreported, undiscovered."[11]

The same thing happened in 2004 when Kay resigned as head of the Iraq Survey Group and said he did not believe that Saddam Hussein had produced weapons of mass destruction on a large scale since the first Gulf War.[12] This statement was immediately taken to mean that he had said Saddam never had any WMD or such programs at all. In Britain, the *Independent* headlined its story: "Saddam's WMD never existed, says chief American arms inspector."[13]

Well, no, he didn't say that. He said he thought *large-scale stockpiles* had not existed.

The distinction was lost on opponents of the war. The former British foreign secretary Robin Cook remarked, "It is becoming really rather undignified for the Prime Minister to continue to insist that he was right all along when everybody can now see he was wrong, when even the head of the Iraq Survey Group has said he was wrong."[14]

Well, no, he hadn't. Indeed, Kay said to the Senate Armed Services Committee and in associated media interviews that "right up to the end" the Iraqis were trying to produce the deadly poison ricin. "They were mostly researching better methods for weaponization," he said. Not only that, Saddam had restarted a rudimentary nuclear program. He had also maintained an active ballistic missile program that was receiving significant foreign assistance until the start of the war.[15] Kay told Fox TV:

> We know there were terrorist groups in state [Iraq] still seeking WMD capability. Iraq, although I found no weapons, had tremendous

capabilities in this area. A marketplace phenomenon was about to occur, if it did not occur; sellers meeting buyers. And I think that would have been dangerous if the war had not intervened.[16]

In other words, what Kay found bore out the concerns set forth by Bush and Blair as the case for going to war in Iraq. Yet his comments were presented as *demolishing* that case. And to this day, people believe that is what David Kay did.

ABSENCE OF EVIDENCE IS NOT EVIDENCE OF ABSENCE

There is an argument that is held to constitute absolute proof that "we were taken to war on a lie." This is that since no WMD were found in Iraq, this proves that they never existed at all. But this is utterly absurd. It is illogical to state that because something hasn't been found, it therefore never existed. If you say this to people, however, they look at you in stupefied disbelief. "If it was there, it would have been found!" they say. "What other explanation could there be for it *not* being found, with the Americans busting a gut to find it? And if Saddam had the stuff, why didn't he use it in the war?"

In fact, there are several perfectly plausible explanations for what might have happened to the missing WMD. Saddam could have destroyed them in the immediate run-up to war. He could have transported them to a neighboring country. They could still be buried somewhere in Iraq: the missing stockpiles were said to have been no more than would fit into a double garage, and Iraq is a huge country. As for why he didn't use the WMD, he may have wanted to avoid revealing that the West had been right all along; or he expected to win easily against the coalition; or he may have put the weapons beyond use for the time being in order to conceal them.[17] Given Saddam's history, and the conclusions of the weapons inspectors during the 1990s that they were being obstructed and lied to, and the intelligence that the world believed in 2002 when it signed up to UN Resolution 1441, which stated that Saddam had WMD, any of these explanations would be rational. But instead, people decided irrationally that absence of evidence of WMD at a certain point in time was evidence that they had never existed.

What's more, evidence suggesting that Saddam must have had something to hide since he had gone to considerable lengths to do so was either not reported at all or brushed aside. Charles Duelfer, the head of the Iraq Survey Group after David Kay, said in 2004 that "deception continued right up until war in 2003." With UNSCOM and UNMOVIC monitored and infiltrated by Iraqi intelligence, "elaborate plans were developed and rehearsed to enable sensitive sites to be able to hide sensitive documents and equipment on as little as 15 minutes notice."[18]

More significant still, the failure by the Americans immediately after they invaded Iraq to secure those sites where it was suspected that work on WMD programs was taking place meant that those sites were looted and destroyed by the Iraqis. As the former CIA director George Tenet said in 2004,

> the Iraqis systematically destroyed and looted forensic evidence before, during and after the war. We have been faced with the organized destruction of documentary and computer evidence in a wide range of offices, laboratories, and companies suspected of WMD work. The pattern of these efforts is one of deliberate rather than random acts. Iraqis who have volunteered information to us are still being intimidated and attacked.[19]

David Kay told the Senate Armed Services Committee how this security failure caused difficulties in gaining accurate knowledge of Saddam's WMD program:

> I regret to say that I think at the end of the work of the [Iraq Survey Group] there's still going to be an unresolvable ambiguity about what happened. A lot of that traces to the failure on April 9 to establish immediately physical security in Iraq—the unparalleled looting and

destruction, a lot of which was directly intentional, designed by the security services to cover the tracks of the Iraq WMD program and their other programs as well. . . . I've seen looting around the world and thought I knew the best looters in the world. The Iraqis excel at that. The result is—and document destruction is, we're really not going to be able to prove beyond a truth the negatives and some of the positive conclusions that we're going to come to. There will be always unresolved ambiguity here.[20]

Why would these sites have been destroyed if Iraq didn't have anything to hide? Clearly, such destruction could not provide any proof that WMD programs had existed there, but it certainly provided one plausible explanation for the failure to find WMD material. It would also explain the subsequent reluctance by the United States to pursue the issue energetically. After all, since it had gone to war in Iraq specifically to make the world safe from the use of such materials, the revelation that it had lost them through a post-invasion failure to secure the suspected sites would have demonstrated a highly damaging degree of incompetence.

Another plausible explanation was that the WMD materials had been moved. Again, evidence to support this scenario was barely reported. In 2003, Kay told Congress that U.S. satellite surveillance revealed substantial vehicular traffic going from Iraq to Syria just before the American attack on March 19, 2003. Investigators couldn't be sure the cargo contained WMD, said Kay, but one of his top advisers called the evidence "unquestionable."[21]

In February 2004, Kay told the *Sunday Telegraph* that he had discovered from interrogating Iraqi scientists that Saddam had hidden components of his WMD program in Syria before the war.[22] This statement reinforced observations made by Lt. Gen. James Clapper (Air Force, retired), head of the National Imagery and Mapping Agency, who said vehicle traffic photographed by U.S. spy satellites indicated that material and documents related to the arms programs were shipped to Syria. According to the *Washington Times* report,

Other goods probably were sent throughout Iraq in small quantities and documents probably were stashed in the homes of weapons scientists. Gen. Clapper said he is not surprised that U.S. and allied forces have not found weapons of mass destruction hidden in Iraq because "it's a big place. . . . Those below the senior leadership saw what was coming, and I think they went to extraordinary lengths to dispose of the evidence."[23]

THE EVIDENCE OF SADDAM'S FORMER AIR VICE-MARSHAL

More detailed claims regarding the whereabouts of Saddam Hussein's WMD emerged from someone who might be considered rather close to the horse's mouth. Georges Sada reported that as Saddam's air vice-marshal he "not only saw these weapons but witnessed them being used on orders from the air force commanders and the president of the country." In his book *Saddam's Secrets*, he explained how these weapons had been concealed:

> I know the names of some of those who were involved in smuggling WMDs out of Iraq in 2002 and 2003. I know the names of officers of the front company, SES, who received the weapons from Saddam. I know how and when they were transported and shipped out of Iraq. And I know how many aircraft were actually used and what types of planes they were, as well as a number of other facts of this nature. . . .
>
> Saddam had ordered our weapons teams to hide the WMDs in places no military commander or United Nations weapons inspector would expect to find them. So they hid them in schools, private homes, banks, business offices and even on trucks that were kept constantly moving back and forth from one end of the country to the other. And then fate stepped in. . . .
>
> On June 4, 2002, a three-mile-long dam collapsed in Syria, causing a disaster over 40 square miles. When Syria asked for help from Jordan and Iraq, Saddam seized his opportunity. For him, the disaster in Syria was a gift, and there, posing as shipments of supplies and equipment sent

from Iraq to aid the relief effort, were Iraq's WMDs. Weapons and equipment were transferred both by land and by air. The only aircraft available at the time were one Boeing 747 jumbo jet and a group of Boeing 727s. But this turned out to be the perfect solution to Saddam's problem. Who would suspect commercial airliners of carrying deadly toxins and contraband technology out of the country? So the planes were quickly reconfigured....

Eventually there were fifty-six sorties. He [Saddam] arranged for most of these shipments to be taken to Syria and handed over to ordnance specialists there who promised to hold everything for as long as necessary. Subsequently I spoke at length to a former civilian airline captain who had detailed information about those flights. At the time he held an important position at Iraqi Airways, which is the commercial airline in Baghdad.... In addition to the shipments that went by air, there were also truckloads of weapons, chemicals and other supplies that were taken into Syria at that time. These weren't government vehicles or military equipment but large cargo trucks and eighteen-wheelers made to look like ordinary commercial operators....

To keep all these transfers under wraps, the operators worked through a false company called SES. This company played a key role in transporting equipment back and forth between Syria and Iraq, as well as in smuggling many former government officials out of Iraq prior to and immediately after the US invasion in March 2003.[24]

I spoke to Sada in 2006. An Assyrian Christian, he had not belonged to the Ba'ath Party. Somehow he had survived Saddam's regime and was now president of the National Presbyterian Church in Baghdad and head of the Iraqi branch of the Centre for Peace and Reconciliation based at Coventry Cathedral. He told me that he had lived and worked with the ever-present daily reality of Saddam's tactics of hiding his WMD from the weapons inspectors. Whole environments were transformed and rebuilt in the largely successful strategy of concealment. The idea that Saddam suddenly stopped hiding the stuff and secretly destroyed it while playing his cat-and-mouse games with the UN was, he said, utterly ludicrous. Hiding WMD was the unchanging pattern of Saddam's regime.

Sada said he had listened to the tapes that had surfaced after the invasion recording Saddam's discussions with his top brass about the problems being caused by the UN weapons inspectors. He said the translations that had so far been made of those tapes were inadequate because the translators did not speak Tikriti Arabic, the dialect in which these discussions were conducted. Sada did speak Tikriti. He had translated a crucial three and a half minutes of those tapes, he said, in which Saddam and his generals were discussing how to outwit the UN inspectors; in which they said that the problem of the chemical weapons was solved but the biological weapons were still causing a problem; that this problem would probably be solved with the help of the Russians and the French; and in which Saddam said: "In the future the terrorism will be with WMD."[25]

With a few exceptions, Sada's claims were totally ignored by the media. His firsthand evidence could not be given any importance because it disturbed the view that had become an unchallengeable dogma: that we were "taken to war on a lie." Of course, Sada may have been mistaken; but shouldn't his claims have been taken seriously and investigated?

THE DENIAL OF SADDAM'S ROLE
AS A GODFATHER OF TERROR

In a further act of collective cognitive dissonance, the argument that Saddam had had no WMD was broadened to include the claim that he had had no connections to either al-Qaeda in particular or terrorism in general, and was therefore no threat at all to anyone outside Iraq. Thus Sir Simon Jenkins wrote in the *Times*, "An equally respectable school, indeed most of the intelligence community, could find no link between Baghdad and international terrorism, however ghastly Saddam might have been to his own people."[26]

Similarly, Richard Cohen wrote in the *Washington Post*, "More to the point is the administration's Westmorelandish insistence on asserting the insupportable—that Saddam Hussein was a grave threat to the United States because he was linked to terrorism and armed to the teeth with those awful weapons. There is no truth to that—none."[27]

Representative John Murtha, a Democrat from Pennsylvania, told NBC's *Meet the Press* in March 2006: 'There was no terrorism in Iraq before we went there. None. There was no connection with al Qaeda, there was no connection with, with terrorism in Iraq itself."[28]

These were quite astounding claims. Saddam was well known to be a godfather of terrorism, a fact which had never been in dispute. He had subsidized the families of Palestinian suicide bombers. His operatives had tried to assassinate the elder President Bush in Kuwait in 1993. He provided a safe haven in Iraq for a string of terrorist groups including the Mujahedin-e-Khalq, the Kurdistan Workers' Party, the Palestine Liberation Front and the Abu Nidal organization. He provided training in weapons, plane hijacking and even suicide bombing at a terrorist training camp at Salman Pak.[29] In 2008, the *Wall Street Journal* revealed some findings from a recent Pentagon report on Iraq's ties to terrorism:

> The redacted version of "Saddam and Terrorism" is the most definitive public assessment to date from the Harmony program, the trove of "exploitable" documents, audio and video records, and computer files captured in Iraq. On the basis of about 600,000 items, the report lays out Saddam's willingness to use terrorism against American and other international targets, as well as his larger state sponsorship of terror, which included harboring, training and equipping jihadis throughout the Middle East.[30]

Yet the "war on a lie" brigade repeatedly denied that any such connections to terrorism existed, and more specifically insisted that there was no evidence of any links between Saddam and al-Qaeda. The evidence that there *were* such links thus had to be misrepresented.

In June 2004, for example, the *New York Times* ran a story on the newly published 9/11 Commission Report under the headline: "Panel Finds No Qaeda-Iraq Tie."[31] But in fact the report detailed several "friendly contacts" between Iraq and al-Qaeda. It did conclude that there was no proof of Iraqi involvement in al-Qaeda terrorist attacks against American interests and said there was "no evidence of a collaborative relationship." That was a very different matter from asserting there were no links at all; the 9/11 Commission actually said there *were* links. Thomas Kean, chairman of the 9/11 Commission, said at a subsequent press conference, "Were there contacts between al Qaeda and Iraq? Yes."[32] A month later, he said more emphatically, "There was no question in our minds that there was a relationship between Iraq and al Qaeda."[33]

George Tenet wrote in his book *At the Center of the Storm* that although in his view the connection between al-Qaeda and Iraq had been exaggerated in some quarters, it had existed and had been a source of anxiety:

> There was more than enough evidence to give us real concern about Iraq and al-Qaeda; there was plenty of smoke, maybe even some fire.... Our data told us that at various points there were discussions of cooperation, safe haven, training, and reciprocal nonaggression.... There was concern that common interests may have existed in this period [mid 1990s] between Iraq, Bin Laden, and the Sudanese, particularly with regard to the production of chemical weapons. The reports we evaluated told us of high-level Iraqi intelligence service contacts with Bin Laden himself, though we never knew the outcome of these contacts.[34]

In Britain, the government-commissioned Butler Report said that contacts between al-Qaeda and the Iraqi Directorate General of Intelligence had dated back as early as 1992, with al-Qaeda seeking toxic chemicals and other terrorist equipment. Although British intelligence in 2001 judged there to have been too much distrust for practical cooperation, by 2002 it decided that "meetings have taken place between senior Iraqi representatives and senior al Qaeda operatives. Some reports also suggest that Iraq may have trained some al Qaeda terrorists since 1998." By March 2003 it noted that "senior Al Qaeda associate Abu Musab al Zarqawi has established sleeper cells in Baghdad, to be activated during a US occupation of the city." It concluded that there were contacts although no evidence of cooperation between al-Qaeda and the Iraqi government.[35]

But the falsehood that the absence of any such ties had been officially established was impervious to mere facts. In June 2004, the Iraqi prime minister, Iyad Allawi, told NBC News, "I believe very strongly that Saddam had relations with al-Qaeda. And these relations started in Sudan." The interviewer, Tom Brokaw, expressed surprise that Allawi should make any such connection. "The 9/11 Commission in America," he claimed, "says there is no evidence of a collaborative relationship between Saddam Hussein and those terrorists of al-Qaida."[36]

A year later, American journalists were still repeating the falsehood. In June 2005, the CNN anchor Carol Costello stated: "There is no evidence that Saddam Hussein was connected in any way to al-Qaeda." Later the same day, another CNN anchor, Daryn Kagan, said: "And according to the record, the 9/11 Commission in its final report found no connection between al-Qaeda and Saddam Hussein." Richard Cohen, in his *Washington Post* column, regularly chided the Bush administration for presenting what he called "fictive" links between Iraq and al-Qaeda. The editor of the *Los Angeles Times* scolded the Bush administration for perpetuating the "myth" of such links. Lesley Stahl, the *60 Minutes* anchor, asserted: "There was no connection."[37]

In 2009, Andrew Sullivan went further still. In the *Sunday Times*, he claimed that the Bush administration had tortured an al-Qaeda suspect, Abu Zubeydah, to make him "confess" falsely that Saddam Hussein and al-Qaeda had a working relationship, "the key casus belli for the Iraq war." According to Sullivan, "The Bush and Cheney ideology was that Iraq needed to be invaded because Saddam had weapons of mass destruction and had an operational relationship with al Qaeda that put America under an intolerable risk. When the facts could not be found to defend that idée fixe, they skewed the intelligence. When there was no intelligence to skew, they tortured people to get it."[38]

But the suspected relationship with al-Qaeda was not the "casus belli" for the Iraq war. And President Bush had never claimed that Saddam had an "operational relationship" with al-Qaeda, only "contacts," which he placed in the context of Saddam's alarming links to terrorists worldwide. In his speech in 2003, he said:

> And we know that Iraq is continuing to finance terror, and gives assistance to groups that use terrorism to undermine Middle East peace. We know that Iraq and the al Qaeda terrorist network share a common enemy—the United States of America. We know that Iraq and al Qaeda have had high-level contacts that go back a decade. Some al Qaeda leaders who fled Afghanistan went to Iraq. These include one very senior al Qaeda leader who received medical treatment in Baghdad this year, and who has been associated with planning for chemical and biological attacks. We have learned that Iraq has trained al Qaeda members in bomb making, poisons, and deadly gases. And we know that after September 11, Saddam Hussein's regime gleefully celebrated the terrorist attacks on America. Iraq could decide on any given day to provide a biological or chemical weapon to a terrorist group or individual terrorists. Alliances with terrorists could allow the Iraqi regime to attack America without leaving any fingerprints.[39]

CONSPIRACY THEORY GOES VIRAL

The sustained distortion, misrepresentation, selective reporting and systematic abandonment of evidence and reason over the war in Iraq clearly reflect something rather more profound than simple opposition to a divisive war. One explanation for the implacable conviction that we were "taken to war on a lie" is a widespread skepticism, especially in Britain, over the true scale and nature of the threat to the West from the Islamic world. People do not believe that a religious "war" is being waged against the West. They "know" that the true reason for Muslim rage lies in the behavior of Israel and its backer, America. That is why they are unable to process facts about the threat posed by Saddam's involvement in terror, and why they have suspended rationality over his WMD programs. Their minds are shut to evidence because they "know" the greater truth: that the whole Iraq mess was cooked up by a conspiracy of neoconservatives stretching from Bush's White House to Jerusalem, who invented the threat from Saddam as a pretext to invade Iraq in order to advance the interests of Israel. The real enemy was to be found not in Baghdad or Tehran or the caves of Tora Bora, but in Washington D.C.

One of the few writers still connected to reality on this subject, Jonathan Foreman, commented in amazement:

> Moreover the British chattering classes are convinced almost to a man
> (or woman) that Guantanamo is at best a gulag in which all the
> detainees are innocent victims of paranoia and aggression, and where the
> quotidian tortures rival those of the Gestapo. They "know" that the war
> in Iraq is really about stealing oil, doing Israel's evil bidding, boosting
> corporate profits, or some vicious combination of all three. The war in
> Afghanistan is equally "pointless" and "unwinnable." They fully buy the
> media line that radical Islamism is somehow a creation of these wars
> rather than a phenomenon that predated 9/11, and that solving the
> Palestinian question will somehow bring peace between Shia and Sunni
> and end bin Ladenite dreams of restoring the medieval caliphate.[40]

In 2004, the head of MI5, Dame Eliza Manningham-Buller, warned: "There is a serious and sustained threat of terrorist attacks against UK interests at home and abroad. The terrorists are inventive, adaptable and patient; their planning includes a wide range of methods to attack us."[41] Yet a strong current of opinion among the intelligentsia held that not only was Saddam no threat to the West but there was no systemic Islamist terrorist threat at all. It was all concocted by Western leaders just to scare us.

Simon Jenkins wrote in the *Spectator*, "Daily life offers many risks but that from terrorist attack is extremely slight."[42] That very day, March 23, 2004, al-Qaeda exploded thirteen bombs on commuter trains in Madrid, killing 192 people and wounding more than 1,700. Not even this horrific corrective could puncture Sir Simon's hermetic insulation from reality. Later that year he sneered, "The vision of the West as facing daily terrorist Armageddon is being seen for the sham it is."[43]

Thus it is not surprising that Jenkins applauded *America Alone*, by Stefan Halper and Jonathan Clarke. He called the book a "fascinating study in power" revealing the truth behind the Iraq war: that "a small group of neoconservatives contrived to take the greatest nation on Earth to war and kill thousands of people." Their first commitment, apparently, was to the defense of Israel; they opposed all Middle East "peace processes," and thought that war was always good and allies always bad. The authors concluded: "The neoconservative fascination with war would make an interesting psychological study."[44]

It is surely the obsession with neoconservatives that would make a fascinating psychological study. The gross misrepresentations of this group, the way they have been invested with near-diabolical powers to subvert American foreign policy and their characterization as a covert global conspiracy of evil, are all evidence of some profound pathology. What is really troubling, however, is the degree to which this irrationality has gripped wide swaths of the Western intelligentsia, blinding them to the objective reality of the threats that confront the free world and unleashing the demons of primitive prejudice instead.

4

THE MISREPRESENTATION OF ISRAEL

The prevailing attitude towards Israel in the West transcends altogether the normal conventions of political debate. People are obviously entitled to criticize Israel as they do any other state, and to hold differing views about whether its actions are justified. But the treatment afforded to Israel in its dispute with the Arab and Muslim world is unique. Among the educated and high-minded classes in particular, Israel inspires an obsessional hatred of a type and scale that is directed at no other country.

I will discuss the virulence of this obsession further on. What is being looked at here is one particular aspect of this phenomenon: the depths of misrepresentation and upside-down thinking that it embodies. Again, it is not uncommon for issues to be misunderstood out of ignorance, laziness or indifference. What is unique about the treatment of Israel is that a conflict subjected to an unprecedented level of scrutiny should be presented in such a way as to drive out truth and rationality. History is turned on its head; facts and falsehoods, victims and victimizers are reversed; logic is suspended, and a fictional narrative is now widely accepted as incontrovertible truth. This fundamental error has been spun into a global web of potentially catastrophic false conclusions. The fraught issue of Israel sits at the epicenter of the West's repudiation of reason.

Many of the errors and misrepresentations about the Middle East conflict not only promote falsehood but turn the truth inside out. This is because the West has swallowed the Arab and Muslim narrative on Israel, which as we will see later acts as a kind of global distorting mirror, appropriating Jewish experience and twisting it into a propaganda weapon against the Jews. What is striking is the extent to which this patently false and in many cases demonstrably absurd account has been absorbed uncritically by the West and assumed to be true.

In Britain and much of Europe, the mainstream, dominant view among the educated classes is that Israel itself is intrinsically illegitimate. Its behavior is thus viewed through that prism. Much of the obsession with Israel's behavior is due to the widespread belief that its very existence is an aberration and a historic mistake, although an understandable one at the time it came into being.

Many people believe that Israel was created as a way of redeeming Holocaust guilt. They assume that European Jews with no previous connection to Palestine—which in this view was the historic homeland of Palestinian Muslims whose ancestors had lived there since time immemorial—were transplanted there as foreign invaders and then drove out the indigenous Arabs, pushing them into the West Bank and Gaza. These are territories that Israel is now said to be occupying illegally (even after its "disengagement" from Gaza in 2005), oppressing the Palestinians and frustrating the creation of a state of Palestine, which would end the conflict.

Every one of these assumptions is wrong. Let's go through them one by one and compare claim with reality to grasp the scale of the delusion.

THE JEWS' HISTORIC CLAIM TO THE LAND OF ISRAEL

In President Obama's Cairo speech to the Islamic world in June 2009, he claimed that "the aspiration for a Jewish homeland is rooted in a tragic history that cannot be denied. Around the world, the Jewish people were persecuted for centuries, and antisemitism in Europe culminated in an unprecedented Holocaust."[1] The president was echoing the Arab claim that Israel was created as a result of the Holocaust, from which it follows that the Palestinians have been forced to pay a price for the Nazi genocide against the Jews. This claim turns the Arabs into victims and sets up their further assertion that the authentic inheritors of the land of Israel are not the Jews but the Arabs. Thus they pose as resisting an alien people foisted onto their land—and this narrative is now accepted as true in the West.

But it is false. The Jews' aspiration for their homeland does not derive from the Holocaust. It derives from Judaism itself, which comprises the inseparable elements of the religion, the people and the land.

Israel did not spring into being after the Holocaust; it was the historic homeland of the Jewish people going back to ancient times. The unique Jewish entitlement to Israel is not just a Biblical story but historical fact. The Jews are the *only* people for whom the land of Israel was ever their national homeland. They first entered the land around 1300 BCE, living under a tribal confederation. By 1000 BCE they established a united monarchy under King David, ruling themselves independently and continuously for over four hundred years—more than a millennium before Islam was established in the seventh century and the Arabs invaded. In 586 BCE, the Jews were conquered and driven out of their kingdom, later returning to rebuild it only to be defeated and finally exiled again in 70 CE.[2]

Even then, the Jews maintained an unbroken presence in the land of Israel through centuries of Roman, Christian and Ottoman occupation, with Jewish majorities in several towns. There was a brief resumption of Jewish rule in Jerusalem after a revolt against the Romans in 135 CE and again in 614 CE; by the ninth century, Jews had re-established communities in Tiberias; in the eleventh century, in Gaza; in the thirteenth century, Jewish families restored the community of Safed; in the sixteenth century, refugees from the

Spanish Inquisition led to a substantial expansion of the Jewish presence in Safed, Hebron and Tiberias; from the mid nineteenth century onwards, there was a Jewish majority in Jerusalem.

The recognition of the Jews' unique claim to the land of Israel was fundamental to the Balfour Declaration in 1917, which committed the British to re-establishing the Jewish national home in Palestine. The legitimacy of Israel rests not on the United Nations vote of 1947, which finally established it as a state, but on the setting up of the Palestine Mandate in 1922 by the precursor to the UN, the League of Nations, which paid recognition to "the historical connection of the Jewish people with Palestine and to the grounds for reconstituting their national home in that country."[3] In 1922, the British government, which was required under the Mandate to re-establish the Jewish national home in Palestine, made the point in its "Churchill White Paper" that Jewish rights in Palestine were not a gift from anyone:

> [I]n order that [Palestine's Jewish] community should have the best prospect of free development and provide a full opportunity for the Jewish people to display its capacities, it is essential that it should know that it is in Palestine as of right and not on sufferance. That is the reason why it is necessary that the existence of a Jewish National Home in Palestine should be internationally guaranteed, and that it should be formally recognised to rest upon ancient historic connection.[4]

Just as it is false to claim that Israel owes its legitimacy to Holocaust guilt, so it is misleading to claim that Israel is populated by the families of European Jews who survived the Holocaust. More than half the Jews who make up its Jewish population are families forced to flee from the Arab and Muslim world; more than 850,000 Jews were ethnically cleansed from countries such as Syria, Transjordan, Egypt, Lebanon, Yemen, Iran, Iraq, Algeria, Tunisia and Morocco, where some Jewish communities had existed for more than 2,500 years *before* the creation of these modern Arab states.[5]

THE FALSE "PALESTINIAN" CLAIM TO THE LAND OF ISRAEL

People who claim that it is mostly European Jews who populate the State of Israel and that the authentic original inhabitants of the land were Palestinian Arabs fail to acknowledge the history of ancient Israel, and they falsely create a historic Palestinian identity. In the *Independent*, Johann Hari wrote a typical summary of this view:

> The Jews who arrived in Palestine throughout the twentieth century did not come because they were cruel people who wanted to snuffle out Arabs to persecute. No: they came because they were running for their lives from a genocidal European antisemitism that was soon to slaughter six million of their sisters and their sons. They convinced themselves that Palestine was "a land without people for a people without land". I desperately wish this dream had been true. You can see traces of what might have been in Tel Aviv, a city that really was built on empty sand dunes. But most of Palestine was not empty. It was already inhabited by people who loved the land, and saw it as theirs. They were completely innocent of the long, hellish crimes against the Jews.[6]

In fact they were not innocent of those crimes at all; as we shall see later, during the 1930s they became Hitler's allies and a beachhead of Nazism in the Middle East. But the real problem with the passage above lies in the claim that Palestine was regarded as "a land without people for a people without land." This is a common misquotation of an aphorism coined by a number of people, starting with various nineteenth-century Christian clergymen who all made more or less the same observation that Palestine was "a land without a people ... [for] a people without a land."[7]

The importance lies in the indefinite article: "without *a* people." No one ever claimed there were no people in Palestine before the Jews started to arrive in the late nineteenth century—although there certainly weren't many, as numerous observers testified. The British consul general, James Finn, wrote in 1857 that "the country is in a considerable degree empty of inhabitants" and that its "greatest need is that of a body of population."[8] Arthur Penrhyn Stanley, the great British cartographer, reached similar conclusions in 1881: "In Judea it is hardly an exaggeration to say that for miles and miles there was no appearance of life or habitation."[9] The Palestine Royal Commission quoted an account from 1913 saying that on the road from Gaza to the north, "no orange groves, orchards or vineyards were to be seen until one reached Yabna [a Jewish village].... [T]he western part towards the sea was almost a desert.... The villages in this area were few and thinly populated."[10] And Sherif Hussein, the guardian of holy places in Arabia, wrote in 1918: "The resources of the country are still virgin soil and will be developed by the Jewish immigrants."[11]

The crucial point, however, is that the Arabs who *were* living in Palestine were not *a* people. They did not consider themselves to have a distinct cultural or national identity rooted in Palestine. Indeed, how could they? "Palestine" had no cultural meaning at all. The original land of Israel had simply been renamed "Palestine" by the Romans, after they destroyed the remnants of the thousand-year Jewish presence, to erase any recognized connection with the Jews. The Arabs ruled merely for around a century, followed by protracted periods of Islamic rule largely through the Turkish or Ottoman Empire, which was brought to an end when the Turks were defeated in the First World War.

But from the time the Jews of Judea were conquered and exiled, the non-Jews who inhabited "Palestine"—who we are told were the ancestors of the Palestinian Arabs displaced in 1948 from their "historic" home—actually included not just Arabs but also Greeks, Syrians, Latins, Egyptians, Turks, Armenians, Italians, Persians, Kurds, Germans, Afghans, Circassians, Bosnians, Sudanese, Samaritans, Algerians, Tartars, Copts, Maronites, Ruthenians, Bohemians, Bulgarians, Georgians and many others.[12]

In the mid seventeenth century, around 20 percent of Palestine's population were Greeks.[13] In the mid nineteenth century, it contained whole villages of Bosnians, Druzes, Circassians and Egyptians.[14] The 1911 edition of *Encyclopaedia Britannica* listed more than fifty languages being spoken in Palestine, including Czech, Finnish, Hindustani, Hebrew, Arabic, Dutch, Kurdish, Russian, Serbian, Syrian and Turkish.[15] A British government handbook from 1920 noted, "The people west of the Jordan are not Arabs, but only Arabic-speaking. The bulk of the population are fellahin. . . . In the Gaza district they are mostly of Egyptian origin; elsewhere they are of the most mixed race."[16]

ARABS THEMSELVES SAY "NO SUCH COUNTRY AS PALESTINE"

Even under the Palestine Mandate, the Arabs who lived there did not regard themselves as a people seeking nationhood at all. Very few had been in Palestine before the Jews arrived; many Arabs moved into the area on the back of the prosperity brought by the returning Jews during the first half of the twentieth century. Between 1922 and 1946, the Arab population of Palestine increased by 118 percent.[17] Franklin D. Roosevelt concluded in 1939 that "Arab immigration into Palestine since 1921 has vastly exceeded the total Jewish immigration during the whole period."[18]

And these Arabs who came to live in Palestine regarded themselves mainly as Syrian. In 1937, the British Peel Commission found that the Palestinian Arabs and their kinsmen in Syria "clung to the principle that Palestine was part of Syria and should never have been cut off from it."[19] Arabs themselves have said over and over again that "Palestinian" identity is a complete fiction. The Syrian leader Auni Bey Abdul-Hadi told the Peel Commission, "There is no such country as Palestine. 'Palestine' is a term the Zionists invented. There is no Palestine in the Bible. Our country was for centuries part of Syria. 'Palestine' is alien to us. It is the Zionists who introduced it."

In 1956, Ahmad Shuqairy, who eight years later would found the Palestine Liberation Organization, told the UN Security Council, "It is common knowledge that Palestine is nothing but southern Syria."[20] Later, the Syrian dictator Hafez Assad told the terrorist PLO leader Yasser Arafat:

> You do not represent Palestine as much as we do. Never forget this one point: There is no such thing as a Palestinian people, there is no Palestinian entity, there is only Syria. You are an integral part of the Syrian people, Palestine is an integral part of Syria. Therefore it is we, the Syrian authorities, who are the true representatives of the Palestinian people.[21]

Thus "Palestinians" were a fictive entity. According to Zuhair Muhsin, who was the military commander of the PLO and a member of its executive council, this fiction was a tool to be used against Israel:

> There are no differences between Jordanians, Palestinians, Syrians and Lebanese. We are all part of one nation. It is only for political reasons that we carefully underline our Palestinian identity.... [Y]es, the existence of a separate Palestinian identity serves only tactical purposes. The founding of a Palestinian state is a new tool in the continuing battle against Israel.[22]

THE MYTH OF THE ARAB EXPULSION FROM PALESTINE

The next myth is that the Jews drove out the Arabs when Israel was created in 1948, with many of the Israelis living in properties stolen from the Palestinians. In the *Guardian*, Seumas Milne wrote of "the nakba, or catastrophe, that led to the destruction of their society and expulsion from their homeland."[23] In the *Independent*, Robert Fisk wrote similarly about the "Palestinians, originally expelled from 1948 Palestine in Israel's initial act of ethnic cleansing."[24]

Once again, however, the Arabs themselves have repeatedly made clear that this is just not true. Far from appropriating Arab property, the Jews bought most of the land from the Arabs—mainly absentee landlords—as many Arab sources have testified, such as King Abdullah of Transjordan, who wrote that the Arabs were "as prodigal in selling their land as they are in useless wailing and weeping."[25]

As for the displacement in 1948, the evidence is that most of the Arabs of Palestine fled during the war to exterminate the State of Israel at birth because they were told to do so by the Arab world, which was confident of victory. The *Economist*, never a friend of Israel, reported that the most potent factors for the Arabs' flight were "the announcements made over the air by the Higher Arab Executive urging the Arabs to quit.... It was clearly intimated that those Arabs who remained in Haifa and accepted Jewish protection would be regarded as renegades."[26] Syria's prime minister after 1948, Khaled al-Azm, acknowledged the Arab responsibility for creating the refugee problem, writing in his memoirs: "Since 1948 it is we who demanded the return of the refugees while it was we who made them leave.... We brought disaster upon the refugees, by inviting them and bringing pressure to bear upon them to leave.... We have rendered them dispossessed."[27] In 2006, a columnist in the Palestinian Authority's official paper, *Al-Hayat al-Jadida*, acknowledged the same thing. Mahmud al-Habbash wrote that in 1948, Palestinian Arabs left their homes willingly under the instruction of their own Arab leaders and with false promises of a prompt return.[28]

Having tried to exterminate Israel at its rebirth in 1948 and told the Palestinian Arabs to flee the fighting on the basis that Israel would soon be wiped out, these Arab states then kept the Palestinian Arabs permanently in squalid conditions in the West Bank and Gaza in order to win a propaganda war against the Jews within the gullible and ambivalent West. The West has swallowed this propaganda, apparently oblivious to the striking Arab tactic of using an event that has actually happened but switching the roles of the principal actors so that the Arabs always end up portrayed as victims of the Jews.

THE MYTH OF ISRAEL'S "ILLEGAL OCCUPATION"

One example of role reversal in Arab propaganda involves Israel's occupation of the West Bank and (previously) Gaza. This occupation is repeatedly said to be illegal, not least by the UN, whose former secretary-general, Kofi Annan, told Israel in 2002, "You must end the illegal occupation of lands captured in the 1967 Middle East war."[29]

This is wrong in law, since under the terms of the seminal UN Resolution 242, Israel is entitled to keep these territories unless the Arabs end their belligerency from within them. But there is a far deeper flaw still in the "illegality" charge. This is because Jewish rights over these territories do not derive from their capture by Israel after the 1967 war. They derive instead from the Palestine Mandate, which prescribed the "close settlement" by Jews everywhere in their historic and ancient homeland of "Palestine"—whose borders then ran from the Jordan to the Mediterranean. In other words, the "occupied territories" of the West Bank and Gaza actually form part of the original land of Palestine within which the British were enjoined to establish the Jewish national home.

That undertaking remains valid under international law even today. Nothing since that time has abrogated the mandatory requirements for territories that have not subsequently come under the sovereignty of any state. Article 80 of the UN Charter expressly preserves such "rights of peoples" as existed under previous League of Nations mandates that remained thus unabrogated. Eugene W. Rostow, former U.S. under-secretary of state for political affairs and one of the framers of UN Resolution 242, has written:

Many believe that the Palestine Mandate was somehow terminated in 1947, when the British government resigned as the mandatory power. This is incorrect. A trust never terminates when a trustee dies, resigns, embezzles the trust property, or is dismissed. . . . In Palestine the British Mandate ceased to be operative as to the territories of Israel and Jordan when those states were created and recognized by the international community. But its rules apply still to the West Bank and the Gaza Strip, which have not yet been allocated either to Israel or to Jordan or become an independent state. Jordan attempted to annex the West Bank in 1951, but that annexation was never generally recognized, even by the Arab states, and now Jordan has abandoned all its claims to the territory.[30]

Many in the West believe that the principal barrier to a Palestinian state is the Israeli settlements in the "occupied" territories. This in itself is bizarre, since these settlements constitute less than 2 percent of the area involved. It is also an article of faith that the settlements are illegal. The British Foreign Office certainly thinks so. In November 2008, the British foreign secretary asserted, "Settlement activity is illegal; it also makes a Palestinian state more difficult to achieve by the week."[31] This is because the Foreign Office claims that Israel is in violation of the Fourth Geneva Convention, which stipulates that "The occupying power shall not deport or transfer parts of its own civilian population into the territory it occupies."

But these territories are not "occupied" in the sense meant by the Geneva Convention, since those rules are designed to assure the reversion of such lands to the sovereign state to which they formerly belonged—a sovereign power which, in the case of the West Bank and Gaza, does not exist. As Eugene Rostow has written, "The West Bank is not the territory of a signatory power, but an unallocated part of the British Mandate. It is hard, therefore, to see how even the most literal-minded reading of the Convention could make it apply to Jewish settlement in territories of the British Mandate west of the Jordan River."[32]

Given this point about the absence of a sovereign power over the West Bank, I asked the Foreign Office for its legal definition of "occupied territories." "As defined by UN resolutions—which everyone accepts," came the breezy reply.[33] Since when did "everyone accepts" become synonymous with objective facts or legal authority?

The West Bank and Gaza were indeed illegally occupied—by Jordan and Egypt between 1948 and 1967, a fact that unaccountably has never been mentioned by those who rage against Israel's "illegal" occupation. Places like Hebron in the West Bank are an important part of the Jews' ancient history; Hebron is an Arab town today only because the Jews who formed the majority of its population were murdered or expelled in a pogrom in 1929. The idea that these territories are Palestinian as of historic right is a myth of historical inversion. Indeed, the original Article 24 of the PLO Covenant explicitly stated that "this organization does not exercise any regional sovereignty over the West Bank." It was only in the wake of the 1967 war, after Jordan had lost the territory to Israel, that the article was revised to assert the Palestinian claim.[34]

The Jews are entitled to these territories by both law and history, and the great injustice has been done to *them*. It is *Jewish* land that has been occupied—a fact that has simply been turned on its head.

THE MYTHS OF ISRAEL'S "GENOCIDE" AND "APARTHEID"

Even more egregiously irrational—and inverted—is the claim that Israel is committing "genocide" against the Palestinians. Despite its demonstrable absurdity, this claim is regularly made, and not just by the Arabs. The president of the UN General Assembly, Miguel d'Escoto Brockmann, condemned Israel's killings of Palestinians in its 2008–2009 Gaza offensive as "genocide."[35] In 2008, Todd May, a philosophy professor at Clemson University in South Carolina, accused Israel of perpetuating a "slow motion genocide" against the Palestinians.[36] In 2006, the Israeli historian Ilan Pappé said Israel had conducted state-sponsored genocide against the Palestinians for decades and intensively in Gaza. In September 2006 he wrote, "A genocide is taking place in Gaza.... An average of eight Palestinians die daily in the Israeli attacks on the Strip."[37] And in 2000, when Israelis were being blown up in cafes and buses in an onslaught from Arab terror, Francis A. Boyle, professor of international law at the University of Illinois, proposed that the "Provisional Government of the State of Palestine and its President" institute legal proceedings against Israel before the International Court of Justice in The Hague for "violating the 1948 Convention on the Prevention and Punishment of the Crime of Genocide."[38]

As a statement that black is white this could hardly be bettered. A mere glance at the Palestinian population reveals that, far from being wiped out, it has vastly *increased*. Gaza has been overwhelmed by a demographic boom that shows no sign of abating. Between 1950 and 2007, its population jumped from 240,000 to nearly 1.5 million.[39] Since 1948, the total Palestinian Arab population has increased from just over a million to over six million, doubling in size with each new generation.

This increase is due not only to large family size but also to dramatic improvements in the health and longevity of Palestinians. In 1967, when Israel took over the administration of the West Bank and Gaza, the average lifespan of a Palestinian was forty-eight years and infant mortality approached 100 per 1,000 live births. Access to clean drinking water was limited and illiteracy was rampant. By 2008, despite the hardships caused by the ongoing conflict, Palestinians were living on average to seventy-two years, infant mortality had dropped to 23 per 1,000, most residents of Gaza and the West Bank had clean drinking water, and literacy was nearly universal among those born after 1967.[40]

While the Palestinians have thrived, the real genocide is being threatened *against* Israel—by Iran, which regularly declares its intention to wipe Israel off the map and out of history,[41] and by

Hamas, which is pledged to destroy Israel and "kill every Jew wherever you can find him."[42] Yet Israel, the designated victim of these genocidal threats, stands accused of committing genocide against people who are visibly increasing year by year.

Equally egregious in its perversity is the claim that Israel is practicing "apartheid"—a claim made by, among others, some of the victims of real apartheid, such as Bishop Desmond Tutu, who said, "The way the Palestinians are treated is the way we were treated in apartheid South Africa."[43] While it can reasonably be argued that there is social and economic discrimination against Israeli Arabs just as there is against Mizrachi (or Eastern) Jews, the fact remains that Israel gives its Arab citizens full civil and political rights. There are Israeli Arab members of the Knesset, soldiers and police officers; Israeli Arabs attend Israeli universities and are treated as equals alongside Jews and others in Israel's hospitals. The Palestinians in the territories—who are also treated equally alongside Jews in Israeli hospitals—do not have the same civil rights for the simple reason that they are not Israeli citizens; their stateless situation derives from the temporary exigencies of war, and the hardships they suffer derive in large measure from the fact that they harbor those who persist in trying to kill Israelis.

The claim of Israeli apartheid is thus demonstrably meaningless. But once again, its real sting derives from the fact that it is *Jews* who are the victims of gross *Arab* discrimination, since Jews are not allowed to live in Arab countries such as Jordan or Saudi Arabia, nor would they be in a future state of Palestine. And in 2009 a ruling by Egypt's Administrative Court required the Egyptian government to strip Egyptians of their citizenship if they married Israelis.[44] When it comes to bigoted discrimination, it is the Israelis once again who are the victims of what they themselves stand falsely accused of perpetrating.

There are many other examples of irrational thinking and demonstrable falsehoods in the animus against Israel. It is a departure from reality to believe, for example, that the Arab/Israel impasse would be ended by the creation of a Palestinian state when the Arabs have repeatedly refused to accept a "two-state solution." They were offered such a state in 1936 and 1947; they were offered the land that is claimed for such a state in 1967 when the West Bank and Gaza were proffered to the Arabs in return for peace, and the response was the famous "three noes"; more than 90 percent of the territories was offered for such a state in 2000, to which the Palestinians responded by launching the "Second Intifada" campaign of mass murder against the Israelis; and by all accounts they were offered much the same thing in 2008 by the Israeli government of Ehud Olmert.

It's also important to realize that two states *were* established. In 1920, the Allied Supreme Council granted the mandate for Palestine to Britain. At that time, Palestine included what is now Jordan. One year later, Winston Churchill gave almost 80 percent of Palestine away to King Abdullah to form what is now Jordan. Therefore, Jordan is eastern Palestine. So the Arabs *were* given a state of Palestine. The core of the problem is that they never wanted the Jews to have a state too.

It is irrational—indeed, uniquely so—to exculpate countries that were artificially created in the postcolonial era, such as Pakistan, from questions about the validity of their existence, while subjecting the State of Israel, the one country whose creation was specifically legitimated by the United Nations, to precisely such questioning. It is irrational—and unique—to expect a country that has been under existential attack for the six decades since its founding to make compromises with its aggressors and agree to at least some of their demands even while they continue to attack it and murder its citizens.

The multiple irrationalities, delusions and falsehoods that constitute the mainstream attitude to Israel within the West make it blind to what is going on in front of its eyes. Time after time, otherwise cynical, reality-hardened journalists have published or broadcast claims of Israeli "atrocities" that are clearly staged fabrications, or allegations whose implausibility should provoke a skeptical response but instead they are presented uncritically as objective accounts. In so doing, these journalists have helped stir up a hysterical hatred of Israel.

FALSE ALLEGATIONS AGAINST ISRAEL

In 2002, Western journalists and United Nations envoys were in an uproar over an alleged Israeli massacre of hundreds of Palestinians in the West Bank town of Jenin. There were supposedly eyewitness accounts of Israeli bulldozers shoveling hundreds of Palestinian corpses into mass graves; stories of Israeli soldiers murdering Palestinian children in front of their parents and throwing their bodies into wells and sewage pits. The European Union's external relations commissioner at the time, Chris Patten, fumed that "Israelis can't trample over the rule of law, over the Geneva conventions, over what are generally regarded as acceptable norms of behaviour."[45] Eventually, however, it emerged that far from a massacre there was a battle in which Israeli soldiers went house to house rooting out terrorists, in the course of which around fifty-six mostly armed Palestinians were killed, as were twenty-three Israeli soldiers.[46] The atrocity claims were total fabrications.

When Israel went to war against Lebanon in 2006, there were many examples of staged events reported as authentic. For example, there were claims that Israeli aircraft intentionally fired missiles at two Lebanese Red Cross ambulances performing rescue operations, causing huge explosions that injured everyone inside the vehicles. This claim, which gave incendiary force to the lie that Israel deliberately targeted civilians, was repeated by ITV News, the *Guardian*, *Time*, the *Boston Globe*, NBC News, the *New York Times*, the *Age*, and thousands of other outlets around the world.

But anyone with even the most cursory knowledge of the kind of missiles used by the Israeli air force would grasp immediately that the hole in the roof of the ambulance whose picture went round the world could not have been caused by such a missile. If a missile had indeed hit it there would have been no roof to inspect; nor would there have been an ambulance anymore. Yet aside from the hole in the roof, the ambulance in the pictures was pretty well intact. And the driver, who allegedly had been seriously hurt, was pictured with only minor injuries, and these had miraculously disappeared without a trace in pictures taken a few days later. Subsequently it appeared that the hole in the roof was almost certainly an air vent.[47]

Undeterred by this encounter with what has been dubbed "Pallywood," after Israel's Operation Cast Lead in Gaza in January 2009 the *Guardian* published a multipage "special investigation" by Clancy Chassay accompanied by three videos claiming that Israel committed "war crimes" by deliberately targeting civilians, medical personnel, ambulances and hospitals.[48] The article presented these allegations as facts, even though they were unsupported by any evidence and were made by people in Gaza who either favored Hamas or would have been controlled and schooled by Hamas to tell lies under pain of torture or death. But the most striking feature of these claims was their inherent implausibility.

For example, Chassay asserted that three young brothers had been used by Israeli soldiers as human shields. But this was hardly likely. The whole point of human shields is that they are a deterrent against attack because the other side will not want to kill civilians being used in such a way. That is undoubtedly true of the Israelis: there have been countless examples of their aborting attacks because Palestinian children were seen or suspected to be present. But children and other civilians were present because Hamas uses them as human shields. The Palestinians deliberately kept families in houses that the IDF warned would be targeted—even putting them on the rooftops—in order that they should be killed as martyrs to the cause of destroying Israel. And as is well known, the Palestinians also turn their own children into human bombs for the same reason. So it was hardly likely that the Israelis would assume that if they used Palestinian children as human shields, Hamas would not fire at them.

Most ludicrously of all, one video displayed what it solemnly stated was an Israeli army magazine found in one of the destroyed houses, with a picture showing one of the three brothers bound and blindfolded before he claimed to have been stripped to his underpants and used as a human shield. Since Operation Cast Lead lasted from December 27 to January 18, Chassay was apparently claiming that the Israelis managed to publish during that time a magazine with a picture of a boy they had captured during that very same operation, and then left it lying around in the rubble, miraculously without so much as a tear in its pages, for the *Guardian* conveniently to find.

The most egregious of the staged "atrocities," however, was the "killing" of a twelve-year-old Palestinian named Mohammed al-Dura by Israeli troops in Gaza in November 2000, a scene depicted in footage transmitted by the France 2 television station at the beginning of the Second Intifada. The iconic image of the child crouching with his father behind a barrel next to a concrete wall, apparently in a vain attempt to shelter from the gunfight raging around them before he was allegedly shot dead by the Israelis, served to incite terrorist violence and atrocities around the world. The death scene has been replicated on murals and posters as well as postage stamps, even making an appearance in the video of Daniel Pearl's beheading.

Yet it is clear to anyone looking at this episode in detail that the whole thing was staged. There is devastating evidence on untransmitted footage that was finally shown in a French courtroom in November 2007, revealing that, during what was said to be forty-five minutes of continuous shooting by the Israelis at a Palestinian demonstration, there was no sign of anyone being killed or injured at all. Most striking of all, Mohammed al-Dura himself was seen to raise his arm and peep through his fingers seconds after the France 2 correspondent Charles Enderlin told the world he had been shot dead.[49]

Granted, the world had not seen this hitherto suppressed footage, which France 2 was forced to produce in the course of a libel case it had brought against a French media watchdog, Philippe Karsenty, for claiming that it had knowingly transmitted a blood libel against the State of Israel. Even so, the film that *was* transmitted, with Mohammed al-Dura apparently cowering with his father in the line of continuous Israeli fire and finally being shot dead, showed no sign of any wound whatsoever. There was no blood. His body was unmarked, as was his father's. And yet no one asked how this could have been so; no one questioned the story that accompanied these pictures. It was believed despite the evidence of people's own eyes. And when the truth finally emerged, that an image which had been the direct cause of untold numbers of murderous terrorist rampages around the world was in fact a staged Pallywood fabrication, no one wanted to know.

There is no other world conflict that is so obsessively falsified. Where Israel is involved, truth and reason are totally suspended. Irrationality and hysteria rule instead.

5

SCIENTIFIC
TRIUMPHALISM

In October 2008, following a debate in Oxford's Natural History Museum between the prominent zoologist and atheist campaigner Professor Richard Dawkins and John Lennox, a professor of mathematics at Oxford, I asked Dawkins whether he believed that the origin of all matter was most likely to have been an entirely spontaneous event. He agreed that he did think so. I put it to him that he seemed therefore to be arguing that something could be created out of nothing—which surely runs counter to the scientific principles of verifiable evidence that he tells us should govern all our thinking.

Although physicists often write as if something *can* arise from nothing, what they actually mean by "nothing" in every such case is actually "something"—like the empty quantum field, the area that exists between two separate physical systems. So Dawkins's belief that matter had probably arisen from literally nothing at all seemed itself to be precisely the kind of irrationality, or "magic," that he scorns.

In reply he said that, although he agreed this was a problematic position, he believed that the first particle arose spontaneously from nothing because the alternative explanation—God—was more incredible. (In focusing on particles, Dawkins overlooked the fact that these emerge spontaneously all the time; he seemed to confuse particle generation with the much more general question I was asking concerning the spontaneous appearance of matter in any form—which term I use here to include the quantum field itself and whatever it is that modern physics accepts as material.)

But then Dawkins vouchsafed something utterly unexpected. He was, he said, not necessarily averse to the idea that life on earth had been created by a governing intelligence—provided that such an intelligence had arrived on earth from another planet. I thought for a moment I must have misheard him. But no, he was indeed suggesting in all seriousness that life on earth might have been imported by beings from outer space.[1]

Leaving aside the question of how that extraterrestrial intelligence had itself been created in the first place, it seemed quite astounding that the arch-apostle of reason appeared to find the concept of God more unlikely as an explanation of the universe than the existence and plenipotentiary power of extraterrestrial little green men. But just as astonishingly, Dawkins is not the first scientist to have suggested such a concept. The theory was put forward by no less a person than Professor Francis Crick, one of the discoverers of DNA, the building block of life.

Crick found it impossible to believe that DNA could have been the product of evolution because of the nature of the genetic code, which is identical in all living things with the exception of mitochondria (cellular power plants), where the differences are small. But as a committed atheist, he did not believe in an intelligent Creator either. Having gone through all the weaknesses of theories of life originating on earth, he put forward the theory of "directed panspermia," the "seeding" of life on earth by beings from another planet—which was first suggested in the nineteenth century by the Swedish physicist Arrhenius. In 1973, Crick and the chemist Leslie Orgel published a paper in the journal *Icarus* suggesting that life may have arrived on earth through directed panspermia,[2] a proposition which Crick subsequently developed in his book *Life Itself*. In this theory, "the micro-organisms are supposed to have travelled in the head of an unmanned spaceship sent to earth by a higher civilisation which had developed elsewhere some billions of years ago. The spaceship was unmanned so that its range would be as great as possible. Life started here when these organisms were dropped into the primitive ocean and began to multiply."[3]

Crick concluded that directed panspermia was a "valid scientific theory," although "premature."[4] Subsequently, he abandoned this theory and returned to the idea that life began spontaneously through purely natural mechanisms.[5] But soon he reaffirmed his interest in directed panspermia in his preface to the first edition of *The RNA World* in 1993.

One has to wonder how scientists such as Francis Crick or Richard Dawkins, who one might have thought would be committed with every fiber of their being to evidence-based reasoning, could possibly entertain such elaborately contrived theories with no more claim to be taken seriously than fantasies conjured up from the imagination. How could the standard-bearers of rational thought have become so irrational?

The answer, paradoxical as it may seem, is that this is precisely because of their belief that everything in the world is governed by what we deduce from the material world. This rules out metaphysics and religious faith, which stand outside that world. But since other planets plainly exist, and since science does not rule out life there as a possibility, it follows, by this thinking, that a theory involving beings from other planets importing life to earth is not to be dismissed—whereas belief in a Creator God is unthinkable. Directed panspermia is thus a dramatic example of how, by fetishizing materialism, supposed rationalists can descend into irrationality. Scorning religious faith as superstition, scientists such as Dawkins or Crick flirt instead with nonsense straight out of science fiction.

SCIENTISM, OR SCIENTIFIC TRIUMPHALISM

The explanation of how a section of scientific thinking has become unreasonable is deeply paradoxical. In Western culture, Christian religious belief buckled under the pressure of scientific materialism. The resulting vacuum was filled by science itself. In a display of over-reach, science then made claims for itself that it could not sustain, venturing beyond its field into the province properly occupied by religion and, in the process, undermining the place of reason within science itself.

When science first developed in the West, it thought of itself merely as a tool to explore the natural world. It made no claim upon the separate spheres of philosophy or religion, which it was content should coexist alongside it. Indeed, scientists were overwhelmingly religious believers (as many still are). As Einstein said, "Science without religion is lame, religion without science is blind."[6] In modern times, however, science has given rise to "scientism," the belief that scientific materialism alone can answer *all* the questions in the world. Thus Peter Atkins, professor of chemistry at Oxford University, has typically claimed: "There is no reason to suppose that science cannot deal with every aspect of existence."[7]

Insofar as scientism has any respectable intellectual antecedents —rather than being merely a crude prejudice that everything derives from elementary particles—it derives from a strain of thought going back to the Enlightenment that became known as positivism. This was the belief that the only authentic knowledge derives from the experience of the senses. It can be traced back to the eighteenth-century Scottish philosopher David Hume and was extrapolated into a fully fledged philosophy of science by Auguste Comte in the nineteenth century.

In *Language, Truth and Logic*, published in 1936, the philosopher A. J. Ayer established positivism as a more generally applicable philosophical doctrine, but one which quickly foundered upon its own internal contradiction. Through the "verification principle," Ayer argued that statements that cannot be tested by rules of science, language or logic have no meaning at all. In itself, this was a nonsensical proposition: since the verification principle cannot itself be verified, by its own standard it too must be meaningless.

Nevertheless the principle set up an apparent conflict between religion and science. Since religion could not be verified, it could have no meaning. Only science could have meaning, and so science alone became synonymous with reason. There could be nothing beyond the natural world; to believe otherwise was irrational. In the words of the astronomer Carl Sagan: "The cosmos is all there is, or was, or ever shall be."[8] Science would therefore answer all the questions in the world.

But science cannot account for everything. Many people—including many scientists—have pointed out that such a view is as absurd as it is arrogant. There are clearly many aspects of existence that cannot be reduced to materialist scientific analysis: love, law, philosophy, appreciation of beauty, belief in right and wrong. It does not follow that these things lie beyond rational understanding. The zoologist Sir Peter Medawar criticized the positivist attitude as the quickest way to discredit scientists and science, saying that the limits to science were demonstrated by its inability to answer questions such as "How did everything begin?" or "What are we all here for?"[9] These questions could properly be addressed through religion, literature or philosophy.

In their book *Philosophical Foundations of Neuroscience*, the neuroscientist M. R. Bennett and the philosopher P. M. S. Hacker mount a monumental attack on materialism or "reductionist science," which they say confuses conceptual questions with empirical ones. Criticizing Richard Dawkins's belief that "science is the only way we know to understand the real world,"[10] they say that there is no such thing as "explaining the world," only different ways of explaining phenomena *in* the world. And the natural sciences do not describe and explain every phenomenon that is somehow describable and explicable. To believe that there is no such thing as *understanding* aesthetic phenomena, for example, or that such understanding apes our understanding of physics or chemistry, is a matter of dogmatism.[11]

Such dogmatism is precisely what is on display among scientists such as Atkins or Dawkins for whom science defines the world. Since they don't accept that there can possibly be any questions that science can't answer, the fact that it cannot answer some questions only proves to them that they should not be asked. The fact that science cannot answer questions of ultimate purpose proves to them that there is no such thing as any ultimate purpose. The fact that science cannot prove the existence of God proves to them that God does not exist. In fact, the only thing that is proved by such conclusions is that scientific rationality disappears into its own black hole.

THE ROOTS OF SCIENTISM DO NOT ACTUALLY LIE IN SCIENCE AT ALL

The conflict provoked by scientific triumphalism is not actually between religion and science, but between materialism—sometimes also called "naturalism"—on the one hand, and science *and* faith on the other. Naturalism holds that the natural or material world accounts for everything in existence. Naturalism, says the mathematician David Berlinski, "comes closest to conveying what scientists regard as the spirit of science, the source of its superiority to religious thought. It is commended as an attitude, a general metaphysical position, a universal doctrine—and often all three."[12]

Yet as the theoretical particle physicist Stephen Barr said in his Erasmus Lecture in 2002, "materialism" is not really science at all but a school of philosophy defined by the belief that nothing exists except "matter"—or, as Democritus put it, "atoms and the void." Crucially, Barr added, materialism was also a "passionately held ideology" with a purpose:

Indeed, it is the ideology of a great part of the scientific world. Its adherents see science as having a mission that goes beyond the mere investigation of nature or the discovery of physical laws. That mission is to free mankind from superstition in all its forms, and especially in the form of religious belief.[13]

Since science is essentially objective, involving the study of how things actually are, "materialism" would therefore seem to be its antithesis, since its starting point is the desire to impose upon the natural world a particular and limited way of looking at it. Moreover, it does so with an ideological end in view: the destruction of religious belief. Its own core principle, however—that the end of the matter is matter—is surely itself a kind of faith since it cannot be proved. Yet as David Berlinski points out, materialism creates the illusion that religion is reasoned away. If all is matter, then God is a material object; if God is not susceptible to materialist evidence, he therefore cannot exist; if he does exist, it follows that he is not God. An inexorable trap, but sprung from a premise that is false.

HOW MATERIALISM LEADS TO UNREASONABLE ASSERTIONS

Scientism destroys itself by its own internal logic. Just as A. J. Ayer's "verification principle" self-destructs because it cannot be verified itself, so the statement that nothing beyond science can be true is also unverifiable. As John Lennox argues, the assertion that science is the only path to truth is not itself deduced from science but is a statement *about* science for which there is no evidence.[14] Scientism is therefore not rational, and it leads scientists into making absurd and unsupported claims.

The most conspicuous exemplar of such reductionism is Richard Dawkins, the high priest at the shrine of empirical reason. He has said, "The universe is nothing but a collection of atoms in motion, human beings are simply machines for propagating DNA and the propagation of DNA is a self-sustaining process. It is every living object's sole reason for living."[15] But if Dawkins's mind were nothing other than a collection of atoms, it would surely have been incapable of producing *The God Delusion* and all his other books arguing that we are merely a collection of atoms. It is hard to imagine how rationality can be arrived at through a collection of random characteristics. The essence of randomness is purposelessness. Things happen by sheer accident. But when we try to unpick rationality, we can't get away from the fact that it is *purposive*. Indeed, some of Dawkins's very own theories about ostensibly random processes, such as his proposition that life is replicated through the "selfish gene," seem to imply as much.

Rationality involves evidence, inference, logic, deduction, proof—and these in turn involve intention and goals. We aim at deducing truth from evidence based on logic. These concepts are also normative: what is true is better than what is false. And in exercising our rationality, we assume that we possess free will by framing our theories and choosing to follow the evidence.

Without purposefulness, then, there can be no rationality. And that is the consequence of Dawkins's proposition, as John Polkinghorne summed it up: "Thought is replaced by electro-chemical neural events. Two such events cannot confront each other in rational discourse. They are neither right nor wrong. They just happen.... The world of rational discourse dissolves into the absurd chatter of firing synapses."[16]

It also dissolves into the absurd chatter of overreach. For those who believe nothing exists beyond the material world, there can be no credible argument for the existence of God. But those people must surely accept the corollary: by the same criteria, there can be no credible materialist argument for the *non*-existence of God. That is because God lies by definition outside the limits of the material world. As the philosopher Roger Scruton has observed, the argument that it is meaningless to ask what caused the conditions for the origin of matter since such things have no scientific answer is a self-serving argument, because the question lies beyond science; it is a philosophical question.[17]

In the natural world, everything must have a beginning. But God by definition does not belong to the natural world because he is said to have created it. Eliezer Berkovits explains why questions about God and the origin of the cosmos necessarily stand apart from the questions that are addressed by science:

> The idea of creation means that God created out of nothing a universe in which every effect must originate in something that was previously in existence. Out of nothing, God created a world in which nothing comes from nothing. One is therefore not justified in drawing conclusions from the observable order of things as to what might have been the "order" prior to creation in the timeless and spaceless state of divine "aloneness". The coming into being of the whole of the cosmos is an essentially different event from the coming into being of particulars within the framework of the already created whole. No deduction of any kind may be made from the one to the other. Therefore, notwithstanding the fact that in all of our experience nothing comes out of nothing, the world itself may well be God's creation *ex nihilo*.[18]

Trying to use science to "prove" the nonexistence of God therefore leads straight into the province of unfounded assertions. That's why scientists such as Dawkins depart from reason by claiming that Darwin's theory of evolution—which sought to explain how complex organisms evolved through unguided natural selection—somehow accounts for the origin of life itself. In *The Blind Watchmaker*, Dawkins wrote that "the evidence of evolution reveals a universe without design." Natural selection was the "blind watchmaker," the "unconscious, automatic process" that was "the explanation for the existence and apparently purposeful form of all life."[19] In *Climbing Mount Improbable*, he wrote: "Nobody knows how it happened but, somehow, without violating the laws of physics and chemistry, a molecule arose that just happened to have the property of self-copy-ing—a replicator."[20] As the late, great comedian/magician Tommy Cooper would have said, "Just like that!" There is no evidence what-ever for this just-so story. It belongs not to science but to Dawkins's imagination.

In *The God Delusion*, Dawkins states that any designer actually came *after* the design, that "any creative intelligence, of sufficient complexity to design anything, comes into existence only as the end product of an extended process of gradual evolution."[21] One might think this is putting the cosmic cart before the horse and expecting the cart to proceed on its own volition. In a similar vein, the chemist Peter Atkins believes the universe simply created itself through a "cosmic bootstrap," in which "space-time generates its own dust in the process of its own self-assembly."[22] Yet as the theologian Keith Ward riposted, it is "logically impossible for a cause to bring about some effect without already being in existence."[23]

The same weakness lies in some of Dawkins's arguments that belief in God is illogical. One of his favorite drum-roll moments is to scoff that it is stupid to believe God created the universe because no one can answer the next question, "So who created God?" Yet in exactly the same way, Dawkins can be asked: "So what created the first particle or the quantum field?" This is a more deadly version of the conundrum, in fact, since the first particle and the quantum field are governed by the laws of science whereas God, by definition, is not.

Because Dawkins's arguments depend on a blinkered view of reality, they become hopelessly stranded at the summit of Mount Improbable. Various scientists have demonstrated that the idea of life or all matter arising spontaneously is mathematically ignorant. The astronomer Sir Fred Hoyle famously quipped that it was as likely as the spontaneous self-assembly of a Boeing 747. "The likeli-hood of the formation of life from inanimate matter is one to a num-ber with 40 thousand noughts after it," he said. "It is enough to bury

Darwin and the whole theory of evolution. There was no primeval soup, neither on this planet nor on any other, and if the beginnings of life were not random they must therefore have been the product of purposeful intelligence."[24]

Harold Morowitz, a Yale University physicist, imagined as an experiment a broth of living bacteria that was superheated so that all the complex chemicals were broken down into their basic building blocks. After the mixture cooled, he concluded, the odds of a single bacterium reassembling by chance was one in 10,100,000,000,000.[25] One common counterargument to this improbability is to say that over a very long period of time, what seems extremely unlikely eventually turns into the inevitable. But writing about Morowitz's calculation in his book *Origins: A Skeptic's Guide to the Creation of Life on Earth*, Robert Shapiro remarked: "The improbability involved in generating even one bacterium is so large that it reduces all considerations of time and space to nothingness. Given such odds, the time until the black holes evaporate and the space to the ends of the universe would make no difference at all. If we were to wait, we would truly be waiting for a miracle."[26]

Dawkins replies scornfully that such claims reveal merely ignorance of evolution. The whole point, he says, is that organisms do not assemble themselves in one great leap but through tiny incremental steps.[27] But as John Lennox demonstrates, tiny incremental steps make spontaneous origin even *more* mathematically improbable. Dawkins attempts to overcome the problem by what is in effect an algorithmic trick, but which appears to undermine his whole argument, as Lennox explains:

> Dawkins tells us that evolution is mindless. What, then, does he mean by introducing two mechanisms, each of which bears *every evidence of the input of an intelligent mind*—a mechanism that compares each attempt with the target phrase, and a mechanism which preserves a successful attempt? And strangest of all, the very information that the

mechanisms are supposed to produce is apparently already contained somewhere within the organism, whose genesis he claims to be simulating by his process. The argument is entirely circular.[28]

Although the view that living systems arose from inorganic matter is widespread enough to amount to an orthodoxy of thought, it is hard to find any evidence to support it. The experiments probing the origins of life all depend crucially on the intervention of the chemist conducting the experiment. If the current orthodoxy is not true, then the only alternative—let us be honest—is some form of designing intelligence. Which leads inescapably to religious or metaphysical belief.

THE FALSE POLARITY BETWEEN SCIENCE AND METAPHYSICS

Dawkins and the scientific triumphalists have succeeded in driving a wedge between science and religion because they have persuaded people that science and materialism, or naturalism, are indistinguishable. But denying any validity to metaphysics in this way actually undermines science itself—counterintuitive as this may seem.

Although Sir Karl Popper's famous doctrine that all scientific theories must be capable of being falsified is itself open to serious criticism, his thinking is widely respected among scientists. Popper strongly opposed positivism, however. He believed that the division between science and metaphysics was false and ahistorical. Statements that metaphysics was meaningless were based on a "naive and naturalistic" view of meaningfulness, one that threw all scientific theories onto the same scrap-heap. The positivists' principle of verifiability would make scientific knowledge impossible, he said, since the fundamental laws of nature were themselves not verifiable and no more derived from observation than did metaphysics.

Moreover, the epistemology of science presupposes something that exists beyond itself. In attempting to squash religious faith, scientists are fond of declaring that just because we don't yet under-stand the origin of the universe, this doesn't mean we won't ever understand it, since everything about the universe is capable of sci-entific discovery. But as the philosopher Leo Strauss observed, this boast undermines those scientists' own doctrine that nothing exists but matter. Science, he says, is understood by positivists as being capable of infinite progress. Every scientific result is provisional and subject to future revisions, and this will never change. But science can sustain infinite progress only if its object possesses an inner infinity. "The belief admitted by all believers in science today—that science is by its nature essentially progressive and eternally progres-sive—implies, without saying it, that being is mysterious."[29] In other words, the concept of infinity implicit in scientific progress places a "mystery" or metaphysical idea at the very core of science itself.

So the conflict between science and religion is totally misplaced —and indeed, unscientific. In reality, the more science explains the world to us and the more we understand how it works, the more it creates the need further to understand and to explain. Far from clos-ing off the questions that take us into the realm of religious faith, sci-ence progressively *increases* them, by leading from questions about "what" and "how" to "why"—which it cannot answer. This was par-ticularly true of the discoveries made by physics during the last cen-tury—such as quantum mechanics—which, as Popper observed, created areas of unproveability and subjectivity that have blown materialism clean out of the water. The view that science was char-acterized by observation while metaphysics relied on speculation was a false demarcation, he said, since modern theories of physics were highly speculative and abstract.

Science has thus left naturalism far behind. Many physicists and mathematicians have accepted that their discoveries inescapably sug-gest a realm beyond the material, but evolutionary biologists seem to be incapable of accepting such an implication. Possibly this is because biologists *are* naturalists: they deal with what they can see in the world of living organisms. Not needing to look at what lies beneath, they assume that what they can see is all there is.

That may be why scientists like Richard Dawkins appear not to grasp the difference between matter and information. "Information" denotes the biological programs that govern all activity in the natural world; it accounts for the difference between inert matter and living organisms. One of the foremost advocates of evolutionary theory, George C. Williams, has acknowledged: "The gene is a package of information, not an object. . . . In biology, when you're talking about things like genes and genotypes and gene pools, you're talking about information, not physical objective reality."[30]

To understand the role and character of biological information is to see the limits of scientific materialism. As the director of the German Federal Physics and Technology Institute, Professor Werner Gitt, has observed,

> A physical matter cannot produce an information code. All experiences show that every piece of creative information represents some mental effort and can be traced to a personal idea-giver who exercised his own free will, and who is endowed with an intelligent mind. . . . There is no known law of nature, no known process and no known sequence of events which can cause information to originate by itself in matter. . . . Information is something different from matter. It can never be reduced to matter. The origin of information and physical matter must be investigated separately.[31]

THE TERROR OF GOING WHERE THE EVIDENCE LEADS

The Dawkins/Atkins school of scientific triumphalists cannot accept the crucial point that information, as opposed to matter, necessarily implies some kind of creative intelligence behind it. They are therefore refusing to go where the evidence leads them—the key characteristic of a discourse based on reason. And what is making them so resistant is of enormous significance. It is not because they are confident that the counterargument is wrong; it is because they are terrified that it *might be right*. The consequence of it being right is too awful for them to contemplate: they would have to acknowledge that God might exist.

Richard Lewontin, a geneticist at Harvard, has been remarkably frank in admitting why a materialist ideology has a powerful hold on scientists:

> Our willingness to accept scientific claims that are against common sense is the key to understanding the real struggle between science and the supernatural. We take the side of science in spite of the patent absurdity of some of its constructs, in spite of its failure to fulfil many of its extravagant promises of health and life, in spite of the tolerance of the scientific community for unsubstantiated just-so stories, because we have a prior commitment, a commitment to materialism.... Moreover, that materialism is absolute, for we cannot allow a Divine Foot in the door.[32]

The terror of allowing even a Divine Toenail to peep over the threshold is so great that these scientists are prepared to put forward theories they know are absurd. Their phobia against religion is so profound that they would rather entertain the possibility of little green men from outer space than the existence of God.

They would rather believe the impossible, as a Harvard University biochemist and Nobel laureate, George Wald, confessed in 1954 when he contemplated the origins of life. "Spontaneous generation of a living organism is impossible," he conceded, and yet he believed it was the cause of our existence.

> When it comes to the origin of life there are only two possibilities: creation or spontaneous generation. There is no third way. Spontaneous generation was disproved one hundred years ago, but that leads us to only one other conclusion, that of supernatural creation. We cannot accept that on philosophical grounds; therefore, we choose to believe the impossible: that life arose spontaneously by chance![33]

Of course, it is irrational to believe what is known to be impossible. So Wald went on to claim that "impossible" didn't mean the same thing in science as it did in colloquial usage. "Impossible" in science actually meant, it appeared, entirely "probable" and indeed "inevitable" given sufficient passage of time, say a couple of billion years or so. The happy feat of verbal legerdemain behind Wald's redefinition of "impossible" unfortunately lost its capacity to suspend disbelief when the research into amino acids on which it was based, wherein the graduate student Stanley L. Miller purported to show how the first elementary life forms had started through random chemical reactions, was demolished by further research in 1979. Wald, in response, published an unprecedented retraction of his earlier claim.[34]

The grim resolve to avoid the concept of a Creator has led into ever more silly and unscientific arguments about the origin of life. For instance, there is the "multiverse" theory propounded by the cosmologist Sir Martin Rees, along with Richard Dawkins, in an effort to explain the inexplicable. According to this theory, there are many different universes with different laws and physical constants; our own just happens to belong to a subset of universes that by happy chance are conducive to the appearance of complexity and consciousness.

But there is no evidence at all for a "multiverse." It is sheer fantasy. As the philosopher Anthony Flew points out, Rees himself acknowledges that the idea is "highly speculative" and might well be wrong.[35] In fact, it is less than speculative—there is no evidence for it at all. Other scientists are more damning in their description. The physicist Paul Davies has said that such an infinitely complicated charade "explains everything and nothing" and makes the whole idea of "explanation" meaningless. "Followed to its logical extreme," he wrote, "it leads to conclusions that are at best bizarre."[36] The philosopher Richard Swinburne was even more cutting: "It is crazy to postulate a trillion (causally unconnected) universes to explain the features of one universe, when postulating one entity (God) will do the job."[37]

Why are some scientists so anxious to deny the possibility of a supernatural Creator that they say ridiculous, unscientific and irrational things? The reason is that their firmly held materialism does not derive from evidence but from "a passionately held ideology," in Stephen Barr's words. A prior commitment to materialism holds sway over scientific thinking, as Richard Lewontin acknowledged:

> It is not that the methods and institutions of science somehow compel us to accept a material explanation of the phenomenal world but, on the contrary, that we are forced by our *a priori* adherence to material causes to create an apparatus of investigation and a set of concepts that produce material explanations, no matter how counter-intuitive, no matter how mystifying to the uninitiated.[38]

This is a devastating admission. It is a confession of intellectual corruption: Facts are made subservient to an idea. Materialism is thus not a means to unlock knowledge, but an ideology. And the cause that it promotes in this devious and manipulative way is the destruction of religion.

THE CREATION MYTH OF SCIENTIFIC NATURALISM

Darwinism—or to be more precise, neo-Darwinism with its additional genetic and other baggage—is the principal vehicle for materialism, since it assumes that the entire natural world is a closed system of material causes and effects. As the law professor and anti-scientism campaigner Phillip E. Johnson has observed, Darwinism has become the most important element in the religion of naturalism, with its own ethical agenda and plan for salvation through social and genetic engineering. Darwinism has turned into "the creation myth of scientific naturalism."[39]

In recent years, Darwinism has found itself challenged on two quite different fronts: a resurgent and muscular Christian religious literalism in America, and discoveries in physics suggesting that beyond science lie mysteries it cannot explain. To beat off this twin challenge to materialism, Richard Dawkins went to war against God under the banners of the blind watchmaker and the selfish gene. Just as scientism had supplanted religion, so Darwinism was now to supplant Genesis as the atheistic creation myth.

But by seeking to colonize another sphere of thinking altogether, the Darwinists have overreached themselves with disastrous results. Trying to use science to prove that religion is irrational, they have instead made science irrational by making grandiose claims for evolution that are not backed up by evidence. Their accusation that their opponents deny the facts of evolution is not true. It is more accurate to say that these critics oppose the totalizing creed of Darwinism, which makes claims for evolution that it cannot sustain.

Evolution is a slippery word that has many meanings: development and change within a population over time; variation within prescribed limits of complexity; the coming into existence of new organs and structures. No one doubts the veracity of microevolution, meaning changes within a population over time. But Dawkins and others intent on proving that materialism explains everything argue that microevolution turned into macroevolution, a process whereby all life evolved from one common ancestor. This in itself is controversial even among the ranks of evolutionary biologists. More fundamentally, however, they also present macroevolution as the explanation for the origin of life itself—and all of this as not mere theory but fact. According to Dawkins, "the sheer weight of evidence totally and utterly, sledgehammeringly, overwhelmingly strongly supports the conclusion that evolution is true."[40] By this he appears to mean the whole macroevolution bag of tricks, including its explanation of the origins of life; but the evidence, with or without sledgehammers, is far less straightforward.

In his sparkling book *Darwinian Fairytales*, the philosopher David Stove—who was himself a fan of Darwin and a supporter of certain forms of natural selection theory—shredded the Darwinian belief that organisms survive and develop through the constant ruthless competition of natural selection.[41] As he pointed out, most members of a species would *lose* the struggle for survival in such a competition. The human race could not have continued to exist unless cooperation had always been stronger than competition. While Darwin's theory had the more fit crowding out the less well adapted, Darwin himself lamented that "the weak members of civilized societies propagate their kind."[42] Moreover, all the theories that Darwinists have come up with to resolve this dilemma are fatally and obviously flawed.[43]

Some prominent evolutionary scientists have candidly acknowledged the absence of evidence for macroevolution (an absence they have tried to finesse). In 1980, the prominent American Darwinist Stephen Jay Gould blew the whistle on the standard claim that "all evolution is due to the accumulation of small genetic changes guided by natural selection and that trans-specific evolution is nothing but an extrapolation and magnification of the events that take place within populations and species." This theory, he said, had "beguiled me with its unifying power when I was a graduate student in the mid-1960s; since then I have been watching it slowly unravel as a universal theory of evolution."[44]

In a similar vein, the British developmental biologist Brian Goodwin wrote that Darwin's assumption of a gradual accumulation of small hereditary differences appeared to lack significant support, and that "some other process is responsible for the emergent properties of life, those distinctive features that separate one group of organisms from another—fishes and amphibians, worms and insects, horsetails and grasses."[45]

The fossil record in particular is problematic in failing to provide evidence of the development of one species from another. Far from showing developmental progress through transitional forms, the fossil record shows complex life forms arriving suddenly, without precursor—most notably in the Cambrian Explosion some 570 million years ago, when most forms of complex animal life emerged seemingly with no evolutionary trail. The paleontologist Harry Whittington, who pioneered the modern study of the Cambrian Explosion, wrote in 1985, "I look sceptically upon diagrams that show the branching diversity of animal life through time and come down at the base to a single kind of animal.... Animals may have originated more than once, in different places and at different times."[46]

In 2007, Eugene Koonin of the National Center for Biotechnology Information at the National Institutes of Health in the United States published a paper saying, "Major transitions in biological evolution show the same pattern of sudden emergence of diverse forms at a new level of complexity."[47] The paleontologist Niles Eldredge was even more candid, saying that evolutionary novelty "usually shows up with a bang" and admitting, "We paleontologists have said that the history of life supports [the story of gradual adaptive change] knowing all the while it does not."[48]

Darwinists have come up with various theories to explain away the missing fossil evidence. But these theories basically boil down to the belief that eventually the gaps will be filled. And that's just what macroevolution is—a belief. It is held so strongly not because the evidence is overwhelming, but because the alternative is unconscionable. Thus it is a form of dogma.

Professor Michael Behe, a biochemist, is one of the main proponents of the theory that the origin of life could not have been a random event but must have been designed by some kind of governing intelligence. As such, he is regarded by Darwinists as public enemy number one. But Behe actually supports the idea of common descent.[49] What he rejects is the belief that the process occurred by random mutation and natural selection. When people hear the claim that "evolution is supported by overwhelming evidence," he wrote, they need to understand that "virtually all of the evidence concerns just common descent. The experimental evidence that natural selection could build a vertebrate from an invertebrate, a mammal from a reptile, or a human from an ape is a bit less than the experimental evidence for superstring theory—that is, none at all."[50]

Certain biologists do appear to realize that Darwinism is built on sand, as the philosopher of science Alexander Rosenberg points out:

> The theory of evolution itself is riven with controversy, and agreement cannot even be claimed on the canonical expression of its central ideas. Indeed, there remain members of the biological community who deny its warrant and even reject its claim to cognitive legitimacy. Leaving aside special Creationists with fundamentalist objections to the theory, there are serious biologists who hold it to be a vacuous and circular triviality. Others insist that, though a respectable theory, it does not provide even in principle the explanatory and predictive results physics has led us to expect of a theory. Moreover, there is no consensus on how this theory is to be related to the rest of biology.[51]

Indeed, is Darwinian evolution actually science at all? Sir Karl Popper didn't think so; he said the theory wasn't testable and therefore was "metaphysical." In his view, moreover, "To say that a species now living is adapted to its environment is, in fact, almost tautological. . . . Adaptation or fitness is defined by modern evolutionists as survival value, and can be measured by actual success in survival: there is hardly any possibility of testing a theory as feeble as this."[52]

To shore up their belief in a universe driven by ruthless competition for survival, Darwinian fundamentalists construct ever more fantastically contrived edifices of sophistry and internal contradiction. Dawkins's signature conceit of the "selfish gene" whose only purpose for being is to replicate itself was taken apart by David Stove in a devastating essay. Stove pointed out, first, that such a "self-replicator" is not acting in its own interest at all, since it is perpetuating not its own survival but merely a copy of itself; and second, that it is patently absurd to invest a gene with such an anthropomorphic trait—which, despite his protestations that this is merely a figure of speech, is precisely what Dawkins does. "Genes can no more be self-ish than they can be (say) supercilious or stupid," Stove observed, and scoffed that elevating such a "transparently nonsensical central thesis" to the title of a book, as Dawkins did, was akin to titling a book *"The Sex Mad Prime Numbers."*[53]

Yet Dawkins has plunged ever further into the realm of fantasy, seeking to explain the persistence of religious faith as a "virus of the mind." This "God-meme" that has "leapt" into people's brains, he states, has a "high survival value, or infective power, in the environ-ment provided by human culture."[54] Dawkins presents the "God-meme" as a naturalistic entity with observable characteristics. But there is no evidence for it whatsoever. It is a sheer flight of fancy. As Stove observed, all Dawkins needed for the pseudoscientific "discov-ery" of the meme was "to remember that some things are transmitted non-genetically from one person to another, to give these things a new name, and then to allow free rein to the demonological bias of his mind."[55]

Alister McGrath, a former molecular biophysicist who is now a professor of historical theology at Oxford, points out that this claim is not based in science at all and has less credibility as a rational proposition than the historical evidence for the existence of Jesus.[56] An interesting comparison indeed, since Dawkins, under pressure from John Lennox in the Oxford debate, was actually forced to retract his previous claim that Jesus had probably "never existed." And in a revealing aside, when Lennox remarked that the Natural History Museum in which they were debating—in front of dinosaur skeletons—had been founded for the glory of God, Dawkins scoffed that of course this was absolutely untrue.

But it *was* true. Construction of the museum was instigated between 1855 and 1860 by the Regius Professor of Medicine, Sir Henry Acland. According to Keith Thomson of the Sigma XI Sci-entific Research Society, funds for the project came from the surplus in the University Press's Bible account as this was deemed only appropriate for a building dedicated to science as a glorification of God's works. Giving his reasons for building the museum, Acland himself said that it would provide the opportunity to obtain the "knowledge of the great material design of which the Supreme Master-Worker has made us a constituent part."[57]

One might raise an eyebrow at Dawkins's seemingly insouciant approach to factual information. But then, for scientific triumphalists mere facts apparently cannot compete with the doctrines laid down by the scientific priesthood. According to the Nobel Prize-winning physicist Steven Weinberg, "Science is what is generally accepted by scientists.... [I]t is the theory of evolution through natural selection that has won general scientific acceptance."[58]

QED. Science is what scientists say it is. But this doctrine might be thought to have less to do with knowledge than with the rather less elevated pursuit of power over people's minds.

6

THE SECULAR
INQUISITION

What have the issues of anthropogenic global warming, the war in Iraq, Israel and scientism got in common? Not a lot, you might think. But in fact a number of threads link them all. Most fundamentally, they all involve the promotion of beliefs that purport to be unchallengeable truths but are in fact ideologies in which evidence is manipulated, twisted and distorted to support and "prove" their governing idea. All are therefore based on false or unsupported beliefs that are presented as axiomatically true. Moreover, because each assumes itself to be proclaiming the sole and exclusive truth, it cannot permit any challenge to itself. It has to maintain at all costs the integrity of the falsehood. So all challenges have to be resisted through coercive means. Knowledge is thus forced to give way to power. Reason is replaced by bullying, intimidation and the suppression of debate.

This makes them all deeply regressive movements of thought, which corrode the most fundamental concept of the Western world. The principal characteristic of Western modernity is freedom of thought and expression and the ability to express dissent. The eighteenth-century Enlightenment ushered in the modern age by breaking the power of the church to control the terms of debate and punish heresy. Church and state were separated, and a space was

created for individual freedom and the toleration of differences—
the essence of a liberal society.

CULTURAL TOTALITARIANISM

While it would be a mistake to idealize the eighteenth and nineteenth centuries, this era in Britain and America did provide a
breathing space between the religious tyranny of the age that preceded it and the horrors that were to follow. Yet the French Revolution and the Terror unleashed by it presented the inescapable
evidence that the Enlightenment, far from consigning murderous
obscurantism to the dustbin of history, contained powerful strands
from the start that would merely secularize tyranny. In the twentieth
century, the political totalitarianism of communism and fascism,
although overtly antireligious, echoed the premodern despotism of
the church by declaring themselves the arbiters of a totalizing worldview in which all dissent would be crushed. Now, with both communism and fascism defeated, the West has fallen victim to a third
variation on the theme of totalitarianism: not religious or political
this time, but cultural. It is what J. L. Talmon identified back in 1952
as "totalitarian democracy," which he characterized as "a dictatorship
based on ideology and the enthusiasm of the masses."[1]

If religious totalitarianism was rule by the church and political
totalitarianism was rule by the "general will," cultural totalitarianism
is rule by the subjective individual, freed from all external authority
and constraints. Morality is privatized so that everyone becomes his
or her own moral authority, while the laws and traditions rooted in
Christianity and the Hebrew Bible have come under explicit attack.
The old order of Western civilization, resting on the external
authorities of religion and culture, has to be destroyed. With no
order or purpose in the world, moral and cultural relativism are the
rule; any attempt to prioritize any culture or lifestyle over any other

is illegitimate. The paradox—and it is acute—is that this relativist doctrine itself assumes the form of a dogmatic moralizing agenda that takes an absolutist position against all who challenge it and seeks to stamp out all deviations.

Medieval Christianity—like contemporary Islamism—stamped out dissent by killing or conversion; Western liberals do it by social and professional ostracism and legal discrimination. It is a kind of secular Inquisition. And the grand inquisitors are to be found within the intelligentsia—in the universities, the media, the law, the political and professional classes—who not only have systematically undermined the foundations of Western society but are heavily engaged in attempting to suppress any challenge or protest.

It is paradoxical but not surprising that the assault on intellectual liberty is taking place within the institutions of reason. For decades, these have been dominated by a variety of wrecking ideologies such as anticapitalism, anti-imperialism, utilitarianism, feminism, multiculturalism and environmentalism. What they all have in common is the aim of overturning the established order in the West. What was previously marginalized or forbidden has become permitted and even mandatory; what was previously the norm has become forbidden and marginalized. As the philosopher Roger Scruton has written, the curriculum in the humanities is "relativist in favour of transgression and absolutist against authority."[2] Because these are ideologies, they wrench facts and evidence to fit their governing idea. They are inimical to reason and independent thought—and thus to freedom, because reason and liberty are inseparable bedfellows.

As Sir Karl Popper has observed, reason grows by way of mutual criticism and through the development of institutions that safeguard the liberty to criticize and thus preserve freedom of thought. Because it treats people impartially, reason is therefore closely linked to equality. Pseudo-rationalism, by contrast, is "the immodest belief in one's superior intellectual gifts—the claim to be initiated, to know with certainty, to possess an infallible instrument of discovery."[3] This pseudo-rationalism, the enemy of reason, is precisely what has the Western intelligentsia in its grip.

It is hard to overstate the influence on our culture that is wielded by the doctrines of anti-imperialism, multiculturalism, feminism, environmentalism and the like. They form the unchallengeable orthodoxy within academia, the base camp for their "long march through the institutions," which they have colonized with stunning success. The center of political gravity has been shifted so that anyone who does not share these values is defined as extreme.

"Progressives" on the left believe that their secular, materialistic, individualistic and utilitarian values represent not a point of view but virtue itself. No decent person can therefore oppose them. In Manichean fashion, the left divides the world into two rival camps of good and evil, creating as the sole alternative to itself a demonic political camp called "the right," to which everyone who challenges it is automatically consigned. Since "the right" is by definition evil, to dispute any left-wing shibboleth is to put oneself beyond the moral pale. There can be no dissent or argument at all. Only one worldview is to be permitted. Anyone who supports Israel or the Americans in Iraq, or is skeptical of anthropogenic global warming, or opposes multiculturalism or utilitarianism, or supports capitalism or is a believing Christian is "right-wing" and therefore evil.

A central doctrine in the progressive orthodoxy is that "discrimination" is the supreme crime. The very idea of a hierarchy of cultures, beliefs or lifestyles is deemed to be discriminatory. According to the ideology of nondiscrimination, all self-designated "victim" groups can do no wrong, while the majority culture can do no right. Morality is redefined around subjective feelings. Any objective evidence of harm that may be done by "victim" groups is swept away; all that matters is that they must not be made to feel bad about themselves, nor be put at any disadvantage even if it results from their own actions.

Activities previously marginalized or considered transgressive are now privileged, while those considered to embody normative values are actively discriminated against. In the cause of nonjudgmentalism, only those who are in favor of moral judgments based on the ethical codes of the Bible are to be judged and condemned. In the cause of antidiscrimination, only those who believe in a level playing field are to be discriminated against. In the cause of freedom, those who seek to limit anarchic behavior in order to prevent harm are to be denied the freedom to do so.

THE ILLIBERALISM OF MINORITY "RIGHTS"

In Britain, the antidiscrimination orthodoxy has led to a systematic campaign against Christians—particularly over the issue of homosexuality, the key area where Christians run up against social libertarianism in the public square. Freedom of conscience, the cardinal tenet of a liberal society, has been swept aside in the cause of gay rights. While true prejudice against homosexuals or anyone else is reprehensible, "prejudice" has been redefined to include the expression of normative values.

A Christian registrar who refused to carry out gay "weddings" was disciplined and forced to resign, in a case in which judges ruled that antidiscrimination law trumped religious belief;[4] a Christian had to step down from an adoption panel because he refused to place children for adoption with gay couples,[5] and Catholic adoption agencies have been forced to close because they had the same approach.[6] When a Scottish heroin addict was judged unfit to care for her four-year-old daughter and five-year-old son, their grandparents' request to adopt them was turned down and the children were instead given up for adoption to a gay male couple against strong opposition by the grandparents—who were told that if they objected they would never see the children again.[7]

The basic crime here is the giving of offense by suggesting that a minority lifestyle may be, in any way or for anyone, worse than that of the majority. But offense seems to be strictly a one-way street. In its 2009 booklet *The Pink Guide to Adoption for Lesbians and Gay Men*, the British Association for Adoption and Fostering described people who oppose gay adoption as "retarded homophobes."[8]

In 2006, an evangelical Christian campaigner, Stephen Green, was arrested and charged (although later acquitted) with using threatening, abusive or insulting words or behavior after merely trying peacefully to hand out leaflets at a gay rally in Cardiff. The offending words in question were those in the 1611 King James Bible forbidding homosexuality.[9]

In the United States, there have been numerous examples of serious inroads into civil liberties by the coercive enforcement of "gay rights." In 2009, the beauty queen Carrie Prejean was deprived of the Miss USA title because, when asked by a gay judge in the contest whether American states should allow same-sex marriage, she replied that although it was good that Americans could vote for the rules they wanted, in her opinion a marriage should be between a man and a woman.[10] In Britain, on a satirical BBC TV show discussing threats made against Carrie Prejean, a gay Conservative MP, Alan Duncan, said, "If you read that Miss California is murdered, you will know it was me." Amidst protests by Christians and others, the MP and the BBC dismissed the remark as a joke that was "not meant to be taken seriously."[11]

In 2008, an African-American woman, Crystal Dixon, was removed from her position as associate vice president for human resources at the University of Toledo because she wrote an article saying that homosexual behavior should not be compared to being black. A community college professor in California, June Sheldon, was fired for leading a brief discussion on the nature-versus-nurture debate in connection with homosexuality. A doctor in California was sued for declining to artificially inseminate a woman in a lesbian relationship. In Georgia, a counselor was fired for referring a lesbian woman to another counselor for relationship advice. In New York City, a school of medicine under Orthodox Jewish auspices was forced to rent married housing to homosexual couples under a "sexual orientation non-discrimination" law. A Lutheran high school in California was sued for expelling two girls who had openly displayed their lesbian relationship. Catholic Charities of Boston was forced out of the adoption business because it did not want to place children with persons engaged in a homosexual relationship.[12]

The assault on bedrock Western moral codes has punished those who embody a moral order that is now deemed to be oppressive. In Britain, the Blair/Brown Labor government systematically legislated in favor of vice while demonizing virtue. It sanctioned and incentivized irregular sexual relationships and out-of-wedlock births, while loading the financial dice against married couples. It liberalized laws and practices regulating drinking, gambling and drugs.

At the same time, it loaded the scales of justice against men, whom it implicitly characterized as intrinsically violent by reversing the age-old presumption of innocence. Thus doctors and midwives were instructed to ask all pregnant women if they were being abused by their husbands or boyfriends.[13] The law on rape was altered to make convictions more likely on the basis that women who claim they have been raped always tell the truth, although there is clear evidence to the contrary.[14] The government poured millions of pounds into women's shelters on the grounds that domestic violence against women was rampant, despite overwhelming research evidence that women instigate violence against men at least as frequently as men instigate it against women.[15]

The issue of racial prejudice routinely results in the demonization of majority culture. In 1997, the British Macpherson inquiry into the police handling of the racially motivated murder of Stephen Lawrence, a black teenager, in south London in 1993 turned into something out of Salem, with the police pressured to confess to their own racism—even though, as the report eventually made quite clear, there was not a shred of evidence of any racist statement or act by any police officer. One of the inquiry advisers, Dr. Richard Stone, required a ritual confession of sins from the police. He urged the Metropolitan Police Commissioner, "I say to you now, just say, 'Yes, I acknowledge *institutional* racism in the police.' . . . Could you do that today?"[16] The failure by the police to declare their guilt could only reflect their lack of "understanding" of "the essential problem and its depth": the "institutional racism" on which Stone had already reached his unalterable verdict. Chillingly, the refusal to confess their guilt therefore served to prove their guilt—just as in the Stalinist show trials of the 1930s.

The antiracism witch-hunt is even more savage in America. In 2006, three white members of the Duke University lacrosse team were accused of raping a black stripper. For more than a year, they were crushed by denunciation as racist and sexual thugs, and the career of their coach was ruined, before their alleged victim was unmasked as a pathological liar.[17]

The classics professor Mary Lefkowitz describes in her book *History Lesson* what happened when she spoke out against one of her faculty colleagues at Wellesley College, Professor Anthony Martin, who had been teaching his students that Greek culture was stolen from Africa and that the Jews were responsible for the slave trade. Even though he had been teaching patently absurd myths—such as that Aristotle himself stole manuscripts from the great library at Alexandria in Egypt, which was built *after* his death—Lefkowitz discovered that the truth was irrelevant. All that mattered was "white racism."

She further discovered that one of the texts being taught, *The Secret Relationship between Blacks and Jews*, published in 1991 by the Nation of Islam, was an anti-Jew polemic that accused Jews of instigating a "black African Holocaust" and was drawn in large measure from Henry Ford's *The International Jew: The World's Foremost*

Problem. As a result of her protests, Professor Lefkowitz in turn was subjected to outpourings of anti-Jewish bigotry. Colleagues who said they didn't care "who stole what from whom" accused her of putting Martin on trial and disrupting campus harmony. When she wrote a book, *Not Out of Africa,* documenting the egregious lies being taught, she was accused of attacking black Afrocentrist scholars because they were black. "During these strange days in the academy," she wrote, "it seemed that race had become knowledge. Descartes had said 'I think, therefore I exist.' ... Now the motto had become 'I am, therefore I know.'"[18]

THE "STUPIDITY OF HUMAN DIGNITY"

Anyone who stands up for the intrinsic respect due to human life against the amoral march of bioethics is demonized for offending against the priestly caste of the dogmatic relativists who inhabit a higher plane of existence altogether. In a *New Republic* article titled "The Stupidity of Dignity," the renowned American psychologist Steven Pinker spoke darkly of "a movement to impose a radical political agenda, fed by fervent religious impulses" that drew upon "quite extraordinary" Judeo-Christian ethics in order to restrict the ability of scientists to do certain forms of research, such as embryonic stem-cell research or human cloning. Outraged by this challenge to "twenty-first-century biomedicine" from "Bible stories, Catholic doctrine and woolly rabbinical allegory," he singled out for abuse the leader of this movement, the philosopher Leon Kass, whom he characterized as "pro-death" and "anti-freedom"—all because Kass had the temerity to champion the cause of human "dignity," which Professor Pinker called a "squishy, subjective notion," "slippery and ambiguous" and "a mess." He considered the concept of "autonomy" to be far better.[19]

One of the notable features of this attack was that the "theocon" ethics that Pinker was demonizing as an offense against the unchallengeable virtue of biomedicine were said to be overwhelmingly Catholic. Kass was accused of bringing forward phalanxes of Catholics to promote his evil agenda. Pinker made no mention of the fact that Leon Kass is a Jew.

It is hard not to conclude from remarks such as Pinker's that just as leftists assume that all evil people are right-wing and all right-wing people are evil, so also all these evil, right-wing people are Christians and all Christians are evil and right-wing. These labels have become self-reinforcing weapons with which to smear opponents, even if they are not Christian or right-wing at all.

THE UNINTELLIGENT ATTACK ON INTELLIGENT DESIGN

The label "creationist" has joined the lexicon of generic and misleading terms of abuse and demonization. All opponents of naturalism are said to be "anti-evolution"; all who are anti-evolution are said to be "creationists"; and all creationists are said to be "right-wing."

Creationism is a form of Biblical literalism that has become common in America (though not in Britain) and holds that the world was literally created in six days or, in the "young earth" version, six thousand years ago. Either way, it is a belief that is demonstrably absurd and flies in the face of scientific knowledge. Most religious believers are not creationists, since they accept that the earth is billions of years old. They do believe, however, that the universe had a Creator.

In recent years a movement has emerged called "intelligent design" (ID). While not signed up to any religious belief in a personal God, ID claims that the "irreducible complexity" of the natural world that science has now revealed suggests that life could not have existed without a governing intelligence having brought it all into being. For propounding this theory, proponents of ID have found themselves on the receiving end of a remarkable campaign of abuse and smears, intimidation and misrepresentation. Proponents of Darwinian evolution, nearly hysterical at the thought of creationism being introduced into the American school curriculum, have repeatedly claimed that ID was invented as a means of smuggling creationism in by the back door.

In 1999, a firestorm erupted when the media reported that the Kansas State Department of Education had banned evolution from the school curriculum. In fact, what the board appears to have wanted schools to do was acknowledge the controversy over Darwinism—to teach that while science had shown that natural selection had created variations in populations over time, it had not produced evidence to back up claims for macroevolution and the development of all species from one common ancestor. But this approach contradicted the plenipotentiary view of evolution put over by scientism, so the distinction was vilified as being part of the "creationist" agenda—even though distinguished Darwinists have themselves been arguing precisely this for years, admitting to major problems with Darwinian theory and the fossil record.[20]

Insults flew. The British writer A. N. Wilson condemned the whole population of Kansas and the Midwest generally as people of boundless "stupidity and insularity" and "simple, idiotic credulity." In his view, "The Land of the Free, telly and burgerfed, has become the Land of the Credulous Moron. And one of the things which the religious Right has been cleverly spooning into these millions of rolypoly, CocaCola-swigging cretins is that they have the last word in complicated matters of theology and science and philosophy."[21]

The argument that intelligent design is a form of creationism was upheld in a court case in 2005 against the school board of Dover, Pennsylvania, when Judge John E. Jones III ruled that teaching ID violated the constitutional ban against teaching religion in public schools. One does not have to be a supporter of intelligent design to conclude from a reading of this judgment that, while the school board may well have been at fault, the thinking of Judge Jones was shallow. For example, he concluded that ID could not be judged a "valid, accepted scientific theory" as it had "failed to publish in peer-

reviewed journals, engage in research and testing and gain acceptance in the scientific community." But ID is not a scientific theory. It
is an inference *from* scientific discoveries and theories, but itself
belongs in the realm of metaphysics or philosophy. Looking at the
complexity of the created world, it says the evidence points
inescapably to a guiding intelligence as the cause of that complexity.
It is therefore merely an idea, the conclusion of a sequence of observation and analytical thought.

While the Darwinists claim repeatedly that intelligent design is
a creationist front, the principal ID proponents, such as the biochemist Michael Behe or the law professor Phillip Johnson, say
explicitly that they have no truck with creationism at all. Moreover,
it is clear from what they have written that their theory derives not
from religious belief, let alone creationism, but from their study of
science and their analysis of its discoveries. Johnson explains it this
way: The information directing the evolution of life processes needs
to be complex, irregular and specified. In all human experience, only
intelligent agency can bring about this combination. This does not
rule out evolution in its meaning of variation or diversification, only
in the creation of new complex genetic information.[22]

Intelligent design therefore grounds itself in what is observably
true or can reasonably be inferred from what science tells us. Those
who have come to believe there is some guiding intelligence behind
Creation have concluded *from the science* that there are limits to scientific knowledge. Their opponents, refusing to accept that science
and faith can be complementary because they see religious belief as
simply nuts, cannot grasp that ID is a metaphysical idea that comes
out of science but stands separate from it—that science leads to this
metaphysical idea with which, *by definition*, it must abruptly part
company.

It is not the intention here to support the concept of intelligent
design, which is merely a theory, and as such should be exposed to
robust interrogation just like any other theory. Many religious

believers scorn ID as neither fish nor fowl, a muddled and timid attempt to have religion without God. But one has to wonder why it generates a reaction among some scientists that is so viscerally hostile and irrational, since all it is effectively saying is that complexity presupposes a purposive intelligence behind it—hardly an irrational proposition. Yet for sinning against the dogma of materialist omnipotence, ID proponents have seen their reputations smashed and their careers jeopardized.

Professor Michael Behe's observations about the "irreducible complexity" of microscopic biological structures—such as the bacterial flagellum, which is like a tiny outboard motor that propels a bacterial cell in different directions—form a central argument for ID. William Dembski, a mathematician, argues that the probability of any accidental co-evolution of multiple independently useless components to create the complex and precise nanotechnology of the living cell is almost infinitely small. The work of Behe and Dembski has been endorsed by none other than Francis Collins, the geneticist who heads the Human Genome Project in the United States. Referring to William Paley, the nineteenth-century philosopher and priest who famously likened the idea that the universe had been designed to the need for a watch to have been fashioned by a watchmaker, Collins wrote that Behe outlined his argument "quite persuasively" and that "the main scientific argument of the ID movement constitutes a new version of Paley's 'argument from personal incredulity,' now expressed in the language of biochemistry, genetics and mathematics."[23]

Nevertheless, the work of Behe and Dembski has been scorned and trashed by Darwinists anxious to discredit their arguments as antiscientific. Similar treatment has been meted out to other scientists propounding ID.

One egregious case of this hounding involved Richard von Sternberg, who holds a degree in theoretical biology and another in molecular evolution. As managing editor of the *Proceedings of the*

Biological Society of Washington, a journal associated with the Smithsonian National Museum of Natural History, he ran the first peer-reviewed article to appear in a technical biology journal laying out the evidential case for intelligent design. The article, published in August 2004, was written by Stephen Meyer, who holds a doctorate from Cambridge University in the philosophy of biology. Meyer cited biologists and paleontologists at universities such as Chicago, Yale, Cambridge and Oxford who were skeptical of certain aspects of Darwinism. He concluded that intelligent design was the most likely explanation for the enormous increase in biological information required to produce the phyla, or major animal body plans, that apparently arrived suddenly in the Cambrian Explosion 530 million years ago.

What happened next was recounted by David Klinghoffer in the *Wall Street Journal:*

> Soon after the article appeared, Hans Sues—the museum's No. 2 senior scientist—denounced it to colleagues and then sent a widely forwarded e-mail calling it "unscientific garbage."
>
> Meanwhile, the chairman of the Zoology Department, Jonathan Coddington, called Mr. Sternberg's supervisor. According to Mr. Sternberg's OSC [US Office of Special Counsel] complaint: "First, he asked whether Sternberg was a religious fundamentalist. She told him no. Coddington then asked if Sternberg was affiliated with or belonged to any religious organization.... He then asked where Sternberg stood politically ... he asked, 'Is he a right-winger? What is his political affiliation?'" The supervisor (who did not return my phone messages) recounted the conversation to Mr. Sternberg, who also quotes her observing: "There are Christians here, but they keep their heads down."...
>
> In October, as the OSC complaint recounts, Mr. Coddington told Mr. Sternberg to give up his office and turn in his keys to the departmental floor, thus denying him access to the specimen collections he needs. Mr. Sternberg was also assigned to the close oversight of a curator with whom he had professional disagreements unrelated to evolution. "I'm

going to be straightforward with you," said Mr. Coddington, according to the complaint. "Yes, you are being singled out." ... Mr. Sternberg begged a friendly curator for alternative research space, and he still works at the museum. But many colleagues now ignore him when he greets them in the hall, and his office sits empty as "unclaimed space." Old colleagues at other institutions now refuse to work with him on publication projects, citing the Meyer episode.[24]

The U.S. Office of Special Counsel, an independent federal agency, later substantiated Sternberg's account of his persecution. As Klinghoffer reported, the office stated:

> Our preliminary investigation indicates that retaliation [against Sternberg by his colleagues] came in many forms. It came in the form of attempts to change your working conditions. ... During the process you were personally investigated and your professional competence was attacked. Misinformation was disseminated throughout the SI [Smithsonian Institution] and to outside sources. The allegations against you were later determined to be false. It is also clear that a hostile work environment was created with the ultimate goal of forcing you out of the SI.[25]

Sternberg was not alone in suffering this kind of victimization. William Dembski was the director of Baylor University's Michael Polanyi Center, which had been set up in 1999 by the university president, Robert Sloan, specifically to investigate the concept of intelligent design in nature. The faculty at Baylor, convinced that ID was "stealth creationism," boycotted a conference at the center in 2000 and then denounced Dembski in the media. Initially protesting that the response seemed to "border on McCarthyism," Sloan subsequently restricted Dembski's ability to say what he wanted and, as the uproar at the university continued, eventually fired him from his post.[26]

In 2003, Dr. Nancy Bryson, head of the Division of Science and Mathematics at Mississippi University for Women, presented an honors forum that included scientific criticisms of chemical and bio-logical evolution. Afterwards a senior biology professor read to the audience a prepared statement calling her presentation "religion masquerading as science." The following day she was told her position as division head would not be renewed and she had to find work elsewhere.[27]

The same year, Dr. Caroline Crocker, a biologist with a doctorate in immunopharmacology and a visiting professor at George Mason University, gave one lecture on evidentiary problems with Darwinian theory and briefly mentioned the controversy over ID. She was promptly told that she was being disciplined for teaching creationism. She protested that she had not done so, but was fired at the end of the semester and then found herself blacklisted when she applied for other jobs.[28]

Dr. Guillermo Gonzalez, a cosmologist at Iowa State University, was denied tenure after he wrote a book suggesting that intelligent design was behind the creation of the universe. The university authorities said they did not want the institution to be associated with ID.[29]

This kind of intellectual repression has been openly advocated by academics. Paul Z. Myers, a professor of biology at the University of Minnesota Morris, recommends "the public firing and humiliation" of teachers who speak approvingly of ID. "I say, screw the polite words and careful rhetoric. It's time for scientists to break out the steel-toed boots and brass knuckles."[30]

Universities are, of course, supposed to be the crucibles of reason and the supreme guardians of free inquiry and debate—a place where theories are tested out against each other in scholarly argument. When universities persecute scientists for putting forward a theory deemed to be prohibited, even though it derives from scientific scholarship, that is a shocking betrayal of academic integrity and the principles of a free society.

Why is this attack so savage? After all, if proponents of an indeterminate "intelligent designer" are so pernicious they have to be run out of the academy, why isn't the same treatment afforded to scientists who believe in God?

The answer is surely that, although ID proponents are smeared as religious nutcases, it is precisely because their arguments *are* based in science that they are viewed as dangerous. While scientific materialists can deal with religious believers by scoffing that they are in a separate domain altogether from the "real"—that is, scientific—world, the suggestion that science might *itself* arrive at the conclusion that there are limits to what it can encompass is a heresy that directly threatens the materialist closed thought system, and therefore must be stamped out. Because this suggestion poses such a threat to "the elect" who falsely claim sole rights to both knowledge and virtue, the academy has turned into an Inquisition, complete with an Index of Prohibited Ideas and a determination to silence every heretic lest his dangerous ideas gain any traction.

THE PERSECUTION OF GLOBAL WARMING SKEPTICS

Like the proponents of intelligent design, those who are skeptical of anthropogenic global warming (a number of whom, as it happens, would take a very dim view of ID) are also vilified, denied funding and persecuted. Their doubts about AGW theory are regarded as totally unsayable. The United Nations special climate envoy, Dr. Gro Harlem Brundtland, declared it "completely immoral, even, to question" the UN's scientific "consensus" on the matter.[31] In Britain, the BBC decided that "the weight of evidence no longer justifies equal space being given to the opponents of the consensus."[32] Its definition of impartiality thus involved promoting the claim of a consensus as fact by failing to report the views of scientists who disagreed.

All those who do question manmade global warming are generally reviled as either corrupt or insane. To appear on a platform sponsored by the oil industry leads to vilification as a stooge of Big Oil. Assertions inimical to science, such as the claim that "the argument is over" or that global warming is the belief of a scientific consensus, are deployed to stifle dissent. But in science, no argument is ever over. Any consensus on AGW—such as it is—has been created through intimidating all challengers.

Dissident scientists report that they don't get funding unless their research supports AGW theory. Having crisply observed that most scientists are unaware that doubling or even tripling CO_2 would have only a marginal impact on global temperature, the eminent meteorologist Professor Richard Lindzen explained at a conference in 2009 why so many have gone along with the manmade global warming scam. Most funding that goes to global warming, he said, would not be provided were it not for the climate scare. It has therefore become standard to include in any research proposal the effect of presumed AGW on the topic, irrespective of whether it has any real relevance or not.

Scientific logic has also been silenced by an abuse of power. The global warming movement has skillfully co-opted sources of authority such as the Intergovernmental Panel on Climate Change and scientific academies; the alarmist statements issued by various professional societies express the views of only the activist few, who often have controlled the IPCC's governing council.[33] This has been the case with the Royal Society, the very heart of Britain's scientific establishment, which has claimed there is a consensus on climate change. In 2006, it tried to intimidate ExxonMobil into withdrawing support for dozens of groups that it alleged had "misrepresented the science of climate change by outright denial of the evidence."[34]

More arrestingly still, Professor Lindzen, himself an IPCC lead author, described conditions under which climate scientists working in the IPCC process were forced to tell lies:

> Throughout the drafting sessions, IPCC "co-ordinators" would go around insisting that criticism of models be toned down, and that "motherhood" statements be inserted to the effect that models might still be correct despite the cited faults. Refusals were occasionally met with *ad*

hominem attacks. I personally witnessed co-authors forced to assert their "green" credentials in defense of their statements.[35]

In the *Wall Street Journal,* Lindzen testified further to the intimidation of scientists who did not toe the AGW line. The reason why more didn't do so, he said, was that they had been "cowed not merely by money but by fear":

> In 1992, [Al Gore] ran two congressional hearings during which he tried to bully dissenting scientists, including myself, into changing our views and supporting his climate alarmism. Nor did the scientific community complain when Mr. Gore, as vice president, tried to enlist Ted Koppel in a witch hunt to discredit anti-alarmist scientists—a request that Mr. Koppel deemed publicly inappropriate. And they were mum when subsequent articles and books by Ross Gelbspan libelously labeled scientists who differed with Mr. Gore as stooges of the fossil-fuel industry.
>
> Sadly, this is only the tip of a non-melting iceberg. In Europe, Henk Tennekes was dismissed as research director of the Royal Dutch Meteorological Society after questioning the scientific underpinnings of global warming. Aksel Winn-Nielsen, former director of the U.N.'s World Meteorological Organization, was tarred by Bert Bolin, first head of the IPCC, as a tool of the coal industry for questioning climate alarmism. Respected Italian professors Alfonso Sutera and Antonio Speranza disappeared from the debate in 1991, apparently losing climate-research funding for raising questions.[36]

Another IPCC expert reviewer, the Dutch economist Hans LeBohm, described the pressure against "non-believers" in the Netherlands, including the case of Henk Tennekes. "My own departure at the Netherlands Institute of International Relations was also connected with my high public profile as a climate skeptic," he said. "Young researchers keep their mouth shut, because of the fear for repercussions for their careers if they come out in favor of climate skepticism. So far climate skeptics have not been able to get one single piece published in the meteorological journal of this country."[37]

Dr. William M. Briggs, a climate statistician who serves on the American Meteorological Society's Probability and Statistics Committee, said that his colleagues have recounted "absolute horror stories of what happened to them when they tried getting papers published that explored non-'consensus' views." Briggs was "shocked" at what he described as "really outrageous and unethical" behavior by some editors of scientific journals.[38]

Dr. Nathan Paldor, a professor of dynamical meteorology and physical oceanography at the Hebrew University of Jerusalem and author of almost seventy peer-reviewed studies, asserted in December 2007 that skeptics had a much harder time publishing in peer-reviewed literature. "Many of my colleagues with whom I spoke share these views and report on their inability to publish their skepticism in the scientific or public media," Paldor wrote.[39]

Those who try to tell the truth about climate change to the general public are subjected to extreme bullying tactics to intimidate them into silence. For example, Michael T. Eckhart, president of the American Council on Renewable Energy, wrote a threatening email to Marlo Lewis, a senior fellow at the Competitive Enterprise Institute:

> It is my intention to destroy your career as a liar. If you produce one more editorial against climate change, I will launch a campaign against your professional integrity. I will call you a liar and charlatan to the Harvard community of which you and I are members. I will call you out as a man who has been bought by Corporate America. Go ahead, guy. Take me on.[40]

Even weather forecasters on television swapped their galoshes for hobnailed boots. In the United States, the Weather Channel's most prominent climatologist, Heidi Cullen, advocated that broadcast meteorologists be stripped of their scientific certification if they expressed any skepticism about catastrophic manmade global warming.[41] In Britain, the popular botanist David Bellamy, a veteran host of around four hundred television programs, claimed he had been shunned by TV producers for a decade after he started saying he did not believe in manmade global warming, a theory he called "anti-science" because there was not a shred of proof.[42]

In 2007, the UK's Channel 4 TV transmitted a documentary by Martin Durkin titled *The Great Global Warming Swindle*, which claimed that AGW theory was bogus and that the principal driver of changes in the earth's temperature was likely to be the sun.[43] The film provoked three hundred complaints to the broadcast regulator Ofcom, the longest of them running to two hundred pages; it took a year for Durkin to reply, in a response that ran to three hundred pages. All the complaints were thrown out and the film received virtually a clean bill of health except for a couple of minor caveats.[44] This inconvenient truth, however, was not to be allowed to get in the way of the big green lie. On the BBC's *Newsnight*, Channel 4 was said to have had "its fingers burnt," while the AGW zealot George Monbiot described the film as a "cruel deception" and asked, "Why is Channel 4 waging war against the greens?"[45]

For Monbiot and his fellow campaigners, questioning manmade global warming was on a par with denying the Holocaust. "Almost everywhere, climate change denial now looks as stupid and as unacceptable as Holocaust denial," said Monbiot.[46] Scott Pelley, a correspondent for *60 Minutes* on CBS, also compared skeptics of global warming to Holocaust deniers.[47] What was claimed to be happening to the planet was thus equated with the documented genocide of the Jews—even though there was no evidence that climate change was causing the slightest distress to a single polar bear, let alone to any Pacific Islanders, who remained obstinately uninundated by any rising seas despite having already been turned into eco-refugees by Al Gore.

Nevertheless, the zealots wanted to jail AGW skeptics for expressing such evil views. "When we've finally gotten serious about global warming, when the impacts are really hurting us and we're in a full worldwide scramble to minimize the damage, we should have our war crimes for these bastards—some sort of climate Nuremberg," said David Roberts of *Grist*, an environmental magazine.[48] In 2008, the prominent Canadian geneticist David Suzuki twice suggested that political leaders be thrown into jail for the "intergenerational crime" of denying manmade global warming.[49]

As under Stalinism, dissenters were judged to be mentally ill or even not human at all. The German psychologist Andreas Ernst theorized that people who failed to reduce their CO_2 emissions were psychologically similar to rats. And Steven Moffic, a professor of psychiatry, proposed the use of aversion therapy involving "distressing images of the projected ravages of global warming" to encourage correct environmental behavior.[50]

There were even threats of murder. Canada's first Ph.D. in climatology, Dr. Tim Ball, who branded Al Gore's movie *An Inconvenient Truth* "an error-filled propaganda piece," received death threats for his apostasy.[51] And George Monbiot raved that "every time someone dies as a result of floods in Bangladesh, an airline executive should be dragged out of his office and drowned."[52]

All this is something quite different from normal debate. It amounts to a regime under which evidence yields to force wrapped in the banner of scientific rationalism. It represents a flight from reason itself, according to Lord Lawson, a member of the UK House of Lords Select Committee on Economic Affairs, which in 2006 declared climate change theory to be unsound:

> We are looking here at a situation in which the essence of scientific rationalism, that conclusions are arrived at only by the application of reason to evidence which is clearly ascertainable, has been systematically overturned by pseudo-science whose methodology is demonstrably flawed, whose conclusions contradict accepted facts and which is clearly not science at all but politicised, ideological propaganda. This bogus science is then used as a political stick with which to beat up opponents through campaigns of vilification, abuse and professional intimidation.[53]

The similarities with the tactics used to suppress dissent in the former Soviet Union are unmistakable. Professor Paul Reiter, head of the Insects and Infectious Disease Unit at the Pasteur Institute in Paris, has been appalled at the "myths" perpetrated by AGW proponents.[54] In particular, he cited the way in which the IPCC produced wholly false claims that global warming would increase the risk from malaria, a disease on which Reiter is a world expert.[55]

Reiter noted the parallels between the global warming scam and "Lysenkoism" in the Soviet Union. Trofim Lysenko was an agricultural scientist who claimed falsely that he could eradicate starvation by modifying seeds before cultivation and thus multiply grain production. He argued that conventional genetics was "fascist genetics." Opposition to him was not tolerated. Between 1934 and 1948, numerous dissenting geneticists were accordingly shot or exiled to Siberia and starved to death, including the director of the Lenin Academy of Agricultural Sciences. Lysenko took his place and in 1948 genetics was labeled "bourgeois pseudoscience." The ban on genetics was lifted in 1965 only after tens of millions had starved to death because Lysenko's agricultural policies had not produced enough food.

Reiter commented, "One of the few geneticists who survived the Stalin era wrote: 'Lysenko showed how a forcibly instilled illusion, repeated over and over at meetings and in the media, takes on an existence of its own in people's minds, despite all realities.' To me, we have fallen into this trap."[56]

The mathematician William Dembski, a proponent of intelligent design, sees exactly the same pattern of scientific corruption, falsehoods and intimidation happening over Darwinism and ID. "Doubting Darwinian orthodoxy is comparable to opposing the party line of a Stalinist regime," he wrote in 2004. "What would you do if you were in Stalin's Russia and wanted to argue that Lysenko was wrong? ... That's the situation we're in."[57]

The president of the Czech Republic, Vaclav Klaus, a man who knows a thing or two about totalitarian ideologies, saw things in the same way. A report of his remarks to a conference on climate change in 2009 noted:

> He likened the situation to his former experience under Communist government, where arguing against the dominant viewpoint falls into emptiness. No matter how high the quality of the arguments and evidence that you advance against the dangerous warming idea, nobody listens, and by even advancing skeptical arguments you are dismissed as a naïve and uninformed person. The environmentalists say that the planet must be saved, but from whom and from what? "In reality," the President commented, "we have to save it, and us, from them."[58]

7

THE MIDDLE EAST
WITCH-HUNT

One of the main weapons used against dissidents by totalitarian regimes is demonization. Those who challenge the party line are not simply opposed—nor even simply jailed or liquidated—but are represented as diabolical. This is because totalitarianism is, as the name suggests, totalizing; it is the embodiment not just of what is correct but of virtue itself. Anything that dissents from it is therefore evil. That's why skeptics of global warming are called "climate change deniers," which brackets them with the most evil event of the twentieth century. In similar fashion, those who supported the war in Iraq were demonized as "neoconservative warmongers" who had fashioned a conspiracy to take America and Britain to war on a lie—all to further the interests of Israel. This was because a number of neoconservatives were Jews. The term "neocon" thus became a synonym for the Zionist/Jewish conspiracy, supposedly a uniquely powerful cabal that was plotting to replace America's multilateralist foreign policy by unilateral military interventionism to serve Israel's purposes.

Despite the fact that this conspiracy theory was straight out of the Nazi playbook of Jew-hatred, it became a mantra of the fashionable left (and appeasement-minded conservatives) on both sides of the Atlantic. The malign influence of the neocons was as pervasive, it appeared, as dry rot. "They have penetrated the culture at nearly every level from the halls of academia to the halls of Congress," shuddered Tom Zeller in the *New York Times*.[1] The "alarming" truth, groaned Michael Lind in *Salon*, was that "the foreign policy of the world's only global power is being made by a small clique that is unrepresentative of either the U.S. population or the mainstream foreign policy establishment," having seized this power by being "at the center of a metaphorical 'pentagon' of the Israel lobby and the religious right, plus conservative think tanks, foundations and media empires."[2]

Neocons were repeatedly accused of divided loyalties, that old staple of anti-Jewish discourse. The Pulitzer Prize winner Thomas Powers, for example, suggested that the supposed arch-neocon Richard Perle was unnecessarily "a little nervous and defensive" in his denial of divided loyalty, since he should simply admit that "of course the fate of Israel is much on his mind."[3] Any diaspora Jew who was anxious about Israel's survival, it seemed, was to be damned as a potential traitor to the country of which he was a citizen. Adding another stereotype to the mix, Naomi Klein accused the neocons of having an "ideological belief in greed" and "pillaging Iraq in pursuit of a neocon utopia," to make it "the one place on Earth where they could force everyone to live by the most literal, unyielding interpretation of their sacred texts."[4] Whether these "sacred" neocon texts were the collected works of Adam Smith or the Torah wasn't clear.

The primitive prejudices were startlingly unbalanced. The American writer David Brooks said he had the feeling that the whole world was becoming "unhinged from reality," with waves of articles alleging outlandish neocon conspiracies, including "a neocon outing organized by Vice-President Dick Cheney to hunt for humans."[5]

The conspiracy theories involved a set of compound misapprehensions: Because neocons supported the war in Iraq, anyone who supported the war in Iraq was a neocon. Because the neocons supported *that* war, they were natural warmongers. Because they opposed the left; they were "the right." Because a lot of them were Jews, all neocons were Jews. And so on. But in fact, many of those most prominent in President Bush's "neocon" administration were not Jews. Many who supported the war in Iraq were not neocons at all; they were simply reacting to events. As for the neocons being natural warmongers, this was utter fantasy. They believed that war was sometimes necessary as a last resort. If there was one idea common to this disparate set of people labeled "neoconservatives," it was the concern that moral relativism based on lies was leading to illiberalism and nihilism at home and surrender to tyranny abroad.[6]

THE MISREPRESENTATION OF NEOCONSERVATIVE THINKING

At the deepest level, neoconservatism was a commitment to restoring objective truth in public life; and yet the neocons were charged with promoting the politics of force and deception. Thus John Walsh, for example, accused them of believing in "lying on principle" in accordance with the thinking of the philosopher Leo Strauss, who had influenced some of neoconservatism's founding fathers. Strauss, claimed Walsh, had concocted the idea of the "noble lie" without which the "vulgar masses" would become ungovernable.[7]

But this was a falsification of Leo Strauss's views. It originated from Shadia Drury, a professor of political theory at the University of Calgary, who had claimed that Strauss was a "profoundly tribal and fascistic thinker" with a "profound antipathy to both liberalism and democracy." He was "secretive and manipulative," she said, because "he was convinced that the truth is too harsh for any society to bear; and that the truth-bearers are likely to be persecuted by society—especially a liberal society—because liberal democracy is about as far as one can get from the truth as Strauss understood it."[8]

This characterization itself bears absolutely no relation to the truth. Strauss, a Jewish refugee from Nazi Germany, was grateful to the United States and deeply committed to liberal democracy; nowhere did he advocate lying. Drury appears to have totally misunderstood an obscure pedagogic point he was making about how best to interpret ancient texts, and misrepresented it as a malevolent doctrine of mendacity. And yet this outrageous falsification was widely used to demonize Strauss and construct the whole neocon conspiracy theory.

This was guilt by association with a myth. The British journalist Will Hutton seized upon Drury's noxious myths about Strauss as early as 2002 in order to demonize the Republican Party as ultra-reactionaries.[9] But the neocon firestorm was really started in March 2003 by the crackpot political agitator and antisemite Lyndon LaRouche, who blamed Strauss for helping steer the United States "into a disastrous replay of the Peloponnesian War."[10]

LaRouche circulated four hundred thousand copies of three pamphlets titled "Children of Satan," in which he claimed that the 9/11 attacks had triggered followers of the "Nazi-like" Strauss to attempt a fascist takeover of the United States from within. He condemned Strauss as subhuman for his antiprogressive reading of Plato. He also accused Strauss of promoting "mass insanity"—but then pinned the charge of insanity on Galileo, Hobbes, Descartes and "the notorious" Adam Smith, before condemning Strauss, Allan Bloom, Donald Rumsfeld, Dick Cheney and other "neocons" as "a type of pseudo-human species ... equivalent to a species whose very existence is morally and functionally worse than that of naturally determined lower forms of life."[11]

These claims were deranged. But weeks after the pamphlets began to circulate, the *New York Times* published a long article about the neocons that drew heavily upon the ideas in them. One day later, Seymour Hersh followed suit in the *New Yorker,* and thus a fully fledged conspiracy theory took wing.[12] Michael Lind wrote that the neocons espoused "Trotsky's theory of the permanent revolution mingled with the far-right Likud strain of Zionism" and thus they "took over Washington and steered the U.S. into a Middle Eastern war unrelated to any plausible threat to the U.S. and opposed by the public of every country in the world except Israel."[13]

In fact, Israel was warning the United States that Iraq was a distraction from the main threat to the world, which was Iran. Not to be deterred, the media continued to blame the Zionist neocon conspiracy for the war in Iraq. In the UK, the BBC's *Panorama* program asked, "Will America's Superhawks drag us into more wars against their enemies?" and painted the neocons as a "mafia" of Zionist Jews who were "plotting" a covert agenda to drag the United States into war in the Middle East so as to produce an environment more congenial to Israel.[14]

A particularly baroque version of this rank prejudice was a three-part BBC TV series called *The Power of Nightmares*.[15] According to the host Adam Curtis, the threat of Islamist terror was a fiction spun by the neocons, who had spent the past thirty years confecting one phantom enemy after another for their own power-crazed ends. This was because the neocons were doing the bidding of their teacher, Leo Strauss, who was presented as more sinister and significant than the leaders of al-Qaeda. Recycling the Drury falsehood, Curtis claimed Strauss had taught that the American people had to be fed "noble myths" to bring them together. Thus the neocons wanted to create myths of good versus evil, to conjure up an artificial threat so they could pose as defenders of the world.

The first such phantom threat they created, claimed Curtis, was communism. The next was Bill Clinton's bad character, invented to make the American people realize that liberal America was decadent. And the third "myth" was the threat of Islamic terror. There was apparently no such thing as al-Qaeda—no international conspiracy, no sleeper cells across the world, just a few disparate terrorists who had run out of steam and hardly presented any great danger to anyone. Curtis's patently absurd claims were backed up by grotesque parallels between the neocons and the radical Islamists, thus equating the former with genocidal fanatics. The conclusion of this farrago was that the neocons had created a politically driven fantasy to terrify people and provide a sense of purpose for politicians who were no longer trusted to deliver the good society.

It was the BBC program's argument, however, that was the real fantasy; it was simply unhinged. This bizarre conspiracy theory had about as much grip on reality as claims that the world was being controlled by the Illuminati. The alarming thing is that it was taken seriously and believed. Indeed, it was turned into a feature film and screened at the 2005 Cannes Film Festival, as well as receiving awards from Bafta, the Directors' Guild of Great Britain and the Royal Television Society.

DEMONIZING ISRAEL AND ITS SUPPORTERS

Undoubtedly, the basic reason why so many people took the ludicrous claims in *The Power of Nightmares* to be true was that it played on beliefs about Israel and the Jews that are as widely believed as they are deeply irrational. At the core of the fury in Britain over the war in Iraq lay the unshakeable belief that the real cause of Arab and Muslim rage against the West was Israel's behavior and even its very existence. Having swallowed the false Arab and Muslim narrative that reconfigured the six-decade Arab and Muslim war against Israel as Israel's oppression of the Palestinians, mainstream opinion in Britain and Europe firmly believed that America under President Bush was in Israel's pocket, that there was a secret cabal linking Washington to Jerusalem, and that any diaspora Jew who stood up for Israel was part of that manipulative and covert network.

Accordingly, anything any Jew said in defense of Israel was disbelieved *a priori* as an attempt to deceive. Such Jews were automatically deemed to be neocons; and neocons, people had been informed over and over again, were incorrigible and reflexive liars. Just as with global warming, Darwinism and the war in Iraq, knowledge of Israel's intrinsic perfidy was unchallengeable. Virtue resided in casting it as villain rather than victim in the Middle East. But if passions ran high—as they did—over climate change, evolution and Iraq, they ran far higher over Israel, which became a touchstone issue for people who considered themselves to be enlightened and progressive. The fact that they were thus allying themselves with Arabs and Muslims who were committed to religious hatred, ethnic cleansing and genocide, and whose whole position rested on demonstrable fabrications and distortions, was dismissed or denied. These inconvenient truths had to be suppressed altogether for fear that otherwise the narrative of ideological virtue would be destroyed; so those who tried to tell the truth often found themselves exiled to a professional and social gulag.

One such case of ideological repression involved Robin Shepherd, who was head of the Europe program at the Royal Institute of International Affairs at Chatham House in London, Britain's premier research institution on foreign affairs. In January 2008, Shepherd published an op-ed in the *Times* defending Israel's right to protect itself. Israel was being excoriated in the West for taking military action in Gaza to stop the rocket attacks on its citizens, attacks which then totaled about four thousand. Criticizing the "wilful distortion" arising from the "obsessive desire to beat the Jewish state with any stick available," Shepherd said that blame for the dire situation of Gaza's residents should rest with Hamas and condemned the "frenzied, rhetorical onslaught against the Jewish state" as lazy and hateful.[16]

That evening, Shepherd received what he has described as an aggressive email from the head of Chatham House, Robin Niblett, accusing him of damaging its reputation by writing a misleading article. Furthermore, he wrote, Shepherd had had no business writing the article because he knew nothing about Gaza; his area of expertise was Europe, not the Middle East. This complaint was particularly remarkable since Shepherd had been hired specifically to write a book about Europe's attitude towards Israel and the Palestinians. Shepherd's real offense was surely to express an opinion that was simply forbidden within Britain's foreign affairs establishment: sympathy for Israel. With Chatham House seen as a pillar of that establishment, there could be no expression of any view running counter to the party line on the neuralgic issue of the Middle East.

Niblett demanded that Shepherd show him the outline of his book. Shepherd refused and a battle ensued, which eventually led to Shepherd being told his contract would not be renewed and departing in March 2009, less than two years after he joined the institute. "It was clear that the *Times* article was simply a game-changer," he said, "after which the relationship could never be repaired and which set in train the events which led to my departure."[17] In response, Chatham House has denied Shepherd's claims that it was anti-Israel and that he had been victimized on account of his pro-Israel views.[18]

The attempt to silence those with the "wrong" views about Israel has been most virulent within institutions of learning and culture. "Israel Apartheid Week" has become a regular event on British and American campuses. In the United States, several campuses are hotbeds of anti-Israel and anti-Jewish activism. One Jewish student activist at the University of California, Berkeley, said there were "many cases of hate crimes, discrimination, vandalism of Jewish centers and a great sense of intimidation from showing support for Israel."[19]

Since 2002, academic trade unions in Britain have repeatedly attempted to boycott Israeli universities and scholars, while similar efforts have been made by other trade unions including the National Union of Journalists and even by representatives of the medical profession. This movement finally crossed the Atlantic in 2009 with the launch of the "U.S. Campaign for the Academic and Cultural Boycott of Israel," whose press release complained about "Israel's ongoing scholasticide"—a reference to alleged restrictions on Palestinian academic freedom. The irony was of course not acknowledged.[20] In 2005, an attempt by the American Association of University Professors to organize a boycott of Israel, led by a prominent figure in American academia, Professor Joan Wallach Scott of Princeton, foundered only when an antisemitic article, "The Jewish War on Nazi Germany," was circulated by AAUP sponsors at a conference to discuss giving a public forum to boycott advocates. Professor Scott blamed the debacle on a Zionist plot.[21]

In Britain, the boycotts have been pushed by a tiny minority of mainly far-left academics, and have been strenuously fought on the grounds that universities of all places should not seek to censor or suppress debate. Ostensibly, the boycotts are aimed at changing Israel's policies, for example, over the "occupation." But in fact, the frequent references to Israeli "apartheid" or to Israel as a "Nazi state" make it clear that the real agenda is to force the end of Israel as a Jewish state.

From time to time this agenda has emerged unambiguously. In 2007, for example, the boycott organizer John Rose was recorded on video explaining why Israel should be disbanded or toppled.[22] Moreover, Professor Shalom Lappin of Kings College London pointed out that the boycott call that the University and College Union had voted to circulate to all its branches was none other than the statement by the Palestinian Campaign for the Academic and Cultural Boycott of Israel, which characterized Israel as a "colonial and apartheid state" from its creation in 1948 and by virtue of its "Zionist ideology." Lappin wrote:

> It is not an instrument for criticizing Israeli government policy or an effort to end Israel's occupation of Palestinian territory beyond its 1967 borders. This movement does not seek a peace between Israelis and Palestinians within the framework of a two-state solution. It is an integral part of a rejectionist programme to dismantle Israel as a country.[23]

So what is being attempted by these persistent calls for an academic boycott is the victimization of Israeli institutions and academics and the suppression of the free exchange of ideas by the supposed custodians of intellectual freedom, for the ultimate purpose of destroying a country. And the reason for this attempt is patent bigotry. The originator of the boycott movement, Professor Steven Rose, remarked that what really bothered him was the "ethnic assumptions underlying the claims of a Jewish republic."[24] Apparently, while other peoples in the world had a right to self-determination in their own country, for the Jews alone a homeland entailed dubious "ethnic assumptions."

What the academic boycott movement inescapably suggests, therefore, is that within the supposed crucible of reason that is the university system an obscurantist movement has taken root—a movement based on prejudice, lies and unreasoning hatred. Increasingly, it has taken on the characteristics of a witch-hunt. In May 2008, yet another boycott call by the University and College Union (UCU) involved singling out Jewish and Israeli academics to explain their politics as a precondition to normal academic contact. The implication was that if they didn't condemn Israel for the "occupation," or for practicing "apartheid" or "genocide" or any of the other manufactured crimes laid at Israel's door, they wouldn't be able to work. Their continued employment would depend on their holding the only permitted views—which were in fact based on lies, distortion, propaganda, ignorance, blood libels and prejudice.

The very idea of conditioning freedom of association on expressing only certain permitted views should be abhorrent in a free society. It is the kind of behavior associated with a totalitarian state. What made it all the more disturbing was that only Israelis and Jews were singled out for this treatment. Eventually, the boycott call was stopped as the result of a legal opinion stating that the motion constituted "harassment, prejudice and unfair discrimination on grounds of race or nationality."[25]

The boycott movement both reflected and exacerbated an ugly mood within the universities. One UCU member, Eve Garrard, who resigned from the union as a consequence, described the effect that the boycott campaign was having on Jewish scholars in particular:

Most, though not all, Jews in the UK, and most Jewish academics, support the existence of Israel, and are extremely concerned that it has been singled out for hostile treatment in this way. Most of them feel that the palpable hostility to Israel and its supporters displayed by the pro-boycotters is based on an astonishingly one-sided, partial, and often quite false account of the troubled history of the Middle East; and that the principal effect, and quite possibly the principal aim, of the boycott project is to demonise and delegitimise Jewish national identity and self-determination.

Most Jewish academics feel that Jews have as much right to self-determination and national aspirations as any other people, and that the UCU has become a place where such rights are being dismissed and denied. They increasingly feel that the Union is no longer a place where they can be as much at home as any other members, and that its increasingly chilling attitude to Jewish self-determination is creating an unwelcoming and even hostile environment for people with their political sympathies. And the Executive of the Union has made no attempt whatever to address such concerns. It has treated the worries and fears of its Jewish members with contemptuous neglect.

There has been a constant deployment of some of the most traditional stereotypes of anti-Semitism, thinly concealed under the fig leaf of anti-Zionism. Repeated (and demonstrably false) claims have been made that Israel is committing genocide, and is comparable to the Nazis. Those who have not shared the dominant hostility to Israel have been compared to members of an alien species. It has been explicitly asserted by Union activists that those members who resist this demonising of the Jewish state, and who are concerned about the double standards being deployed in the boycott project, are manipulatively trying to distract others from Israel's crimes, and are indeed part of a conspiracy to do so.[26]

The boycott movement was part of a broader climate of intimidation and bullying felt by many Jews on campus. Students felt threatened by virulent anti-Israel motions and the intimidation of those who supported Israel. At the School of Oriental and African Studies during 2005, one speaker referred to the burning down of synagogues as a "rational act"; articles in the student newspaper supported suicide bombings; the student union told the Jewish society that it was not allowed to invite an Israeli embassy representative to speak since it contravened union policy—a ban that was lifted only after a legal warning.[27]

The Parliamentary Inquiry into Antisemitism reported that in 2002, the University of Manchester Students' Union proposed a motion saying that anti-Zionism was not antisemitism and that Israeli goods should be boycotted. A Palestinian leaflet that was distributed to students queuing up to vote described Jews as vampires and warned that unless they were expelled from the UK they would enslave the country and control its economy. Following the defeat of the motion, a brick was thrown through the door of a Jewish student residence and a poster saying "slaughter the Jews" was pasted on its front door.[28]

At the time of writing, the formal boycott movement had been beaten back by opposition, but less formal boycotts of Israeli institutions and individual Israelis are increasing in number.

In 2002, Mona Baker, an Egyptian-born professor of translation studies at the University of Manchester Institute of Science and Technology, sacked two Israeli academics from the editorial boards of two journals owned by herself and her husband, simply because they were Israelis.[29] In June 2003, Andrew Wilkie, Nuffield Professor of Pathology and a fellow of Pembroke College, rejected the application of an Israeli Ph.D. student to study at Oxford University because he was Israeli and had therefore served in the armed forces.[30]

In May 2006, Richard Seaford, an English professor at Exeter University, was asked to review a book for an Israeli classical studies magazine. He refused the request and explained that he, along with many other British academics, had signed an academic boycott call against Israel in light of what he described as the "brutal and illegal expansionism, and the slow-motion ethnic cleansing." Two months previously, the *Jewish Chronicle* reported that the British magazine *Europe Dance* had refused to publish an article about the choreographer Sally Ann Freeland and her dance troupe because she was an Israeli and the editor "opposed the Israeli occupation."[31]

In 2009, four hundred people including the Nobel Peace laureate Mairead Maguire signed a letter to the *Guardian* arguing that the Science Museum in London should cancel its planned "Israel Day of Science," aimed at sixth-form students. They charged that the event, billed as a "celebration of science," was in fact "an attempted celebration of Israel," which they believed should not be permitted in the immediate aftermath of "the indiscriminate slaughter and attempted annihilation of all the infrastructure of organised society in Gaza."[32]

This was a reference to the war in Gaza in January 2009. But there had been no "indiscriminate slaughter" nor any "attempted annihilation of all the infrastructure." Most of those killed had been terrorists, and the war had been waged to stop the barrage of rocket attacks from Gaza on Israeli citizens. Yet on the basis of false and hateful propaganda claims made by Hamas and reproduced by the *Guardian* signatories, scientists were to be prevented from educating the young. This sacrifice of knowledge to ideology was endorsed by none other than a former chairman of the House of Commons Science Select Committee, Dr. Ian Gibson, who candidly declared: "Science is not neutral. It is part of the political process."[33]

In the event, the bullies were faced down at the Science Museum and the "Israel Day of Science" went ahead as planned. But the bullying continues elsewhere. In April 2009, University College's Bloomsbury Theatre in central London bowed to pressure by anti-Zionist groups and canceled an Israel Independence Day celebration on the grounds that an entertainment troupe from the Israel Defense Forces was scheduled to take part.[34]

Tali Shalom Ezer, a graduate of Tel Aviv University, was due to go to the Edinburgh International Film Festival in 2009 for a screening of her film, *Surrogate*. This film had nothing to do with politics. It was a romance set in a sex-therapy clinic. Yet simply because she was Israeli and had received a grant of £300 from the Israeli embassy to enable her to travel to Scotland, the celebrated British movie director Ken Loach said the festival should be boycotted on account of "the massacres and state terrorism in Gaza."

The terrorism was of course being perpetrated *by* Gaza against Israel. Loach did not seek to boycott those who try to murder Israeli innocents; he wanted to punish their victims instead. A movie director, who surely should be promoting free artistic and cultural expression, was trying to stifle it. And he was attempting to penalize someone who had no responsibility whatever for Israeli policy, simply because she was an Israeli citizen. What was more shocking was that the festival organizers meekly capitulated and returned the funding provided to Ezer by the Israeli embassy—although the embassy subsequently funded her trip itself.

THE PATHOLOGY OF PSYCHOLOGICAL PROJECTION

The attempts to suppress dissent over the issues of Israel and the Iraq war, as well as global warming and Darwinism, all involve heavy use of what Freud termed "psychological projection." When people don't want to admit certain unpleasant things about themselves, they project these unbearable characteristics onto other people instead.

Proponents of anthropogenic global warming, for example, regularly claim that climate-change skeptics are "flat-earthers" who deny the evidence of science. But it is the AGW proponents themselves whose claims fly in the face of scientific principles and demonstrable evidence, while real science and objectivity are on the skeptics' side. Similarly, Darwinists claim that religious believers are superstitious and irrational; but it is the Darwinists who make claims that are not supported by any evidence and thus break the rules of scientific materialism to which they purport to adhere. As for those who claim that neocons are enemies of liberalism who tell lies in order to capture society by stealth, it is these critics who embody the abandonment of liberal values to relativism and the destruction of the very idea of truth.

Perhaps the most mind-twisting example of psychological projection is the claim that the people you victimize are actually victimizing *you*. Thus, those trying to silence Israelis or Jews who support Israel turn around to claim that any protest against their boycotts or other acts of suppression is a threat to *their* freedom of speech—even while they dominate the media and their books are regularly displayed in bookshops. In a letter to the *Guardian* following the boycott attempt in 2007, for example, Professor Jacqueline Rose and others wrote:

> The opponents of the boycott debate argue that a boycott is inimical to academic freedom, yet they are engaged in a campaign of vilification and intimidation in order to prevent a discussion of this issue. While defending academic freedom, therefore, they seem only too willing to make an assault on the freedom of speech.[35]

It appears that vilifying Israel or suppressing the academic freedom of its citizens is a principled position; but when the insults or protests fly the other way, that is "shutting down debate."

The *British Medical Journal* used the same ploy when in 2009 it accused pro-Israel lobby groups of organizing a mass campaign of hostile and often abusive emails in response to an article by Dr. Derek Summerfield that ran in 2004. Among other things, this article had accused Israel, falsely, of having killed more unarmed Palestinians than the number of people killed on 9/11, and claimed equally falsely that Israeli soldiers were "routinely authorised to shoot to kill children in situations of minimal or no threat."[36] In a piece analyzing the emails received in response, Karl Sabbagh wrote:

> The ultimate goal of some of the groups that lobby for Israel or against Palestine is apparently the suppression of views they disagree with.... [T]he abuse hurled at the *BMJ* and its staff, and the egregious misuse of "facts," could well be a justification for a return to the subject matter of the original contribution and a fuller account of why it was justified.[37]

The claim that such protests were an assault on free speech was visibly disproved by the fact that the substance of Summerfield's original article was now being rehashed all over again by the *British Medical Journal* five years later. So much for the alleged pressure to shut down the debate.

"Psychological projection" is a (doubtless instinctive) tactic to shut down debate, which arguably derives from a profound insecurity among these ideologues about the positions they promote with such ferocity. What is surely so intolerable for the proponents of global warming or Darwinism, and for the opponents of neocons or Israel, is a particular form of knowledge or reasoning that at some level they know to be true but which is lethal to their worldview. Because that worldview is a closed thought system that can admit to no flaw, any reasoning that challenges it must be denied and opposed so as to prevent their whole moral and intellectual identity from being destroyed. This process sets up a pattern of thinking that turns truth and lies inside out. It is a mind-bending phenomenon that is also one of the key characteristics of the West's enemies, as we shall shortly see.

8

THE JIHAD AGAINST
WESTERN FREEDOM

When we think of modernity, what comes into our mind? Rationality; the separation of religion and state; individualism; equal rights and tolerance; freedom of thought and action. These are the characteristics associated with the West. And these are what the Islamic jihad wants to destroy—paradoxically, by using modern Western science and technology.

The Twin Towers of the World Trade Center, which were pulverized on 9/11 by al-Qaeda, were not chosen at random. They were considered to be the supreme symbol not just of America but of the Western freedoms for which America stands proxy. Osama bin Laden declared, "The values of this Western civilization under the leadership of America have been destroyed. Those awesome symbolic towers that speak of liberty, human rights, and humanity have been destroyed. They have gone up in smoke."[1]

Many Muslims around the world are keen to embrace Western freedom and the prosperity to which freedom gives rise. Among those who have emigrated to the West, it is usually the reason why they have done so. In Islamic states as well, movements for democracy and equal rights—particularly for women—have been given huge impetus by the ferment of questioning since 9/11. For the Islamic jihad is a war not just against the West, but also within Islam itself. At the heart of modern jihadi Islamism—the form of repoliticized Islam that developed from the 1920s onwards—lies the fear that the Islamic world is being seduced by the siren song of individual freedom. While the jihadis have eagerly embraced the technology of modernity and use it ruthlessly to service their terrorist onslaught, they seek to destroy the values of the society that enabled such technology to be created—and which they fear as a threat to the continued existence of Islam.

Since 9/11 there has been a tumultuous debate within the Islamic world about democracy and Islam, producing tentative and fitful moves towards freedom. This is a battle for the future of Islam between those who want to accommodate it to Western ideas of liberty and human dignity, and those who wish to impose Islamic theocracy upon the world instead. No one can say what the result of this battle will be. But the difficulties facing those who wish to bring about an Islamic reformation to harmonize Islam with human rights are formidable because, although many Muslims emphatically reject the Islamists' interpretation of their faith, that interpretation is founded in the religious precepts of Islam. And fundamental to those precepts is a belief about the place of mankind in the world that sits awkwardly with reason.

THE HERESY OF THE ENTIRE UN-ISLAMIC WORLD IS THE REAL GRIEVANCE

Many still think erroneously that the Islamic jihad is motivated by grievances arising from various flashpoints of the world—the Middle East, Kashmir, Chechnya and so on. This is not so. These grievances are ancillary to the real reason the Islamists have declared war on the West: that it embodies the freedom of the individual and the negation of theocratic authority. In a globalized world, this freedom is viewed as a contagion that threatens Islam everywhere.

When a group of Muslim scholars wrote to the Americans saying there should be equality, justice and freedom between the West and Islam, Osama bin Laden rejected their "humanistic" declaration, for it did not mean "equality, freedom, and justice as was revealed by the Prophet Muhammad [Sharia]. No, they mean the West's despicable notions, which we see today in America and Europe, and which have made the people like cattle."[2] Western freedom is regarded as a secular heresy, one that is embodied particularly in America, as Suleiman Abu Gheith, a spokesman for al-Qaeda, makes clear:

> America is the head of heresy in our modern world, and it leads an infidel democratic regime that is based upon separation of religion and state and on ruling the people by the people via legislating laws that contradict the way of Allah and permit what Allah has prohibited. This compels the other countries to act in accordance with the same laws in the same ways ... and punishes any country [that rebels against these laws] by besieging it, and then by boycotting it. By so doing, [America] seeks to impose on the world a religion that is not Allah's.[3]

Islam is a Manichean religion that inflexibly divides the world into the spheres of good and evil. Only the realm of Islam, where all exists in submission to God, is good; the rest is evil. Thus bin Laden defined his struggle as one between Islam and global heresy: "The conflict is a conflict between two ways, and a deep struggle between two beliefs: a conflict between the divine, perfect way, submitting full authority to Allah in all matters ... and the grossly secular way."[4] For the jihadists, this evil world has to be conquered for Islam or else destroyed, as exemplified by Mohammed's conquests in the Qur'an.

There are Muslims who disagree with this interpretation and draw upon Islam's spiritual and mystical elements to live in peace with people of other faiths and none. Many Muslims are resolutely opposed to the jihad, particularly if they live in the West, which they have chosen to do precisely because they want to live in peace and freedom. There are also Muslim reformers who—with conspicuous courage—are trying to reconcile the central tenets of their faith with freedom, tolerance and human rights. Their difficulty is that Islam's warlike history testifies to its signature characteristic as a religion of conquest that denies human rights; and it is that tradition which, after the constraints of colonialism were lifted, was revived by modern-day Islamism and now convulses the world.

Believing that everything other than the most austere and exclusive version of Islam must be rejected and destroyed, the Islamists have set out not merely to conquer the West but to purify the world and redeem it for Islam. Within the Islamic world itself, that means targeting any evidence of contamination by the main political precept of modernity: human rights guaranteed by the separation of religion and state. The distinction between public and private spheres—a precondition for the liberal, tolerant society that defines the West—is impossible in Islam. No dissent whatever can be permitted.

Although the worst internal oppression has been inflicted on apostates, women and homosexuals within the Muslim world, *all* backsliders and unbelievers everywhere have to be brought into line or else destroyed, including the Christian and Hindu civilizations and, of course, the Jewish State of Israel. In the use of terror and tyranny against the "enemies of God," the Islamic jihad exceeds the fanatical but more localized Inquisition by the medieval Catholic Church—and is equipped furthermore with the technology of modern warfare. Thus Sheikh Omar Abdel-Rahman (also known as the "Blind Sheikh") declared:

> There's no solution [for our problems], there's no treatment, there's no medicine, there's no cure except with what was brought by the Islamic method which is jihad for the sake of God ... and the Koran makes it, terrorism, among the means to perform jihad in the sake of Allah, which is to terrorize the enemies of God and who are our enemies too.[5]

The push for religious purification has historically gone hand in hand with the desire to regain the lost political power of Islam. Taqi al-Din ibn Tammiyah, a thirteenth-century Islamic jurist, was the key influence over modern Islamism. Wanting to purify Islam of "distortions" from later commentaries, he said that Muslims must rebel against insufficiently pious leaders. He believed that a decline in piety had facilitated divisions that had enabled the Mongol advance in the seventh century and the capture of Baghdad, the notional capital of the Islamic empire.[6]

In the eighteenth century, a spiritual descendant of ibn Tammiyah emerged in Arabia in the person of Muhammad ibn Abd al-Wahhab. After Islam was beaten back from Europe at the gates of Vienna in 1683, it had gone into decline as European civilization embraced modernity and started its ascendancy. Wahhab, who believed Muslim society had regressed to pre-Islamic days, wanted purification and renewal by returning to the religion's Qur'anic core.[7]

Wahhab's thinking came into vogue after the defeat of the Ottoman Empire, when the ferment of nationalism and anticolonialism revived Arab and Islamic imperialism. In the nineteenth century, under European economic penetration and cultural influence, the dominant discussion had been how to reconcile Islam with democracy, reason and modernity. At the turn of the twentieth century, the focus dramatically changed. Radical Islamic thinkers modeled themselves on Islam's early conquerors and aspired to replace the existing international system with Islam. One of these thinkers, Rashid Rida, argued that only an Islam purged of impurities and Western influences could save Muslims from subordination. He detested Muslim rulers who substituted Western laws for Sharia, and he used the Qur'anic term *jahiliyya*, denoting the barbarity of pre-Islamic Arabia, to describe contemporary Muslim lands that submitted to manmade law.[8]

From 1928, the Islamists of the Muslim Brotherhood followed the same line. They rejected the view that Islam could be compatible with democracy and proposed instead a comprehensive Islamic system. Their view was endorsed by another thinker, Maulana Abul ala

Maududi, who agitated for an Islamic state ruled by God's law alone and said it should be universal. "The objective of the Islamic jihad is to eliminate the rule on an un-Islamic system, and establish in its place an Islamic system of state rule," he wrote. "Islam does not intend to confine this rule to a single state or to a handful of countries. The aim of Islam is to bring about a universal revolution."[9]

It was this goal of Islamization that bin Laden explicitly laid out in his "Letter to the American People" as the first priority of the jihad:

> The first thing that we are calling you to is Islam.... The second thing we call you to, is to stop your oppression, lies, immorality and debauchery that has spread among you. We call you to be a people of manners, principles, honour, and purity; to reject the immoral acts of fornication, homosexuality, intoxicants, gambling, and trading with interest.... You separate religion from your policies, contradicting the pure nature which affirms Absolute Authority to the Lord and your Creator.[10]

For bin Laden and other Islamists, the decadence and moral disintegration they see in America and the West are proof of the evil of a society that does not live in submission to the will of God. However, since they believe that everything outside of Islam is forbidden and evil, they fail to acknowledge important distinctions in the Western society that they anathematize. As a result, the catalogue of crimes they lay at its door is incoherent and contradictory.

ISLAMISTS CONFUSE BEDROCK WESTERN VALUES WITH THEIR REPUDIATION

America is the principal target of the Islamists because it is the fount of modernity. It is therefore immoral, because modernity is identified with secularism, which has led away from God's laws. The Islamists use secularism to mean both atheism *and* separation of religion from state. To them, both are equally reprehensible. In the Western world, they are very different. America is a secular society in that it rigorously separates church and state, keeping religion out of public life. But in cultural terms, it is also still a deeply religious, Christian society. The idea that the political separation of religion and state can coexist with a religiously inclined popular culture is, however, not understood by the Islamists because in Islam that distinction does not exist. They assume that any society that is not a theocracy is by definition godless and thus immoral.

Nor do they understand that the extremes of behavior that so offend them are due in large measure not to mainstream Western culture, which is shaped by Judeo-Christian ethics, but to a direct *challenge* to that culture from the postmodern brew of atheism, nihilism and Marxism, which is eroding it from within. Certainly, that challenge has made significant inroads in America and the West; yet it is by no means universal, and it has provoked a "culture war" between opponents and defenders of the bedrock, religiously rooted principles of Western society. But to the Islamists, all these things are equally offensive and equally characteristic of Western society.

These confusions in the Islamists' discourse about the West tend to conceal the most fundamental problem they have with modernity. The muddled mindset encasing this problem was graphically illustrated by the writings of the most influential twentieth-century Islamist of all, Syed Qutb. As the ideologue of the Egyptian Muslim Brotherhood in the 1950s and 1960s, Qutb called for revolt against all kinds of manmade government, which meant "destroying the kingdom of man to establish the kingdom of heaven on earth."[11] He was tortured and executed by President Nasser for his theocratic incitement against the state.

Originally secular, Qutb was changed by a year he spent in America—in New York City, Washington D.C. and Greeley, Colorado. Founded in 1870 as a self-declared utopian community, Greeley was still a proud exemplar of moral rigor, temperance and civic-mindedness when Qutb stayed there in 1948. And yet it was Greeley that he felt epitomized American debauchery and materialism. He was disgusted, for example, by the care its residents lavished on their lawns, which to him typified America's obsession with selfish individualism. And it was after a church hop that Qutb exploded in disgust at American moral degradation. After a regular evening service, the pastor dimmed the lights in the church hall to create a "romantic, dreamy effect" and put on the current hit "Baby It's Cold Outside" so that people could dance. Qutb reacted in horror upon seeing that "the dance floor was replete with tapping feet, enticing feet, arms wrapped round waists, lips pressed to lips, chests pressed to chests. The atmosphere was full of desire."[12]

Qutb wrote vivid descriptions of the moral degradation he had found in America's heartland:

> Humanity today is living in a large brothel! One only has to glance at its press, films, fashion shows, beauty contests, ballrooms, wine bars and broadcasting stations! Or observe its mad lust for naked flesh, provocative pictures and sick, suggestive statements in literature, the arts and mass media![13]

> The American girl is well acquainted with her body's seductive capacity. She knows it lies in the face, and in expressive eyes, and thirsty lips. She knows seductiveness lies in the round breasts, the full buttocks, and in the shapely thighs, sleek legs—and she shows all this and does not hide it.[14]

One might speculate that this absurdly intemperate reaction suggests a pathological sexual repression. But the indiscriminate lumping together of the church hop with sexual licentiousness and lawn care as examples of the deadening effect of Western materialism owed more to the belief that everything other than submission to Islam was inherently degraded and debauched. As Qutb himself declared: "In this respect, Islam's stand is very clear. It says that truth is one and cannot be divided; if it is not the truth, then it must be falsehood. The mixing of truth and falsehood is impossible.

Command belongs to Allah or else to *jahiliyya*. The sharia of Allah will prevail or else people's desires."[15]

In other words, it was a choice between Sharia and debauchery. Of course, these are false alternatives. There is another option: a secular state in which moral rules still apply. But the breakdown of morality in Western society has lent itself to the Islamists' false (and patently ahistorical) belief that Western culture is intrinsically debauched, and it has enabled the most manipulative of contemporary Islamist thinkers to hoodwink some Western leaders who are desperate to find a way of bringing Islam into the secular fold.

Tariq Ramadan, the charismatic Swiss-born academic and grandson of the founder of the Muslim Brotherhood, Hassan al-Banna, is supposedly the thinker who reconciles Islam with modernity. In fact, as the Dominican priest Jacques Jomier has put it, his real project is not to modernize Islam but to Islamize modernity.[16] He tries to pull off the trick by characterizing the modern West as intrinsically debauched. Caroline Fourest observes that Ramadan berates Western "modernism" as excessive and proposes instead a countermodel of Islamic "modernity."[17] By Western "modernism," what he actually means is libertarianism and libertinism: the breakup of the family, homosexual priests, increasing expressions of androgyny and so forth.

Thus far he would raise cheers among Christian and other social conservatives. But he goes much further by refusing to accept any freedom at all from religious authority. "We cannot conceive of progress that runs counter to revelation," he says, "only a progress that is guided by revelation." In case there is still uncertainty about what he means by "progress," Ramadan finds it "extremely heartening" that his grandfather's Islamism is gaining ground. "For the last fifty years," he wrote enthusiastically, "although no-one foresaw it, there has not been a single society in majority Muslim, nor a single minority Muslim community, that has not been living the revival of its faith."[18] He says he wants to create *dar el shahada*, or "land of witnessing," which is a euphemism for conversion.[19] That is Tariq Ramadan's vision of modernity.

Those who charge that Islamist puritans are saying much the same thing as social conservatives—who also rail against contemporary licentiousness—have missed the crucial distinction between modernity and libertinism. Social conservatives want to repair the Judeo-Christian principles underpinning Western civilization, which are being eroded. The Islamists want to destroy that civilization and those principles. Social conservatives have no problem with modernity based on objectivity and rationality, but a lot of problems with postmodernism based on subjective relativism and emotion. Islamists have a problem with both and do not acknowledge the difference between them. Social conservatives want to uphold the dignity and human rights of every individual and the primacy of truth and reason. Islamists have a problem with all those things.

This is because the key division between Western civilization and Islam lies in the status of the individual. To the Western mind, the individual has free will and power over his or her own actions. As far as the Islamists are concerned, the individual has *no* status except as a vehicle for God's will. That means there can be no place for temporal governance. Since Islam holds that submission to God means "freedom," the democratic systems that actually give rise to freedom are considered a form of subjugation. Thus, language is turned inside out.

Qutb said that Islam was "a general declaration of liberation of mankind from subjugation to other creatures, including his own desires, through the acknowledgment of God's lordship over the universe and all creation," and thus liberation involved "the destruction of every force that is established on the basis of submission to human beings in any shape or form."[20] As Efraim Karsh has noted, for Qutb *all* systems of governance created by man including capitalism and communism "are inevitably affected by the results of human ignorance, human weakness and human folly." So believers must enter into a state of war with state and society to bring about the eventual "conquest of world domination."[21]

ISLAM AND REASON

With the individual's status in the world so downgraded and the power of God absolute and omnipresent, Islam's view of knowledge is entirely different from that of the West. Rather than being something people discover for themselves about the world, knowledge in Islam belongs to God alone; all that human beings can do is work out what that divine knowledge is. And this belief has profound implications for the development of reason. While it is true that there have always been Islamic thinkers who have tried to reconcile their religion with reason, the fundamental precepts of Islam make the task extremely difficult.

Ali Allawi, formerly a minister in the Iraqi cabinet and now a fellow of Princeton University, has written that Islam conceived of three forms of knowledge. The first relied on the Qur'an and religious texts. The second was mystical knowledge from esoteric branches of Islam such as Sufism and Shi'ism. The third derived from observation and empirical evidence, a kind of knowledge that is connected to rationality and is found in the West. According to the Islamic scholar 'Abid al-Jabiri, this last form of knowledge didn't get anywhere in the Islamic world because it was held to be of secondary value to the other two forms; it developed only in Western Islam based in Spain and the Maghreb, a tradition that was attacked and died out. So Islamic thought instead revolved inside knowledge systems that were fixed.[22]

In the West, Allawi notes, knowledge is based on a constant challenge to the existing verities, and progress is achieved through questioning and the exercise of reason. But as Matthias Küntzel observes, the claim that human reason is the source of knowledge is considered sacrilegious by orthodox Muslims, for whom the only real knowledge derives from the study of holy texts. Religious faith and knowledge are thus one and the same, since knowledge essentially is nothing other than a clearer interpretation of the signs given by God.[23] There can be no doubt that the Qur'an is the literal truth.

Western science, based on questioning and doubt, merely splits the world. Thus it constitutes an intellectual invasion of the Islamic world—the real "Western imperialism." According to the Islamist Syed Attas, "The contemporary challenge of western civilization ... is the challenge of knowledge ... which promotes skepticism, which has elevated doubt and conjecture to 'scientific status' in its methodology."[24] The goal of academic Islamism is thus to de-Westernize the sciences and free them from doubt and conjecture. Sadiq al-Asm, a Syrian philosopher, was jailed and lost his professorship at the University of Beirut because he wrote in his book *Critique of Religious Discourse*, published in 1969, that human reason is the source of knowledge.[25]

Reason in the Islamic world thus means something very different from the Western understanding. In the West, reason is inextricably connected to freedom and autonomy. But as Allawi writes, the individual as an autonomous entity endowed with free will does not exist in Islam outside that individual's relationship with God. The Arabic word for "individual," *al-fard*, denotes solitariness or aloofness; it does not have the implication of a purposeful being imbued with the power of rational choice. Man's ability to reason and to distinguish right from wrong is derived merely from the belief that God acts justly and does so by empowering man with the faculty of reason.[26]

It follows that when man acts in accordance with Islamic precepts, God is acting through him, and he cannot be at fault because Islam is perfect. "Muslims are always innocent," declared the British Islamist extremist Anjem Choudary after a mini riot erupted when a meeting in London where he was speaking was ambushed by his banned group al-Muhajiroun.[27] Virtues such as equality, freedom and justice are defined strictly on the basis of submission to Allah. Therefore they embody the precise *opposite* of equality, freedom and justice as understood in the Western world. Servitude is freedom and freedom servitude.

Qutb explained that only when sovereignty belongs to God alone and every person is free from "servitude to others" does a person find true freedom.[28] According to this view, the true meaning of "defense" is not the guarding of a homeland or resistance to aggression, as it is generally understood, but instead "a universal proclamation of the freedom of man from servitude to other men, the establishment of the sovereignty of God and His Lordship throughout the world, the end of man's arrogance and selfishness and the implementation of the rule of the Divine Shari'ah in human affairs."[29] Similarly, peace does not mean the "superficial peace" where Muslims live in security; it means "that the religion (i.e. the law of the society) be purified for God, that the obedience of all people be for God alone, and that some people should not be lords over others."[30]

That is why for the Islamists freedom can exist only in a theocracy—where there is no freedom. Defense is attack, freedom is servitude, peace is war. And that is why they claim that the jihad against the West is not aggressive or threatening to life and liberty, but rather a way of delivering freedom to the West.

Many Muslims vehemently disagree with all this. They are horrified by the aggression and the violence of the jihadis; they want to live in *real* freedom and enjoy the benefits of a culture that safeguards individual rights. But even they struggle to escape from the implications of the doctrine that Islam is perfect. This means that in conflicts where Muslims are the aggressors they believe Muslims are instead the victims: Israel, Sudan, Iraq, Algeria, Afghanistan, Kashmir, Indonesia, the Caucasus. They never mention the Islamic wars of conquest that took place from the seventh century onwards. They claim that the Crusades were an exercise in Christian aggression against Islam; but although the Christian Crusaders were setting out to reconquer Jerusalem and were slaughtering Jews, Muslims and other non-Christians along the way in acts of great barbarity, they were in fact attempting to retrieve the Christian world from Muslim conquest. Professor Raphael Israeli explains how this inverted thinking is applied to conflicts involving Muslims:

> The Muslims can, and indeed are called upon, to expand, conquer, kill, enslave, dominate and rule, for the entire universe is theirs to be included in Dar-al-Islam, but woe to the one who resists that "noble" process entrenched in the Will of Allah, and if he does, he is decried as "aggressor," "killer of civilians and children," "arrogant," and a perpetrator of "massacres."
>
> ... For that reason, they do not recognize the difference between intentional damage and collateral casualties. It is the result that counts, no matter what the intention of the enemy planners may have been. America and Israel are always "children killers," "heretics," aggressors, arrogant, and perpetrators of massacres.... Thus, a reversal of roles is effected, whereby the West and Israel become the "terrorists" and the Muslims the victims thereof; it is the West who terrorizes the Muslim world and is arrogant and condescending towards it, and the Muslims merely act in self-defense.
>
> ... The idea of fair play, of attack and counter-attack, and in consequence of casualties inflicted on both parties to a conflict is misunderstood in Muslim circles.... According to these rules, any attack by non-Muslims on Muslims is inherently illegal and immoral, and therefore it is incumbent upon all Muslims to assist their co-religionists, regardless of what they did to provoke the attack. Conversely, any Muslim attack on the West, for example, since it can be justified as a defensive war against the heretical West, or as an act of self-defense against the spiritual invasion of the West, or as a battle to repulse the enemy from Dar-al-Islam (for example Palestine, Andalusia, Kashmir, and Southern France), is *eo ipso* a just war that all Muslims are called upon to sustain.[31]

THE INVERSION OF LANGUAGE

Conversation with many Muslims in the West today has no correspondence with reality or rationality. The dialogue proceeds on two separate planes with no intersection between them, because the Islamic mindset is governed by a closed thought system that cannot acknowledge anything beyond its own inverted structure.

The absurdity of its circular logic is exemplified by the common complaint that Muslims are wrongly associated with terrorism, a complaint backed up by the threat of violence if the association persists. This amounts to declaring, in effect: "Say one more time that I'm violent and I'll kill you." It proves the charge that is being denied. And while bad behavior by Muslims is denied, that very behavior is imputed to its victims, in a kind of psychological projection of forbidden characteristics that is a staple of Islamic discourse. Islamists declare war against the West, but then accuse the West of trying to destroy the Islamic world. Some Muslims vow that they will have nothing to do with "unbelievers," but then the "infidel" world is accused of "Islamophobia" if it objects to Muslim prejudice or hostility.

Israel in particular is the target of frenzied psychological projection. Islamic countries such as Saudi Arabia, Jordan or the putative state of Palestine refuse to have Jews living within their borders; yet Israel is falsely accused of "ethnic cleansing" and "apartheid." The Muslim world tells lies about Jews; but it is Jews who are accused of telling lies about Islam. Nazi-style antisemitism pours daily out of the Muslim world; yet that world accuses Zionism of being "racist." Iran threatens to wipe Israel off the map; yet Israel is accused of "genocide" against the Palestinians, whose numbers have actually multiplied.

Raphael Israeli gives a horrifying example of this projection at work. The Palestinians along with Hezbollah, al-Qaeda and Ansar al-Islam, he writes, are known to have experimented with gas and poisons in the shells and bombs they use against Israeli civilians. As they were doing so, they spread rumors that Israelis were using depleted uranium in the territories, "like NATO in Kosovo," or distributing "poisoned sweets" to Palestinian children or contaminating them with HIV. Thus, before they themselves used poisons for mass killings, the Palestinians wanted to inject in the minds of the world the idea that they were only responding to the "crimes, atrocities and massacres" carried out by Israel and the Jews, with American connivance.[32]

This kind of projection is closely linked to the serial lies and libels put out by the Islamic world, which in the words of Raphael Israeli reflect the rich seam of fantasy that it inhabits:

> [L]ies are made up to cover up deficiencies (Palestinians' economic suffering is due to Israel's policies, not to terrorist activities by the Palestinians), and denial is exercised when one is faced with facts (no *Karine A*, no blowing up of the Twin Towers). History is invented (Palestinians are the descendants of Canaanites), false analogies are made (Palestinian leaders are comparable to the founding fathers of America), facts are denied (the Holocaust, or involvement in terrorism).
>
> ... Each of the fantasies undergoes several stages: first the fabrication of a web of lies that has no relation to facts, and which Muslims think that if repeated often enough, it becomes a reality, in which they begin to believe themselves, even when they cannot prove it. Because no rules of evidence apply to them, and what matters is the manufacturing of "facts" and the diffusion of such in their midst and across the world, which swallows the stories, unsuspecting that hoaxes of that dimension can be invented.
>
> ... Perhaps the most chilling hoax that was fabricated by the Palestinians, actively supported by all Arabs and Muslims, and passively accepted by much of the European press, was the "Poison Affair" of 1983, when the Israelis were blasted for "poisoning Palestinian schoolgirls in Jenin," and then in other areas of the West Bank, with a view to "sterilizing them before their age of reproductive activity" and thus

"battle against Palestinian demography." These condemnations were made throughout the press of the world, and even when it was proved that the "poisoning" was a case of mass hysteria.[33]

The Islamic world is also consumed by unhinged conspiracy theories—all expressing variations on the belief that the rest of the world is a cosmic conspiracy against it. Many Muslims believe there is a Jewish conspiracy to control the world. The arch-exposition of this fantasy, the tsarist libel *Protocols of the Elders of Zion*, not only is a standard text in Islamic countries but is sold in Islamic bookshops and on university campuses in the West, and is believed as solid fact.

Ahmad Thomson, a member of the Association of Muslim Lawyers in Britain, claimed that a secret alliance of Jews and Freemasons had shaped world events for hundreds of years and now controlled governments in both Europe and America. He said the prime minister, Tony Blair, was the latest in a long line of British politicians to come under the control of this "sinister" group, and that the invasion of Iraq and the removal of Saddam Hussein were part of a master plan by Jews and Freemasons to control the Middle East. "Pressure was put on Tony Blair before the invasion," he said. "The way it works is that pressure is put on people to arrive at certain decisions. It is part of the Zionist plan and it is shaping events."[34]

Crazy—but as we have already seen and will see further, such theories find many echoes in the supposedly rational West.

Many Muslims also believe 9/11 was a conspiracy between Jews and Americans. In a poll conducted in August 2006, 45 percent of British Muslims thought that 9/11 was a conspiracy between the United States and Israel.[35] One of the most popular claims in these theories is the fantasy that four thousand Jewish employees skipped work at the World Trade Center on September 11. This rumor was first reported on September 17 by the Lebanese Hezbollah-owned satellite television channel Al-Manat. In fact, the number of Jews who died in the attacks is variously estimated at between 270 and

400.[36] Dr. Abd al-Hamid al-Ansari, former dean of the Faculty of Sharia at the University of Qatar, criticized the belief that the Jews and the Israeli Mossad were behind the 9/11 attacks. He pointed out that when reality intruded into such a fantasy, the response was to create ever more deranged theories:

> The Arabs keep insisting on their innocence and accusing the Mossad of planning the deed with the aim of launching an aggressive war against the Muslims in Afghanistan and Iraq. . . . But this tale clashes with the fact that Jews are cowards and do not commit suicide. So the theory was amended, and it was claimed that the Mossad had planned and funded [the operation], and a group from among our innocent young people was deceived and ensnared by the Mossad, and that it was they who carried out [the operation].[37]

Several Arab columnists have written that the global economic crisis is the result of a conspiracy by the U.S. government, by American Jews, and/or by the Zionists. They have alleged that this plot was aimed to prevent the establishment of a Palestinian state, to seize Arab wealth and to take over the global economy. Thus Dr. Mustafa al-Fiqqi, head of the Egyptian Parliamentary Foreign Liaison Committee, wrote in the London daily *Al-Hayat*:

> In my opinion, the current economic crisis, which is expected to get worse, is a new kind of conspiracy. It started in September, only seven years after the first [conspiracy, i.e. the September 11 attacks]. This time, the aim is to take over the property and capital of the Arabs, and to create a new climate of economic plundering in the wake of the political plundering. . . . The Bush administration was trained and impelled, by the American conservative right and by Jewish circles, to carry out this mission [in two stages]—at the beginning of [Bush's] first term in office, and at the end of his second term in office. The aim is to achieve two major goals—a global political [goal] in 2001, and a global economic [goal] in 2008.[38]

The Lebanese columnist Fuad Matar wrote in the Lebanese daily *Al-Liwa* and the Saudi daily *Al-Yawm* that the Jews and the global Zionist movement had deliberately instigated the financial crisis in order to prevent President Bush from fulfilling his promise to establish a Palestinian state before the end of his presidency. According to him, the Jews brought to power the Israel-sympathetic French president Nicolas Sarkozy and were plotting to replace the British prime minister Gordon Brown—who he noted was in political difficulties—by another Sarkozy, after which the Jews would "attempt to press other governments in to their service."[39]

Syed Qutb believed there was a worldwide conspiracy of the crusading Christian West, Marxist communism and world Jewry against true Islam. These three forces were the enemies of God, always plotting the destruction of Islam, and they united all Western cultures.[40] According to Dr. al-Ansari, the roots of this conspiracy theory lie within Islam itself and specifically in the Muslim attitude to the Jews. In particular, he cites:

+ The words of the Koran regarding the deception of the Children of Israel against their prophets and against the other nations.
+ The words of the Sira [biography of the Prophet Muhammad] with regard to the dangerous conspiratorial role [played by the Jews] already in the early days against Islam, against the Prophet Muhammad, and against the Muslims and their new empire....
+ The words that our culture implants in the souls and minds of the Muslims, [i.e.] that the Jews are the source of evil in the world. It appears we are the only nation that still thinks that *The Protocols of the Elders of Zion* are real—even though they were compiled by the Russian intelligence service in order to torment the Jews of Russia in the days of the Tsar, [as] the expert in Jewish affairs Abd Al-Wahhab Al-Masiri [wrote] in his famous encyclopedia.
+ The words of the stories of the final days, concerning the eternal conflict between the Arabs and the Jews, until the Day of Judgment when the Jew will hide behind [the tree] and the rock, and [the rock] will

say [to the Muslim], "O servant of Allah, O Muslim, a Jew is hiding behind me, come and kill him."

These traditions make the Muslim suspicious, and he interprets every event as if a Jew is behind it. This is why Sheikh Fadhlallah and others have not ruled out a Jewish role in the tragic incident that took place in the school in Beslan. These are the deep roots that arbitrarily control both us and how we see the world around us.[41]

Dr. al-Ansari was surely correct. Prejudice against the Jews within the Islamic world is not a tangential issue; it is fundamental to the Islamic outlook and to Muslim hostility and paranoia towards the West. It is a principal driver of both Islamic terror and the irrationality that has so calamitously twisted the discourse of nations.

9

ISLAMIC
JEW-HATRED

In November 2008, the Indian city of Mumbai suffered a major terrorist attack carried out by the Islamist group Lashkar-e-Taiba. In the middle of this horror in which 172 people were killed and around 300 injured, one curious feature stood out. Eleven targets were attacked in a multiple onslaught, including prominent city landmarks such as the Taj Mahal and Oberoi hotels, the Café Leopold and the Chattrapati Shivaji railway terminus. But the attackers also singled out Nariman House, a nondescript, out-of-the-way building housing a small ultra-orthodox Jewish outreach center, where they murdered six Jews including a rabbi and his wife and some Israeli visitors.

Lashkar-e-Taiba's aims are to establish an Islamic state in South Asia and achieve independence from India for the Muslims of Kashmir. So why would they target a tiny, obscure Jewish center, which wasn't even Israeli?

It had certainly not been hit at random. The synchronized attacks in Mumbai were precisely calibrated and the targets were all chosen for a reason. The controllers of the operation, it was later revealed through retrieved tape-recordings, gave exact instructions about killing the Jewish hostages in Nariman House.[1] There were also reports that, with evidence that the terrorists had tortured some of their victims before murdering them, the bodies of the Jewish victims bore the most severe marks of such treatment.[2]

The Indian authorities came to believe that the Nariman House had actually been the *prime focus* of the attack. The Mumbai police found that the terrorists' handlers in Pakistan were clear that the Nariman House attack should not fail under any circumstances. The other operations—at the Taj, the Oberoi and the railway station—were intended to amplify the effect. Under interrogation one of the terrorists, Mohammed Amir Iman Ajmal, revealed that their team leader, Ismail Khan, briefed them intensely on what to do at Nariman House:

> When asked during interrogation why Nariman House was specifically targeted, Ajmal reportedly told the police they wanted to send a message to Jews across the world by attacking the ultra orthodox synagogue. According to the statement by Ajmal, Khan told Babar and Nasir [two other terrorists] that even if the others failed in their operation, they both could not afford to. "The Nariman House operation has to be a success," the officer said, quoting from Ajmal's statement. "Khan also said that as far as Nariman House was concerned, there should not be even a minimal glitch in finding it and capturing it," the officer quoted Ajmal as saying.[3]

So why should an obscure, ultra-religious Jewish outreach center have been the focus of this enormous operation? Some claimed it had been hit in an attempt to disrupt the alliance between Israel and India. The real reason, however, is likely to have been much deeper.

Lashkar-e-Taiba has repeatedly claimed that its main aim is to destroy India and to annihilate not only Hinduism but Judaism. Its political wing, the Markaz Dawa al-Irshad, has declared both Hindus and Jews to be "enemies of Islam," just as India and Israel are "enemies of Pakistan."[4] Given its political hostility to India, the animosity to Hinduism might be explicable on that account. Yet Jews are given equal place with Hindus as enemies. And that is because

Jews are seen as an existential enemy not just on political but more fundamentally on religious grounds.

This fact was graphically demonstrated by the massacre in February 2008 carried out by an Arab on the Mercaz Harav yeshiva (or seminary) in Jerusalem, in which eight young Talmudic scholars were gunned down as they studied Torah. In a scene as symbolic as it was horrific, the terrorist shot and ripped to pieces the Talmudic books that the students had been studying and left them stained with blood.[5]

The yeshiva has been a leading center of religious Zionism for the past century and a half. Its significance for the Arabs was not only, as Israel's enemies in the West claimed, that it was linked to the Israeli settlers. It was because religious Zionism makes explicit the link between Israel and the Jewish religion; it affirms the historic Jewish claim to the land, which is in turn the pivot of Jewish people-hood and thus the Jewish religion, all of which the Arabs and Islamists seek to deny and to eradicate.

Islamists make no bones about the fact that what motivates them above all is their hatred not just of Israel but of the Jews. The leader of Hezbollah, Sheikh Hassan Nasrallah, stated this point unambiguously: "If we searched the entire world for a person more cowardly, despicable, weak and feeble in psyche, mind, ideology and religion, we would not find anyone like the Jew. Notice, I do not say the Israeli."[6] All Jews were to be targeted, declared al-Qaeda's number two, Ayman al-Zawahiri: "We promise our Muslim brothers that we will do the best we can to harm Jews in Israel and the world over, with Allah's help and according to his command."[7]

After the lynching of two Israeli soldiers who had taken a wrong turn in Ramallah in 2000, Sheikh Ahmad Abu Halabaya drew on the Qur'ran to condemn Jews comprehensively in a live broadcast on PA TV from a Gaza City mosque:

The Jews are the Jews. Whether Labor or Likud the Jews are Jews. They do not have any moderates or any advocates of peace. They are all liars.

They all want to distort truth, but we are in possession of the truth....
They are the terrorists. They are the ones who must be butchered and
killed, as Allah the Almighty said: "Fight them: Allah will torture them
at your hands, and will humiliate them and will help you to overcome
them, and will relieve the minds of the believers."

... The Jews are like a spring: as long as you step on it with your
foot it doesn't move. But if you lift your foot from the spring, it hurts you
and punishes you.... It is forbidden to have mercy in your hearts for the
Jews in any place and in any land. Make war on them any place that you
find yourself. Any place that you meet them, kill them.[8]

To many in the West, Israel's behavior and even its very existence
are the root cause of the global Islamic jihad. The reality is in fact
precisely the other way round. Muslim hatred of the Jews is the root
cause of the war between Israel and the Arabs. Certainly, Israel plays
a large part in the Muslims' vilification of the Jews. But to assume
this means they hate the Jews only because of Israel is a grievous and
fatal misunderstanding, which has prevented the West from grasp-
ing not just the true nature of the impasse in the Middle East but
the wider Islamic threat to the world.

A tirade by the Egyptian cleric Muhammad Hussein Ya'qoub,
transmitted on Al-Rahma TV in January 2009, made explicit the
fact that the real reason for the Muslim war against the Jews had
nothing to do with Israel:

If the Jews left Palestine to us, would we start loving them? Of course
not. We will never love them. Absolutely not. The Jews are infidels—not
because I say so, and not because they are killing Muslims, but because
Allah said: "The Jews say that Uzair is the son of Allah, and the Christians say that Christ is the son of Allah. These are the words from their
mouths. They imitate the sayings of the disbelievers before. May Allah
fight them. How deluded they are."

It is Allah who said that they are infidels. Your belief regarding the
Jews should be, first, that they are infidels, and second, that they are

enemies. They are enemies not because they occupied Palestine. They would have been enemies even if they did not occupy a thing. Allah said: "You shall find the strongest men in enmity to the disbelievers [sic] to be the Jews and the polytheists." Third, you must believe that the Jews will never stop fighting and killing us. They [fight] not for the sake of land and security, as they claim, but for the sake of their religion....

This is it. We must believe that our fighting with the Jews is eternal, and it will not end until the final battle—and this is the fourth point. You must believe that we will fight, defeat, and annihilate them, until not a single Jew remains on the face of the Earth. It is not me who says so. The Prophet said: "Judgment Day will not come until you fight the Jews and kill them. The Jews will hide behind stones and trees, and the stones and trees will call: Oh Muslim, oh servant of Allah, there is a Jew behind me, come and kill him—except for the Gharqad tree, which is the tree of the Jews." I have heard that they are planting many of these trees now.... As for you Jews—the curse of Allah upon you. The curse of Allah upon you, whose ancestors were apes and pigs.

You Jews have sown hatred in our hearts, and we have bequeathed it to our children and grandchildren. You will not survive as long as a single one of us remains. Oh Jews, may the curse of Allah be upon you. Oh Jews ... Oh Allah, bring Your wrath, punishment, and torment down upon them. Allah, we pray that you transform them again, and make the Muslims rejoice again in seeing them as apes and pigs. You pigs of the earth! You pigs of the earth! You kill the Muslims with that cold pig [blood] of yours.[9]

Osama bin Laden too, in 1998, left no doubt about the deep and total hostility toward Jews that motivated him, saying, "the enmity between us and the Jews goes back far in time and is deep rooted. There is no question that war between us is inevitable.... The hour of resurrection shall not come before the Muslims fight Jews."[10] Hatred of Jews even figured in the 9/11 attacks, as was revealed at a trial in Hamburg related to that event in 2002–2003. It was said that

that in the social circles around the principal plane hijacker, Mohammed Atta, there had been much talk about attacking New York "because so many Jews lived there.... They saw that city as the center of world Jewry."[11]

THE RELIGIOUS BASIS FOR THE HATRED OF JEWS

What is often not appreciated in those parts of the West where religion is not taken seriously and religious fanaticism not understood at all is that the vilification of the Jews within the Muslim world—the accusations, epithets, metaphors, sentiments, the incitement to violence against them—is taken straight from the Qur'an.

Many non-Muslims claim that any aggressiveness in the Qur'an is no big deal. After all, they say, isn't the Old Testament also full of blood-curdling calls to wipe out whole populations? And doesn't the New Testament contain the denunciations of the Jews that caused centuries of anti-Jewish persecution? Well, the latter is certainly true, because the New Testament accuses the Jews of deicide and curses them for all time—a particular extremity that cannot be laid at the door of the Qur'an. But the New Testament does not contain, as the Qur'an does, a purportedly divine injunction to kill Jews and other "unbelievers." As for the Hebrew Bible, its wars are merely a historical record and its injunctions to smite the foes of the Jews are specific and confined to the participants in those historic events. There are *no* divine injunctions in the Hebrew Bible to kill unbelievers. On the contrary, Judaism does not demand converts, nor has it ever sought to possess any lands beyond its own. It has no problem with other faiths, provided they leave it alone.

But Islam has a huge problem with Judaism and always has. Many in the West believe the claim, endorsed by revisionist historians, that Muslims had no problem with the Jews until the State of Israel was created. The classic example of this mythology is the repeated assertion that the Muslim conquest of Spain in the Middle Ages brought about a "golden age" for the Jews who lived there. While it is true that there were periods when Jews rose to positions of great prominence and wealth under Muslim rule, writers such as Jane Gerber and Richard Fletcher have pointed out that these were exceptions to normal conditions in which the Jews were kept in humiliating subservience, forced to pay special taxes and subjected to repeated forced conversion, pogroms and massacres of thousands.[12]

The true facts have been set out in scrupulous studies such as Bat Ye'or's pioneering scholarship on the subjugation and oppression of Jews under Islamic rule as second-class "dhimmi" people, and the monumental *The Legacy of Islamic Antisemitism* by Andrew Bostom.[13] These works and others have shown that modern Islamic Jew-hatred has deep roots within Islam and unique characteristics, as discovered by S. D. Goitein in his analysis of the Cairo Geniza documentary record from the High Middle Ages. This record revealed, for example, that the intensity of Muslim Jew-hatred motivated Jews of the time to coin two unique Hebrew words: *sinūth* for Muslim anti-semitism and *sōnē* for the Muslims who promulgated it.[14]

The great medieval Jewish philosopher Moses Maimonides was forced to flee his native Cordoba in Spain after it was conquered in 1148 by the Muslim Almohads, who gave the Jews a choice of conversion, death or exile. In his *Epistle to the Jews of Yemen*, written in about 1172, Maimonides wrote that news of compulsory conversion for the Jews in Yemen had "broken our backs" and "astounded and dumbfounded the whole of our community." The Arabs, he said, had "persecuted us severely and passed baneful and discriminatory legislation against us." And further, "Never did a nation molest, degrade, debase and hate us as much as they."[15]

The reasons for this treatment of Jews lay in what Islam itself teaches. A great deal of the Qur'an is virulently anti-Jew. True, it is hostile to all other religions and to atheism—everything, in short, that is not Islam. The foundational texts of Islam express hostility to four religious groupings: Jews, Christians, pagans and Muslim renegades. Although it is more merciless against the pagans and the Muslim renegades—only Jews and Christians are to be allowed to keep their faith (albeit as subject peoples) after Islamic conquest—of the two "Peoples of the Book" it is the Jews who attract the most intense expressions of hatred.[16]

As Raphael Israeli writes, there is less anti-Christian sentiment in the Qur'an and hadiths than there is anti-Jewish sentiment, and in Mohammed's biography his dealings with the Jews of Arabia—leading to a genocide of Jewish tribes in Medina and the bloody conquest of the Jewish oasis of Khaybar—loom much larger and are much more negative than his dealings with Christians.[17] Haggai ben Shammai also highlights the centrality of the Jews' abasement and humiliation in the Qur'an and the divine rage decreed upon them forever, transforming them into apes and swine.[18] True, the Qur'an also contains warmer words towards Jews; but they are from Mohammed's early period in Mecca, and Islam holds these passages to have been "abrogated," or superseded, by what he said in his later period in Medina. That was when he went to war against the Jews because they refused to accept his re-interpretation of Judaism. And here surely is the heart of the problem.

The Arab and Muslim hatred of Israel and the Jews can be understood only if it is realized that Islam is a supersessionist religion, which believes it replaces both Christianity and Judaism; and of the two it is Judaism—to which it is closest—that it feels the most urgent need to subjugate. Indeed, this is more than mere supersessionism. For Islam, unlike Christianity, does not merely want to replace Judaism's authority by itself as a later and superior model of Abrahamic monotheism. Islam seeks to obliterate Judaism altogether by appropriating its foundational story and doctrines, radically altering them, and claiming them to be authentic Judaism, while accusing the Jews of falsifying their own sacred text so as to disguise the alleged priority of Islam. Maimonides observed this last accusation at work in the twelfth century:

Inasmuch as the Muslims could not find a single proof in the entire
Bible, not a reference or possible allusion to their prophet which they
could utilise, they were compelled to accuse us, saying: "You have altered
the text of the Torah and expunged every trace of the name of
Mohammed therefrom." They could find nothing stronger than this
ignominious argument.[19]

THE CENTRALITY OF ISLAMIC SUPERSESSIONISM

Without wishing to sound as if Sigmund Freud has turned up at the
UN, Judaism is both parent and stepbrother to Islam. The Jews are
the descendants of Abraham, his wife Sarah and their son Isaac. The
Muslims are the descendants of Abraham, his concubine Hagar and
their son, Ishmael, whom Abraham sent away into the desert to die.
This was obviously not a recipe for extended-family harmony. Islam
reacted to the fact that the Jews became a people with a religion and
a land by claiming that Islam predated it—which was difficult, since
Judaism actually predated Islam by more than two millennia.

Nevertheless, Muslims claim not only that they inhabited the
land of Israel before the Jews but that Islam was somehow the real
Judaism before the Jews corrupted their own religion. The Islamist
thinker Maulana Abul ala Maududi even associated the origins of
Islam with the origins of mankind: "This was the simple beginning
of Islam," he claimed. "Adam and Eve invited their children to follow
the Islamic way of life. They and their children and their later generations followed the teachings of Islam as propounded by Prophet
Adam (peace be upon him) for quite a long period."[20]

This demonstrable absurdity is embedded in the foundational
religious texts of Islam. The Qur'an says that Islam came before
Judaism and Christianity, and that it was the faith practiced by
Abraham (3:67–68). It refers to Islam as the religion of Abraham
many times (2:130, 135; 3:95; 4:125; 6:161). It teaches that Jews and

Christians corrupted their scriptures, so Allah sent a fresh revelation through Mohammed. This revelation canceled out Judaism and Christianity, bringing people back to the one true religion of Islam that Abraham had practiced.

After the Jews rejected Mohammed, the Qur'an says, they were cursed by Allah (5:78) and transformed into monkeys and pigs (2:65, 5:60, 7:166). The Qur'an accuses the Jews of corrupting their own holy books and removing the parts that spoke of Mohammed (2:75, 5:13). It says the Jews are the greatest enemies of Islam (5:82), that they start wars and cause trouble throughout the earth (5:64), and even that they claim to have killed the Messiah (4:157).

As the historian of religion Professor Paul Merkley observes, the Qur'an declares that the whole of Jewish scripture from Genesis 15 onwards is full of lies. The Qur'an offers a supersessionist counter-history wherein God's promises devolve upon Ishmael, not Isaac. Accordingly, in the story seminal to the Hebrew Bible of the binding of Isaac, Islamic tradition teaches that it is Ishmael, not Isaac, whom God orders Abraham to sacrifice. Islam teaches that the destiny of the faithful has been unlinked forever from the destiny of the Jews.[21] It maintains that Islamic scripture is authentic precisely *because* it rejects Jewish scripture. But it goes further. In its attempt to wipe out Jewish scripture, it also has to wipe out the Jews.

When the Jews refused to accept Islam, Mohammed denounced them as not people of faith. The outcome was the eradication of the Jewish-Arab tribe called the Banu Qurayza. Unable at first to break them, Mohammed entered into a truce with them but then slaughtered the entire tribe. Unlike the wars between tribes in the Hebrew Bible, which are merely a historical account with no practical application today, the annihilation of the Banu Qurayza is constantly alluded to by the Islamists, for whom it remains an exemplary and timeless call to arms against precisely the same enemy and with similar tactics.

THE APPROPRIATION AND INVERSION
OF JEWISH PRECEPTS AND EXPERIENCE

The religious teachings of Islam make false claims about Jewish history and religion, hijacking its doctrines and turning them into their precise opposite. The Talmud states, for example: "Whoever destroys a single soul, he is guilty as though he had destroyed a complete world; and whoever preserves a single soul, it is as though he had preserved a whole world."[22] The Qur'an appropriated this precept, but altered it to mean something very different (5:32–35):

> That was why we laid it down for the Israelites that whoever killed a human being, *except as punishment for murder or other villainy in the land,* shall be regarded as having killed all mankind; and that whoever saved a human life shall be regarded as having saved all mankind. *Our apostles brought them veritable proofs: yet many among them, even after that, did prodigious evil in the land. Those that make war against God and His apostle and spread disorder in the land shall be slain or crucified or have their hands and feet cut off on alternate sides, or be banished from the land.* [My emphasis.]

This turns a Talmudic precept affirming the value of preserving human life into a prescription for violence and murder against Jews and "unbelievers."

Much of Muslim discourse today involves a similarly obsessive appropriation and inversion of Jewish experience. Thus while Muslims deny the Holocaust, they claim that Israel is carrying out a holocaust in Gaza. While antisemitism is central to Jewish experience in Europe, Muslims claim that "Islamophobia" is rife throughout Europe. Israel gives all Jews the "right of return" to Israel on account of the unique reality of global Jewish persecution; Muslims claim a "right of return," not to their own putative state of Palestine but to Israel. They even claim that the Palestinians are the world's "new Jews." These and many other examples are attempts to negate

Jewish experience and appropriate it to obtain what Muslims want from the world in terms of status and power. And while it must not be forgotten that many Muslims reject Islamism, it remains uncomfortably the case that many so-called "moderate" Muslims do subscribe to this inverted thinking.

Many in the West fail to grasp that what drives the Arab and Muslim hatred of Israel is the desire to stamp out Jewish identity—a desire rooted in religious belief. The former Palestinian terrorist (and now Christian) Walid Shoebat says he was brought up to understand that killing Jews was proof of being a good Muslim. The existence of Israel as a Jewish state is anathema because Islam teaches that the Muslims are the real, authentic Jews. Thus Osama bin Laden declared in his "Letter to the American People":

> It is the Muslims who are the inheritors of Moses (peace be upon him) and the inheritors of the real Torah that has not been changed. Muslims believe in all of the Prophets, including Abraham, Moses, Jesus and Muhammad, peace and blessings of Allah be upon them all. If the followers of Moses have been promised a right to Palestine in the Torah, then the Muslims are the most worthy nation of this.[23]

Consequently, says bin Laden, when the Jews maintain that *they* are the historic and rightful inhabitants of "Palestine," they are lying. And he believes it is a lie because he has been taught by his religion's holy book that the Jews lie about everything. Repeatedly quoting the Qur'an, bin Laden stated in a sermon in 2003:

> Come let me tell you who the Jews are. The Jews have lied about the Creator, and even more so about His creations. The Jews are the murderers of the prophets, the violators of agreements, of whom Allah said: "Every time they make a promise under oath, some of them violated it; most of them are unbelievers." These are the Jews: usurers and whoremongers. They will leave you nothing, neither this world nor religion.[24]

Therefore, quoting the Qur'an again, bin Laden has declared war to the death against the Jews *as a religious duty*:

> The prophet has said, "The end won't come before the Muslims and the Jews fight each other till the Jew hides between a tree and a stone. Then the tree and stone say, "Oh, you Muslim, this is a Jew hiding behind me. Come and kill him." He who claims there will be a lasting peace between us and the Jews is an infidel.[25]

DESTROYING WESTERN CIVILIZATION MEANS DESTROYING THE JEWS

Believing themselves to be engaged in the final apocalyptic battle that presages the end of time, when Islam will rule the earth, Islamists see the Jews as the diabolical and cosmic evil to be destroyed. The Jews are seen as the enemy of Islam. They possess demonic powers. They are behind all the ills of the world, including modernity, which is a threat to Islam. Every single development in the post-Enlightenment world is put down to the Jews.

In his 1950 diatribe *Our Struggle with the Jews*, Syed Qutb declared that the Jews were the adversary of God, and "the enemies of the Muslim community from the first day.... This bitter war which the Jews launched against Islam ... is a war which has not been extinguished, even for one moment, for close on fourteen centuries, and which continues until this moment, its blaze raging in all corners of the earth."[26] Qutb claimed that the Jews were conspiring to penetrate governments all over the world so as to "perpetuate their evil designs." One of the tricks they were playing on the world, it appeared, was the development of philosophy, no less, whose purpose was to eliminate all restrictions imposed by faith and religion so that Jews could penetrate the body politic of the entire world. Topping the list of tricks was usury, the aim of which was that all the wealth of mankind should end up in the hands of Jewish financial institutions.[27]

To Qutb, as Matthias Küntzel has noted, not only was every-thing Jewish evil but everything evil was Jewish—particularly sensu-ality. Alluding to Karl Marx, Sigmund Freud and Emile Durkheim, Qutb wrote:

> Behind the doctrine of atheistic materialism was a Jew; behind the doc-trine of animalistic sexuality was a Jew; and behind the destruction of the family and the shattering of the sacred relationship in society ... was a Jew. ... They free the sensual desires from their restraints and they destroy the moral foundation on which the pure Creed rests, in order that the Creed should fall into the filth which they spread so widely on this earth.[28]

This was surely an amplification of the revulsion that Qutb had felt at the Greeley church hop two years previously.

Islamists harbor an obsessive antipathy towards free sexual expression, which they identify with equality for women. It is seen as the cardinal threat posed by modernity, and it has always been of the highest significance in Islamist hostility towards the West. Indeed, anxiety about female sexuality was a factor in the earliest expressions of Arab rejectionism towards those Jews who started returning to Palestine in the early years of the last century. As Professor Robert Wistrich has written, many of these new Jewish arrivals were from Russia and imbued with secular and socialist ideals. The Muslims of Palestine wanted them to be expelled so that, among other concerns, the "holy land" should not become "a fount of immorality." Wistrich writes, "The charge of 'immorality' was particularly instructive, for the sight of Jewish women dressed in shorts, enjoying relative sexual and political freedom and near equal status with men in the new immigrant society, was profoundly unsettling to the mores of a Mus-lim culture. It seemed to herald nothing less than the overturning of family life, social order and religion."[29]

This horror of human sexuality—and particularly female sexual-ity—clearly goes deeper than anxiety about the perceived breakdown of moral order. Women embody fecundity, earthiness, a bodily commitment to this world and to the human senses. Female sexuality is therefore essentially life-giving and life-affirming. To Islamists such as Qutb, however, sexuality was intrinsically "animalistic"—precisely because it affirms *this* life and not the next world. And there is no people more committed to this life on earth than the Jews. So the Islamists hate them because the Jews love life, have tenaciously hung on to it and have pursued happiness and fulfillment as the highest goals of existence. Islamists by contrast define death and the afterlife as the highest goal and believe in the abnegation of the self and the denial of humanity. As Paul Berman has pointed out, Qutb thought that a "contemptible characteristic of the Jews" was a "craven desire to live, no matter at what price, regardless of quality, honor and dignity."[30]

Qutb's deranged and paranoid ranting gained traction in large parts of the Islamic world and became the rocket fuel behind Islamist ideology. According to Wistrich, it was Qutb's invective that turned antisemitism into the marker of Islamist movements and infected mainstream Muslim society with the virus. The Jews became a metaphor for Western domination and immorality, and thus represented a threat to the integrity of Islam.[31]

As Wistrich observed, these beliefs are not confined to the Islamist fringes but are mainstream within Muslim society. They are, however, hugely amplified and reinforced by Islamist demagogues. The Hamas Charter, for example, rages about the Jews:

> With their money they stirred revolutions in various parts of the globe.... They stood behind the French Revolution, the Communist Revolution and most of the revolutions we hear about.... With their money they formed secret organizations—such as the Freemasons, Rotary Clubs and the Lions—which are spreading around the world, in order to destroy societies and carry out Zionist interests.... They stood behind World War I, so as to wipe out the Islamic Caliphate ... and formed the League of Nations through which they could rule the world.

They were behind World War II, through which they made huge financial gains.... They inspired the establishment of the United Nations and the Security Council to replace the League of Nations, in order to rule the world by their intermediary. There is no war going on anywhere without them having their fingerprints on it.[32]

Since the Jews were behind modernity, and since America was the principal carrier of modernity, it followed that the Jews were the puppet-masters pulling America's strings. Thus bin Laden said in 1998 of President Clinton's administration: "We believe that this administration represents Israel inside America.... The Jews ... make use of America to further their plans for the world, especially the Islamic world."[33] And when the Bush administration attacked Iraq, bin Laden predictably stated: "There is no doubt that the treacherous attack has confirmed that Britain and America are acting on behalf of Israel and the Jews, paving the way for the Jews to divide the Muslim world once again, enslave it and loot the rest of its wealth."[34]

Thus when the West attempts to defend itself against an onslaught fueled by a conviction that the Jews must be destroyed, it reinforces the belief that Islam is under attack and that the Jews are behind it. In this bizarre circular argument, war upon the Jews becomes the overwhelming driver of the jihad. To halt the threat from modernity, Western civilization has to be overthrown and the perceived puppeteers of progress, the Jews, have to be destroyed everywhere.

GENOCIDAL JEW-HATRED IN THE ISLAMIC WORLD

The Islamist view of Jews is, of course, highly reminiscent of Nazi ideology; and it was no coincidence therefore that the precursors of today's Islamists, the Muslim Brotherhood in 1930s Palestine, were Nazi accomplices. Today's Nazi-style indoctrination in hatred of the Jews and incitement to murder, purportedly fired by divine authority, has produced mass genocidal hysteria throughout the Islamic world. As Raphael Israeli observes, there has been no other society since the Nazis that so boasted of its hatred towards the Jews as Muslim society today. Its preachers denigrate and humiliate them, incite against them, justify massacres against them. Israeli analyzes three layers of Muslim Jew-hatred, beginning with

> the immense anti-Jewish literature, which is enshrined in Qur'anic verses, in the *hadith* stories, in accounts of the *sirah* (the biography of the Prophet) and in treatises of jurisprudence, which have the force of law. The second is the massive Christian antisemitic literature, which was adopted by Muslims in later centuries as a result of the interaction between the two civilizations. The third is the wealth of reports and commentaries, which accompany, day after day, the fortunes of the Arab-Israeli dispute, and [tend] to intensify or quiet down in accordance with the swing of the war-and-peace pendulum....

These three layers, he says, "have merged into one major cataract of hatred and calumny, which submerges all the compartments of Judaism, Zionism, and Israel without distinction."[35]

Thus in 1983 the Syrian defense minister, Mustafa Tlas, published *The Matzah of Zion*, which promulgated the Damascus blood libel of 1840 in which eight Jews were falsely accused of murdering a Capuchin monk and his servant and using their blood to bake *matzot*, the unleavened bread eaten at Passover. Such blood libels have regularly been repeated. In March 2002, for instance, Dr. Umayma Ahmed al-Jalahma stated in the Saudi government daily *Al-Riyadh*, "The Jews spilling human blood to prepare pastry for their holidays is a well-established fact, historically and legally, all throughout history. This was one of the main reasons for the persecution and exile that were their lot in Europe and Asia."[36]

The Protocols of the Elders of Zion is sold throughout the Muslim world along with Hitler's *Mein Kampf*.[37] In 2003, Egypt TV transmitted a series in forty-one parts, syndicated to more than twenty other Arab television stations, updating the *Protocols*. Muslim children throughout the Arab world are taught to hate the Jews and regard them as malevolent and diabolical. Syrian school textbooks portray the Jews as the enemies of Islam, of mankind and of God himself.[38] In Egypt, a booklet for children states that the Jews "persistently attempted to spread hate among the Muslims" and that "the only way to eliminate the Jews is through holy war (jihad) for the sake of Allah because they are the most villainous among Allah's creatures."[39] Another book says, "No other nation in ancient and modern times has carried the banner of fraud, evil and treachery as has the Jewish nation." It accuses the Jews of behaving throughout history in a "cruel and corrupt manner," and of using "conspiracy and deceit" to carry out their plans for "establishing their rule over the world."[40]

In the Palestinian Authority, state-controlled television sermons and newspaper articles label the Jews as the enemies of God and humanity, and present their annihilation as legitimate self-defense and a service to the world. In a sermon on PA TV, Dr. Muhammad Mustafa Najem, a lecturer in Koranic interpretation at Gaza's Al-Azhar University, preached that Allah described the Jews as "characterized by conceit, pride, arrogance, savagery, disloyalty and treachery ... [and] deceit and cunning." Dr. Khader Abas, a lecturer in psychology at Gaza's Al-Aqsa University, taught that Jewish evil was innate: "From the moment the [Jewish] child is born, he nurses hatred against others, nurses seclusion, nurses superiority."[41]

In 1999, a cartoon in the official PA daily *Al-Hayat al-Jadida* depicted a Jew as a subhuman dwarf with the caption: "The disease of the century." An opinion piece in the same paper commenting on the Jewish festival of Passover said, "There is nothing in history more horrible than the theft, the greatest crime in history, that the Jews carried out the night of their Exodus [from Egypt].... In other words, robbing others is not only permitted, it is considered holy. Especially since this thievery was done under the direct command of

God, [that is,] the God of the Jews." According to the writer, one of the meanings of Passover was: "Murdering foreigners is a godly virtue that should be emulated."[42]

Hezbollah presents the struggle between Islam and Judaism as one between good and evil. Thus: "The Jews are the enemy of the entire human race"; "The Torah inspires the Jews to kill"; "Zionism dictates the world and dominates it"; and "The Jews constitute a financial power. . . . They use funds to dominate the Egyptian media and infect its society with AIDS." Typically, Israel's alleged ruthlessness is illustrated by a soldier with a long, crooked nose, long teeth and ears and a prickly chin, wearing an armband with the Star of David and a steel helmet on his head, and holding a dagger dripping with blood.[43]

Likewise, Hamas calls the Jews "killers of the Prophets, blood-suckers, warmongers"; "barbaric"; "cowards"; a "cancer expanding in the land of Isra' [Palestine] and Mi'raj [Mohammed's ascent to heaven] threatening the entire Islamic world"; "a conceited and arrogant people"; "the enemy of God and mankind"; "the descendants of treachery and deceit"; Nazis "spreading corruption in the land of Islam"; "the Zionist culprits who poisoned the water in the past, killed infants, women and elders"; and "thieves, monopolists, usurers."[44]

Government-controlled media in Syria have described the Jews repeatedly as "blood-suckers." In his column in the Syrian government daily *Al-Thawra*, Jallal Kheir Bek wrote in 2009: "They kill, uproot, and eradicate, because deep within them, Judas does not slumber, and he instructs them to live off the blood of innocents. Further, they live off the blood that they suck, and make a living off the Christians in the U.S. and in other Western countries who have become Zionists." In an article in *Teshreen*, Mustafa Antaki wrote:

> The Zionists showed solidarity with those responsible for the Cold War, and perpetuated hostile activities within the U.S.S.R. and outside it. The

loathsome role played by the Zionists in the Ukraine and in Bolivia cannot be ignored—they flagrantly embezzled the economic and political resources of both countries. Perhaps one day the world will awake and realize that these Zionist elements are the blood-letters who hang on the peoples, sucking their blood and consuming their resources.[45]

On and on it goes, the hysterical lies and calumnies building one on top of another in fantastic pyramids, all with the same fundamental motif: that the Jews are the enemies of God and therefore must be destroyed. This is the driving impulse behind the Islamists' war against the West.

10

WESTERN
JEW-HATRED

The Arab and Muslim world is consumed by a virulent, theologically based prejudice against the Jews, which generates hallucinatory levels of genocidal hatred towards the Jewish people as well as serial fabrications and distortions about Israel. One might have expected the supposedly rational West, so quick to condemn religious obscurantism, to understand this hatred for what it is. One might have expected Western progressives, for whom prejudice in any form is the cardinal sin, to find this hatred abhorrent and say so in the strongest terms. On the contrary: they ignore, dismiss or excuse it. And worse, they have internalized and reproduced many of the same tropes, which they appear to believe are true.

The main reason why Muslims insist that "Palestine" is theirs is the belief that Islam represents a perfected world, and so the Jews can have no rights within any land that Muslims have ever conquered. The Western intelligentsia have bought heavily into the Arab and Muslim narrative of "Palestine" without understanding the fanatical theological sophistry from which it derives. Consequently, they believe that Israel lies at the root of some of the world's most intractable problems through its behavior and even its very existence. They therefore propagate a view that is as divorced from reality as it is murderously unjust.

Instead of attacking Arabs and Muslims for their irrationality and falsehoods, the Western intelligentsia accuse Israel's defenders of lies and even insanity. Instead of backing Israel while Hezbollah rockets were raining down on its northern towns in 2006, the British took to the streets with placards declaring "We are all Hezbollah now."[1] Within three years this contagion had spread to Fort Lauderdale, Florida, where demonstrators against Israel's war on Gaza in early 2009 chanted "Nuke, nuke Israel!" and carried placards accusing Israel of "ethnic cleansing" and bearing such messages as: "Did Israel take notes during the Holocaust? Happy Hanukkah." To the dozen or so supporters of Israel gathered across the street, one demonstrator shouted, "Murderers! Go back to the ovens! You need a big oven."[2]

Such incitement has consequences. In Europe, the Associated Press reported in 2009:

> Molotov cocktails have been hurled toward synagogues in France, Sweden and Belgium. Jews have been beaten in England and Norway, and an Italian union endorsed a boycott of Jewish-owned shops in Rome. In Amsterdam, a Dutch lawmaker marched in a demonstration where the crowd hollered "Hamas, Hamas, Jews to the gas." Socialist lawmaker Harry van Bommel said he did not repeat calls for another Holocaust and only chanted, "Intifada, Intifada, Free Palestine" . . . [S]imilar protests have also taken place in the United States. In San Francisco, protesters burned Israeli flags and carried banners reading "Jews are terrorists," "Zionism Nazism," and "Gaza Holocaust." Some read "Zionazis."[3]

In Norway, one of the most ferociously anti-Israel countries in Europe, Siv Jensen, chairwoman of the main opposition Progress Party and a leading pro-Israel politician, received death threats after she spoke at a pro-Israel rally and was placed under twenty-four-hour security guard. A witness who was also present at the rally commented, "I have never experienced this kind of hatred in Norway. There were people throwing stones at and spitting on rally-goers. Afterward, people carrying Israeli flags were randomly attacked in the streets."[4]

In Britain, all Jewish communal events have to be guarded. Jewish schools are fitted with shatterproof glass and reinforced walls, and some Jewish children are abused on their way to and from school. In February 2009, a twelve-year-old Birmingham schoolgirl was terrorized on her way home by a mob of twenty youths chanting "Kill all Jews" and "Death to Jews."[5]

The Community Security Trust, the defense organization run by British Jews, recorded a steep jump in anti-Jewish incidents in 2006 during the Lebanon war. The number of such incidents that year, 598, was the highest since records began in 1984. During the next two years, the number dropped back only slightly.[6] In 2006, the Parliamentary Inquiry into Antisemitism said that violence, desecration of property, and intimidation directed towards Jews was on the rise and that British Jews as a result were now "more anxious and more vulnerable to abuse and attack than at any other time for a generation or longer."[7]

A poll by the American Anti-Defamation League in 2007 revealed that half of all respondents in the UK believed it was "probably true" that "Jews are more loyal to Israel than their own country," a rise of 28 percent from the proportion two years earlier; 22 percent believed it was "probably true" that "Jews have too much power in the business world," compared with 14 percent who believed so two years previously; and 34 percent agreed that "American Jews control US foreign policy."[8] In the wake of Israel's Operation Cast Lead in Gaza, antisemitic incidents recorded in Britain leapt in the first six months of 2009, to 609, more than the previous record annual high of 598 for the whole of 2006.[9]

BLAMING THE JEWS FOR THEIR OWN PERSECUTION

Attacks on Jews spike whenever Israel is coming under fire in the media. So great is the animosity towards Israel, however, and so reluctant are people to acknowledge that the attacks signify a re-emergence of "the oldest hatred," that Israel itself is blamed for the rise in Jew-hatred. According to the British film-maker Ken Loach, who claimed that Israel was guilty of a "massacre" in Gaza in 2009, the rise in antisemitism was "perfectly understandable because Israel feeds feelings of antisemitism."[10] Popular hostility towards Jews is said to result from Israel's "oppression" of the Palestinians, its "disproportionate" attacks on them and its "violations" of international law. Jews collectively are held responsible for Israel's perceived misdeeds—even as Israel itself is routinely accused of imposing "collective punishment" on Palestinians. Jews are thus deemed to be responsible for their own persecution.

In fact, it is not Israel's behavior that is responsible for the extraordinary animosity towards Israel within the West. It is the *presentation* of that behavior, which amounts to a collective libel of unprecedented malevolence, scope and intensity. Israel is charged with behavior of which it is the *victim*, not the perpetrator. The treatment of Israel is a spectacular example of "psychological projection," a phenomenon that characterizes totalitarian ideologies in both the Western and Islamic worlds.

Of course, history is littered with causes that have been misrepresented through ignorance or false assumptions, ideology or prejudice. These are, however, generally issues that attract little attention or where the facts are difficult to obtain. The Israel conflict is unique because it is dwelt upon obsessively and disproportionately, more than any other conflict in the world, and because the true facts are open for all to see. Yet the more attention it receives, the more irrational its presentation becomes—and the more this distorts the way many view what is going on in the world more generally.

Those who view Israel through this distorting prism often try to defend themselves by asking why that country should uniquely be exempt from criticism. But this argument is a straw man. Of course Israel should be open to criticism, just like any other country, and called to account for its behavior. Sometimes, like any other country, it behaves badly. What we are looking at here, however, is not "criticism." It is a pathological malice that is meted out to no other country on earth.

In his novel *The Counterlife*, Philip Roth's hero comments on England's "peculiarly immoderate, un-English-like Israel-loathing." As Howard Jacobson wrote two decades later, "The peculiarly immoderate Israel-loathing that Roth remarked upon in 1987 is now a deranged revulsion, intemperate and unconcealed, which nothing Israel itself has done could justify or explain were it ten times the barbaric apartheid state it figures as in the English imagination."[11]

England—or to be more accurate, Britain—is indeed the brand leader of this "deranged revulsion" in the West. That is not to say it is alone; the prejudice is widespread throughout western Europe. There are countries where Jew-hatred is more violent, such as France, and where Israel-hatred is more virulent even than in Britain—Norway and Sweden especially.[12] It has also put down deep roots on campuses in the United States and is spreading into the American mainstream.

But Britain is the brand leader, not only because it is the mothership of the English-speaking world, disseminating its culture way beyond that world, in particular through the unique global reach and authority of the BBC. It is also the country where the whole intellectual, political and religious establishment—the universities, the Foreign Office, the Church of England, the theatrical and publishing worlds, the voluntary sector, members of Parliament across the political spectrum, as well as the media—has signed up to the demonization and delegitimization of Israel. The combination of these two factors has meant that Britain has effectively become a kind of global laundry for the lies about Israel and the Jews that pour out of the Arab and Muslim world, sanitizing them for further consumption throughout English-speaking, American and European society, and turning what was hitherto confined to the extreme fringes of both left and right into mainstream views. Where Britain has led, the rest of the West has followed.

REASON AS THE INCUBATOR OF PREJUDICE

While the prejudice against Israel and the Jews is global, it is also specific to the intelligentsia. It correlates overwhelmingly with education and social class. The higher up the educational and social scale, the more virulent and extreme the prejudice. In the UK, it unites conservatively minded "Middle Britain" with liberal metropolitan salon society. In the United States, it extends from Noam Chomsky on the far left, through the former Democratic president Jimmy Carter, to John Mearsheimer and Stephen Walt on the "new realist" right.

Polling data from Europe reinforces the link between demonization of Israel and higher educational attainment. A 2002 Pew survey in France, Germany, Italy and Britain found that sympathy for the Palestinians rose among more educated groups and fell among the less educated. In France, it rose to 51 percent among the highly educated from 36 percent in the general population. In Germany it rose to 40 percent from 26 percent. In Italy it rose to 34 percent from 30 percent. In Britain it rose to 36 percent from 28 percent.[13]

The disconcerting fact is that an obsessional prejudice and hatred against Jews has been incubated in the supposed citadel of reason: the university. Far from promoting enlightenment, Western universities are the prime breeding ground of falsehoods about the Middle East and bigotry towards Israel—a mutant virus born of reason itself—as well as intimidation against those who try to present a balanced and factual picture. In the universities, where leftism is the orthodoxy, a dominant narrative of Israeli perfidy and Palestinian victimization has sprung from the left's romance with radical Islamism, its hatred of the very same West that gives it the freedom to proclaim these ideas, and its deconstruction of the concept of truth itself (all discussed more fully later in the book).

One of the principal drivers of Israel-hatred in the universities has been the extraordinary grip that the work of Edward Said has had on the academic mind. A professor of English and comparative literature at Columbia University until his death in 2003, Said has shaped not just Middle Eastern studies but the humanities more generally ever since his book *Orientalism* was published in 1978. Said accused Western academics who studied the Orient of perpetuating negative racial stereotypes and anti-Arab and anti-Islamic prejudice, and thus constructing an entirely false impression of Islam and its civilization. Zionism, he taught, was an imperialist conspiracy created for the purpose of "holding Islam at bay."[14]

Said was the prime popularizer of the belief that Arabs and Muslims in general and Palestinians in particular, as victims of imperialism, were not responsible for their own destiny. More than anyone else, he made Israel-hatred and the myth of Palestinian victimization academically mainstream and fashionable. He invested this crude propaganda with a scholarly hinterland that was as mendacious as it was mesmerizing. Accusing Said of systematically misrepresenting the work of many scholars and Western civilization as a whole, the Islam expert Ibn Warraq has parodied Said's view thus: "If only the wicked west and those Zionists would leave us alone, we would be great again as in the time of our forefathers when one Muslim could fell ten infidels with one blow of the sword."[15]

Despite Said's countless "contradictions" and "howlers" and much "intellectual dishonesty," as Ibn Warraq describes them, his influence in the academy was enormous in promoting the cause of "Palestine," demonizing Israel and engendering a climate in which honest and truthful discussion of Islam became all but impossible. One German Arabist observed that academics were now wearing "a turban spiritually in their mind" and practicing "Islamic scholarship" rather than scholarship about Islam.[16]

University humanities graduates, with their heads stuffed full of this propaganda and unable as a result to think straight about the Middle East, have gone on to swing the intelligentsia as a whole behind their anti-Israel, pro–Third World ideology. And the media are bursting with such graduates, whose groupthink has turned newspapers and broadcasting outlets—not to mention those sacred citadels of the intelligentsia, the *London Review of Books* and the *New York Review of Books*—into the propaganda arm of the jihad against Israel and the free world. In recent years, the American media have increasingly disseminated this twisted groupthink on Israel. Despite the overwhelming support for Israel among the American public, the big media players such as CNN and MSNBC, the *New York Times* and *Boston Globe* have been falling in with the view that Israel is responsible for the impasse in the Middle East. American reporting on Israel has become far more tendentious than it once was—undoubtedly emboldened, at least in part, by the mainstreaming in the British media of canards about Israel that would previously have been considered beyond the pale.

THE BRITISH MEDIA AS THE GLOBAL LAUNDRY FOR BIGOTRY

While some reporting on Israel in the American media is tendentious, it is nothing compared with the British media—the global leaders in frenzied attacks on Israel. In the BBC, this virulence attains unparalleled power and influence since it is invested with a worldwide imprimatur of objectivity and trustworthiness. The false narrative of Arab propaganda is now so deeply embedded in the consciousness of journalists that they cannot see that what they are saying is untrue even when it is utterly absurd. In the "massacre" of

Jenin, they parroted Palestinian claims of atrocities that had left hundreds of civilians dead but where in fact only fifty-two Palestinians, who Israel said were mostly armed men, had been killed along with no fewer than twenty-three Israeli soldiers—an enormous Israeli attrition rate, which to this day has never been acknowledged by Israel's accusers.[17]

Reading the British papers and listening to the broadcast media on Israel is like experiencing a verbal pogrom. Israel's every action is reported malevolently and ascribed to the worst possible motives. Even though every military action by Israel is taken solely to protect itself from attack, these actions are misrepresented as violent oppression of the Palestinians. Israel is dwelt upon obsessively, held to standards of behavior expected of no other country, while tyranny around the world goes almost unreported—such as the twenty-year genocide in southern Sudan, or the persecution of Christians in Africa or Asia, or indeed Palestinian violence upon other Palestinians. While Israel is falsely accused of imposing wanton suffering, its own victimization is glossed over or ignored altogether.

The war against Hamas in Gaza in 2008–2009 was a case in point. The British media had scarcely reported the constant rocket bombardment from Gaza. Most of the public were simply unaware that thousands of rockets had been fired at Israeli citizens. But when Israel, in Operation Cast Lead, finally bombed Gaza to put a stop to the attacks, it was denounced for a "disproportionate" response and for wantonly and recklessly killing "civilians"—even though, according to Israel, the vast majority of those killed were targeted terrorists. Figures of four or five hundred child casualties were regularly bandied about. Heartrending pictures of children who had been killed were incessantly transmitted by the BBC. There was scant reference, if any, to the calls by Hamas for civilians to form human shields, or to the fact that Hamas deliberately put women and children on the rooftops to maximize casualties.[18] Instead, the media repeated claims put out by Hamas and its patsies, the UN Relief and Works Agency, of Israeli atrocities against civilians—as in the allegedly "deliberate" shelling of a school where forty Gazan civilians taking shelter were said to have been killed in a direct hit, a claim later revealed to be totally untrue since the shells had missed the school and killed only a handful of people in the neighboring street, including a number of Hamas terrorists who were firing mortars at Israeli soldiers.[19]

Moreover, according to the Israel Defense Forces, which eventually traced the names of virtually everyone killed during the war, of the 1,166 Palestinians killed, 709 were Hamas terrorists. Of the rest, 295 were "uninvolved Palestinians," of whom *only 89 were under the age of sixteen* and 49 were women. In addition, there were 162 names of men that had not yet been attributed to any organization.[20] Given that fully half of Gaza's population is under age sixteen, it is clear from these figures that far from launching a "disproportionate" attack that wantonly killed children, Israel had indeed targeted terrorists and had striven to avoid civilian casualties to a degree that is unprecedented in warfare.

Nevertheless, the media gave the impression that the Israelis were a bunch of bloodthirsty child-killers. Israel was further accused of causing a humanitarian catastrophe in maintaining a blockade of Gaza. But there was no mention of the many supplies Israel was in fact allowing through, nor the steady stream of Gazans being routinely treated in Israeli hospitals.

Defenders of the media might say that during Operation Cast Lead many of the media were largely taking their cue from the UN, which was putting out Hamas propaganda as if it were the truth; or that they were merely too naive and trusting in their anxiety to get "the story" out. And undoubtedly there's something in that. But no such excuse can begin to explain the unparalleled malice with which British journalists and intellectuals approach the subject of Israel month in, month out.

To much of the media, Israel's self-defense is regarded as intrinsically illegitimate. It is routinely described as "vengeance" or "punishment." Thus Sir Max Hastings wrote in the *Guardian* in 2004: "Israel does itself relentless harm by venting its spleen for suicide bombings upon the Palestinian people."[21] Israel's attempt to prevent any more of its citizens from being blown to bits on buses or in pizza parlors was apparently nothing other than a fit of spiteful anger. The Israelis were presented by Hastings not as victims of terror but as Nazi-style butchers, while the aggression of the Palestinians was ignored altogether.

In 2007, the BBC's Middle East editor Jeremy Bowen wrote a piece marking the fortieth anniversary of the Six-Day War, in which he suggested that the Israeli generals "had been training to finish the unfinished business of Israel's independence war of 1948—the capture of East Jerusalem—for most of their careers." He also said that Zionism had an "innate instinct to push out the frontiers" and that Israel was "in defiance of everyone's interpretation of international law except its own."[22] In other words, rather than fighting a defensive war to prevent Israel from being wiped out in 1967—as it was terrified might happen[23]—its generals saw a golden opportunity to complete a conquest begun at its founding in 1948.

Bowen's claim was a distortion of breathtaking malevolence, since in 1948 a war of extermination had been waged *against* Israel. And the suggestion that Zionism is innately expansionist was untrue, as was the statement that Israel's actions were all illegal. For this disgraceful abuse of journalism, Bowen received a rare public censure in 2009 by the BBC Trust Editorial Standards Committee, in response to two complaints, for breaching the BBC's rules on impartiality and accuracy. This ruling nevertheless failed to acknowledge the most egregious elements of his piece and amounted to no more than a mild rap over the knuckles.[24]

Even so, the very fact that *any* ground had been given to Israel's cause sent various prominent British journalists into a tailspin. Hailing Bowen as one of the BBC's most "courageous, authoritative and thoughtful broadcasters," the BBC presenter Jonathan Dimbleby fumed that "the BBC's international status as the best source of trustworthy news in the world has been gratuitously—if unintentionally—undermined."[25] The idea that Bowen himself might have undermined this status would of course not be considered. In the *Independent*, Richard Ingrams wrote that the BBC, by censuring Bowen, had upheld "the complaints of wealthy American lobbyists who seek to promote the cause of a foreign government."[26] Previously, Ingrams had distinguished himself by writing in the *Observer*, "I have developed a habit when confronted by letters to the editor in support of the Israeli government to look at the signature to see if the writer has a Jewish name. If so, I tend not to read it."[27] Also in the *Independent*, Robert Fisk raged that the Bowen ruling was "pusillanimous, cowardly, outrageous, factually wrong and ethically dishonest" and that the BBC Trust was "now a mouthpiece for the Israeli lobby which so diligently abused Bowen."[28]

When Muslims around the world go on the rampage at the publication of cartoons they deem disrespectful to Islam, they are "protesters" reacting spontaneously to offense. When two Jews complain at a collective libel of Israel, they are the "Israel lobby" which seeks to silence a worthy reporter.

Any doubts that the British media's attitude towards Israel was pathologically hostile would surely have been dispelled by a piece written by the *Independent*'s Johann Hari. Explaining why he couldn't praise Israel on its sixtieth birthday, he wrote: "Whenever I try to mouth these words, a remembered smell fills my nostrils. It is the smell of shit."[29] In associating Israel with excrement, Hari justified this particular form of scatological and dehumanizing imagery by holding Israel to blame for flooding the West Bank with raw sewage. But as had been reported elsewhere, this problem had been caused in part by the Palestinians themselves; indeed, Israel was also being polluted by municipal waste from the West Bank seeping into the groundwater,[30] a problem that Israelis and Palestinians were jointly attempting to rectify.[31] These facts were simply brushed aside by Hari in his eagerness to present Israel in the most degraded and disgusting light possible.

According to Hari, a state founded on the promise to be "a light unto nations" had ended up "flinging its filth at a cowering Palestinian population" because it was really established on a plan to void itself of the Arabs living within its borders. Drawing on claims by the Israeli "revisionist" historian Ilan Pappé that Israel's founding fathers had devised a plan for expelling the Arabs, Hari alleged that Israel was built on the ruins of ethnic cleansing. But when Hari had made the same claim two years previously, another "revisionist" Israeli historian, Benny Morris, pointed out in an outraged letter to the newspaper that it was "an invention, pure and simple," as there had never been such a plan or policy.[32] Nevertheless, Hari chose to repeat the falsehood.

But then, demonstrable evidence seems to count for nothing where Israel is concerned. Sheer fantasy takes over instead. For example, Israel is repeatedly accused of practicing "apartheid." Jimmy Carter devoted an entire book, *Palestine: Peace Not Apartheid*, to making this claim, alleging that Israel was perpetrating "worse instances of apartness, or apartheid, than we witnessed even in South Africa."[33] In 2006, the *Guardian* published a purportedly serious and considered comparative analysis of apartheid South Africa and Israel by Chris McGreal, who had extensive experience reporting from both countries. Among other things, McGreal said, "There are few places in the world where governments construct a web of nationality and residency laws designed for use by one section of the population against another. Apartheid South Africa was one. So is Israel."[34] Israel's security barrier is repeatedly referred to as its "apartheid wall"; and in 2009, the charity War on Want published a book by Ben White titled *Israeli Apartheid: A Beginner's Guide.*[35]

But such a claim is bizarre. South African apartheid was a form of discrimination against the country's own black population that forced them to live apart from white people. One glance at Israel's free, open and democratic society tells you that the claim it practices apartheid is utterly ridiculous. While Israeli society is not immune from racist attitudes or discrimination against both its Arab citizens and Sephardi (or Eastern) Jews, Israeli Arabs have full and equal political rights. Arab students attend Israeli universities; there are Arab members of the Knesset, they serve in the courts, as police officers and in the army. There are *no* discriminatory nationality and residency laws in Israel. (The fact that the "right of return" confers automatic citizenship on Jews alone in respect of their unique global and historic victimization does not mean that Israel disbars other cultures from citizenship.) What Carter, McGreal and all the rest do—disgracefully—is to conflate Israel's population with the Arabs who live outside its borders. Clearly they do not have citizenship since they are not Israelis. And the *only* reason they are prevented from traveling freely is to stop them from blowing up more Israelis in buses and cafes.

THE DISTORTION OF REALITY BY THE NGOS

There are countless examples of such malice against Israel in the media. But journalists are not alone in this. As influential, if not more so, are the NGOs such as Save the Children, Oxfam or Christian Aid, which almost without exception whip up hatred by putting out a steady stream of grossly unbalanced or mendacious claims about Israeli repression while ignoring or sanitizing actual Palestinian aggression. They systematically invert reality by turning victim into victimizer and vice versa. They back up their version of events with a wholly misleading account of Jewish history, which fails to acknowledge that the Jews are the *only* people for whom Israel was its national home.

According to NGO Monitor, more than fifty NGOs claiming to promote human rights and humanitarian agendas issued more than five hundred statements about Israel's Operation Cast Lead in Gaza.

These statements exhibited egregious bias and double standards, focusing overwhelmingly on condemning Israel while ignoring or paying little attention to Israeli human rights and casualties. Under the façade of morality and universality, NGO Monitor said, they exploited international legal terminology while airbrushing violations of international humanitarian law by Hamas—such as the extensive use of human shields—out of the picture altogether. Speaking for Amnesty International, Donatella Rovera disingenuously argued that Hamas's violations were so clear as to demand little attention, while "Israeli authorities deny everything, so one has to prove what happened in a way that you don't need to do with the Palestinian rockets."[36]

The NGOs push Palestinian propaganda about Israel year in, year out. In 2008, on the sixtieth anniversary of the creation of the State of Israel, War on Want issued a press release saying:

> It also marks the 60th anniversary of the "nakba," or catastrophe, in which hundreds of thousands of Palestinians were driven from their homes in the displacement that made the state of Israel possible.... [I]nstead of supporting the rights of the occupied, the UK and other Western governments have given their consistent support to Israel. This stance is morally unacceptable, and a dereliction of our own responsibility under international law.[37]

In response to protests over War on Want's misleading and ideologically twisted statements, its director, John Hilary, resorted to Jewish conspiracy theory by complaining that these complaints were "part of an ongoing strategy by an organised pro-Israel lobby and the Jewish press."[38]

In a similar vein, John Prideaux-Brune, Oxfam's country program manager in Jerusalem, said in a press release about Operation Cast Lead: "The international community must not stand aside and allow Israeli leaders to commit massive and disproportionate violence against Gazan civilians in violation of international law."[39]

Human Rights Watch has a history of peddling false "massacre" claims as true. According to NGO Monitor, during the Lebanon war in 2006, HRW promoted the myth of a "massacre" at Qana, inflating the death toll to fifty-four although officials knew at the time that the Red Cross was only reporting twenty-eight casualties. HRW eventually retracted its false report. Similarly, its major report on that conflict, *Fatal Strikes*, claimed it had "found no cases in which Hezbollah deliberately used civilians," despite a wealth of documentary and video proof of the extensive Hezbollah activity in many of the specific villages where HRW claimed it was absent. "Nine out of 21 cases described in *Fatal Strikes* were contradicted by later HRW reports—a remarkable inaccuracy rate of 43%—even before independent analysis of the evidence," NGO Monitor said.[40]

In March 2008, CARE International, Cafod, Amnesty International, Christian Aid and Oxfam (among other organizations) published a report called *The Gaza Strip: A Humanitarian Implosion*.[41] About this report, the historian Andrew Roberts wrote:

> The authors did not bother to hide their political bias against Israel, repeating standard Palestinian political rhetoric and including claims that Israeli policy "constitutes a collective punishment against ordinary men, women and children" and is "illegal under international humanitarian law." The report was wrong on many counts, including allegations over the availability of food and basic necessities, which were later contradicted by both the World Bank and World Health Organisation. The fact that Hamas chose to pursue war with Israel rather than the welfare of its people was omitted. There was no reference to the fact that any of these claims might be disputed by the other side or by genuinely neutral observers.[42]

EVEN THE MEDICAL PROFESSION
IS A SUITABLE CASE FOR TREATMENT

The hostile fixation on Israel extends even into areas with no professional interest in foreign affairs. Britain's medical establishment, for example, as expressed through its house organ, the *British Medical Journal*, devotes wholly disproportionate attention to the perceived suffering of the Palestinians compared with any other people. In a search of the medical literature for citations relating to victims of international conflicts, the media watchdog Honest Reporting discovered the following:

> When Europeans kill Europeans (Bosnia), the BMJ allocates one citation for every 2000 deaths; when Africans kill Africans (Rwanda), the BMJ allocates one citation for every 4000 deaths; when Muslim Arabs kill Christian Africans (Darfur), the BMJ allocates one citation for every (minimum) 7000 Christians who are killed; when Israelis, in the process of combating terrorists, kill Palestinians, the BMJ allocates one citation for every 13 Palestinians killed (including terrorist combatants); when Arab Muslims kill Kurds, the BMJ fails to give this any attention whatsoever.[43]

As part of this strange obsession, the medical profession appears itself to require treatment for a clear loss of reason. In 2009, the *Lancet* published a blog post by Dr. Ghassan Abu Sittah and Dr. Swee Ang that it took down one month later "because of factual inaccuracies."[44] This blog post had claimed, among other things:

> People in Gaza described a silent bomb which is extremely destructive. The bomb arrives as a silent projectile at most with a whistling sound and creates a large area where all objects and living things are vaporized with minimal trace. We are unable to fit this into conventional weapons but the possibility of new particle weapons being tested should be suspected.... The wounds of Gaza are deep and multi-layered.

The blog also talked about "the execution of 35,000 prisoners of war by Israel in 1967."[45]

But this was all fabrication. The supposed "silent bomb" was straight out of science fiction. As for the 35,000 Egyptian POWs allegedly killed, Egyptian sources give the total casualty figure for the 1967 war as just over 9,800 Egyptian soldiers killed, wounded or missing in action.[46] As a group of eminent Israeli doctors wrote in response to the "silent bomb" claim and other aspects of this travesty:

> Of course, no facts are brought to remotely support such an absurd accusation, other than "unnamed people in Gaza" who supposedly witnessed such an event. The same goes for purported executions of innocent children, old people and women who were supposedly killed in cold blood. No such thing occurred. What did occur, according to an orthopedic rehabilitative surgeon in one of Israel's leading hospitals, is that Hamas made PLO policemen and others stand against a wall while they shot their legs with a machine gun and then stabbed their legs to finish the job. Most of these Palestinians were treated in Israeli hospitals such as Ichilov, Sheba and Barzilai Medical Centers to save their lives and treat their fractures, amputations and neurological damage.[47]

The *Lancet* took down the post about the "silent bomb"; but how could it have allowed such a poisonous and paranoid fantasy to be posted in the first place? And before it was consigned to the cyber-bin, the piece managed to pump a little more hatred of Israel into the world, as indicated by messages posted in response:

> Many people were dreading to read a report such as this, knowing full well what horrific actions has been carried out by Israel over the years.
>
> I have no words appropriate to describe my horror and revulsion. It is almost unbelievable that the people of Israel, many of whom are descended from Jews who died in the Nazi holocaust, should have a government practising today's holocaust.

The Israeli government gets away with these atrocities for one main reason: the US backs them to the hilt.[48]

THE OLDEST HATRED ASSUMES A FRESH FORM ONCE AGAIN

The malice shown towards Israel is unique in its nature and scope. No other conflict in the world than that between Israel and the Arabs attracts such a frenzy of falsification, distortion, selective reporting, moral inversion, historical fabrication, viciousness and imputations of bad faith. And there is an adamantine refusal to acknowledge that this is the latest manifestation of the unique prejudice of antisemitism.

People think of antisemitism as a prejudice towards Jews as people and believe that this prejudice died with Hitler. The argument that attitudes towards Israel may be anti-Jewish strikes them as absurd because they think you can't be antisemitic about a country. They also are often decent people for whom the idea of prejudice against the Jews is abhorrent and offensive. And they point out that among those who criticize Israel most harshly are people who themselves are Jews.

The semantic question, however, is in one important sense a red herring. As Robin Shepherd rightly observes in his book *A State Beyond the Pale*, the animus against Israel is bigotry because it is irrational, hateful and dishonest discourse. One doesn't make that bigotry any better by protesting that it isn't antisemitism.[49]

True enough; and yet there is a reason why it *is* important to say whether this animus is a type of Jew-hatred. This is because Jew-hatred is a particular species of irrationality that tells us something important about the depths of unreason to which the human mind is capable of descending, and about the society in which it manifests itself. Indeed, since Jew-hatred usually stands proxy for other disorders of the *Zeitgeist*, the Jews often serve as the canaries in the mine of history. And there is overwhelming cause to believe that the phenomenon of the unreasonable hatred of Israel is, as it has often been described, a "new antisemitism."

This does *not* mean that all those who subscribe to the demonization and delegitimization of Israel are prejudiced against Jews,
or even "the Jews" (although some undoubtedly are). Indeed, as has
been noted already, some of the people who demonize Israel are Jews
themselves. It means rather that they have all bought into a governing set of ideas about Israel that are in themselves a type of Jew-
hatred, albeit in ways that may not be recognized.

The key point is that antisemitism is not simply a form of racial
or ethnic prejudice like any other, but one with unique characteristics. It applies expectations to the Jews that are applied to no other
people; it libels, vilifies and dehumanizes them; it scapegoats them
not merely for crimes they have not committed but for crimes of
which they are in fact the victims; it holds them responsible for all
the ills of the world.

The gross misrepresentation of Israel exhibits precisely these
characteristics. Antisemitism has simply mutated from prejudice
against Jews as people to prejudice against Jews as *a* people. First,
theological antisemitism wanted the Jewish religion to disappear;
then racial antisemitism wanted the Jews themselves to disappear;
now the latest mutation wants the Jewish state to disappear.

There is also at work here a uniquely hybrid animus. The hostility towards Israel on account of its presumed behavior has developed into an open hostility towards Israel's very existence and
towards Zionism. Thus it crosses an important line, because it singles out the Jews alone as having no right to assert their own people-
hood. Yet Jewish peoplehood, the Jewish religion and the land of
Israel are the three legs of the tripod of Jewish identity. The attack
on Zionism and Israel's existence is an attack on the Jewish people as
a people, and thus on Judaism itself. This applies equally to those
Jews who have led the charge against Israel, most of whom have only
a tangential or conflicted attachment to their Jewish identity—
which they often assert *only* in order to bash Israel, wrapping themselves in the mantle of Holocaust victimology while doing so—and

who display almost total ignorance of Judaism, if not actual hatred towards it.

The Jews are a unique people with a unique history. The treatment of the Jewish state is also unique. There is no other nation in the world that, having been the target of annihilatory attack for six decades, is expected to make concessions to its attackers even while the assaults continue. There is no other nation in the world whose right to existence is deemed to be forfeit through its behavior. There is no other nation in the world whose right to existence is deemed to be forfeit through *someone else's* behavior, for which it is made the scapegoat.

MOTIFS OF DEHUMANIZATION

The continuity between the old and new forms of the "longest hatred" is visible through various ancient motifs of Jew-hatred. One such is the medieval blood libel, centered on the idea that the Jews are child-killers—a trope that was much labored by the Palestinians and their willing dupes in the media during Operation Cast Lead and other wars. Closely allied to it is the image of the Jews "poisoning the wells," which was on startling display in the scatological animus of Johann Hari. Other hoary chestnuts are the belief that the Jews do "vengeance" and "punishment," a belief that reflects a view of the Hebrew Bible as hostile as it is ill-informed; or that the Jews are some kind of global conspiracy with a fiendish power to manipulate events for their own ends.

All these motifs are on conspicuous display in the verbal pogrom against Israel. In 2003, the blood libel was given graphic representation by the cartoon in the *Independent* by Dave Brown—published on Britain's Holocaust Memorial Day—depicting the former Israeli prime minister Ariel Sharon in monstrous form biting the head off a Palestinian baby. This cartoon pointedly won first prize in the UK Political Cartoon Society's annual awards.[50]

In 2009, in the fevered atmosphere of Israel-loathing in Britain following Operation Cast Lead, a ten-minute play was put on at London's fashionable Royal Court Theatre. Caryl Churchill's *Seven Jewish Children* dealt in oblique fashion with seven seminal episodes in modern Jewish and Israeli history: the Holocaust, its aftermath in Europe, the creation of the State of Israel, the Six-Day War, the rise of the settlements in the West Bank and Gaza, the Second Intifada and Operation Cast Lead. The underlying message was that the Jews who had started as victims of the Nazis claimed the land of Israel out of a sense of superiority, dispossessed its rightful Arab inhabitants, and thenceforth set about killing them in hatred, blood-lust and rapacious colonialism; and that as the "chosen people" they were "better haters" than the rest of the world and were thus happy to kill Arabs.[51]

The Jews were presented as literally dehumanized, feeling no pity or sorrow for all the babies they had killed because they claimed a monopoly on suffering; indeed, they supposedly laughed at their victims. This portrayal of Jews as not only monstrous child-killers but "better haters" because they were the "chosen people" was straight out of the hallucinatory lexicon of medieval Jew-hatred. *Seven Jewish Children* was in short a modern "mystery play," an update on the medieval productions that unleashed bloody pogroms against Jews in Europe. The cutting edge of London theater had taken us back to the murderous anti-Jewish passions of the Middle Ages. This went down very well indeed with progressive London—and even in America, where the play was staged in New York. Michael Billington, theater critic for the *Guardian*, wrote that "Churchill also shows us how Jewish children are bred to believe in the 'otherness' of Palestinians" and praised the Royal Court for "connecting with the big issues."[52]

But what Britain and the West are being bred to believe in, through this play and countless other examples of Israel-loathing and Jew-hatred, is the diabolical "otherness" of the Jews. As Professor Efraim Karsh observed,

> the Palestinians are but the latest lightning rod unleashed against the Jews, their supposed victimization reaffirming the millenarian demonization of the Jews in general, and the medieval blood libel—that Jews delight in the blood of others—in particular. In the words of David Mamet, "The world was told Jews used this blood in the performance of religious ceremonies. Now, it seems, Jews do not require the blood for baking purposes, they merely delight to spill it on the ground."[53]

The next dominant motif from the ancient lexicon of Jew-hatred is the "Jewish conspiracy" theory: the belief that the Jews have demonic power, which they use covertly to disadvantage everyone else. There was a time not long ago when this canard was confined to the loonier elements among fascists and white supremacists. Now it is a commonplace in the West. It underpins discourse not just about Israel but also about the war in Iraq and against Islamist terror, since it holds that a Jewish conspiracy stretches from Jerusalem to Washington to subvert U.S. foreign policy in the interests of Israel and put the rest of the world in danger. The risk to the world therefore comes not from global Islamism but from the Jews.

In Britain this is said repeatedly, with no more than a slap on the wrist—if that—in response. In 2002, the *New Statesman* magazine printed an investigation into the power of the "Zionist" lobby in Britain, which it dubbed the "Kosher Conspiracy." In 2003, the Labor backbencher Tam Dalyell claimed that Tony Blair was "being unduly influenced by a cabal of Jewish advisers."[54] The Liberal Democrat politician Jenny Tonge, who was honored by her party with a peerage after sympathizing with suicide bombers and comparing Arabs in Gaza to Jews in the Warsaw Ghetto, told her party conference in 2006: "The pro-Israel lobby has got the Western world in its financial grips. I think they've probably got a certain grip on our party."[55]

A distinguished British general told me, in words as confident as they were false, that Rupert Murdoch had ordered that opposition to the Iraq war in the *Times* newspaper should be drastically limited "on the instruction of the Jewish lobby in America." Furthermore, claimed this general, George Bush had invaded Iraq because "he had Ariel Sharon's hand up his back."

In the *Guardian* in 2007, Geoffrey Wheatcroft lamented that the British Conservative Party leader David Cameron had fallen under the spell of neoconservatives with their "ardent support for the Iraq war, for the US and for Israel." He urged Cameron to ensure that British foreign policy was no longer based on the interest of "another country"—Israel.[56]

In 2009, Brian Reade bemoaned Britain's "cowardly subservience to the all-powerful pro-Israel lobby in America. We looked away as Israel bombed the crap out of Gaza," he wrote in the *Daily Mirror*. "When the 1,314 dead Palestinians temporarily sated Tel Aviv's bloodlust, we sent a third-rate politician to pledge millions to replace all the buildings flattened by Israel's military machine."[57]

A column by John Pilger in the *New Statesman* in 2004 began by blaming Israel for causing the Madrid train bombings and for being "the guiding hand" behind American foreign policy, and then went on to draw "middle-class Jewish homes in Britain" into the circle of "destructive" Zionist complicity.[58]

In November 2009, the Channel 4 program *Dispatches* claimed that a "cabal" of wealthy British Jews had bought up both the Labor and Conservative parties in order to hijack British politics for the cause of Israel.[59]

Even Richard Dawkins got in on the act, saying, "When you think about how fantastically successful the Jewish lobby has been, though, in fact, they are less numerous I am told—religious Jews anyway—than atheists and [yet they] more or less monopolise American foreign policy as far as many people can see."[60]

Such comments served to normalize the hitherto unsayable and create a climate of acceptability, which crossed the Atlantic to enable "Jewish conspiracy" theory to attain the status of scholarship. In 2006, two previously uncontroversial Harvard academics, John Mearsheimer and Stephen Walt, published an explosive article on the "Israel Lobby" in the *London Review of Books*,[61] followed a year later by a book, *The Israel Lobby and U.S. Foreign Policy*, that amplified their argument.[62] Their thesis—as summarized by the law professor Alan Dershowitz in response to the original paper—was that the "Israel Lobby," a cabal whose "core" was composed of American Jews, had a "stranglehold" on mainstream American media, think tanks and government, through which it put the interests of Israel ahead of those of the United States. Jewish political contributors used "Jewish money" to blackmail government officials, while "Jewish philanthropists" influenced and "policed" academic programs and shaped public opinion. America's terrorism problem was directly attributable to "the Lobby," and Israel was responsible for America's involvement in wars that were not in its interest, particularly in Iraq. Furthermore, Israel lacked any moral claim to American support, because the "creation of Israel entailed a moral crime against the Palestinian people"; Israel had continued to commit crimes including "massacres" and "rapes"; it was a "colonizing regime" based on the principle of "blood kinship," and its conduct was "not morally distinguishable from the actions of its opponents."[63]

As Gabriel Schoenfeld remarked, this astounding farrago had effectively "put a scholarly cap and gown on every hoary calumny ever devised about Jewish influence."[64] Virtually every single "fact" the authors adduced as the ostensibly scholarly basis for their paranoid claim of undue Jewish influence was untrue or distorted. One of the scholars whom they cited, the Israeli "revisionist" historian Benny Morris, said that Mearsheimer and Walt's work was "riddled with shoddiness and defiled by mendacity."[65]

Such was the flexible nature of the authors' connection with the truth that when the very heart of their argument was exposed as false, they executed a stunning volte-face without a blush. As Martin Kramer pointed out, their main argument was that America had gone to war in Iraq largely because of the influence of the "Israel Lobby" and its neoconservative wing. In their original article, they argued that Israel pushed "the Lobby," which pushed the neocons, which pushed the Bush administration into war. Various people then pointed out that this was clearly nonsense, since there was a large body of evidence that Israel had not been particularly worried about Saddam Hussein and wanted the United States to neutralize the threat from Iran instead.

In their book, Mearsheimer and Walt actually admitted that Israel had wanted Iran to take precedence over Iraq; subsequently they claimed that Israel joined the Iraq bandwagon only when the Bush administration seemed set on invasion. In response to the facts contradicting their claim, they still stuck to their original thesis but with a new gloss that, in the lead-up to the war, Israel and its "Lobby" worked overtime to ensure that Bush didn't get "cold feet"—an assertion backed up by no evidence at all.[66] It was also illogical; if Israel had merely gone along with America's plan for Iraq, it could not have been the puppet-master of American foreign policy and the instigator of the war. Indeed, the core premise that American foreign policy revolved around Israel was itself ridiculous; given America's dependence on oil, any rational person would realize that the lobby with real clout was Saudi Arabia.

The Israel Lobby and U.S. Foreign Policy was in effect a modern version of *The Protocols of the Elders of Zion*, the difference being that unlike the tsarist conspiracy theory, the modern version wasn't a forgery. Moreover, the appearance of this thesis dressed up in the trappings of scholarship had the effect of making people think that the obviously crazy stuff in the *Protocols* or the Hamas Charter, for example, wasn't so crazy after all. The only thing more astounding than the publication of this mendacious and malicious book by two mainstream Harvard academics was how respectfully it was received in intellectual circles. Certainly, its arguments were often shredded and its manifold illogicality and shoddiness repeatedly exposed. But bookstores displayed it prominently, and the authors were attentively interviewed or offered platforms to justify their argument in newspapers and periodicals.

Nevertheless, when Jews responded to the book with outrage, Mearsheimer and Walt claimed that this reaction proved their argument that Jews use the charge of antisemitism to close down debate. The fact that Jews protested against the charge of an "Israel Lobby" was used to demonstrate the existence of that "Lobby." But far from being stifled, these authors' voices were in fact constantly being heard. Their circular argument was a tactic that is regularly used in the service of closed thought systems, for which all dissent merely confirms the infallibility of the dogma. It is a tactic used repeatedly against those who object to the demonization of Israel, who find that if they call it anti-Jewish prejudice they are dismissed as proving once again that Jews respond to criticism by "playing the anti-semitism card."

A corollary is the assumption that anyone who raises a protest over the resurgence of antisemitism—or indeed takes the part of causes thought to be Jewish—must therefore be a Jew. When the gentile British journalist Richard Littlejohn made a documentary about antisemitism for Channel 4 TV, the reaction of some people was to assume that he was therefore Jewish. "They simply couldn't comprehend why a non-Jew would be in the slightest bit interested in investigating antisemitism," he wrote. "If I had been making a film about Islamophobia, no one would have asked me if I was Muslim." The Labor MP John Mann had the same experience when he instigated a parliamentary inquiry into antisemitism. As soon as he set it up, the first MP who commented to him about it said, "Oh, I didn't know you were Jewish, John." He is not. The implication was that only Jews would complain about antisemitism, with the further insinuation that they made it up for their own purposes—an assumption made about no other victim group.[67]

The left-wing *Observer* journalist Nick Cohen, who caused consternation among his comrades when he supported the Iraq war, wrote that he was assumed to be part of the "Jewish conspiracy" on account of his name. Although Cohen has Jewish ancestry on his father's side, he is not himself a Jew. "I learned it was one thing being called 'Cohen' if you went along with liberal orthodoxy, quite another when you pointed out liberal betrayals. There had to be a malign motive," he wrote. "You had to be in the pay of 'international' tycoons or 'neo-conservatives'. You had to have bad blood. You had to be a Jew."[68]

Cohen elaborated on this point in 2009, in the wake of the BBC's decision not to screen a charity appeal for Gaza on account of the tendentious nature of the message:

> Fight back and you become a Jew, whether you are or not. [The broad-caster] Mark Lawson recently described an argument at the BBC over the corporation's decision not to screen the charity appeal for Gaza. His furious colleague declared that the only reason Lawson supported the ban was because he was Jewish. Lawson had to tell him that he was, in fact, raised a Catholic. A furious Labour MP was no different when he told a colleague of mine that I had gone off the rails when I married a "hard-right" Jewish woman from North London. My friend replied that this would be news to my wife, a liberal Catholic from Stoke-on-Trent.[69]

THE "NAZIFICATION" OF ISRAEL ENTAILS DEMONIZING JEWS WHO DEFEND IT

It has become virtually impossible to draw attention to the phenomenon of resurgent antisemitism, even when Israel is accused of being a Nazi state—a pernicious claim that is indeed outright Jew-hatred.

It is far worse than the "Israeli apartheid" claim. At least it is possible to argue that those who accuse Israel of "apartheid" do so out of ignorance—of Israel, or apartheid, or the status of Arabs in the disputed territories. No such excuse can apply to the equation of Israel with Nazi Germany. Israel is patently not committing genocide. There is no persecution, there are no concentration camps, there is no extermination of the Arabs; there is merely an attempt by Israel to defend itself against attack by *them*.

To equate Israel with Nazi Germany is not merely to perpetrate a cruel and grotesque collective libel against Israeli Jews; it is also effectively to deny the Holocaust by redefining it. Equating the Nazis with Israeli Jews—whose behavior towards the Arabs accords with the rule of law, human rights and democracy—is effectively to deny that Jews were the victims of anything malevolent under the Nazis. Equating Israel with the Nazis takes the worst single crime ever to have afflicted the Jewish people and fashions it into a weapon against them—an unparalleled act of ethnically targeted malice.

Yet this odious gibe is used in the West with astonishing frequency. In Britain in 2001, the poet Tom Paulin referred to the "Zionist SS" in his poem *Killed in Crossfire*, which was published in the *Observer*.[70] He subsequently told the Egyptian paper *Al-Ahram Weekly* that Brooklyn-born Jewish settlers in the West Bank and Gaza "should be shot dead" as "they are Nazis, racists. I feel nothing but hatred for them."[71]

During the Lebanon war in 2006, a senior Conservative MP, Sir Peter Tapsell, claimed that Tony Blair was colluding with President Bush "in giving Israel the go-ahead" to commit "a war crime gravely reminiscent of the Nazi atrocity on the Jewish quarter of Warsaw."[72] The *Daily Telegraph* repeated the libel by publishing a cartoon depicting two scenes of devastation, one captioned "Warsaw 1943" and the other "Tyre 2006."[73] And Deborah Orr wrote in the *Independent*, "As for the great and terrible wall Israel is building around the West Bank, comparisons with the Warsaw ghetto are heartbreakingly painful."[74]

In January 2009, a senior Norwegian diplomat in Saudi Arabia was publicly exposed sending out emails making direct comparisons between Israel's behavior in Gaza and the actions of Nazi Germany. The email, sent from a Norwegian foreign ministry account, said, "The grandchildren of Holocaust survivors from World War II are doing to the Palestinians exactly what was done to them by Nazi Germany."[75] This comparison between Israelis and Nazis was illustrated with more than forty pictorial attachments.

The "Israelis as Nazis" analogy sometimes veers directly into hatred of the Jews as Jews. For instance, when the UK's National Union of Journalists voted in 2007 to boycott Israeli goods (a move that was subsequently reversed), one of its members, Pamela Hardyment, described Israel as "a wonderful Nazi-like killing machine backed by the world's richest Jews." Then she referred to the "so-called Holocaust" before pouring venom on Jews generally, saying, "Shame on all Jews, may your lives be cursed."[76]

The linkage between the Israelis-as-Nazis theme and hatred of Jews as Jews was made quite explicit by no less a luminary than the Portuguese Nobel Prize-winning novelist José Saramago. Visiting Yasser Arafat's compound in Ramallah in 2002, Saramago opined, "What is happening in Palestine is a crime which we can put on the same plane as what happened at Auschwitz, at Buchenwald. Even taking into account the differences in time and place, it is the same thing."[77] But clearly, it was *not* the same thing at all. So how could a Nobel Prize-winning author say this? How could he "see" a genocide among people who were clearly alive, not incarcerated, not being murdered but actually increasing in number? Later that year, Saramago provided the answer in an article in the Spanish newspaper *El Pais*, and Paul Berman provided translations of the most significant passages in an article in *The Forward*. Here Saramago revealed the deep roots of his hatred for Israel:

> Intoxicated mentally by the messianic dream of a Greater Israel which will finally achieve the expansionist dreams of the most radical Zionism;

contaminated by the monstrous and rooted "certitude" that in this catastrophic and absurd world there exists a people chosen by God and that, consequently, all the actions of an obsessive, psychological and pathologically exclusivist racism are justified; educated and trained in the idea that any suffering that has been inflicted, or is being inflicted, or will be inflicted on everyone else, especially the Palestinians, will always be inferior to that which they themselves suffered in the Holocaust, the Jews endlessly scratch their own wound to keep it bleeding, to make it incurable, and they show it to the world as if it were a banner. Israel seizes hold of the terrible words of God in Deuteronomy: "Vengeance is mine, and I will be repaid." Israel wants all of us to feel guilty, directly or indirectly, for the horrors of the Holocaust; Israel wants us to renounce the most elemental critical judgment and for us to transform ourselves into a docile echo of its will.[78]

Saramago's hatred of Israel arose therefore from his openly expressed hatred of Biblical Judaism and of the Jews on account of their having been "chosen by God." Israel was monstrous on account of its monstrous doctrines and the monstrous words of the God of the Hebrew Bible. To Saramago, Israel was therefore not just a country that behaved badly; it was a country that represented the metaphysical evil of the religion in which it was rooted. This was not the "new antisemitism." This was the old kind: pure, unadulterated, theological hatred of Judaism. It was Saramago's detestation of Judaism and of Jews that lay behind his unhinged perception of a genocide in Ramallah.

The tidal wave of incitement against Israel and the Jews has created an atmosphere of hysterical hatred among the Western intelligentsia. This is obvious from newspaper websites. On a readers' thread on the *Independent* site, for example, following a story about the proposed boycott of the Science Museum on account of its hosting Israeli scientists to teach schoolchildren about Israeli contributions to science, readers left these comments:

In some ways the brutality of the Israelis exceeded [that] of the Nazis.

Since its procreation by Zionist terrorists this stillbirth entity has been a cradle of hatred, violence, and war. Israel should cease to exist as an independent state.

The Jews—may as well call a spade a spade—have shown themselves not only as unprincipled thieves in their appropriation of Palestinian land, but as wanton, vicious, twisted murderers of civilians, in the process.

Killing people is a national past [sic] amongst Jews.

Zionism is a cancer that needs radiation.[79]

In September 2009, a high-ranking Foreign Office diplomat, Rowan Laxton, was found guilty of racially aggravated harassment for launching into a screaming anti-Jewish tirade while watching TV reports of the Israeli attack on Gaza while he used an exercise bike in a gym. Stunned staff and gym members heard him shout: "Fucking Israelis, fucking Jews." He also said that Israelis should be "blown off the fucking earth" if they got in the way of the international community.[80] Laxton was no minnow. He was head of the South Asia Group at the Foreign Office, a former deputy ambassador to Afghanistan and before that the head of chancery in Islamabad. In other words, he was a very senior diplomat. Yet he hated Israelis and Jews with such unbridled venom that he lost control and started raving.

Incitement of this kind has led to violence and intimidation against diaspora Jews. At San Francisco State University in 2002, Professor Laurie Zoloth wrote in a widely circulated email, "I cannot fully express what it feels like to have to walk across campus daily, past posters of cans of soup with labels on them of drops of blood and dead babies, labeled 'canned Palestinian children meat, slaughtered according to Jewish rites.'" That May, following a "Peace in the Middle East" rally sponsored by the campus Hillel House, Jewish students staying on for afternoon prayers were set upon by a mob. Zoloth wrote, "Counter-demonstrators poured into the plaza, screaming at the Jews to 'Get out or we will kill you' and 'Hitler did not finish the job.'.... There was no safe way out of the plaza. We had to be marched back to the Hillel House under armed SF police guard and we had to have a police guard remain outside Hillel."[81]

In June 2009, Jonathan Hoffman of the UK Zionist Federation attended the launch of Ben White's book *Israeli Apartheid: A Beginner's Guide* at a meeting in the House of Commons sponsored by the Labor MP Brian Idden. Hoffman later wrote of his experience:

> I remonstrated at the lies and Idden threatened me with eviction (the third time at Israel hate-fests in nine days). My friend was jeered at when she said her (Jewish-sounding) name before she asked her question. Idden said he would take statements after the questions, then refused to let me talk saying they were out of time. On my way out, I was told that "the Nazis should have finished the job."[82]

The antisemitism researcher Dave Rich has pointed out that although demonizing Israel as a Nazi state is intended to delegitimize it altogether and thus advance the agenda of its destruction, there is also a further consequence:

> If Israel is a Nazi state, then anybody who does not oppose Israel is morally no better than a Nazi. There is only one place this train of thought can end: with the demonisation and social isolation of the vast majority of ordinary British Jews. It means that when mainstream Jewish community leadership bodies organise a rally with the slogan, "Stop Hamas Terror: Peace for the people of Israel and Gaza", and launch a Jewish community fundraising campaign for hospitals in both Gaza and Israel during the fighting, [blogger] Richard Seymour accuses them of "cheerleading the massacre" and concludes that anybody who goes on the rally "ought to be shunned, and treated as the moral and political degenerates that they are."[83] It means that a research paper published by the School of Oriental and African Studies to investigate "legal aspects of economic and trade issues arising from Israel's occupation of the OPT

[Occupied Palestinian Territories]" lists the names, addresses and contact details of kosher food shops in London and Manchester. Once the central argument of anti-Israel campaigning in this country is that Israel is Nazi Germany, then this is no longer an anti-Zionist movement: it is an antisemitic one, with an antisemitic politics as its driving force.[84]

The insistence that Israel is to blame for any hostility towards Jews in the West thus encloses them within a Kafka-esque trap in which they will be blamed for whatever harm may befall them. As Nick Cohen has put it:

> They are the only ethnic minority whose slaughter official society will excuse. If a mass murderer bombed a mosque or black Pentecostal church, no respectable person would say that the "root cause" of the crime was an understandable repulsion at the deeds of al Qaeda or a legitimate opposition to mass immigration. Rightly, they would blame the criminal for the crime. If a synagogue is attacked, I guarantee that within minutes the airwaves will be filled with insinuating voices insisting that the "root cause" of the crime was a rational anger at the behaviour of Israel or the Jewish diaspora.[85]

Of course, "rational" is the one thing it is not. Like all other prejudices, Jew-hatred is quintessentially irrational. The question remains, however, why it has erupted in this way at this point in history. All kinds of theories can be adduced to explain it. Antisemitism is protean and never goes away; it merely mutates. Israel has turned in the eyes of the world from "David" into "Goliath." The anti-imperialist left needed a fresh cause after the implosion of communism. Progressives have embraced a postnational agenda that has replaced justice by "human rights," cultural continuity by multiculturalism and warfare by lawsuits. High levels of Muslim immigration in Britain and Europe have resulted in a supine acceptance of the Islamist agenda on Israel. Europe is trying to sanitize its role in the Holocaust by demonizing Israel as a Nazi state.

All these explanations are plausible to some extent, but they still don't really explain what has happened. When such patent derangement affects Harvard professors, Nobel Prize-winning novelists, senior diplomats, politicians, playwrights, physicians and others across the political spectrum—not to mention the wretched media—one has to sit up and take notice because something big is happening. The puzzle is the obsessional nature of this hatred and its location firmly within the sphere of reason. Why are the Western intelligentsia Israel's enemies—and why do they care so much?

11

THE RED-BLACK-GREEN-
ISLAMIC AXIS

One reason why people find it so difficult to acknowl-edge the resurgence of antisemitism in the West is that hatred of Jews has been associated with the "far right." But those who are deeply hostile to Israel are often also deeply hos-tile to the "far right," which they believe stands for racism, obscuran-tism, irrationality and bigotry.

Those left-wingers and liberals who march against Israel and America, denounce the neocons, promote the green agenda and raise the standard of atheistic reason against religious superstition think of themselves as progressive and enlightened. Their Manichean approach means they define themselves in large measure by what they are not. Most people are resolutely un-ideological and recoil from extremist attitudes. But for those activists within the intelligentsia whose voices are the most shrill, to be on the left, as we have already seen, is to inhabit the sphere of unassailable virtue. Everyone outside it belongs to the party of the damned, otherwise known as "the right"—which quickly shades into the "far right" with scarcely a breath drawn. And "the right" is invested with stupidity, ignorance, prejudice and authoritarianism, so that the left can think of itself as the opposite, waging a principled fight for reason, progress, tolerance and liberty. The left portrays itself historically as fighting heroically against tyranny and fascism.

Except it's not as simple as that. Indeed, this division is itself ignorant and ahistorical. The fact is that, today as in the past, left and right have common roots and share many characteristics. The idea that one side represents reason and liberty and the other their antithesis is false. In many ways, both left and far right form an axis of unreason, antimodernity and intolerance; and thus they share a number of characteristics with revolutionary Islamism. Indeed, the "reasoned" West has more in common with the "obscurantist" East than people care to recognize.

THE LEFT AND THE ISLAMISTS

On its face, the love affair between sections of the left and the Islamists is a most unlikely pairing, as has been noted by commentators such as Nick Cohen.[1] Much of the left stands for militant secularism and the social agenda that follows: sexual libertinism and gay rights, as well as the bedrock issue of equality for women. Yet behind the banners of "Free Palestine" and "No Blood for Oil," they have marched shoulder to shoulder with Islamists who believe in the subservience of women, stoning adulterers and executing homosexuals and apostates.

Some on the left have not only marched alongside the Islamists but also embraced them, literally. Thus the former mayor of London, the far-leftist Ken Livingstone, publicly embraced Sheikh Yusuf al-Qaradawi, the legal authority of the Muslim Brotherhood, who has openly supported Islamist terrorism, voiced extreme prejudice against Jews *and* justified the execution of homosexuals under Islamic rule and domestic violence against women. In May 2006, Noam Chomsky traveled to Beirut and there embraced Sheikh Hassan Nasrallah, the head of Hezbollah, which repeatedly calls for the destruction of the United States. In 1983, Hezbollah murdered 241 American Marines in Lebanon along with numerous Israelis and Jews—activities which Chomsky described as "a justified deterrent against aggression."[2]

In Britain in 2003, a series of huge antiwar rallies was organized by the Stop the War Coalition, an alliance between the Socialist Workers Party, the Communist Party and the Muslim Association of Britain, an offshoot of the Muslim Brotherhood. At the rallies, people screamed their support for Hezbollah and Hamas. The British "Respect" MP George Galloway, speaking at the University of Damascus in 2005, called for victory for the Iraqi terrorists over the coalition forces. To amplify his pan-Islamic credentials, he also told Syria to face its enemies with dignity, saying, "I believe, God willing, we will prevail and triumph, *wa-salam aleikum*."[3]

A few days before 9/11, radical Islamists were joined by NGOs and other Western leftists at a United Nations conference in Durban, South Africa, in an anti-Israel, anti-Jew hate-fest whose sole purpose was to demonize and delegitimize Israel under the banner of "human rights." A similar alliance emerged in the United States as the internet-based progressive movement called MoveOn.org, whose ostensible aim of defeating the Republican Party stood proxy for its deeper animus against Zionism and American "imperialism."

As David Horowitz has chronicled, the roots of the left's alliance with Islamism lie in a logical progression of its core animus against America and the West. After communism imploded, those on the left did not conclude they had been mistaken—indeed, they could never think such a thing—but instead simply reshaped their belief system to perpetuate their revolutionary illusions by encompassing new nihilistic and anti-Western agendas, of which Islamism was one, alongside environmentalism, feminism and gay rights.[4] From Harold Pinter to Naomi Klein and Noam Chomsky, the luminaries of progressive thinking stood alongside the enemies of liberty and said to the defenders of the West, "not in our name."

THE NEOFASCISTS AND THE ISLAMISTS

Leftists are not the only people whose alliance with Islamists is surprising. There is also a third party to this love affair. Among neofascists and white supremacists, many of whom express their loathing for Islam and Muslims on the grounds that they loathe anyone who is not white, there is nevertheless a significant number who make common cause with the Islamists against the Jews and America. It is the left-wing-dominated Western intelligentsia that has enabled this to happen, since its claim that American foreign policy has been hijacked by a Jewish or Zionist cabal putting the world in danger for its own evil ends comes straight out of *The Protocols of the Elders of Zion*—the conspiracy theory whose grip on the imagination of neofascists and white supremacists is exceeded only by its grip on the Arab and Muslim world.

Thus the British National Party advised its members to read the *Guardian* for information about "the Zionist cabal around President Bush."[5] In 2003, websites of groups such as the National Front, Combat 18 and the White Nationalist Party reproduced articles by the left-wing journalist John Pilger and the Islamist group Hizb-ut-Tahrir. The story of the Office of Special Plans, a supposed secret unit inside the Pentagon that was said to have acted as a backdoor channel for Israel to manipulate American foreign policy through the neocons, appeared in the *Guardian*, the *New Statesman* and the *Morning Star*—the latter two pieces written by John Pilger.[6] Yet it had first appeared in Lyndon LaRouche's *Executive Intelligence Review*, a magazine devoted to antisemitic conspiracy theories.[7]

When George Galloway led a British delegation to a conference in Baghdad in May 2002, he found himself (doubtless to his discomfiture) in the company of the ultranationalist Russian politician Vladimir Zhirinovsky, the French far-right activist Serge Thion, and James Thring, a friend and confidant of the late Lady Birdwood, a veteran hate propagandist of the British neofascists.[8] At a conference in Italy the previous month, Galloway reportedly participated in a round-table discussion with yet more ultranationalists—Olivier Wyssa, an elected official of the French Front National, and Francis Van den Eynde, a Belgian MP from the Vlaams Blok.[9]

Neofascist and white supremacist groups also reproduced antisemitic cartoons taken from Arab websites; they issued a call for White Nationalist Party members to phone the Malaysian embassy in London and express their support for Mahathir Mohamad after he claimed that "Jews rule the world"; they reproduced boycott lists from Islamist or anti-Zionist websites of "Jewish controlled companies, used to prop up Zionism around the world," as one White Nationalist Party supporter put it; and they made frequent use of the logo of the Boycott Israeli Goods campaign, an Israeli flag in a red circle with a line through it.[10]

These ultranationalist, racist and anti-Jewish groups saw in the Islamists something beyond their wildest dreams: a global force, armed and trained, committed to the destruction of both Jews and the Western political order. In a letter posted on its website, the head of the white supremacist group Aryan Nations, August Kreis, offered his thanks to radical Islamic terrorists:

> We as an organization will also endeavor to aid all those who subvert, disrupt and are malignant in nature to our enemies. Therefore I offer my most sincere best wishes to those who wage holy Jihad against the infrastructure of the decadent, weak and Judaic-influenced societal infrastructure of the West. I send a message of thanks and well-wishes to the methods and works of groups on the Islamic front against the jew [sic] such as al Qaeda and Sheikh Usama Bin Ladin, Hamas, Islamic Jihad, Hezbollah and to all Jihadis worldwide who fight for the glory of the Khilafah and the downfall of the anti-life and anti-freedom System prevalent on this earth today.[11]

The National Alliance, America's largest neo-Nazi organization, published an essay in 2002 by its founder, William Pierce, which claimed that the 9/11 attacks had "forced the whole subject of U.S. policy in the Middle East into the open: the subject of American interests versus Jewish interests, of Jewish media control and its influence on governmental policy." Because Osama bin Laden broke the "taboo" about questioning Jewish interests, Pierce claimed, "[i]n the long run that may more than compensate for the 3,000 American lives that were lost."[12]

Leftists were therefore not merely in bed with Islamists—who, after all, they could tell themselves were victims of the West because they were the oppressed from the Third World—but with the very people it was supposedly their life's work to fight: neofascists and white supremacists.

THE ANTIGLOBALIZATION PROTESTERS AND THE ISLAMISTS

There is yet another "progressive" member of this unholy alliance: the environmental movement. Under the banner of antiglobalization—a synonym for anticapitalism—greens have joined with ultraleftists, neofascists and anarchists in a philosophically incoherent "rainbow coalition" whose only common characteristic is their aim to destroy the established capitalist order. Protesters at the G20 meeting in London in March 2009, for example, smashed the windows of the Bank of England because they wanted to oust the bankers, abolish all borders, get rid of corrupt politicians and overhaul democracy, as well as promote the cause of "Palestine" and push for action against climate change.[13]

The French-Jewish leader Roger Cukierman has identified an anti-Jewish "brown-green-red alliance" among ultranationalists, greens and communist fellow travelers.[14] Racist and ultranationalist groups are antiglobalization in the interests of preserving racial and national purity. Matt Hale, leader of the U.S. white supremacist World Church of the Creator, praised the 1999 antiglobalization protests in Seattle for having "shut down talks of the Jew world order

WTO and helped make a mockery of the Jewish occupational government around the world. Bravo."[15]

Islamists too are antiglobalization, although they mean something rather different again. In a lecture on "Our Islamic Rhetoric in the Globalisation Era," Sheikh Qaradawi, the Muslim Brotherhood's *éminence grise*, described globalization as "spreading the culture of seduction, sex, pornography, and deviation, the culture of abortion according to the wishes of the pregnant woman, and the culture of peace that Israel wants.... [E]conomic invasion is always followed by cultural invasion by the United States and the West. There is the culture of fast-food restaurants, like McDonalds, Kentucky Fried Chicken, Pizza Hut, and others.... [A]ll these globalisation efforts serve the interests of Israel and Zionism."[16]

THE PROJECTED PATHOLOGY OF UTOPIA

These curious coalitions are frequently explained as merely opportunistic alliances, where certain groups make common cause with ideological opponents in pursuit of the shared aim of bringing down Western society. This explanation surely is only partly correct. What these various movements have in common goes much deeper: they are all utopian. Each in its own way wants to bring about the perfect society, to create a new man and a new world.

Each therefore thinks of itself as progressive; the supporters of each believe themselves to be warriors in the most noble of causes. The greens believe they will save the planet. The leftists believe they will create the brotherhood of man. The fascists believe they will purge mankind of corruption. And the Islamists believe they will create the Kingdom of God on earth.

What they all have in common, therefore, is a totalitarian mindset in pursuit of the creation of their alternative reality. These are all worldviews that can accommodate no deviation and must therefore be imposed by coercion. Because their end product is a state of perfection, nothing can be allowed to stand in its way. This is itself a projected pathology. As Eric Hoffer suggested in *The True Believer*, the individual involved in a mass movement is in some way acutely alienated from his own society, an alienation to which he is completely blind. Projecting his own unacknowledged deficiencies onto his surroundings, he thinks instead there is something wrong with society and fantasizes about building a new world where he will finally fit.[17] This belief that humanity can be shaped into a perfect form has been the cause of the most vicious tyrannies on the planet from the French Revolution onwards.

As Jamie Glazov notes in his book *United in Hate*, the totalitarian believer publicly denies the violent pathologies within the system that he worships. Privately, however, these are what drew him towards that system in the first place because he is aware that violence is necessary to destroy the old order so that utopia can arise from its ashes. Pretending he is attracted to "peace," "justice" and "equality," he actually stands for their opposite. He needs to empathize with the "martyrs" and the downtrodden in order to validate himself vicariously. The Third World, intrinsically noble since it is uncorrupted by the developed world, provides an apparently inexhaustible supply of such validation. That's why the image of the Palestinian youth armed with only a slingshot touches the radical soul so deeply, and why the radical does not want to hear—why he even denies—the guns that are ranged just behind that youth as he throws his stones.[18]

COMMON ROOTS OF THE "PROGRESSIVE" LEFT AND THE NEOFASCISTS

The mindset of the totalitarian true believer creates networks between groups that might be thought to have little in common— anticapitalists and Islamists, greens and neofascists. It builds common ground between ostensible political opposites from the "far left" and the "far right," which are thus revealed to have deep similarities. The British Conservative politician Lord Tebbit remarked on these similarities in writing about the neofascist British National Party:

> I have carefully re-read the BNP manifesto of 2005 and am unable to find evidence of Right-wing tendencies. On the other hand, there is plenty of anti-capitalism, opposition to free trade, commitments to "use all non-destructive means to reduce income inequality", to institute worker ownership, to favour workers' co-operatives, to return parts of the railways to state ownership, to nationalise the Royal National Lifeboat Institution and to withdraw from Nato. That sounds pretty Left-wing to me.[19]

Indeed it is, and this left-wing character has roots in the history of fascism, which originally derived from the left. Not for nothing were the Nazis called the National *Socialist* Party.

Fascism was made possible by a way of thinking that swept across Europe at the turn of the nineteenth and twentieth centuries, the first outcome of which was communism. As Ze'ev Sternhell has written, fascism was not some aberration; it was in keeping with the avant-garde and revolutionary trends in the wider European culture. Not only did it compete with Marxism for the allegiance of the masses, but its origins lay in a revision of Marxism. Whereas Marxism had opposed liberalism, which was in turn a revolt against clerical absolutism, fascism rejected both liberalism and Marxism to create a communal, anti-individualistic and antirationalist culture. Fascism wanted to rectify what it saw as the disastrous consequences of modernization: the atomization of society and the alienation of the individual in a free market economy. Although it was eager to retain the benefits of technological progress, it rebelled against modernity insofar as modernity was associated with rationalism and the optimistic humanism of the eighteenth century. Fascism disdained both universalism and individualism, as well as human rights and equality.[20]

The French Revolution held that society was made up of a collection of individuals. Fascism replaced this idea with a theory of the organic unity of the nation, which was perceived as an organism comparable to a sentient being. Absolute moral norms such as truth, justice and law existed only to serve the collective. Subconscious instinct, intuitive and irrational sentiment, emotion and enthusiasm were considered superior to rationality, which was said to deaden sensitivity. Just like communism, pre-1914 fascism expressed disgust for "materialist" capitalism; and because fascism attacked the existing system and aimed to destroy bourgeois culture and to reform the world by transforming the individual, it had a fascination for a lot of idealistic young people. As Sternhell writes, "In addition to a political revolution, fascism sought to bring about a moral revolution, a profound transformation of the human spirit . . . a desire to create a new type of man."[21]

The association of fascism with antisemitism also found echoes in communism. Despite being born into a Jewish family, Marx—who was raised as a Lutheran—was a committed Jew-hater whose "new man" would be created through society's renunciation of Judaism altogether. His letters contain dozens of derogatory references to Jews.[22] His essay On the Jewish Question, published in 1844, uses a discussion about how the Jews could achieve political emancipation to launch a sustained and venomous attack on the Jews as being motivated only by money and self-interest:

> What is the worldly religion of the Jew? *Huckstering.* What is his worldly God? *Money.* . . . An organization of society which would abolish the preconditions for huckstering, and therefore the possibility of huckstering, would make the Jew impossible. . . . We recognize in Judaism, therefore, a general *anti-social* element of the *present time.* . . . Money is the jealous god of Israel, in face of which no other god may exist. Money degrades all the gods of man—and turns them into commodities. . . . The bill of exchange is the real god of the Jew. His god is only an illusory bill of exchange. . . . The groundless law of the Jew is only a religious

caricature of groundless morality and right in general, of the purely *formal* rites with which the world of self-interest surrounds itself.[23]

Sir Isaiah Berlin observed, "The violently antisemitic tone ... became more and more characteristic of Marx in his later years ... and is one of the most neurotic and revolting aspects of his masterful but vulgar personality."[24]

The progression from communism to fascism in the creation of the new world was bridged by Nietzsche, the thinker whose impact on our modern age cannot be overestimated. Mussolini understood both the importance of communism and the significance of Nietzsche in showing how Marx's belief that society had to be destroyed in order to build a new one could be put into practice. Indeed, Mussolini described socialism as "the greatest act of negation and destruction." His own followers were "new barbarians," he declared, and "like all barbarians" they were "the harbingers of a new civilization." Mussolini believed that while the proletariat would not bring about Marx's socialist utopia, the revolt by a Nietzschean "superman" would destroy bourgeois institutions.[25] Thus fascism was born.

Since fascism and communism were joined at the hip, as it were, in seeking to create utopia, both gathered a significant following among the Western avant-garde of the early twentieth century, who thought of themselves as progressive thinkers.

EVOLUTION FED INTO BOTH PROGRESSIVE AND FASCIST THINKING

In the nineteenth century, the progressive intelligentsia had bestowed the "enlightened" label on a body of thought that was to feed directly into communism and later into the obscenity of the Nazi killing machine. Indeed, after reading Darwin's *Origin of Species*, Marx called it "the book that contains the foundation in natural history for our view."[26] The thinking that led Darwin to formulate his theory of evolution contributed not only to Marxism but also to fascism, by way of "social Darwinism" and its offshoot in eugenics, which were the orthodoxy among progressive thinkers.

The roots of social Darwinism and eugenics lay in the ideas of the eighteenth-century economist Thomas Malthus, who had argued that the world's human population would increase faster than the food supply unless checked by restraints such as war, famine or disease. As a result, he thought, most people should die without reproducing.[27] Darwin admitted that his own ideas were an extension of Malthusian thought to the natural world; in turn, intellectuals developed the thinking of both Darwin and Malthus into social Darwinism.

Applying the theory of evolution to the organization of human society, social Darwinism represented progress as a kind of ladder on which humanity could climb towards perfection. This meant that the "unfit," or lesser breeds of humanity, had to be discarded on the way up. Thus eugenics, the "science of selective breeding," came into being. In Victorian and Edwardian Britain, the main targets of eugenic thinking were the poor, whom the intelligentsia regarded as overbreeding throwbacks to an earlier stage of evolution. There was a fear that those higher up the evolutionary ladder would be overwhelmed by lesser forms of human life. The concept of the inherent value of every individual life was therefore seen as a sentimental block to the progress of humanity. In 1880 a German zoologist, Robby Kossman, declared that the "less well-endowed individual" should be destroyed for humanity to reach a higher state of perfection.[28]

Eugenics was therefore seen as a vital tool of social progress. Early socialists were imbued with eugenic thinking. Sidney and Beatrice Webb, George Bernard Shaw, Havelock Ellis, Eden and Cedar Paul, Harold Laski, Graham Wallas, Joseph Needham, C. P. Snow and Maynard Keynes were all eugenicists, as were the editors of the *New Statesman* and the *Manchester Guardian*.[29]

It would not be until the full horror of Nazism became apparent, with its extermination programs against mental defectives and the Jews, that both eugenics and fascism finally became discredited. Before then, however, fascism did not just appeal to convinced Nazis but gained a large following among intellectuals in the humanities from a variety of political positions. As Jonah Goldberg documents, in the 1920s the fascist ideas that had surfaced in Mussolini's Italy were very popular on the American left, where they even influenced elements of Franklin D. Roosevelt's New Deal.[30] In Britain, although Oswald Mosley's British Union of Fascists was always very small and marginalized, early in the century a group of intellectuals around Wyndham Lewis, T. S. Eliot, Ezra Pound, D. H. Lawrence and W. B. Yeats had flirted vogueishly with the repudiation of modernity and with fascist ideas.

Following World War II, fascism was consigned beyond the pale of respectable thinking. And yet certain elements of both fascist and social Darwinist thinking have deep resonances with today's Western culture. The denigration of reason, the horror of stoicism and the promotion of mass emotion course through all levels of society and lie behind the irrational and hysterical cults surrounding both Princess Diana and Barack Obama. "Atomization" and "alienation" are contemporary obsessions. A modern form of eugenics is being practiced in the abortion of defective fetuses at the beginning of life and the withdrawal of food and fluids from the elderly and very infirm at the other end.

THE CONTINUUM OF FASCISM AND ENVIRONMENTALISM

Perhaps the most striking continuation of fascist ideas under the guise of left-wing progressive thinking lies in the modern environmental movement, with its desire to call a halt to dehumanizing modernity and return to an organic harmony with the natural world.

Veneration of nature and the corresponding belief that civilization corrupts man's innate capacity for happiness and freedom go back to the eighteenth century and Jean-Jacques Rousseau—who bridged the Enlightenment and the counter-Enlightenment, the world of reason and the world of emotion, movements of the left and the right. His idealizing of a primitive state of nature, along with a theory of human evolution through survival of the fittest that predated Darwin by a hundred years, became a galvanizing force in the nineteenth century among those who were sounding a retreat from modernity and reason, into the darkness of obscurantism and prejudice. And one of the principal routes they took was through the natural world.

In the mid nineteenth century, Darwinism was sowing the seeds of environmentalism, and in doing so it also fed into fascism. The critical figure in making this crossover was Ernst Haeckel, the most famous German Darwinist of the nineteenth and twentieth centuries. Haeckel believed that the theory of evolution would transform human life by dethroning man from the pinnacle of Creation. He and his followers saw Darwinism as far more than just a biological theory; it was the central ingredient of a new worldview that would challenge Christianity. His Darwinist views led him and his followers to espouse scientific racism, the belief that racial competition was a necessary part of the struggle for existence and—even though he opposed militarism—that the extermination of "inferior" races was a step toward progress.[31]

Haeckel also believed that mind and matter were united everywhere, and he ascribed psychic characteristics to single-celled organisms and even to inanimate matter.[32] As the authoritative historian of the ecological movement Anna Bramwell relates, it was Haeckel who in 1867 coined the term "ecology" to denote a scientific discipline focusing on the web that links organisms with their environment.[33] With his disciples Willibald Hentschel, Wilhelm Bölsche and Bruno Wille, Haeckel deeply influenced subsequent generations of environmentalists by binding the study of the natural world into a reactionary political framework.[34]

The twentieth-century philosopher Ludwig Klages was firmly in the Haeckel mould. In 1913, he wrote an essay titled "Man and Earth" for a gathering of the Wandervögel or Free German Youth, the prewar movement that rejected materialism for excursions in more basic outdoor living. According to Peter Staudenmaier,

> "Man and Earth" anticipated just about all of the themes of the contemporary ecology movement. It decried the accelerating extinction of species, disturbance of global ecosystemic balance, deforestation, destruction of aboriginal peoples and of wild habitats, urban sprawl, and the increasing alienation of people from nature. In emphatic terms it disparaged Christianity, capitalism, economic utilitarianism, hyperconsumption and the ideology of "progress." It even condemned the environmental destructiveness of rampant tourism and the slaughter of whales, and displayed a clear recognition of the planet as an ecological totality.[35]

A political reactionary and virulent antisemite, Klages was described as a "Völkish fanatic" and an "intellectual pacemaker for the Third Reich" who "paved the way for fascist philosophy in many important respects." Denouncing rational thought itself, he believed that the intellect was parasitical on life and that progress merely represented the gradual domination of intellect over life.[36]

During the interwar period, most ecological thinkers subscribed to this way of thinking. There was a particularly close association between ecologists and German nationalists, among whom a number subsequently became Nazis. Their thinking was that nature was the life force from which Germany had been cut off, ever since the days of the Roman Empire, by the alien Christian-Judaic civilization, the source of all the anti-life manifestations of urbanism.

In 1932, the proto-fascist intellectual Oswald Spengler wrote about the deadening effect of "machine technology" on the natural world and humanity:

The mechanisation of the world has entered on a phase of highly dangerous over-extension. . . . In a few decades most of the great forest will have
gone, to be turned into news-print, and climatic changes have been
thereby set afoot which imperil the land-economy of whole populations.
Innumerable animal species have been extinguished. . . . Whole races of
humanity have been brought almost to vanishing point. . . . This machine
technology will end the Faustian civilisation and one day will lie in frag-
ments, forgotten—our railways and steamships as dead as the Roman
Roads and the Chinese Wall.[37]

Such ecological fixations were further developed in German
Nazism. According to Ernst Lehmann, a leading Nazi biologist,
"separating humanity from nature, from the whole of life, leads to
humankind's own destruction and to the death of nations."[38] The
Nazis thus fixated on organic food, personal health and animal welfare. Heinrich Himmler was a certified animal rights activist and an
aggressive promoter of "natural healing"; Rudolf Hess, Hitler's
deputy, championed homeopathy and herbal remedies; Hitler
wanted to turn the entire nation vegetarian as a response to the
unhealthiness promoted by capitalism.[39]

There was top-level Nazi support for ecological ideas at both
ministerial and administrative levels. Alwin Seifert, for example, was
a motorway architect who specialized in "embedding motorways
organically into the landscape." Following Rudolf Steiner, he argued
against land reclamation and drainage; said that "classical scientific
farming" was a nineteenth-century practice unsuited to the new era
and that artificial fertilizers, fodder and insecticides were poisonous;
and called for an agricultural revolution towards "a more peasant-
like, natural, simple" method of farming "independent of capital."
Himmler established experimental organic farms including one at
Dachau that grew herbs for SS medicines; a complete list of home-
opathic doctors in Germany was compiled for him; and antivivisec-
tion laws were passed on his insistence. As Anna Bramwell observes,

"SS training included a respect for animal life of near Buddhist proportions."[40]

They did not show such respect, of course, for the human race. Neither does the ecological movement, for which, echoing Malthus, the planet's biggest problem is the people living on it. Even though our contemporary era has been forged in a determination that fascism must never rise again, certain *völkish* ideas that were central to fascism—about the organic harmony of the earth, the elevation of animal "rights" and the denigration of humans as enemies of nature—are today presented as the acme of progressive thinking.

This astounding repackaging was accomplished during the 1970s. While Western politicians were committed to growth and consumer society was taking off, the dread of overpopulation also grew. It is probably no coincidence that the fear of global immiseration coincided with the end of empire and the West's loss of control over the developing world. Reports by Barbara Ward and René Dubos presented to the UN World Conference on Human Environment in 1972 preached imminent doom as a result of rising technological capacity and argued that man had to replace family or national loyalties with allegiance to the planet. The Club of Rome, which was founded also in 1972, prophesied imminent global catastrophe unless resource use was curbed, a view that the oil shock of 1973 served to validate and embed in Western consciousness.

If ecology was to take off, however, it had to shed altogether its unhappy links with fascism, racial extermination and ultranationalism. It took a number of different opportunities to do so. During the 1960s in both Europe and North America it identified itself with radical left-wing causes, latching onto "alternative" politics such as feminism and, in Britain, Celtic nationalism. In the 1970s, the "small is beautiful" idea of the anti-Nazi émigré Fritz Schumacher took hold.[41]

In 1971, Schumacher became president of the Soil Association in Britain, which was critical in both promoting deeply antirational ecological ideas and laundering them as fashionably progressive. Rudolf Steiner was the arch-proponent of "biodynamic" agriculture, which eschewed artificial fertilizers and promoted self-sufficient farms as preserving the spirit of the soil. When the Soil Association was created in 1946, it embodied this "organic farming" ideal. But Steiner was the also the founder of a movement called anthroposophy, which was based on the development of a nonsensory or so-called supersensory consciousness. It held that early stages of human evolution possessed an intuitive perception of reality, including the power of clairvoyance, which had been lost under the increasing reliance on intellect. It promoted the belief that the human being passed between stages of existence, incarnating into an earthly body, living on earth, leaving the body behind and entering into the spiritual domain before returning to be born again into a new life on earth.[42]

These essentially pagan and irrational ideas were, as we shall see later, intrinsic to ecological thinking. But they were also to surface in a remarkable new alliance between neo-Nazi doctrines and radical left-wing, anticapitalist and New Age ideas. Towards the end of the 1960s, finding itself criticized for espousing reactionary views, the Soil Association turned sharply leftwards and developed an egalitarian socioeconomic perspective instead. It published articles admiring Mao's communes in China and suggested that plots of land a few acres in size should be distributed similarly among the British population.[43]

In Germany, the green movement that emerged from the student protests of 1968 bitterly attacked the "biodynamic" organic farmers for their perceived authoritarianism and social Darwinist beliefs. Thus German Greens of the 1970s, with a considerable communist element, had less to do with ecology than with participatory democracy, egalitarianism and women's rights.[44]

Among radicals in America, there was a split after 1968 between those favoring organized terrorism and alternative groups. Young radicals in the latter camp, galvanized by Rachel Carson's *Silent Spring* (1966), claimed that multinational capitalism was responsible for pollution. Environmental concerns offered up a radicalism for the middle classes. The anarcho-communist Murray Bookchin wrote of a utopian future in communes when scarcity would disappear and man would return to living close to the land. American feminists in particular took up ecology, drawing upon its foundational belief in a primitive matriarchal paradise to support their attacks on patriarchal oppression.

The result of all this ferment was that the green movement became not just radical but radically incoherent. It became the umbrella for a range of alternative, anti-Western causes and lifestyles. But its constant factor was a strongly primitive, pagan and irrational element. As Anna Bramwell caustically comments, "The new paganism, often based on Atlantean theories of a lost golden age and theories of cultural diffusion via a vanished super race, is open to all and especially attractive to the semi-educated, semi-rational product of today's de-naturing educational process, stripped of religion, reason, tradition and even history."[45]

Despite a veneer of fashionable progressivism, the fact is that environmentalism's fundamental opposition to modernity propels it straight into the arms of neofascism. For just like their precursors in the twenties and thirties, today's ultranationalist and neo-Nazi groups chime with many of the ideas that also march under the green banner. In France, Italy and Belgium, the Nouvelle Droite combined Hellenic paganism with support for the dissolution of national boundaries; it was anticapitalist and anti-American, adopting sociobiological arguments to stress the uniqueness of each race and culture *within* national boundaries and to oppose colonization and empire. In Germany, the radical-right journal *Mut* was pacifist and ecological.[46] Such groups met the left on the common ground of New Age paganism, expressed in particular through the religions and cultures of the East.

From the 1970s onwards, neofascist extremists began to repackage the old ideology of Aryan racism, elitism and force in new cultic guises involving esotericism and Eastern religions. Some groups mixed racism with Nordic pagan religions, celebrating magical signs of ancestral heritage and mystical blood loyalty. In the United States, Britain, Germany and Scandinavia, racial pagan groups today ponder runes, magic and the sinister mythology of the Norse gods Wotan, Loki and Fenriswolf. Like the Nazis, these groups resort to the pagan world to express their antipathy to any extraneous organisms that disturb their idea of racial or national purity. As Nicholas Goodrick-Clarke writes, "The racial interpretation of these esoteric ideas, cosmology and prophecies betrays these groups' overwhelming anxiety about the future of white identity in multiracial societies."[47]

In Italy, Julius Evola, who inspired a whole generation of postwar neofascists, embraced Hinduism and Tantrism, a radical Hindu cult focusing on women, goddesses and sexual energy, and revolving around the notion of breaking all bonds. By means of taboo and spiritually dangerous practices such as orgies and intoxication, the superior adept can raise his consciousness to supreme levels of unity with the divine female power of "Shakti," which animates and inspires the whole universe, thereby acquiring exceptional knowledge and power. Tantrism's secrecy and elitism, writes Goodrick-Clarke, negates the modern world of rationalism and democracy.[48]

In Chile, the diplomat, explorer and poet Miguel Serrano adopted the mystical doctrines of Savitri Devi, the French-born Nazi-Hindu prophetess who described Hitler as an avatar of Vishnu and likened Nazism to the cult of Shiva because of its emphasis on destruction and new creation. Tracing semidivine Aryans to extraterrestrial origins, Serrano recommended kundalini yoga to repurify "mystical Aryan blood" to its former divine light. He also proposed a gnostic war against the Jews, promoted the idea of the "Black Sun" as a mystical source of energy capable of regenerating the Aryan race, and believed that the Nazis built UFOs in Antarctica. In the United States, Nazi satanic cults from the 1970s onwards linked anti-Christian paganism to transgressive praise of Hitler. As in Europe and Australia also, "dark side" lodges promoted the worship of force backed by anti-Christian, elitist and social Darwinist doctrines.[49]

THE NEW AGE REPACKAGED
FASCIST PAGANISM AS PROGRESSIVE

The London-based New Age magazine *Rainbow Ark*, which has a range of far-right supporters and links, has printed excerpts from David Icke's conspiracy theories about the "Global Elite," and has helped organize his lectures and meetings. It has also speculated that many old Nazis have been reincarnated as modern Israelis as a way of "karmically balancing former hatreds." The Australian New Age magazine *Nexus* offers a mix of "prophecies, UFOs, Big Brother, the unexplained, suppressed technology, hidden history and more." Its topics range from macrobiotic cooking, aromatherapy and water fluoridation to CIA mind-control experiments, pharmaceutical drug rackets and American militias. According to Goodrick-Clarke, *Nexus* editor Duncan Roads visited Muammar Qadaffi in 1989 and is a close friend of Robert Pash, the Libya promoter and convert to Islam who has tried to forge links between extreme right and left in Australia. In the late 1970s, Pash was the Australian contact for the U.S.-based Aryan Nations and distributed Ku Klux Klan material.[50]

To people accustomed to thinking of New Agers as vegetarian, pacifist tree-huggers, such connections may come as something of a surprise. But as we have seen, nature-worship, paganism and organic mysticism were closely associated with Nazism and antisemitism through prewar German *völkish* thinking. Goodrick-Clarke explains how New Age turned from a left-liberal movement to a fascist style of paganism:

As long as the idealized groups were perceived as marginal, foreign or oppressed, such New Age sentiment was generally left-wing or liberal. However, once the models were sought closer to home in the pre-rational, mythical past of western culture, *völkisch* ideas could make a fashionable return. In the New Age movement, numerous groups and workshops are now devoted to reviving the lore of the ancient Celts and Teutons. Books on ogham, runes, prophecy and pagan gods proliferate. Shamanism, magic and superstition are in. Nostalgia for a lost golden age and apocalyptic hopes of its revival recall the ideological foreground of earlier demands for fascist renewal.[51]

THE DEBT OF ISLAMISM TO BOTH COMMUNISM AND FASCISM

The apocalyptic revivalism of neofascism corresponds precisely to the agenda of radical Islamism. We noted earlier how Islamism, as a form of revolutionary utopianism, marches alongside the left. But as a revolt against liberalism and modernity, it is closely allied with both communism and fascism. That is because, just like these two secular Western movements which also led to fanaticism, terror and mass murder, Islamism repudiates modernity and reason in the interests of creating a perfect world. And so—ironically, considering it believes itself to be a hermetically sealed thought system owing its influence only to God—Islamism has drawn heavily upon and formed alliances with communism and fascism, both representing a heretical world it despises and aims to destroy.

The common interest with communism was first made evident when the Muslims of the Russian Empire were conscripted into the Red Army. In 1920, the Second Congress of the Communist International summoned the "enslaved popular masses of Persia, Armenia and Turkey," as well as Mesopotamia, Syria, Arabia and elsewhere, to gather in Baku, Azerbaijan. During the first session, the president of the International, Grigory Zinoviev, called in his speech five times for "holy war" against the British and the French "colonialists" and "the rich in general—Russian, German, Jewish, French." Thus the "Bolshevik jihad" was launched against the common enemy, the "materialist West," in the mountains of Afghanistan and elsewhere that the Russians faced the forces of imperialism.[52]

The Muslims found much in common with communism. Not only did they have a common enemy, but they shared a utopian vision for transforming the world by negating all distinctions between peoples. As Hanafi Muzaffar, a prominent Volga Tatar intellectual, put it, "Muslim people will ally themselves to Communism. Like Communism, Islam rejects narrow nationalism. Islam is international and recognises only the brotherhood and the unity of all nations under the unity of Islam."[53]

Ali Shariati, a prominent ideologue of the Islamic Revolution in Iran, was an Islamo-Marxist who drew heavily upon the anticolonial radical Franz Fanon and his conception of creating a "new man." Shariati borrowed Fanon's description of "the wretched of the earth" and translated it into Persian by reviving the Qur'anic term *mostazafin,* or "the disinherited." Under Shariati's influence, Iranian radicals became Marxists and read Che Guevara, Regis Debray and the Brazilian urban guerrilla theorist Carlos Marighela. Others studied revolutionary activity in Russia, China, Cuba and Algeria and interpreted Qur'anic verses according to the theory of class struggle. Also under Shariati's influence, Ayatollah Khomeini introduced into radical Islamic thought the pivotal Marxist concept of a world divided into oppressors and oppressed. As the Iranian Islamic Revolution developed, it established a totalitarian apparatus including a morals police, a ministry of intelligence, and Islamic societies acting as watchdogs for Islamic conformity. By 1980, Khomeini had established a communist-style Islamic "cultural revolution" to purge all traces of Western influence from high schools and universities.[54]

As Laurent Murawiec noted, there was also an eerie similarity between the Marxist-Leninist and Islamic outlooks in their Orwellian inversion of aggression and self-defense. For communism, aggression was specific to class society while the Soviet Union was by definition peaceful. Likewise, Islamic thinkers held that Islam represented peace on earth and so anything un-Islamic must trouble the peace by its very existence. As a corollary, since neither the Soviet Union nor the Islamic world could be guilty of aggression, any terror committed by either was by definition self-defense, while self-defense by the outside world was aggression.[55]

In seeking to harness modern revolutionary insights to the jihad, the Islamists made equal use of fascism as a doctrine of bloody nihilism. Muhammad Navvab Safavi's manifesto foreshadowing the Iranian Revolution, writes Laurent Murawiec, resembled fascist and Nazi propaganda: a mixture of romantic-reactionary yearning for an idealized past, violent rejections of anything modern or Western, panic about female sexuality, statist and redistributionist economic and social views, along with radical demands for clerical executive power.[56]

Like Nazism, Islam promotes a subordination of the individual to the collective, celebration of the leadership principle, hostility to liberal democracy and to capitalism, male supremacy, sexual repression and glorification of death in the war with unbelievers.[57] It was therefore not surprising that Arab nationalism in Palestine, Syria and Iraq during the 1930s modeled itself on Italian and German fascism. In prewar Palestine, the Arab mob was inflamed by the grand mufti of Jerusalem, Haj Amin al-Husseini, to commit massacres of Palestinian Jews. When Hitler came to power, Haj Amin avidly courted the Nazis.

Landing up eventually in Berlin after securing a commitment by Mussolini and Hitler to work for the "elimination of the Jewish national home in Palestine," the mufti became active in the Nazi war effort: rallying Muslims everywhere to rise up against the Allies, dispatching Bosnian Muslims to fight under German command, urging the foreign minister of Hungary to prevent Jews from coming to Palestine and send them to Poland instead—with the result that hundreds of thousands of Jews were sent to the extermination camps.[58] During the war, the Muslim Brotherhood distributed *Mein Kampf* in Arabic throughout Palestine, along with German money and weapons to help the Arab revolt against Jewish immigration from Nazi-occupied Europe. Husseini also supported the Nazis via short-wave Arabic broadcasts from Germany to the Arab world. And yet at the very same time, when the mufti was already receiving substantial support from Fascist Italy and Nazi Germany, the Communist Party of Palestine taught him communist agitprop and Marxist-Leninist concepts of imperialism and colonialism that were previously unknown.[59]

As Matthias Küntzel has pointed out, there was an even more striking correspondence between fascism and Islamism. The idea of using suicide pilots to destroy the skyscrapers of Manhattan originated in Nazi Germany. Nazis planned to fly explosive-crammed light aircraft without landing gear into Manhattan skyscrapers. Hitler, according to Albert Speer, was in a "delirium" of rapture at the thought of New York going down in towers of flame. "He described the skyscrapers turning into huge burning torches and falling hither and thither, and the reflection of the disintegrating city in the dark sky."[60] Hitler wanted to kill Jews in order to liberate mankind. He deemed America a "Jewish state";[61] and New York—or more precisely Wall Street—was, as a Weimar Republic bestseller put it, "so to speak, the Military Headquarters of Judas. From there his threads radiate across the entire world."[62]

In Syria and Iraq, Ba'athism was a synthesis forged in the 1930s and 1940s of fascism and a romantic nostalgia for an "organic" community of Arabs. The Ba'athist ideologue Sati' Husri was a keen student of German Romantic thinkers such as Fichte and Herder—who provided the philosophical antecedents of fascism—and their notion of an organic *völkisch* nation rooted in blood and soil. His idea of pulling the Arab world together in a huge organic community bound by military discipline and heroic individual sacrifice was directly inspired by pan-German theories that held sway in fascist circles in Vienna and Berlin in the 1930s. In Iraq, Michel Aflaq, a Syrian Christian and founder of the Ba'ath Party, was to refashion Arab society around the cultivation of hatred and violence and annihilation of all opposition. Ernst Jünger, who fought in World War I and celebrated military heroism and the pleasure gained from the closeness of death, also had great influence on the Muslim world. His book *Über der Linie* was translated in the 1960s by Al-e Ahmed, a prominent Iranian intellectual, who coined the term "Westoxification" for the pernicious influence of Western ideas.[63]

Today's Western Islamists continue to draw upon neofascism. Since 2000, the Muslim Association of Britain and the General Union of Palestinian Students have both published the so-called "Franklin Prophecy," an antisemitic hoax manufactured by the American Nazi William Dudley Pelley and first published in his own publication, *Liberation*, in February 1934.[64] The Muslim Public Affairs Committee has used its website to reproduce material taken from the sites of both David Irving and the Heretical Press (a far-right UK-based publisher), while the pro-Hamas *Palestine Times* has promoted work by Michael Hoffman II, a revisionist historian whose website has links to Holocaust denial material.[65]

As cannot be emphasized too strongly, the reason for these otherwise bewildering alliances between groups that appear to be mortal enemies ideologically—left-wingers and fascists, Islamists and greens—is that they all harbor a utopian vision of perfecting the world. The prominent Islamist Abul ala Maududi, for example, stressed the comprehensive scope of his ideology when he wrote, "Islam is not the name of a mere 'religion,' nor is Muslim the title of a 'nation.' The truth is that Islam is a revolutionary ideology which seeks to alter the social order of the entire world and rebuild it in conformity with its own tenets and ideals."[66]

WHY THE MOST HIGH-MINDED TURN
INTO BIGOTED TOTALITARIANS

The unsettling fact is that it is possible for bad deeds to be done for the highest of ideals. Those wanting to bring about the perfect society see no higher ideal than that. Ever since the French Revolution, all such impossible agendas have led straight to persecution, tyranny and totalitarianism—to the French Terror, to the gulags, to Auschwitz and to the use of children as human bombs; yet the true believers in each case believed they acted from the highest of motives.

The Islamists committing mass murder in New York's Twin Towers or a Jerusalem cafe really do believe they are fighting for justice and to bring about the Kingdom of God on earth. The communists and the fascists really did think they were ending, respectively, the oppression and the corruption of man. The environmentalists really do think they are saving the planet from extinction. The radical left really do think they will erase prejudice from the human heart and suffering from the world. And those who want Israel no longer to exist as a Jewish state really do believe that as a result they will turn suicide bomb belts into cucumber frames, and that they are moving in the way that history intended.

That is why those who promulgate hatred of the Jews are generally to be found among the high-minded, since they are devoted to the most lofty and admirable of ideals. That is why lies about global warming or irrationality about the defense of the West against Islamism are associated with the intelligentsia. That is why those with the most highly developed faculty of reason so often end up promoting the most diabolical of agendas.

But there is yet another factor linking these various ideologies of Islamism, environmentalism, Darwinism, anticapitalism and anti-Zionism. In their very different ways and in very different contexts, they are all attempts to address a spiritual emptiness in the human condition—and that gives them a further common characteristic that moves them away from the sphere of reason altogether, into the province of belief.

12

THE QUEST
FOR REDEMPTION

This may come as a surprise to some, but we are living through a millenarian age in the West.

Millenarianism is a religious belief in the perfectibility of mankind and life on earth. It is a doctrine of collective and total salvation that derives from the belief of some Christians in the "end times" or "last days," based on the Book of Revelation (20:4–6). According to these verses, after the Second Coming, Christ will establish a messianic kingdom on earth and reign for a thousand years before the Last Judgment. This belief in turn is rooted in ancient Jewish prophecies of intolerable tyranny and a Day of Wrath, followed by the resurrection of the righteous in Israel.[1] Millenarianism came to mean any belief that the struggle between the forces of good and evil would climax in a triumph of the good, when injustice and oppression would end and its perpetrators be punished.

Historically, millenarianism became a way of coping with large-scale disasters, and it surfaced in highly charged periods of change and stress. In the Middle Ages, it flourished among marginalized people against the background of natural disasters such as famine or plague, particularly the Black Death, when millenarian exaltation and unrest were whipped up by would-be prophets and false messiahs. The desire of the poor to improve their lives was transfused

with fantasies of a world reborn into innocence through a final apocalyptic massacre. The evil ones—usually the Jews, the clergy or the
rich—were to be exterminated, after which the righteous would
establish a world without suffering or sin.[2]

In our present era, we are enduring the effects of the paradig-
matic millenarian creed of Islam. Its central precept is the need to
establish Islam as God's kingdom on earth. Only when Islam rules
everywhere will the world be brought into a state of perfect justice
and peace. The millenarian myth accepted by pious Muslims in
every epoch is that an Expected Deliverer called the Mahdi will
make his appearance at the end of time, followed at the Day of Judgment by the Antichrist, who will then be killed, and thus the Kingdom of God will arrive on earth. Among Shia Muslims, the Mahdi
is an even more central figure known as the Hidden Imam, whose
expected return is the backbone of the faith. His reappearance will
be preceded by "a long period of chaos and degeneracy," accelerating
until "evil, falsehood and wickedness dominate earth. The disintegration is to be complete and universal and will be characterised by
political unrest, immorality, falsehood and a total disregard for the
principles of religion."[3]

Islam in its radical manifestation is also apocalyptic, holding that
this disintegration describes precisely the condition of the world
today, and that the establishment of God's kingdom on earth is
imminent. Ali Shariati, the principal ideologue of the Iranian Revolution, fused Hidden Imam millenarianism with Marxism to turn
Islam into a revolutionary ideology that would not only conquer the
world but bring about the return of the Hidden Imam to earth. This
view is shared by Iran's president, Mahmoud Ahmadinejad, who
appears to believe in giving the apocalypse a bit of a helping hand in
order to hasten the Mahdi's appearance.

At the heart of Islam is the belief that it embodies the absolute
and unchallengeable truth. Unlike Judaism and Christianity, which
teach that divine intentions are revealed through a historical process

of interrogation and discovery, Islam holds that sacred doctrines were fixed in time by Mohammed, with no further development possible.[4] Ever since Islamic advocates of reason were defeated in a seminal battle in the thirteenth century, the belief in a fixed and unchallengeable truth has made the dominant strains of Islamic theology inimical to rationality and to freedom. It has also made inescapable the view that everything else is unreasonable and tyrannical.

Building on the belief that Islam is perfection, radical Islamists are the "elect," a small core of the righteous whose superior knowledge of this perfection is absolute and cannot be challenged. Hence the Islamist ideologue Abul ala Maududi wrote, "We must ... create out of nothing a minority of pure upright and educated men.... There must exist an upright community, devoted to the principle of truth, and whose sole goal in the world is to establish, to safeguard and to realise correctly the system of Truth."[5]

Islamists draw a Manichean division between the perfect state of Islam and the alternative realm of evil—the non-Islamic or not-Islamic-enough world, which has to be conquered for purified Islam. And since this rival realm belongs to the devil, Islamists see diabolical conspiracies everywhere trying to thwart the arrival of God's kingdom on earth. Syed Qutb expressed this notion of a worldwide battle between good and evil, and a fanatical certainty that the world can be made perfect and whole if Truth is imposed upon it:

> This struggle is not a temporary phase but a perpetual and permanent war. This war is the natural corollary to this eternal verdict that Truth and Falsehood cannot coexist on the face of this earth.... The struggle between Truth and Falsehood, Light and Darkness, is continuing since the beginning of the universe and the surging tide of the *jihad* for freedom cannot cease until the Satanic forces are put to an end and the religion is purified for God in toto.[6]

In an Orwellian inversion, the tyrannical imposition of Islam upon the world is viewed as its liberation. Just as Lenin believed, whatever fosters the revolution is good; whatever hinders it is bad. In the millenarian and totalitarian mind, there is never any middle ground; and truth and reason are turned upside down to fit.

In the face of the Islamists' replication of medieval apocalyptic movements, their ecstatic application of unhinged messianic beliefs, and the terrifying extinction of rationality and freedom in their revolutionary agenda, one might think the West would resist with every fiber of its being and defiantly uphold reason and liberty. Remarkably, the opposite is the case. The Western intelligentsia largely fails to recognize this millenarian fanaticism—not least because this intelligentsia embodies many secular permutations of the same phenomenon.

Thus, at the high tide of the Second Intifada terrorist attacks on Israelis in 2002, fury *against* the Israelis reached fresh peaks in the West, and at the Socialist Scholars' Conference in 2002 the crowd applauded a defense of Palestinian suicide bombing. Pondering the conundrum, Paul Berman suggested that an "unyielding faith in universal rationality" among Western progressives led them to conclude falsely that the desire to blow up Israeli children as a passport to paradise must be caused by real-world grievances.[7] The rationality of Western liberals meant they simply didn't understand the fanatical religious mind, and so they were guilty of a gross naivety.

But surely it's Berman who was being naive in assuming that the Western liberal is always rational. As the Marxist apostate David Horowitz has noted, Western progressives are themselves often utopians with a millenarian program for the salvation of the world. "Like the salvationist agendas of jihad, the Left's apocalyptic goal of 'social justice' is the equivalent of an earthly redemption. A planet saved, a world without poverty, racism, inequality or war—what means would not be justified to achieve such millennial ends?" Horowitz asks.[8]

SECULAR WESTERN MILLENARIAN FANTASIES

There is an assumption that Western society since the Enlightenment has embodied a belief in the power of reason, which acts as a kind of inoculation against the virus of religious obscurantism that characterized life in medieval Europe and is so obviously on display in the Islamic world today. But in fact, the Enlightenment served in part to *secularize* millenarian fantasies. A key idea of certain Enlightenment thinkers was that reason would bring about perfection on earth and that "progress" was the process by which utopia would be attained—a view satirized by Voltaire, Alexander Pope and Jonathan Swift.

According to Condorcet, an editor of the *Encyclopédie*, the bible of Enlightenment humanism, "No bounds have been fixed to the improvement of the human race. The perfectibility of man is absolutely infinite."[9] This idea was further developed in the nineteenth century by Herbert Spencer, the apostle of social Darwinism, who believed that life would get better all the time. "Progress is not an accident but a necessity," he wrote. "Surely must evil and immorality disappear; surely must man become perfect."[10]

It was reason that would redeem religious superstition and bring about the Kingdom of Man on earth. This idea infused the three great secular tyrannical movements that were spun out of Enlightenment thinking: the French Revolution, communism and fascism. Professor Richard Landes, a scholar of apocalyptic movements, notes that for the French revolutionaries the millennial hope lay not in scripture but in Jean-Jacques Rousseau's theories of freedom and the "general will," as expressed by the liberated voice of the people. On November 10, 1793, the Committee of Public Safety abolished the worship of God and substituted for it the "Cult of Reason." At the same time, this committee of twelve men summarily executed thousands of people, from aristocrats, no matter how innocent, to internal dissenters, no matter how loyal—a Terror which ended only with the execution of its two masterminds, Robespierre and Saint-Just, in 1794.[11]

Professor Landes remarks that "the French Revolution was a progressive demotic millennial movement—one inspired by a desire to perfect the world through egalitarian ideals." Landes identifies a variety of religious and cultish streams that fed into it:

> Demotic strains of Christian religiosity, from the Huguenots and their Catholic cousins, the Jansenists, informed such work as the "Declaration of the Rights of Man" and the anti-monarchical reasoning that justified regicide. The Rights of Man adhere closely to the principles of demotic millennial legislation: equality before the law, dignity of manual labor, freedom (of speech) for the individual. One of the earliest paintings publishing the Rights has them surrounded by Masonic symbolism and inscribed on two tablets of stone: the new universal legislation.[12]

The millenarian French Revolution had a direct link with the Russian Revolution of 1917. As J. L. Talmon noted, Gracchus Babeuf, a Jacobin of no great importance, rose to prominence after the Terror in a small group of radicals who articulated a theory of history as a class struggle between those with and those without property, and he predicted the imminent conclusion of this battle with the elimination of all property. In grafting this "terrible simplification" onto Rousseau's *Discourse on Inequality*, Babeuf produced "a crude prototype of Marxist analysis."[13]

Landes observes that Marx's most important contributions to the millennial thought of his age concerned his development of a "scientific" reading of history, the historical dialectic, that resembled in some important ways the thinking of the twelfth-century monk Joachim of Fiore, who viewed history as a process that promised collective salvation. Subsequently, Kant and Hegel developed the notion that the historical process drove towards a collective salvation defined in secular terms. Marx offered a further variant of such a process, where history is "but a continuous transformation of human nature."[14]

Fascism brought yet another secular variation of millenarian fantasies. As Landes writes, the shock of defeat in World War I led to the feeling in Germany that it had been betrayed by evil forces. Many of the returning soldiers, Hitler among them, had what one historian has called a "messianic-revolutionary outlook: a synthesis of nationalist ideology and an apocalyptic Christian mythology. The warrior-dictator can lead Germany to the Promised Land only once he has destroyed evil, sin, and death in their earthly embodiment as the potent, satanic Jew."[15] This vision came to center on the messianic leader who conjured up the utopian prospect of a "thousand-year Reich," with humanity attaining perfection by shedding all departures from the mythologized "Aryan" template. In his public performances this leader resembled, as commentators at the time described it, "a popular preacher turned savior."[16] Indeed, Landes observes:

> Nazism is a religious phenomenon in its own right: a *political religion* that, whatever its content, appealed to the same critical issues and emotions that religion does: faith, ultimate meaning, redemption. And among those links are some of the most powerful forms any religious movement can take—the apocalyptic and messianic traditions that date back to the earliest centuries of Christian-Germanic relations.[17]

THE PURSUIT OF UTOPIAS IN THE CONTEMPORARY WEST

Secular millenarian impulses did not stop at communism and fascism but today infuse the progressive mind. From multiculturalism to environmentalism to postnationalism, Western progressives have fixated on unattainable abstractions for the realization of utopia. The world of everyday reality is rejected. All that matters is a theoretical future that is perfect and just, without war or want or prejudice—a future where fallen humanity has returned to Eden. And since that future is perfect, the idea of it may not be changed or challenged in any way. Which is why the progressive mind, in pursuit of the utopia where reason and liberty rule, is very firmly closed.

In that respect, an intriguing comparison can be made between the sexual libertarians of today and a fourteenth-century European sect known as the Heresy of the Free Spirit. They were gnostics, believing they possessed perfect knowledge. Strictly speaking, gnostics are not true millenarians since they anticipate a state of perfection *beyond* this world rather than within it. Nevertheless, as Norman Cohn observed, the Free Spirits, intent on their own individual salvation, played a significant part in the revolutionary millenarian ferment of the Middle Ages. And the similarities with today's "free spirits" are striking.

Adherents of the fourteenth-century sect believed they had attained a perfection so absolute that they were incapable of sin. Thus they repudiated moral norms, particularly those pertaining to sexual behavior, as Cohn explains:

> The "perfect man" could always draw the conclusion that it was permissible for him, even incumbent upon him, to do what was commonly regarded as forbidden. In a Christian civilisation, which attached particular value to chastity and regarded sexual intercourse outside marriage as particularly sinful, such antinomianism most commonly took the form of promiscuity on principle.... [W]hat emerges then is an entirely convincing picture of an eroticism which, far from springing from a carefree sensuality, possessed above all a symbolic value as a sign of spiritual emancipation—which incidentally is the value which "free love" has often possessed in our own times.[18]

Indeed; and since Cohn's book was first published in 1957, the adoption as permissible of what was previously forbidden has progressed way beyond free love into such formerly transgressive areas as illegitimacy, homosexuality and sadomasochism. This trend has been driven by the "elect" of the intelligentsia who, like the Free Spirits of the Middle Ages, regard themselves as the embodiment of absolute virtue. It is a delicious irony that such people, who consider themselves to be at the cutting edge of modernity, reflect in certain respects such a wildly irrational, obscurantist medieval Christian sect.

The very condition of the modern world provides emotional rocket fuel for the belief that it can and must be transformed. Anomie—the state of radical rootlessness caused by the snapping of attachments in a postreligious age that leaves people without meaning or purpose in their lives—can find its antidote in apocalyptic beliefs that galvanize people and make them feel alive. As Eric Hoffer observed in his classic analysis of mass movements, "Passionate hatred can give meaning and purpose to an empty life. Thus people haunted by the purposelessness of their lives try to find a new content not only by dedicating themselves to a holy cause but also by nursing a fanatical grievance. A mass movement offers them unlimited opportunities for both."[19]

THE QUASI-RELIGIOUS IMPERATIVE OF MODERN MASS SECULAR MOVEMENTS

The mass movements of today are not so much political as cultural: anti-imperialism and anti-Americanism, anti-Zionism, environmentalism, scientism, egalitarianism, libertinism and multiculturalism. These are not merely quasi-religious movements—evangelical, dogmatic and fanatical, with enforcement mechanisms ranging from demonization through ostracism to expulsion of heretics. They are also millenarian and even apocalyptic in their visions of the perfect society and what needs to be swept aside in order to attain it—even if, while embodying certain characteristics of medieval heretics, they simultaneously embody the authoritarianism of the persecutors of those heretics in the medieval church.

Their view of the human condition is essentially one of sin and redemption. They name the crimes committed by humanity—

oppression of Third World peoples, despoliation of nature, bigotry, war—and offer redemption and salvation by a returning to the true faith. Dissenters are heretics forming diabolical conspiracies against the one revealed truth. It is believed that the decision to invade Iraq, Israel's military operations, manmade global warming and the persistence of religious faith cannot possibly have any reasonable basis because they deny the unchallengeable truths of anti-imperialism, environmentalism and scientific materialism, and so the explanations must lie in conspiracies by the neocons or the Jews, or Big Oil, or the creationists, whose various hidden hands are detected everywhere.

The left-wing intelligentsia, the environmentalists and the Darwinists are today's gnostics; their knowledge of a higher truth puts them on a plane above the rest of humanity, who have to be exhorted to change their ways in order to be saved from blood-curdling apocalyptic scenarios: war and social disorder, floods and famine and pestilence, genocidal slaughter perpetrated (solely) by religious fanatics.

The environmentalists, through their scientific credentials, possess exclusive access to the truth that the planet is being destroyed. They preach that the earth has been sinned against by capitalism, consumerism, the West, science, technology, mankind itself. Only when these are purged and economic materialism is rejected will the earth be saved and the innate harmony of the world restored; otherwise we will descend into the hell of a drowned and parched planet where the remains of the human race battle it out for the few remaining resources.

The language and imagery conjure up a secular witch-hunt. In the *Guardian*, for example, the environmental campaigner George Monbiot celebrated the "recanting" of both the tabloid *Sun* and the *Economist* on the issue of global warming, on which they had previously been heretically skeptical.[20] In a similar vein, the atheist evangelist Richard Dawkins asserts that all must comply with his pronouncements on pain of excommunication from the realm of

rationality. Dawkins is surely the Robespierre of evolutionary thinking, crushing in a Darwinian Terror all who stand in the way of an
age of perfect reason. But Dawkins's vision of this utopia, as he
expounds it in *The God Delusion*, achieves all the profundity and
insight of a vacuous pop lyric:

> Imagine, with John Lennon, a world with no religion. Imagine no suicide
> bombers, no 9/11, no 7/7, no Crusades, no witch-hunts, no Gunpowder
> Plot, no Indian partition, no Israeli/Palestinian wars, no
> Serb/Croat/Muslim massacres, no persecution of Jews as "Christ-
> killers", no Northern Ireland "Troubles", no "honour killings", no shiny-
> suited bouffant-haired televangelists fleecing gullible people of their
> money ("God wants you to give till it hurts"). Imagine no Taleban to
> blow up ancient statues, no public beheadings of blasphemers, no flog-
> ging of female skin for the crime of showing an inch of it.[21]

In other words, by redeeming its original sin of religious belief,
mankind can create a paradise with no war, bigotry, persecution,
tyranny, violence—apparently no ills of any kind.

This is a view whose ignorance and absurdity make the weeping
statues of the Virgin Mary look like the first law of thermodynam-
ics. Dawkins is a gnostic *par excellence*, who sees creationist conspiracies lurking beneath every bacterial flagellum—the "outboard
motor" of the cell, whose "irreducible complexity" lies at the heart of
intelligent design theory. And just as medieval apocalypticists were
fearful that Satan would pollute their innocence and sully their
purity, Dawkins believes that the only explanation for the persistence of religious faith is that the purity of human reason has been
contaminated by a "virus," otherwise styled as a "meme"—a concept
that has as much connection to science as does the Antichrist.

Richard Dawkins and George Monbiot are surely secular incar-
nations of those itinerant preachers who traveled around medieval
Europe urging the terrified peasantry to repent of their sins in order
to usher in the Kingdom of God on earth.

MASS SCAPEGOATING AND THE COERCION OF VIRTUE

The crucial element in all millenarian movements is the reaction that sets in when the prophecy of utopia fails—which of course it has done every time throughout human history. The inevitable outcome is that the disappointment turns ugly. Adherents of the cult create scapegoats upon whom they turn with a ferocity fueled by disorientation, anger and shame, in an attempt to bring about by coercion the state of purity that the designated culprits have purportedly thwarted.

When the classless utopia failed to materialize in the Soviet Union, Stalin murdered dissidents and sent them to the gulag. When Germany failed to achieve its apparently rightful place as the paradigm country in Europe, Hitler committed genocide against the Jews. When Mao failed to bring about universal justice and the Confucian ideal of harmony, he killed, jailed or otherwise terrorized millions of Chinese.

In current times, the failure of the environmental vision of spiritual oneness between man and nature has seen mankind blamed for despoiling the planet and imperiling the survival of life on earth. The failure to arrive at a perfect state of reason in which all injustice and suffering are ended has been blamed on religious believers. The failure of the apparatus of international law and human rights to prevent war and tyranny has been blamed on America. And the failure of the existence of Israel to bring about the end of "the Jewish problem" has been blamed on the Jews themselves.

Having identified scapegoats upon whom they can project their anger and shame, disappointed millenarians have tried to carve out their perfect society through coercive measures against the people they hold responsible for the failure of their vision. In the French Revolution, when religious folk showed too much attachment to their old ways, the revolutionaries tried to do away with Christianity altogether. This was done in accordance with Rousseau's dictum that if the general will failed to be accepted, the people would have to be "forced to be free." In other words, they would be coerced for their own good, as Landes notes is characteristic of totalitarian revolutions:

> [I]t is precisely the "good conscience" of the totalitarian, the conviction that he does this for his *victims*, that he is "saving" both them and others, that marks the true believer, whether it be Torquemada, Saint-Just, or Lenin. The numerous differences between Bolsheviks and Jacobins should hardly blind us to the critical and disturbing similarities: for they both represent demotic secular millennial movements which, at the highest pitch of apocalyptic time, turned to state terror as a solution to the disappointments they faced.[22]

In our own time, the left forces people to be free in myriad different ways. In Britain, left-wing totalitarianism wears the pained smile of "good conscience" as it sends in the police to enforce "hate crime" laws, drags children from their grandparents to place them for adoption with gay couples, or sacks a Christian nurse for offering to pray for her patient. In America, school textbooks are censored by "bias and sensitivity" reviewers who remove a reference to patchwork quilting by women on the western frontier in the mid nineteenth century (stereotyping of females as "soft and submissive"); an account of a heroic young blind mountain climber (bias in favor of those living in hiking and mountain-climbing areas but against blind people); and a tale about growing up in ancient Egypt ("elitist" references to wealthy families).[23]

Some would call all this a form of tyranny; but to the progressive mind, tyranny occurs only when their utopia is *denied*. Virtue thus has to be coerced for the good of the people at the receiving end. There can be no doubt that it *is* virtue, because progressivism is all about creating the perfect society and is therefore inherently and incontestably virtuous; and so—like the Committee of Public Safety, like Stalinism, like Islam—it is incapable of doing anything bad. Unlike everyone else, of course, who it follows can do nothing *but* bad.

Progressives feel justified in trying to stifle any disagreement with their agenda on the grounds that the people they are trying to stifle are "fascists," a term they employ without irony. (A sense of humor is not known to be a millenarian trait.) Never engaging with the actual arguments of their opponents, they demonize them instead through gratuitous insults designed to turn them into pariahs (while they themselves characterize all reasoned arguments against them as outrageous "insults"). Dissent is labeled as pathology—homophobia, xenophobia, Islamophobia—with phobia, or irrational fear, used as a synonym for prejudice. There are even outright accusations of insanity, a weapon used by totalitarian movements from the medieval Catholic Church to the Jacobins to Stalin's secret police.

Calling today's conservatives "fascists" is particularly absurd since such people tend to believe in *limiting* state power and giving more freedom to the individual, a position that shades off into libertarianism. Nevertheless, leftists see the alternative to themselves as "fascist" by definition. So the more that conservatives believe government should be limited and the more freedom they want for individuals, the more "fascist" they become in the eyes of the left.

Even more fundamental is the trap that is sprung over the issue of truth. Any fact that challenges the worldview of the left is ignored, denied or explained away, because to admit even a scintilla of such a truth would bring the entire utopian house of cards crashing down and with it the left-winger's whole moral and political identity. That's why progressives refused to acknowledge the French Terror, Stalin's gulags or the millions dead under Mao; that's why today they refuse to acknowledge black racism, Arab rejectionism of Israel or the fact that the climate was warmer a thousand years ago. But here's what follows from this denial: Anyone who objects to the falsehoods of the left and points out the truth must be right-wing, and thus "fascist." In this way, truth itself is demonized—and the bigger the truth that is told, the more demonized the teller becomes.

THE UNTHINKABLE TERROR OF A CHALLENGE TO THE IDEA

Eric Hoffer believed that at the heart of the ideological true believer invariably lay a deep self-contempt, which was transmuted into hatred of others, since "mass movements can rise and spread without belief in a god, but never without belief in a devil."[24] In other words, it is essential for the true believer to have someone or something to hate. The believer is defined in large measure by what he or she is not. Positions are then taken not necessarily because they are so believable, but principally because the alternative is so unthinkable.

This is particularly evident among scientific materialists, who are driven to take manifestly ridiculous positions simply because the alternative—belief in God—is unacceptable. As we saw earlier, the geneticist Richard Lewontin admitted that scientists sometimes put forward absurd theories purely to prevent the "Divine Foot in the door." They cannot tolerate the slightest possibility of a metaphysical explanation. Such an approach betrays the most basic principle of scientific inquiry: that you always go where the evidence leads. Instead, it makes evidence dependent on a prior idea, in the manner of dogmatic ideology.

Surely this betrayal of science has occurred because scientism, or scientific materialism, is an ideology whose goal is not to gain knowledge and truth but to *suppress* knowledge and truth if these threaten its governing idea. The priority is to safeguard the materialist worldview in the teeth of any evidence to the contrary and thus maintain with it the prestige of science as the source of all the knowledge in the world. Defenders of this idea must preclude opposing points of view, for materialism is a closed thought system which cannot be challenged. Anything outside it is deemed non-science and relegated to the status of fantasy. Any true scientific challenge to materialism is labeled "bad" science, and skeptics can be dismissed as not understanding "how science works."[25]

Richard Dawkins goes even further. He doesn't only dismiss opponents' arguments: he maintains that such opponents *could not possibly have meant what they said.* His own gnostic infallibility apparently means that he alone knows what was really in someone's mind. Confronted by the fact that many scientists are religious believers, he dismisses most of these beliefs as not really religious except in the sense that Einstein professed a religious sensibility, which he says wasn't really religious belief at all; he claims to have to scrape the barrel to find genuinely distinguished modern scientists who are truly religious.[26] Really? How about Francis Collins, who heads the Human Genome Project; or the botanist and former director of Kew Gardens, Sir Ghillean Prance; or the physicist Allan Sandage, considered to be the father of modern astronomy; or the Nobel Prize-winning physicists William Phillips and Arno Penzias—all of them religious believers?

Materialists such as Dawkins set up an absolute dichotomy between science and religion, which are presented as engaged in a battle unto death: reason versus faith, good versus evil. Any scientist who accepts the integrity of religious arguments or any religious believer who accepts evolution is therefore deemed not to be telling the truth. So when the evolutionary biologist Stephen Jay Gould wrote in his book *Rocks of Ages* that Darwinism was compatible with both religion *and* atheism because science and religion were "non-overlapping magisteria, dealing respectively with empiricism and questions of ultimate meaning," Dawkins said, "I simply do not believe that Gould could possibly have meant much of what he wrote in *Rocks of Ages*."[27] And after Pope John Paul II said in 1996 that he supported the general idea of biological evolution while entering reservations about certain interpretations of it, the philosopher Michael Ruse recorded that "Richard Dawkins's response was simply that the Pope was a hypocrite, that he could not be genuine about science and that Dawkins himself simply preferred an honest fundamentalist."[28] Thus it was with consummate if unwitting irony that Dawkins in 1989 wrote,

> I don't think it is too melodramatic to say that civilization is at war. It is a war against religious bigotry. In Britain recently our newspapers have shown crowds of fundamentalists (they happen to be Muslim rather than Christian, but in this context the distinction is of no importance) baying for the death of the distinguished novelist Salman Rushdie, displaying his effigy with its eyes put out and publicly burning his books. The truly appalling thing all such people have in common, whether they are incited to murder by ayatollahs or to less violent observances by television evangelists, *is that they know, for certain, that their particular brand of revealed truth is absolute and needs no reasoned defense.*[29] [My emphasis.]

A gnostic knows that reprehensible behavior can by definition be practiced only by others, never by himself.

REDEEMING MANKIND BY ATTACKING THE WEST

For the millenarian, the high-minded belief in creating a perfect world requires the imperfect world to be purified by the true believers. From the Committee of Public Safety to Iran's morals police, from Stalin's purges of dissidents to British and American "hate crime" laws, utopians of every stripe have instigated coercive or tyrannical regimes to save the world by ridding it of its perceived corruption.

The symmetry today is as obvious as the paradox. At a time when radical Islam is attempting to purify the world by conquering it for Islam and thus create the Kingdom of God on earth, the West is also trying to purify the world in order to create a secular utopia in which war will become a thing of the past, hatred and selfishness will be eradicated from the human heart, reason will replace superstition, humanity will live in harmony with the earth, and all division will yield to the brotherhood of man. The paradox is that, while it might be thought that the liberal West is trying to eradicate the kind of hatred and killing that radical Islam brings in its wake, the drive to purify inevitably results not in harmony but in strife.

But there is a further curiosity—that in doing so, the secular West is not merely adopting a quasi-religious posture but a specifically Christian one. The governing story of Islam is the imposition of its doctrines through conquest and submission. Accordingly, it is today attempting to fashion its utopia through conquest and submission. The governing story of Christianity, by contrast, is of sin, guilt and redemption. And remarkably, that is precisely the pattern lying behind the utopian agendas of Western secular progressives— even though by severing these concepts from their transcendent Christian context, they have perverted their meaning and turned them from the engines of truth and justice into their antithesis.

For the left, the West is guilty of exploiting the poor, the marginalized and the oppressed. Britain has to do penance for the sins of imperialism and racism. Israel has to do penance for the sins of colonialism and racism. America has to do penance for the sins of imperialism, slavery and racism.

For the environmentalists, the West is guilty of the sins of consumerism and greed, which have given it far more than it needs. So these things must be taken away and the West must return to a simpler, austere, preindustrial way of life.

Because of its sins, the West is being punished through the wars and terrorism against it. The West "had it coming" on account of its manifold iniquities. America is responsible for Islamic terrorism. Israel is responsible for Palestinian terrorism. And Britain is responsible for the radicalization of British Muslims and the 7/7 attacks on the London transit system because it has backed America and Israel and "lied" about the threat posed by Saddam Hussein.

As a result of all this sin, guilt and punishment, the Western progressive soul yearns for expiation and redemption. By electing Barack Obama as president of the United States, Americans wanted to redeem their country's original sins of slavery and racism. Through its strictures against Israel, post-Christian Europe wants to redeem its original sin of antisemitism. By campaigning against carbon dioxide emissions, environmentalists want to redeem the original sin of human existence. As for the scientific materialists, the sin to be redeemed is not by man against God but by God against man. Their governing story is that uncorrupted man fell from the Garden of Reason when he partook of the forbidden fruit of religion—which now has to be purged from the world to create the Kingdom of Man on earth.

For all these millenarians and apocalypticists and utopians, both religious and secular, the target is the West. As Ian Buruma and Avishai Margalit write in their book *Occidentalism*, the West is seen as an enemy "not because it offers an alternative system of values but because its promises of material comfort, individual freedom and dignity of unexceptional lives deflate all utopian pretensions. The anti-heroic, anti-utopian nature of western liberalism is the greatest enemy of religious radicals, priest-kings and collective seekers after purity and heroic salvation."[30]

That's why the West is squarely in the sights of all who want to create utopia and are determined to remove all the obstacles it places in the way. For environmentalists, that obstacle is industrialization. For scientific materialists, it's religion. For transnational progressives, it's the nation. For anti-imperialists, it's American exceptionalism. For the Western intelligentsia, it's Israel. For Islamists, it's all the above *and* the entire un-Islamic world. And in their desire for redemption and their suppression of dissent from the one revealed truth, Western progressives and radical Islamists are closer than either would like to think.

13

HOW ENLIGHTENMENT
UNRAVELED

How is it that people who are devoted to reason and liberty and who are living in the most rational era known to man have descended into irrationality and intolerance? What has caused them to turn their most cherished beliefs upside down and inside out?

The key to the puzzle is that ever since the eighteenth-century Enlightenment, the West has made the mistake of thinking that reason can exist detached from the civilization that gave it birth. In particular, it has made the fundamental error of thinking that to be "enlightened" necessarily entails a repudiation of religion. It has created the impression that the Enlightenment was a kind of historical thunderclap. Once upon a time there were the Dark Ages when people were irrational and superstitious and ignorant and went round killing each other in wars of religion, and then there was the Enlightenment, after which they became—well, enlightened. They created science and put religion inside a box, devoting themselves to progress, life, liberty and happiness.

But it wasn't like that. History is a complex process, a constant eruption of ideas that both flow out of each other and conflict with each other, sometimes simultaneously. The seismic struggle between reason and irrationality well predated the Enlightenment; and the ideas generated by the Enlightenment created historical feedback loops of reaction and counter-reaction that continue to this day. To understand just how our civilization has turned everything upside down, we need to try to unravel—if only tentatively—the intricate tapestry of Western thought from the eighteenth century onwards.

The Enlightenment had many strands. It arose in large measure as a reaction against the abuse of clerical authority, in response to which it laid down a template for liberty by redefining the relationship between political authority and the private individual. Despite its image as the solvent of religion, however, it could not have taken place without the foundational insight of the Bible that all of humanity was equal, having been fashioned in the image of God.

Many Enlightenment thinkers were religious, even if a number of them were not so much Christians as deists who believed in an impersonal god who didn't interfere in human life. Leibnitz argued that the universe was composed of individual units existing in harmony under God's divine ordinance. John Locke, who laid down the foundations of the rule of law and the principle of religious tolerance, thought that man's duty to God to preserve mankind as part of his Creation was the basic moral law of nature.[1] Isaac Newton was a devout Christian, as was the chemist Joseph Priestley; like Locke they were also Dissenters, and there was indeed a close bond between Protestant dissent, heterodoxy and Enlightenment thinking.[2]

There was also, however, a powerful strand of Enlightenment thinking, particularly in France, that repudiated not just clerical authority but religion itself. Voltaire led the charge with the battle cry *"Ecrasez l'infâme"*—the infamy being not just the Catholic Church but Christianity itself, which he wanted to replace with the religion of reason, virtue and liberty, "drawn from the bosom of nature." Building upon the Reformation, in which Luther had constructed a new orthodoxy around the relocation of spiritual authority within the individual, Enlightenment thinkers believed that individual reason would now explain what had previously been obscure. The real world was governed by intelligible laws and the totality of all observable phenomena was "nature." All laws could be discovered by reason, moral law was written in everyone's conscience, and any dogma that purported to replace reason had to be destroyed.[3] The reorganization of society by such laws would end superstitious reliance on dogma and the cruelties and oppression that had resulted.

But although reason was the leitmotif of all Enlightenment thinking, it did not play the same role in Britain or America as it did in France, where the Catholic Church with its infrastructure of repression was viewed as the enemy and reason as the antidote. As Gertrude Himmelfarb has noted, the driving force of the Enlightenment in Britain was "social virtue," while in America it was political liberty.[4] In those countries, religion was seen not as an enemy but as an ally. Indeed, the historian Roy Porter found that the Enlightenment in England thrived "*within* piety."[5] British Enlightenment thinkers did not form an ideology of reason explicitly to challenge and replace the authority of religion. French thinkers, by contrast, invested reason with the same dogmatic status as religion.[6] In this way they created a secular reflection of the Catholic Church. Reason became a civil religion.

Consequently, the seeds of authoritarianism and worse were sown in France from the start. As Isaiah Berlin noted, the seminal philosophe Condorcet believed that the application of mathematics and statistics to social policy would usher in a reign of happiness, truth and virtue, and would end forever the subjection of mankind through cruelty, misery and oppression. His disciple Saint-Simon correctly predicted the replacement of religious by secular propaganda, into which artists and poets would be drafted just as they had once worked for the glory of the church. Saint-Simon's secretary and collaborator, Auguste Comte, saw a need for a type of secular religion, dedicated to rational rather than liberal or democratic ideals.[7] This in turn would result in scientific materialism, or "positivism" as it was called—the authoritarian thinking that shapes our modern-day secular "priesthood," with their doctrinaire insistence that science has the explanation for all things.

THE CONFLICT BETWEEN REASON AND LIBERTY

The inevitable consequence of creating an apparatus of ideological enforcement was that reason, far from being the guarantor of liberty, was destined to be in conflict with it. The imposition of reason would lead to an *attack* on liberty, something which thinkers such as Edmund Burke perceived very clearly. The philosophes propounded that "enlightened despotism" should be embodied in the general will—effectively a formula for oppression ranging from the "tyranny of popular opinion" to the "dictatorship of the proletariat."

Although this tyrannical concept has been popularly ascribed to Jean-Jacques Rousseau, he himself said he had taken it from the article on "Natural Law" by his contemporary Diderot, who was featured in the same volume of the *Encyclopédie* as Rousseau in 1762. Here Diderot chillingly set out the template for the totalitarianism of reason under which we are living today. "We must reason about all things," he wrote. Whoever refused to seek out the truth thereby renounced the very nature of man and "should be treated by the rest of his species as a wild beast." Once the truth had been discovered, whoever refused to accept it was "either insane or wicked and morally evil." And although there could be no good and evil, right and wrong without freedom, it was not the individual who had "the right to decide about the nature of right and wrong," but only "the human race," which expressed the general will.[8]

As the French Revolution was to prove, this doctrine was more despotic than enlightened. The spirit of the revolution was Rousseau. Proclaiming the arrival of the Republic of Virtue (the euphemism for the Terror), Robespierre echoed Rousseau's call for the "reign of virtue" that would make particular wills conform to the general will—and Rousseau had advocated death to anyone who did not uphold the common values of the community.[9] Rousseau had written of the radical reshaping not just of society but of humanity; Robespierre spoke of "the necessity of bringing about a complete regeneration and, if I may express myself so, of creating a new people."[10]

As J. L. Talmon suggested in 1952, this kind of thinking lay behind what he termed "totalitarian democracy," or "political messianism," which was based on a false identification of reason with virtue. Although this phenomenon was set in train by the French Revolution, it had roots in Enlightenment thinking.

Many Enlightenment thinkers viewed man as a kind of abstraction: not so much an individual as the sum total of reasoning beings. In this view, the existing customs and traditions were unnatural, and man needed to be freed from them. All established institutions had to be remade according to the rules of reason, with the purpose of securing man's natural rights and freedoms. All differences and inequalities had to be eliminated so that nothing remained between man and the state, which was the expression of the general will.[11]

But this view rested on a serious conceptual error. There can be no such thing as free-floating reason; for it to have any meaning, reason has to be grounded in a prior concept. On what basis otherwise does reason exist? There has to be something on which it rests that is generally taken for granted. As Talmon observed, enforcing a meaningless abstraction of "reason" inevitably leads to totalitarianism—which it did, first in the Jacobin Terror, then in Stalinism. And as it has today in our various abstract ideologies, none of which has any claim to the absolutism it demands; they are simply attempts by part of the population to impose its will upon the rest, albeit by less draconian or violent means than the totalitarian tyrannies of the past.

At the same time, what is generally overlooked is that—in an apparent contradiction—much of the Enlightenment actually consisted of a *rejection* of the scope and power of reason, a belief that man, as David Hume put it, was "the slave of the passions,"[12] or emotion and the senses. Hume concluded that there was no way of deducing logically that there was an external, objective world at all. Such thinking lent itself—whether Hume intended it or not—to the view that everything was therefore subjectively created. Experience grounded in the senses may give the appearance of solid reality, but it is compromised by its subjective roots. And without an objective reality, what may then take over is fantasy in which rationality has no place.

Hume, the quintessential Enlightenment thinker, thus unwittingly lent substance to the revolt *against* reason by the "counter-Enlightenment"—as did Rousseau, guiding spirit of the Jacobins' "republic of reason" but also inventor of the "noble savage," the idea that man was free and virtuous only in his natural state, since the world that he had created merely fettered and corrupted him. Perhaps the most tortured (and towering) figure in this regard was Immanuel Kant, who tried to square the Enlightenment belief in universal reason with individual subjectivity by proposing, as a universal moral rule, that autonomous individuals should accept no external moral authority but should act as their own moral arbiters.

THE BACKLASH AGAINST REASON IN GERMAN ROMANTICISM

Whether they intended to or not, some Enlightenment thinkers put forth ideas that had the consequence of undermining objective truth and reason by elevating subjective feelings and passions grounded in the senses. These ideas fed into the great backlash against reason that took the form of German Romanticism in the nineteenth century. Rousseau's idealization of nature contributed to the development of Romanticism, but what fueled it in Germany was resentment and a sense of inferiority towards the French, who were dominant at that time in virtually every aspect of life. Romanticism accordingly fused nationalist feelings with a repudiation of the rationality at the heart of the French Enlightenment, instead stressing emotions and elevating the particular over the universal.

German Romanticism owed much to pietism, a retreat into individual spirituality and a personal relationship with God, which were thought to be undermined by reason and scientific thinking. Romanticism attacked the idea that virtue was knowledge. In the Romantic view, people created their own values out of nothing. There was no pattern to the universe, just an endless flow of creativity that could be understood only through myths and symbols.

The influence of Romanticism on all subsequent thinking cannot be overestimated. A deeply complex movement of thought, it gave rise to a tremendous flowering of German cultural and intellectual life. And yet as the nineteenth century wore on, it also resulted in the submerging of reason by emotion and intuition.

In the emphasis on the individual will and the need for individuals to be free to be themselves to the fullest degree, the greatest virtue became authenticity. There was admiration for minorities, for defiance of authority, for every kind of opposition to normative values. Thus Romanticism led directly to moral and cultural relativism, the belief that there can be no objective cultural standards or hierarchies of behavior—the creed that defines contemporary Western society. In the twentieth century, it led also to existentialism and the idea that life was meaningless. Although relativism today is associated with progressive thinking, its trajectory furnished the intellectual antecedents of fascism.

The Romantic attack on reason began in the late eighteenth century and progressed through a series of thinkers—Lessing, Kant, Herder, Fichte, Schelling—who were towering figures in German culture, yet they also swelled the currents of thought that led to fascism and Nazism. According to Isaiah Berlin, the first and most savage was an obscure figure named Johann Georg Hamann, whose thinking contained many of the motifs that were to characterize the Romantic movement. He believed that people's faculties should be given free rein in the most violent possible fashion. Words were inadequate because they classified things and were too rational; myths were better at conveying the mystery of the world through images and symbols that connected man with nature. "What is this highly praised *reason*, with its universality, infallibility, overweening-ness, certainty, self-evidence?" he asked. "It is a stuffed dummy which the *howling* superstition of unreason has endowed with *divine attributes*."[13]

The attack on reason and elevation of the subjective self went hand in hand with an assault on science, modernity and universal values, and a corresponding embrace of myth, tradition and the particulars of nation. Herder held that every society possessed its own way of living and there were no fixed criteria to rank one above any other. The natural unit of human society was the *Volk*, or the people, who were defined chiefly by soil and language. Fichte said in essence that the self was the center of its own world and created its own reality; life began not with knowledge but with action. He conjured up the mystical idea of a body of men lunging forward to purify and transform themselves, exalting the power of the state to embody the national will. Schelling agreed that the external world was an adjunct to the mind, and developed the concept of a mystical vitalism that saw nature in anthropomorphic terms as being alive in itself. Hegel, while claiming to uphold reason, nevertheless maintained that knowledge was subjective and that nothing was wholly false and nothing wholly true.[14] What was real was in the mind or spirit, or *Geist*, and history was the progressive development of *Geist* through successive ages.

Perhaps the greatest apotheosis of Romanticism was Nietzsche; even though he himself denounced Romanticism as a kind of sickness, he stood firmly against reason and modernity and exalted the irrational and instinctive. Nietzsche pronounced that God was dead and so man now had to provide his own meaning for life. Those who achieved this would be *Übermenschen*, embodying virtues of courage, honor, power and love of danger. Judeo-Christian precepts were excoriated as "slave morality," which kept people subjugated by appealing to virtues such as altruism and egalitarianism. Reason and morality were merely the vehicles of the will to power.

As the supreme prophet of nihilism, Nietzsche is today much in vogue among left-wing opponents of Judeo-Christian "slave morality." And the destruction of objectivity and the veneration of instinct and emotions at the heart of Romanticism constitute the governing creed for contemporary Western progressives. Yet such ideas also fed the antirational, antimodern, "organic" and racist fervor that developed into fascism and Nazism.

As Isaiah Berlin noted, the terrible consequences of this thinking were foreseen as early as 1832 by the German poet Heinrich Heine. He warned that one day the Germans, fired by a combination of absolutist metaphysics, historical memories and resentments, fanaticism and savage fury, would destroy Western civilization. Berlin recorded Heine as predicting that

> "Implacable Kantians ... with axe and sword will uproot the soil of our European life in order to tear out the roots of the past. Armed Fichteans will appear ... restrained neither by fear nor greed ... like those early Christians whom neither physical torture nor physical pleasure could break." And most terrible of all would be Schelling's disciples, the Philosophers of Nature who, isolated and unapproachable beyond the barriers of their own obsessive ideas, will identify themselves with the elemental forces of "the demonic powers of ancient German pantheism."[15]

HOW PROGRESSIVE THINKING DESTROYED MAN AS A FREE AND RATIONAL BEING

Heine's prescience foretold not just Nazism a century later but the eruption in his own century of a host of irrational movements, with the "philosophers of nature" at their core. As J. W. Burrow has recorded, the search for new myths that would transcend daily existence and take the self to a higher plane through purification resulted in movements such as vegetarianism, teetotalism, sexual liberation, mysticism and monism—the religion of nature-worship propounded by the proto-fascist Ernst Haeckel, the founder of ecology, who believed that all matter was alive and possessed mental attributes. In monism, Haeckel brought together hostility to Christianity and propaganda for Darwinism, the Romantic cult of nature, an optimistic evolutionism, theories of hygiene and selective breeding.[16]

The occult was widely practiced by initiates on a mission to discover a redemptive inner truth, as Burrow writes. There was much enthusiasm for secret societies and mystical cosmological doctrines, for pursuing evidence of the afterlife and paranormal powers of the mind. Theosophy supposedly provided an antidote to materialism by fusing the essence of the world's religions to express the omnipotence of the spirit. The self-designated leader of modern theosophy, Madame Blavatsky—said to have been taught by invisible Indian spirit instructors—drew on Hindu doctrines and stressed reincarnation. Mme Blavatsky remained immensely influential despite being unmasked by the English Psychical Research Society as a fraud.[17]

The eruption of irrationality around ecology, "organic" wholeness, mysticism and paganism resulted in the racial theories that were prominent in the twentieth century. Holistic or "Gestalt" theory gave pseudoscientific credibility to the mystical and pagan Dionysian idea of "primal unity" that was so prominent in fascist thinking. As the Talmudic scholar Joseph Soloveitchik has observed, "No concept ever degenerated to such a degree and became so powerful a weapon in the hands of fanatics as did the Gestalt. An untrammeled path led from Gestalt and group psychology through typology, philosophical anthropology and characterology (in conjunction with graphology and physiognomics) into the welter of racial theory."[18]

There were attempts to reassert reason in the face of all this irrationality. A key thinker of the 1840s was Ludwig Feuerbach, who straddled both Romanticism and its antithesis, materialism. Feuerbach held that man had created God, not the reverse, and had then alienated himself from his true rational being by subscribing to religion. Feuerbach had two important disciples. One, Karl Marx, took from him the idea that man dictated consciousness and ideas to satisfy his material needs; on this basis, Marx set out to restructure society around dialectical materialism. The other, Auguste Comte, tried to build a secular religion of science through positivism.

In fact, science itself was to undermine this materialism. For example, the Austrian physicist and philosopher Ernst Mach sought to give science a firm foundation away from metaphysics, but ended up in a very different place from reason. This was because he held that all knowledge was merely sensation, that human selves were essentially fictions, and that knowledge was merely a serviceable means to an end. In the hands of Ernst Haeckel, evolutionary biology undermined materialism with the belief that everything in nature possessed mental attributes, a view that propelled both Darwinism and ecology into an irrational psychic netherworld. For thinkers like these, the slipperiness of experience contrasted with the fixed attributes of the "collective unconscious," as expressed in nature or the heritage of the human race. From about 1900, the surrender of the rational self to the creative force of the unconscious became a mark of the intellectual avant-garde.[19]

The nineteenth century and to a large extent its successor were dominated by the governing assumptions of Romanticism: that reality resided in the subjective mind and that man was swept along by the unstoppable forces of historical progress, in which that subjective experience developed. These assumptions led to a profound irrationality, which clothed itself in scientific and materialist garb.

Darwinism reduced human reason to a mere mechanism for survival, since genetic determinism left no basis for humans to have a disinterested impulse to discover the truth for its own sake. Marxism said that humans were prisoners not of their genes but of society. Since Marxism "unmasked" all of society's thinking as capitalist propaganda, it followed that nothing in capitalist society could be believed and all knowledge that emerged from it had to be destroyed. Freudian psychology held that individuals were all the prisoners of their unconscious, and that what appeared to be the exercise of reason was actually the working out of psychopathology. Thus Darwin, Marx and Freud all undermined the idea of humans as free and rational beings.[20]

Indeed, reason didn't just die but was turned on its head. As the philosopher Alain Finkielkraut has observed, the thinkers of the counter-Enlightenment believed that the sleep of individual reason produced not obscurantism but a form of *collective* reason. In their hatred of modernity and their desire to restore man to his "proper" place in the organically harmonious universe, they discovered his unconscious. And so they founded the sciences of the unconscious, which revealed how culture had gripped and corrupted the human mind. The Enlightenment thinkers who had extolled reason and its cultural artifacts were then cast as hidebound ignoramuses. Thus the irrational became the rational, and vice versa.[21]

For much of the twentieth century, European philosophy was dominated by anti-intellectualism and subjective, intuitive ideas that turned reason upside down. The most elevated intellectual circles created philosophical superstructures as rarified as they were ridiculous. There was little distinction, wrote Soloveitchik, between the mysticism of the medieval German theologian Meister Eckhardt and contemporary emotionalism dressed up as philosophy.[22] The French philosopher Henri Bergson and the American psychologist/philosopher William James rejected the concept of objective reality, which they labeled essentially irrational. Bergson sought to replace the natural sciences with biological myths. Philosophical irrationalism, wrote Georg Lukács (ironically a Marxist, given the role of Marx in undermining human rationality), blurred the boundaries between epistemology, or the theory of knowledge, and psychology, turning knowledge and ethics into subjective psychological problems.[23] Twentieth-century philosophy, in other words, had experienced a collective nervous breakdown.

A DEMORALIZED INTELLIGENTSIA
TURNS AGAINST REASON AND MODERNITY

Into this crisis of modern thought erupted the seismic shocks of two terrible world wars and the Nazi Holocaust. The First World War did not merely remake the map of the world and alter the course of global politics, but within Europe delivered a body blow to religious belief along with trust in authority and faith in human progress. The subsequent experience of fascism, Nazism and the Holocaust gave rise to an even more profound loss of optimism in man's innate goodness and faith in the power of reason. After all, had not prewar Germany been considered the natural home of enlightened learning? Had not the architects of the Jewish genocide dispatched their victims to the gas chambers to the accompaniment of Mozart played by string quartets?

This deep demoralization made the West vulnerable to ideologies derived from a revolutionary cocktail of cultural Marxism and nihilism, which themselves drew deeply upon the antirational, antimodern thinking of the German Romantic movement. A group of theorists that gained immense influence after the Second World War was known as the Frankfurt School, including Theodor Adorno, Max Horkheimer, Erich Fromm and Herbert Marcuse, whose roots were in Marxism but whose thinking owed more to nihilism.

Marcuse, a refugee from Nazi Germany, used the freedom given to him at the universities of Columbia, Harvard, Brandeis and California to proclaim that freedom was actually tyranny in the form of "repressive tolerance." Freedom of expression was not actually toler-ance at all, but oppression, because it enabled people to articulate the wrong sort of views. "Liberating" tolerance apparently meant tolerat-ing all left-wing thinking and not tolerating anything else.[24]

In their book *The Authoritarian Personality*,[25] Adorno and his col-leagues vilified bourgeois culture by arguing that conforming to middle-class norms suggested a predisposition to fascism. The pointers to an antidemocratic personality were obedience and respect for authority. Conservatism was identified with fascism, which in turn was identified as a personal pathology. Anyone not belonging to the self-constituted cultural vanguard of left-wing pol-itics was therefore to be considered psychologically damaged.[26]

In another influential book, *Dialectic of Enlightenment*, Adorno and Horkheimer correctly identified the overreach of Enlighten-ment thinking into rationalist reductionism, but they signally failed to separate out the different strains of thinking that had caused it, particularly through the counter-Enlightenment, and ignored alto-gether the repudiation of religion. They thus effectively blamed the entire Enlightenment project and reason itself for the rise of fascism.[27]

This attack on reason and the Enlightenment by arguments that themselves turned reasoning inside out paved the way for the whole-sale rejection of rationality by postmodernism. Essentially, this was a radical skepticism of truth itself, based on the Marxist concept that whatever held sway was by definition an example of "power" and therefore automatically suspect. Adapting this doctrine to the field of culture, postmodern theorists such as Jacques Derrida, Michel Fou-cault and Jean-François Lyotard maintained that words had no actual meaning other than as a grab for power by the writer or speaker. All thinking was thus labeled a "narrative," on the basis that none of it amounted to any more than a story, or myth, with no claim to objec-tive truth. So all knowledge was worthless. Since there were no objec-tive truths, nothing that was written or said was to be taken seriously.

The flaw in this argument is obvious. For if all knowledge were worthless, why should anyone believe or take seriously a word that Derrida, Foucault or Lyotard ever wrote? Derrida said that texts had no meaning—and wrote so in a text. Fittingly perhaps for theorists whose *raison d'être* was the denial of reason, this logical objection cut no ice at all. The irony that was their stock-in-trade abruptly stopped at their own work.

Postmodernism became orthodoxy among those in the academy who considered themselves to be in the vanguard of progressive thinking, but for whom the inescapable evidence of the horrors of Stalinism had turned Marxist-Leninism into a no-go area. A new way had to be found of undermining the basic tenets of Western society. French intellectuals, believing that modernism led either to discredited Marxist totalitarianism or to loathsome American capitalism, turned for inspiration to those whose opposition to reason and modernity had paved the way to fascism in a previous era. Thus the intellectual icons of postmodernism were Nietzsche and Heidegger, Paul de Man and Georges Bataille—the mystic, occultist libertine who had wanted to fight fascism during the 1930s by using essentially fascist means, saying it was "time to abandon the world of the civilized and its light."[28]

At one time, it was reason, the pursuit of liberty and optimism about progress that had been the lodestars of all who considered themselves to be progressive; now, cynicism about reason and democracy—once the hallmark of reactionary and fascist thinking—became the stock-in-trade of the postmodern left. Foucault believed that reason was a mechanism of oppression, operating through exclusions, constraints and prohibitions; Derrida condemned "logocentrism" or the tyranny of reason; Lyotard argued that there was no such thing as uncoerced rational agreement.[29] In 1960, the German philosopher Hans-Georg Gadamer, a nationalist who had enthusiastically embraced Nazism, argued in *Truth and Reason* that historical understanding lay in the never-ending subjective interchange between the interpreter and the text. This became the defining tenet of postmodernism. "It is not so much our judgments as our prejudices that constitute our being," Gadamer wrote elsewhere, saying he wanted to restore "a positive concept of prejudice that was driven out of our linguistic usage by the French and English Enlightenment."[30]

Nor did the great march backwards to premodernism stop at language. Just like their counter-Enlightenment forebears who were drawn to the primitive and the pagan, the postmodernists believed that going back to the rituals and practices of primitive societies would redeem mankind from the soul-destroying fragmentation of modern life. In 1962, Claude Lévi-Strauss, the anthropologist and founder of the postmodern offshoot called "structuralism," argued that there had been no universal human history and no linear progress, and that the "savage" mind was just as complex as the "modern" mind. Condemning Eurocentrism, he lauded the harmony of tribal peoples and declared that modern societies were to primitive ones as viruses were to higher animals, invading other cultures and forcing them to adapt to their ways.[31]

As Richard Wolin observes, because postmodernists blamed reason and humanism for colonialism and fascism, they replaced tolerance with cultural relativism. When combined with Western self-hatred, cultural relativism resulted in the kind of uncritical Third Worldism that led Foucault to endorse Iran's Islamic Revolution—precisely because it was antimodern, anti-Western and antiliberal.[32]

Postmodernism may seem an egregious example of academic narcissism, but its impact has been huge and profound, and its effects are all around us. Putting it simply, its "deconstruction" of the idea of truth has produced a public discourse built upon a repudiation of objective knowledge and a concomitant openness to the falsehoods of ideology or propaganda.

POSTMODERNISM AND A CULTURE
OF MANDATED MENDACITY

Foucault taught that truth was not disinterested or neutral, but rather an instrument of power, an attempt to conceal biases under a mask of objectivity.[33] In his view, "all knowledge rests upon injustice"; and further, "there is no right, not even in the act of knowing, to truth or a foundation for truth; and the instinct for knowledge is *malicious* (something murderous, opposed to the happiness of mankind)."[34]

The idea that objectivity is dishonest and malicious found its way into British journalism during the 1980s. Suddenly, what cub reporters had learned on day one in journalism school—that journalists should always strive for objectivity and fairness and should tell the truth as they saw it as honestly as they could—was redefined as an attempt to dupe the public. Real integrity was said to lie in practicing a "journalism of attachment," slanting reports in accordance with a prior point of view. If there was no such thing as truth or objectivity, then it was more "authentic" to be openly biased. Fabrications were put forward as representing a "greater truth" than mere factual accounts of what had actually happened. Patently false propaganda claims—by Hamas or Hezbollah, for example—were reported as true, and anyone who pointed out the obvious errors or impossibilities in such claims was told that their counterclaims based on facts were only "a matter of opinion."

The substitution of lies for objective information in the service of the "greater truth" of prior conclusions has taken deep root in those areas of the academy where ideology rules. This is the case even in scientific fields such as climate change, where a whole new branch of postmodernism has been invented, called "post-normal science." Normal science discovers facts and then constructs a theory from those facts. Post-normal science starts with a theory that is politically sensitive, and then makes up the facts to influence opinion in its favor. This practice was revealed in a display of commendable frankness by Mike Hulme, a professor in the school of environmental sciences at the University of East Anglia, founding director of the Tyndall Centre for Climate Change Research, and a guru of manmade global warming theory. In 2007, Hulme confided to the *Guardian*:

> Philosophers and practitioners of science have identified this particular mode of scientific activity as one that occurs where the stakes are high, uncertainties large and decisions urgent, and where values are embedded in the way science is done and spoken. It has been labelled "post-normal" science.... The danger of a "normal" reading of science is that it assumes science can first find truth, then speak truth to power, and that truth-based policy will then follow.... *Self-evidently dangerous climate change will not emerge from a normal scientific process of truth seeking,* although science will gain some insights into the question if it recognises the socially contingent dimensions of a post-normal science. But to proffer such insights, *scientists—and politicians—must trade (normal) truth for influence. If scientists want to remain listened to, to bear influence on policy, they must recognise the social limits of their truth seeking and reveal fully the values and beliefs they bring to their scientific activity.* ... Climate change is too important to be left to scientists—least of all the normal ones.[35] [My emphasis.]

So global warming theory did not seek to establish the truth through evidence. Instead, truth had to be traded for influence. In areas of uncertainty, scientists had to present their beliefs as a basis for policy.

It was a brazen admission that scientific reason had been junked altogether in the name of science, but for the sake of promoting ideological conviction. In other words, science had short-circuited. Where science failed to support an ideology, the overriding imperative of the ideology meant that science had to suspend its very essence as a truth-seeking activity and instead perpetrate fictions.

To support the bogus claim that we face the imminent destruction of the planet from global warming, science has to be reconceptualized as an instrument of propaganda, which is justified by mendacious and obfuscating postmodernist jargon. Thus the leading proponents of "post-normal science," Silvio Funtowicz and Jerry Ravetz, argue that the concept of "quality" should replace "truth" in dealing with issues related to science:

> PNS provides a response to these crises of science and philosophy, by bringing "facts" and "values" into a unified conception of problem-solving in these areas, and by replacing "truth" by "quality" as its core evaluative concept.... Rather than proofs that one side is right and the other wrong, there will be tools displaying to each and to all the legitimate presuppositions and commitments of the parties.[36]

The doctrine of mandated intellectual mendacity also infects global politics, and nowhere does it do more damage than the State of Israel. Professor Edward Said was lionized throughout the intelligentsia as having "told truth to power" with his hugely influential thesis that the West had consistently lied about the East. But as Efraim Karsh and Rory Miller documented in the *Middle East Quarterly* in 2008, it was Said who had *subordinated* truth to power.

Karsh and Miller showed that Said, time after time, had displayed "antipathy for integrity and scholarship" and often sought to "pass off sweeping and groundless assertions as historical fact." For example, he had asserted that "the town of Hebron is essentially an Arab town. There were no Jews in it before 1967." But this statement ignored a long history dating from Biblical days to the 1929 Arab massacre and expulsion of the Jewish population of Hebron. He had claimed that "every kibbutz in Israel is on Arab property that was taken in 1948"; in fact, Zionists established Kibbutz Deganya in 1909 and an additional 110 kibbutzim and 99 moshavim (cooperative villages) by 1944. He had staked his personal, and by extension, national claim to victimhood and dispossession by describing his childhood years in Mandatory Palestine; and yet he had actually grown up in Egypt and made only periodic visits to his family in Jerusalem.[37] And so on.

The revisionist Israeli historian Ilan Pappé, the most famous exponent of the charge that Israel has systematically used ethnic cleansing against the Palestinians—who has influenced countless British students from his current base in the University of Exeter—is brazen about the fact that he doesn't tell the truth. "I admit that my ideology influences my historical writings, but so what? I mean it is the same for everybody," he said in an interview with a Belgian newspaper in 1999. Pappé asserted that "the struggle is about ideology, not about facts. Who knows what facts are? We try to convince as many people as we can that our interpretation of the facts is the correct one, and we do it because of ideological reasons, not because we are truth seekers." The agenda comes before the facts.[38]

Ideology represents the triumph of power over truth. Far from telling truth to power, a dismaying number of people in the contemporary West—on issues from climate change to anti-Zionism, from anti-imperialism to scientific materialism—have allowed truth to become subordinate to the governing power of an idea. Isaiah Berlin lamented that it was with German Romanticism that truth died. The eighteenth century, he said, "saw the destruction of the notion of truth and validity in ethics and politics, not merely objective or absolute truth but subjective and relative truth also—truth and validity as such—with vast and indeed incalculable results."[39]

It was the French Revolution that introduced secular ideology to the Western world. The destruction of freedom and truth that this entails has left a bloody trail across the world. It is a lesson which, despite all the vast and incalculable horrors that ideology has brought in its wake, we have still not managed to learn.

14

THE ATTACK ON WESTERN CIVILIZATION

In the West, the forces of ideology are well on the way to unstitching the fabric of society. With Britain in the lead, and to varying degrees in other Western countries, the precepts that we most prize and take for granted are being turned inside out. To the bewilderment and dismay of many, freedom is giving way to coercion, order to anarchy, progress to obscurantism, modernity to medievalism, tolerance to bigotry, rationality to dogma, truth to lies.

This is not widely understood because the hijacking of reason has created a fundamental confusion. People assume that to be secular is to be enlightened and to be religious is to be irrational. Since the West keeps religion in a box—if not repudiating religion altogether—it tells itself that it is a culture quintessentially founded on reason. What it fails to grasp is that, as a result of the thinking outlined in previous pages, some of what currently marches under the banner of enlightenment is not reason at all but ideology, which has replaced truth by power.

The objectivity that once allowed us to be sure what we were and what we stood for has been all but eroded. Our culture has been upended by moral and cultural relativism, the doctrine that denies any hierarchy of values—but is doctrinaire in its own enforcement. Faced with an onslaught from an Islamic world that correctly recognizes Western culture as decadent, we no longer know what it is we want to defend. We tell ourselves that we stand for human rights, freedom, democracy, tolerance—and yet we also tell ourselves that we cannot uphold those rights because to prefer one culture over another is racist or xenophobic, even if the culture being so preferred is one's own. So a liberal society by definition cannot defend itself but, in the interests of equality, must apparently accept its own obliteration.

The immediate causes of our confusion are complex. Many are rooted in the profound changes in Western society that occurred after the Second World War. The horrors of Nazism provoked a visceral reaction against authoritarianism and nationalism. There was a strong belief that a new world had to be built free of prejudice and war so as to prevent such monstrous developments from ever happening again. In America, the Nazi atrocities stirred up guilt over the country's racist treatment of its black citizens. Discrimination became a taboo and equality became a fetish. In Britain, there was guilt over the treatment of native peoples under colonialism. Any kind of hierarchical authority came to be viewed as oppressive. Throughout the Western world there was an explosion of consumerism and individualism, fed by a therapy culture which told people that being free meant that constraints on behavior were illegitimate and that emotion trumped all.

All this had rocket fuel put behind it in the 1960s, when the personal wealth generated in suburbia was fused with an all-out assault on the moral codes of its bourgeois denizens. With opposition to the Vietnam War providing the perfect pretext, the forces of cultural Marxism and nihilism seized their moment and started their long march through the institutions to embed the attack on Western norms as the orthodoxy within the political, intellectual and cultural elites.

The result was that reality was reshaped around individuals' needs and desires. With religious authority waning under the assault from materialism, nothing was to be allowed to interfere with an individual's right to instant gratification. Alternative lifestyles became mainstream and the counterculture became the norm. The fundamental institution of society, the family, was profoundly undermined as the crucible of emotional and moral growth.

THE NEGATION OF MORAL AGENCY

When morality became privatized, the questions "what is right" and "what is true" turned into "what is right or true for me." Instead of moral codes acting as chains on people's appetites, "anything goes" became the only song in the secular hymnbook. With external authority rejected, it was feelings rather than reason that became the supreme arbiters of behavior. As taboos fell like ninepins, only religiously based moral judgment was deemed taboo. The harm caused to abandoned spouses or children by adultery or desertion, for example—harm that could be objectively measured in rates of ill health, depression, educational underachievement and so on—was all but ignored, while the damage done to people's feelings by the condemnation of their adultery or desertion was considered unforgiveable. Love was emptied of altruism, sentimentality replaced genuine emotion, and a culture of narcissism took up residence in serial relationships of mutual self-regard.

The sense of the sacred and the concept of intrinsic worth were all but destroyed by the prevailing utilitarianism, which elevated the achievement of the happiness of the greatest possible number to the highest virtue. Outcomes thus came to trump motives. Moral agency was negated when actions were judged only in light of consequences, without regard for intentions. So there was said to be no difference between a doctor administering pain relief to a dying person, which might have the unintentional consequence of hastening that death, and administering a drug or removing feeding and hydration tubes with the intention of ending the life of someone who was *not* dying. All that mattered was that the consequences of all these actions—that a person would die—was the same. As a result, the debate about legalizing euthanasia, or "mercy killing," became reconfigured as a debate about "allowing someone to die." But it wasn't. It was about whether there were circumstances in which the law might agree they could be killed.

Similarly, the issue of embryonic stem cell research was presented by its supporters as entirely about the consequences of such research in curing or preventing appalling afflictions. Leaving to one side whether or not embryonic stem cells were likely to produce such results, the question of whether it was morally justifiable to instrumentalize and destroy early human life in this way was not only dismissed as having no value but painted as a cruel and heartless attempt by religious bigots to thwart the alleviation of human suffering. The moral question was ruled out of court altogether by the superior claim to happiness. In America, the ever-incendiary issue of abortion rests on much the same premise: that the moral question about the intrinsic value of an early human being and the respect that should be afforded it was trumped altogether by the "right" to happiness of the woman whose body was its custodian.

This "right to happiness" has paradoxically undermined the very liberalism that brought it into being. Classical liberalism, the optimistic doctrine that gave us progress, liberty and democracy, was above all a moral project. It held that human society could always better itself by encouraging the good and diminishing the bad. It rested therefore on a very clear understanding that there was a higher cause than self-realization: that there were such things as right and wrong and that the former should be preferred over the latter. But the belief that autonomous individuals had the right to make a subjective judgment about what was right for *them* in pursuit of their unchallengeable entitlement to happiness—which was identical to the entitlement to happiness of every other individual—destroyed that understanding and put liberalism on a trajectory of self-destruction.

Progressive opinion interpreted the concept of liberty at the heart of liberalism to mean license—thus destroying the moral rules that make freedom a virtue within constraints that prevent harm to others. Onto license it then spliced the doctrine of equality. The result was a toxic combination of egalitarianism and permissiveness: a marriage between the old left and the new nihilism.

TOLERANCE SUPPLANTED BY AN INTOLERANT "RIGHTS" AGENDA

On the great cultural battleground issues of family, education and social order, the networks of formal and informal legal and social sanctions that restrain behavior in the interests of others were progressively dismantled. They were supplanted by a culture of "rights," in which groups designating themselves as marginalized or oppressed by the majority demanded equal status and the end of moral "judgmentalism."

Elements of this process were highly commendable. Some groups were indeed the victims of bigotry or discrimination. True prejudice against people on the basis of their race or religion is obnoxious and should be vigorously opposed. And lifting both the legal and the social taboos against homosexuality was in itself an enlightened development. In a liberal society, people's sexuality and what they do in the privacy of their bedrooms should remain a private matter and be of no concern to anyone else.

But what started out as an eminently decent impulse for tolerance turned into something quite different. Core liberal beliefs about the difference between public and private and the need to tolerate deviations from the norm were effectively torn up and replaced by deeply illiberal nostrums. Sexual behavior was hauled out of the private realm and turned into enforceable public "rights." And because of the absolute taboo against hurting people's feelings, the very idea of normative behavior had to be abolished so that no one would feel abnormal.

So behavior with harmful consequences for others or for society in general, such as sexual promiscuity or having children without fathers, was treated as normal. Correspondingly, those who advocated mainstream, normative values such as fidelity, chastity or duty were accused of bigotry because they made those who did not uphold these values feel bad about themselves—now the ultimate sin. Alternative lifestyles became mainstream. The counterculture became the culture.

With personal choice and self-realization trumping everything else, people were taught that authority was bunk. Parents lost their confidence to guide their children when they were battered by "experts" who told them in myriad different ways that the worst thing that could happen to a child was to be "repressed." Teachers, influenced by the "child-centered" doctrines first propounded by the educational theorist John Dewey—which in turn were drawn from Rousseau's theory that the innate creativity of children had to be protected from the corrupting influences of the adult world—no longer saw education as the transmission of a body of knowledge but as a therapeutic exercise in self-realization. Antisocial, harmful or illegal behavior among children, such as drug use or underage sex, was either tolerated or even promoted by the adult world on the basis that children had the right to make their own "informed" judgments, relegating parents and teachers to neutral providers of information.

With the traditional family disintegrating into a series of relationship transit camps, Western children increasingly emerged from backgrounds of emotional, moral and intellectual chaos knowing precious little about the world, unable to think for themselves and unaware of what a moral boundary actually was. Those children themselves grew into parents and teachers who had no idea what they didn't know and what had been lost—or what their own children and pupils in turn needed to know.

The result is a Lewis Carroll world in which the idea of responsibility has been twisted into its very opposite and morality has been turned inside out. The values of marginalized or transgressive groups have been substituted for the values of the majority and their historic culture, leading the intelligentsia to embrace postmodernism, multiculturalism, feminism and gay rights. The crucial point is that, despite the rhetoric of "antidiscrimination," these are all part of a victim culture that does *not* seek to extend tolerance to marginalized groups, but instead to transfer power to such groups in order to destroy the very idea of a normative majority culture rooted in the morality of Christianity and the Hebrew Bible. Just as Rousseau laid down in the eighteenth century, people are being "forced to be free."

MORAL INVERSION AND THE BETRAYAL OF THE VULNERABLE

In Britain, the brand leader in the repudiation of the West's bedrock Christian faith and the deconstruction of its moral precepts, changes have been driven forward that are deeply harmful to vulnerable children and adults, on the spurious grounds that such developments *protect* the most vulnerable. Through a range of policies that provide incentives to lone parents while penalizing married couples, family disintegration was effectively encouraged. This has resulted in mass fatherlessness and misery for children on a widening scale, leading to a range of social ills from crime to educational underachievement to teenage pregnancy, and a replication of dysfunctional behavior from one generation to the next.

In the United States, widespread recognition of the link between welfare and family breakdown led to important welfare reforms, while the British Labor government refused to acknowledge the connection.[1] Similarly, academic research studies long ago demonstrated conclusively that children are ill served by family breakdown, a fact that was eventually widely recognized in the United States, but in Britain such evidence is still routinely ignored or even denied within the intelligentsia. Even the Conservative Party, branded as heartless for highlighting this fact when in government during the 1990s, did not dare restate it for almost a decade.

Official attitudes in Britain towards illegal drugs are now similarly polarized between the belief that their use should be actively discouraged and the belief that such use can only be managed rather than reduced. The government has shifted from trying to eradicate unlawful drug use to a strategy of "harm reduction," the implicit logic of which—explicitly backed even by some senior police officers—is the decriminalization of drugs, despite the obvious fact that this would mean millions more young people becoming enslaved to them. Professor David Nutt, the British government's former chief adviser on drugs, claimed absurdly that taking the drug ecstasy is less dangerous than horseback riding. Since the pleasure of riding meant that people were prepared to risk death or brain damage from falling off a horse, he said, the risks from taking ecstasy and other drugs could be seen to be much exaggerated in comparison.[2] Yet as the UK's leading expert on ecstasy, Professor Andy Parrott of Swansea University, has written, the drug causes intensely serious harm including depression and aggression and, in the longer term, damage to the cognitive part of the brain and to the immune system.[3]

Riding horses is not inherently harmful. Taking drugs is. Riding horses is not addictive. Taking drugs is. Most people who ride horses do not come to any harm. The only reason there are not many more deaths from ecstasy is that, unlike horseback riding, it is illegal. The comparison was clearly ridiculous. So how can experts such as Professor Nutt possibly make such absurd claims?

At least part of the answer surely lies in profound cultural changes that for many have undermined respect for absolute rules constraining how people behave. The assault on moral codes and the authority that underpins them has led to the enshrining of radical individualism and autonomy as the supreme virtues. The pursuit of personal gratification drives all before it. Concepts such as truth and justice have been stood on their heads, with the result that irrationality and perversity are now conspicuous in public life.

For example, as the unchallengeable orthodoxy in Britain today, human rights law has institutionalized injustice and led people to think they are living in a world that has taken leave of its senses. Courts allow criminals to roam the streets, while their victims often may be arrested if they try to defend themselves. Teachers attempting to impose discipline in the classroom find themselves handicapped by fear that if they so much as lay a restraining hand on a pupil they will be accused of breaching the child's human rights. Illegal immigrants are given welfare benefits, and terrorist suspects who are held to pose a mortal danger to Britain cannot be deported to any country where there is a possibility that *their* human rights may not be protected.

The perversity extends much further than absurd or self-destructive policy initiatives, into the province of thought itself. In Britain and America, dominant ways of thinking have simply reversed the notions of right and wrong, normal and abnormal, victim and victimizer, truth and lies. Political correctness, which grips Western culture by the throat, ordains that any self-designated "victim" group, a definition that broadly includes all minorities and women, can never do harm, while those with power, who by definition are "victimizers"—white people, Christians, heterosexuals, men—can never do good. This has resulted in an inversion of justice, in discrimination against the mainstream, and in a negation of truth itself. In Britain, an elderly evangelical preacher, Harry Hammond, was convicted of a public order offense after he held up a poster calling for an end to homosexuality, lesbianism and immorality. Although he had been the *victim* of a physical attack when a crowd poured soil and water over him, he alone was prosecuted.[4]

Truth and biological reality took a direct hit in 2004 with the Gender Recognition Act, which was passed to conform to a ruling by the European Court of Human Rights. This ruling laid down that a transsexual had the right to claim that his or her gender at birth was whatever he or she now deemed it to be. The act gave transsexuals the right to a birth certificate that does not record the actual gender into which they were born, but states instead that they were born in the gender that they now choose to be. While the plight of transsexual identity obviously deserves sympathy, this means that such birth certificates—the most basic guarantee that we are who we say we are—would be a lie. Someone who was born a man, married as a man and fathered children as a man may have a birth certificate, if he so chooses, that says he was born a female.[5]

This coercion of "virtue"—at least as defined by self-styled progressives—has been achieved through a process immortalized by the late U.S. senator Daniel Patrick Moynihan as "defining deviancy down."[6] What was once considered transgressive has now become normal and even mandatory. Anyone who disapproves of elective single-motherhood or the gay rights agenda, for example, is demonized as a bigot. If it were simply a matter of removing prejudice and discrimination, as is claimed, no decent person could object. But it is not. The real agenda has been to use sexuality as a battering ram against the fundamental tenets of Western culture in order to destroy it and replace it with a new type of society altogether.

THE POST-FAMILY, POST-MORAL, POST-NATION UTOPIA

In her book *Sexual Politics*, the feminist Kate Millett wrote in 1977 that the enormous change involved in a sexual revolution was "a matter of altered consciousness, the exposure and elimination of social and psychological realities underlining political and cultural structures. We are speaking, then, of a cultural revolution."[7] Even more dramatically, the gay liberation movement was all about destroying the normative role of the heterosexual family and the sexual and moral norms for which the family was the crucible. In 1979, the Gay Liberation Front manifesto declared: "We must aim at the abolition of the family," which was founded upon the "archaic and irrational teachings" of Christianity.[8]

The common aim of both sexual and gay liberationists was to create a relationship free-for-all in which every kind of sexual union would have the same value as every other. It was indeed to be a cultural revolution. One of the ways this has been achieved has been through the indoctrination of the young. Teachers piously invoke the doctrines of individual autonomy and choice to justify their refusal to teach children that sexual continence and marriage are better or more moral than the alternatives, but they have had no such reservations about bombarding children with sex education materials that proselytize for sexual freedom, abortion and the normalcy of same-sex relationships.

Behind this indoctrination lies a clear agenda of destroying Western sexual morality and the traditional family. The Sex Information and Education Council of the United States, which was set up in 1964 to deliver sex education in schools, supported ideas such as merging or reversing sex roles, liberating children from their parents and abolishing the traditional family.[9] Dr. Brock Chisholm, the first director of the World Health Organization, which has promoted global family and sex education programs, believed that the most persistent barrier to civilized life was the concept of "right and wrong." Children had to be freed from national, religious and other cultural "prejudices" forced on them by parents and religious authorities. Dr. Chisholm saw parents as dictators and suppressors of children's better nature, and believed that sex education should be introduced from the age of nine, eliminating "the ways of elders—by force if necessary."[10]

At the same time as Judeo-Christian values were being attacked by moral relativism, subjective thinking was undermining the very idea of Western culture. With hierarchies of values now taboo and "antiracism" a dominant preoccupation in postsegregation America and postcolonial Britain, multiculturalism and transnationalism became the progressive orthodoxies. The nation was seen as the cause of all the world's ills. Nations caused nationalism; nationalism caused prejudice and war and suffering. Therefore the way to avoid these things was to transfer legitimacy from individual nations to supranational institutions, such as the United Nations, the European Union and the International Criminal Court. The fact that this was an attack on democracy—the ability of a country to govern itself in accordance with the expressed wishes of its own population—barely registered in the stampede for the transnational utopia.

The very idea of a majoritarian culture, intrinsic to the identity of the nation, was now deemed to be racist. The only legitimate society was multicultural. This did *not* mean tolerating all cultures; it meant instead *not* tolerating the majority one. Multiculturalism decreed that all minorities should have equal value to the majority, which therefore could no longer assert the dominant position of its own values. This was a suicidal creed for liberalism, since it became impermissible to assert liberal values such as freedom of speech, for example, or equality for women in the face of minorities claiming their right not to be offended or the right to force girls into marriage.

Multiculturalism also took a sledgehammer to the idea of truth. Since it embodied the Marxist formulation that the powerful could never do anything right and the powerless could never do anything wrong, it followed that Arabs and Muslims could not be held responsible for their terrorism, which must instead be the fault of their Western victims. (On the plight of the Arab and Muslim victims of this terrorism, Western multiculturalists were silent.) So America had it coming on 9/11, and Israel was responsible for its own children being blown to bits in cafes and for the rocket attacks from Gaza. After the murder in the Netherlands of the radical filmmaker Theo van Gogh as the result of his insulting Islam, the organization Index on Censorship effectively blamed him for his own death on the grounds that he had made a career out of insulting various groups. It was left to the gay rights activist Peter Tatchell to identify the fifth column working to undermine civilized values. "In this current epoch of post-modernism and live-and-let-live multiculturalism, moral relativism is gaining ground," he said. Tatchell called the article by Index on Censorship "one more instance of this relativism. Liberal humanitarian values are under threat. Much of this threat comes not from the far Right, but from the Left's moral equivocation and compromises."[11]

FORWARD INTO THE PAST WITH THE NEW AGE

Under the creed of multiculturalism, Third World cultures were viewed as not merely equal to the West but superior by virtue of the fact that they were less advanced. This way of thinking was promoted by the United Nations Educational, Scientific and Cultural Organization, founded in the wake of the Second World War to protect for all "the unrestricted pursuit of objective truth" and "the free exchange of ideas and knowledge." But as Alain Finkielkraut has pointed out, what began as a critique of fanaticism turned into a critique of Enlightenment thinking about the universal values of civilization.

It was back to Rousseau's "noble savage," fueled by anthropologists' claims about the practices of primitive societies. Calling them primitive or backward was held to be a form of prejudice; the idea that mankind had progressed from primitive to enlightened was held to be colonialist bigotry. According to a UNESCO report written by Claude Lévi-Strauss in 1951, this was "ethnocentrism." So at the very moment that UNESCO promised to open a new chapter in human history, it was saying that Western enlightenment was as bad as Nazism. "Prejudice was to be destroyed," writes Finkielkraut, "but to do this it was necessary, not to open others to reason but rather to open oneself to the reason of others." Obscurantism was redefined: rather than the absence of Enlightenment values, it was the "blind rejection of what is not us." The barbarian was not the opposite of the civilized man, but "the man who believes there is such a thing as barbarism."[12]

So once again the values of the Enlightenment went into reverse under the banner of progressive thought. Instead, it was the premodern, the primitive and the pagan whose values were to be extolled. The most influential sociologists of the 1960s combined these anthropological theories with Marxism to produce the astounding insight that primitive societies were in the vanguard of progress. Marxist-inspired feminism, in particular, held that primitive patriarchal societies had upset humanity's balanced communion with nature by destroying the matriarchal societies that had preceded them.

Like Engels, who promoted the idea of patriarchal oppression, feminists drew upon the theory of nineteenth-century anthropologists such as Johann Jacob Bachofen that most prehistorical societies had been matriarchal and dominated by a mother-goddess figure— and had started out promiscuous and then passed through many stages before arriving at monogamy, the state that embodied an illegitimate shift of power from women to men. These ideas were seized upon by feminists such as Marilyn French, who in her 1985 book, *Beyond Power: Men, Women and Morals*, asserted that women once presided over a world of compassionate, moon-worshipping matriarchs. This became the orthodoxy.

It was total rubbish, however. Bachofen—whose theories became grist for the Nazis' pagan mill—was wrong. As Bronislaw Malinowski scathingly explained, such matriarchal societies had never existed; these false theories had been used to misrepresent the facts of sexual organization and undermine the traditional family. Savages had been made "pawns and props" in a false picture.[13]

Nevertheless, the false theories of matriarchy played into the explosion of irrational ideas that united the New Left and the New Age around the issues of feminism, paganism, ecology and the occult, in a virtual rerun of the thinking that had led from the organic nature-worship of German Romanticism to Nazi pagan mythology. Largely because of their association with Nazism and fascism, environmental and ecological ideas had fallen into disfavor in left-wing circles after World War II. But during the 1960s, the growth of consumer society generated enough materialist guilt to fixate on an appropriate capitalist scapegoat. The scapegoat was duly provided by two seminal books: Rachel Carson's *Silent Spring* in 1962, which claimed that pesticides and other forms of pollution were getting into the food chain and killing off species, and Paul Ehrlich's *The Population Bomb* in 1968, another apocalyptic prophecy of punishment for inherently destructive humanity.[14]

In the late 1960s, American anarchists and Marxists took up ecological ideas as part of their critique of Western "alienation." In particular, Herbert Marcuse fused Marxism with environmental concerns, arguing that since efforts to dominate nature had led to political enslavement, humanity had to reconcile itself with nature. As the philosopher Michael Zimmerman has written, Marcuse saw the possibility not only of resistance but of a new beginning in the counterculture, with its revolutionary music, consciousness expansion, sexual libertarianism, celebration of previously marginalized peoples and lifestyles, universal brotherhood, anarchic individualism and ecological concerns. "His leftist counter-culturalism led some to conceive of nature as a new dimension of the class struggle."[15]

Two other books, in 1970 and 1971, marked the fusion of ecological concerns with the New Age. Ivan Illich's *Deschooling Society* was saturated with predictions of the coming global catastrophe caused by pollution, while Charles Reich's *The Greening of America* addressed issues such as pollution and environmental degradation with Marcusian arguments that work was artificial and democracy a fraud. Ecology provided left-wing revolutionaries with a conveniently radical and anti-Western cause that enabled them to hide their blushes over the collapse of the class struggle. It was none other than the founder of Greenpeace, Dr. Patrick Moore, who stated that after the failure of world communism, neo-Marxists used green language to cloak agendas that had more to do with anticapitalism and antiglobalization than with the science of ecology.[16]

Similarly, feminism merged with deep ecology around myths of the earth-goddess and the conviction that the enslavement of women was an integral element of the domination of nature by men. An influential text was *The Great Cosmic Mother* by the feminist pagans Monica Sjöö and Barbara Mor, which stated that "in the beginning was a very female sea, a 'womb-like' planetary ocean full of parthenogenic life forms which eventually result in a microcosmic egg on land. By contrast the penis, 'a mechanical device for land reproduction' emerged a mere 200 million years ago into a world in which the male was essentially secondary and drone-like in comparison with female capacities."[17]

Witchcraft rituals were said to provide a haven from the evils of a patriarchal society deeply influenced by Christianity, which had devalued and dominated women and nature. Vivienne Crowley, the English high priestess of Wicca, the religion of witchcraft, has written that from the 1970s onwards Wicca was given a strong boost by the environmental movement. As an example, she cited a founder of the Dragon organization, which was established to practice "eco-magic," meaning "rituals and spells to oppose road-building programs and other projects with negative environmental impact." While studying philosophy and literature at the University of Essex, he had gotten involved in environmental campaigning, which led him to paganism and thence to witchcraft.[18] Thus the fruits of reason as provided by a British university education.

What all these ideas had in common, apart from their nihilistic and anti-Western agendas, was a profound and spectacular irrationality. God was dead, apparently; and yet secular progressives were seeking spiritual expression by going backwards in time to the paganism that had preceded the Hebrew Bible and Christianity— texts which they called reactionary. The pantheism or nature-worship that had characterized the most regressive movements of thought since the Enlightenment now resurfaced in an eruption of primitivism, which purported to be at the cutting edge of radical thought.

Deep ecology, as Michael Zimmerman has written, was a variety of counterculture that opposed modernity in the form of urbanization, technology and ecological destruction—but was happy to make full use of the freedom that modernity also offered. It concocted a "mix of occultism, post-modern science, irrationalism, millennial fervour, utopian aspirations and valuable insights." It had its own pseudoreligious dogma, the "Gaia hypothesis," thus named by the earth scientist James Lovelock, a fellow of the Royal Society and environmental guru, after the ancient goddess of the earth, to symbolize his theory that the earth is a single self-regulating organism that sustains life on its own. Psychotropic drugs were used to trigger an ecstatic, mystical sense of interrelatedness with the "living" universe. The personal transformation deemed necessary to bring about cultural change, wrote Zimmerman, led to the widespread charlatanism of esoteric studies, meditation, Eastern religions, body work, yoga, holistic health, New Age science, alternative psychotherapies, neoprimitivism and paganism.[19]

The ecological savant and physicist Fritjof Capra held that "anomistic, militaristic, mechanistic, patriarchal and nationalistic" modernity was being transformed by the "spiritual, human potential, feminist and environmental movements," which were creating the "social and perceptual context" for a new politics.[20] His own personal transfiguration came when he was sitting by the ocean one summer afternoon and suddenly became aware of his whole environment as a "giant cosmic dance." Capra recalled, "I 'saw' cascades of energy coming down from outer space, in which particles were created and destroyed in rhythmic pulses." And he *knew* this was the dance of the Hindu god Shiva.[21]

THE HUMAN RACE BECOMES ENEMY NUMBER ONE

All this deep green irrationality invites ridicule, but it also has a darker side. It targets the one creature in all of nature whose distinguishing characteristic is reason: man himself. Deep ecology—like its less extreme manifestation, environmentalism—is founded on the premise that the only thing wrong with the planet is the human race. The earth is important and has value; mankind merely corrupts and destroys it. That is why ecologists had so much in common with Nazism, with *its* hostility to modernity, reason and progress.

The antihuman agenda of ecology was spelled out clearly by Edward Goldsmith, founder of *The Ecologist*, who wrote in the green manifesto *The Way: An Ecological World View* that ecology was a religion that would displace science and halt human progress. The most desirable type of human organization, he stated, was "temporary settlements of nomads" because they had "the smallest impact on the environment." He rejected modernism because it was closely associated with "the paradigm of science" and the assumption that progress was achievable and desirable. Goldsmith saw progress as bad because it disrupted the evolution of the planet. "Human evolution, or progress, is the very negation of evolution, or the Gaian process, and is best referred to as anti-evolution," he wrote. In his view, "it is the paradigm of science itself that must be abandoned, and hence the world view of modernism which it faithfully reflects; and they must be replaced by the world view of ecology. . . . It must, in fact, involve a change akin to a religious conversion."[22]

Whereas the religions of Judaism and Christianity place man at the center of Creation, the religion of ecology seeks to boot man out of Eden. Fueled by rage at man's pre-eminence in the world, it aims to knock him off that perch by undoing civilization. Environmentalists, as Christopher Manes puts it, believe that "by exposing the myths of civilization, its unwarranted anthropocentrism, its privileging of technological progress, its claims of hegemony over the natural world, radical environmentalism may have begun the unmaking of the civilisation complex and its institutional power."[23]

Thus John Davis, the editor of *Earth First!*, advocated a return to the hunter-gatherer lifestyles of fifteen thousand years ago. Lynton Caldwell, a sociologist, believed the environmental movement represented a second Copernican revolution: the first required us to give up the idea that the earth was at the center of the universe, and in the second we were asked to give up the idea that man was superior to the rest of Creation.[24]

Rupert Sheldrake, the former biochemist who now writes on parapsychology, attacked the Judeo-Christian tradition for having "always emphasised the supremacy of the male God" in contrast to mother earth and called for a "new renaissance" in which we "acknowledge the animistic traditions of our ancestors."[25] And to Carl Sagan, the purpose of science was to dethrone man from a position of any significance whatever. The advance of science, he said, was a "series of Great Demotions, downlifting experiences, demonstrations of our apparent insignificance."[26] One reviewer commented that the title of Sagan's final bestseller, *Pale Blue Dot*, was itself "a reminder that the Earth, rightly understood, is merely a 'dim and tiny planet in an undistinguished sector of an obscure spiral arm' of the equally fourth-rate Milky Way."[27]

This desire to downgrade the human race, and even run it out of Creation altogether, has united environmentalism with population control, the movement that went underground after being discredited by fascism. The irrational nature of this deeply inhuman movement was dramatized by none other than the husband of Queen Elizabeth II, Prince Philip, Duke of Edinburgh, who in 1988 made this notable remark: "In the event that I am reincarnated, I would like to return as a deadly virus, in order to contribute something to solve overpopulation."[28] Clearly he felt strongly about this, for he had written the same thing in 1986:

I just wonder what it would be like to be reincarnated in an animal whose species had been so reduced in numbers that it was in danger of extinction. What would be its feelings toward the human species whose population explosion had denied it somewhere to exist.... I must confess that I am tempted to ask for reincarnation as a particularly deadly virus.[29]

And tipping his hat to paganism, he told the North American Conference on Religion and Ecology in 1990:

It is now apparent that the ecological pragmatism of the so-called pagan religions, such as that of the American Indians, the Polynesians, and the Australian Aborigines, was a great deal more realistic in terms of conservation ethics than the more intellectual monotheistic philosophies of the revealed religions.[30]

Prince Philip's pagan leanings, not to mention his apparent predilection for both reincarnation and extermination, might be dismissed as merely another example of the limitless eccentricities of the British royal family (the Prince of Wales was famously reported to talk to his plants). This would be an error. The obsession with population control has long been central to the environmental movement even though—ever since Thomas Malthus started this hare running in the nineteenth century—the dire predictions of catastrophic global overpopulation have proved false over and over again.

In 1968, in *The Population Bomb*, Paul Ehrlich predicted apocalypse if the Third World's population was not curbed. "The battle to feed humanity is over. In the course of the 1970s the world will experience starvation of tragic proportions—hundreds of millions of people will starve to death," he claimed, adding that in the United States alone, famine would kill 65 million people in "a great die-off."[31]

Despite the fact that this scenario patently did not occur, the apocalypse continued to be predicted as imminent. In its 1972 report *The Limits of Growth*, the global think tank the Club of Rome predicted that the exhaustion of natural resources would prevent economic growth from continuing indefinitely. By 1993, it was proposing a kind of fascistic, antihuman new world order, declaring in *The First Global Revolution* that a "new type of world society" was needed to fill the vacuum after the expiry of communism and fascism. A common adversary was needed to unite humanity—and incoherent and contradictory as this may seem, humanity was apparently to be united by attacking itself:

> The common enemy of humanity is man.... In searching for a new enemy to unite us, we came up with the idea that pollution, the threat of global warming, water shortages, famine and the like would fit the bill. All these dangers are caused by human intervention, and it is only through changed attitudes and behaviour that they can be overcome. The real enemy then, is humanity itself.... Sacrilegious though this may sound, democracy is no longer well suited for the tasks ahead.[32]

In Britain, the main organization making the links between population, immigration and climate change is the Optimum Population Trust (OPT). The force behind this group is Sir Jonathon Porritt, head of the British government's Sustainable Development Commission. The OPT argues that population growth is a main driver of greenhouse gas emissions and accordingly has suggested that the UK population must be cut by half if the country wants to feed itself sustainably. "Each person in Britain has far more impact on the environment than those in developing countries so cutting our population is one way to reduce that impact," Porritt said.[33] But like much of the West, Britain's birthrate is currently *below* the replacement level. Far from running out of food for hungry mouths, Britain is not producing enough mouths to feed.

Nor was it clear quite how Porritt proposed to reduce Britain's population by half. While demurring at the idea that China's draconian one-child policy could be applied in the UK, he nevertheless spoke approvingly of the fact that since 1979 China had averted 400 million births, calling it "the biggest CO₂ abatement since Kyoto came into force." He failed to mention the corresponding policy of forced abortion or that, until 2002, Chinese women were given no choice about contraceptive method, with the result that 37 percent of married Chinese women have been sterilized.[34]

Hand in hand with the desire to reduce the world's population has come the representation of humanity as some kind of disease. Prince Philip was not alone: environmentalists have compared the human race to an infectious disease;[35] a "super-malignancy on the face of the planet";[36] and "the AIDS of the earth."[37] Sir Crispin Tickell, a former British diplomat and a patron of the Optimum Population Trust, described "constantly increasing growth" in human population as "the doctrine of the cancer cell."[38]

The belief central to environmentalism that mankind must no longer be allowed to dominate the planet has had further inevitable consequences. As the value of human beings has gone down, that of animals has gone up. Prioritizing humans over animals has been labeled "speciesism," which according to the prominent anti-speciesist and bioethicist Professor Peter Singer is as bad as sexism or racism. From this moral equivalence between animals and humans, it follows that if animals can be killed for reasons of utility, so too can human beings. Thus according to the dramatist and animal rights activist Carla Lane, "If you harm an animal you might as well harm a child. There's no difference whatsoever."[39] For Ingrid Newkirk, director of People for the Ethical Treatment of Animals, "When it comes to feelings, a rat is a pig is a dog is a boy,"[40] and the millions who died in the Nazi Holocaust were equivalent to broiler chickens dying in slaughterhouses.[41] Yet while animals apparently deserve our protection, people apparently do not. Newkirk said, "I don't believe that human beings have 'the right to life.' . . . This 'right to human life' I believe is another perversion."[42]

Singer invested such indifference or even antagonism towards human life with the trappings of an antireligion of inhumanity, saying, "Once the religious mumbo jumbo surrounding the term 'human' has been stripped away ... we will not regard as sacrosanct the life of each and every member of our species, no matter how limited its capacity for intelligent or even conscious life may be." It would then be much easier to take the life not only of the unborn but of those with a "low quality of life," including new-born children who did not have certain capacities for "intelligent or even conscious life."[43]

Environmentalism, let us remind ourselves, is considered fashionably progressive in the West. A proper concern to avoid pollution and steward the earth's resources in a responsible manner is indeed a forward-looking, ethical position. Yet the modern environmental movement has become associated—just as it was in Nazi Germany—with indifference or contempt for humanity. It draws upon the most reactionary and regressive trains of thought since the Enlightenment. Those who express skepticism at its apocalyptic predictions of climate catastrophe are called antiscientific "flat-earthers," yet it is environmentalists who are consumed by irrationality and a determination to stop science in its tracks, as well as disdain for the bearer of reason, mankind.

Indeed, the history of thought since the Enlightenment might be summed up as man first dethroning God in favor of reason, then dethroning reason in favor of man, and finally dethroning man himself. This was done by replacing objective knowledge with ideology, which grew out of the belief that man was all-powerful and could reshape the world in whatever image he chose. Paradoxically, this belief fed into the idea that history was merely the inexorable procession of subjective forces—the successive expressions of the collective will, which individuals could not resist. This idea in turn created a permanent sense of determinism and reductionism, the belief that human beings had no control over the course of events, which always boiled down to one single explanation, whether it was expressed through Marxism or materialism or Darwinism.

When expressed through Darwinist genetics, this reductionism was used explicitly to dehumanize mankind. In Richard Dawkins's formulation, "We are survival machines—robot vehicles programmed to preserve the selfish molecules known as genes."[44] A Darwinist determinism contributed no small part to the brutal inhumanities of social systems devoted to the ruthless propagation of one's own and the extermination of others. In *The Descent of Man*, Darwin himself had predicted that in some future period "the civilised races of man will almost certainly exterminate and replace throughout the world the savage races."[45] Anthropology subsequently gave rise to the belief that savage races were equal to the civilized world that had oppressed and slaughtered them; and so in due course, the civilized world came to believe that the savage race to be exterminated and replaced was none other than itself.

THE SANCTIFICATION OF SELF-REGARD

In delivering the message that man is a helpless tool of forces beyond his control, determinism suggested that man had no free will. His behavior was to be explained by social or economic circumstances, or by his genes. Mankind was therefore free of moral responsibility.

Now we are surely starting to get close to explaining why the hyper-rational but also hyper-individualistic and hedonistic West has embraced irrational and patently ludicrous doctrines and beliefs in such large measure. The expression of conscience and spirituality has turned inwards. Instead of the monotheistic codes of ethics, which placed constraints on their behavior, people turned to religions of the self, which gave the individual pretty well a free pass.

Which is why so many were drawn to paganism and to the religions of the East—Confucianism, Taoism, and Shintoism, which made no tiresome moral demands. Rather than improving the lot of fellow human beings, these were essentially concerned with self-realization. Many Westerners who signed up to these religions did not subscribe in any meaningful way to their doctrines but went along with their superficial manifestations, such as yoga, zen or feng shui, in the belief that they were promoting the organic harmony of the universe. They could thus tell themselves that they were being "spiritual" and that meditation was a means to enlightenment. But there was no duty to fulfill—other than to the earth, which in practice meant little besides cycling to work or recycling paper and plastic.

At the same time, they were tapping into doctrines of deep irrationality. Neither the Far Eastern religions nor the worship of nature offers evidence of truth; indeed, they peddle claims about the physical reality of reincarnation, for example, with no evidence at all. They present themselves as noble, beautiful and uplifting ways of life because they create feelings of oneness with nature. Thus they offer an ostensibly desirable lifestyle, but supply no account of the world that is logically consistent and factually verifiable. On the contrary, their emphasis on the unity of experience means a resistance to the very idea of contradiction, upon which reasoned argument—not to mention moral discrimination—is based. As a result, they make a virtue out of *not* knowing and *not* understanding.

Moreover, Eastern practices such as meditation or yoga, which have become popular in the West as an antidote to the pressures of a materialistic society, further erode the capacity for rational and independent thinking. Some of them teach visual techniques that are intended to replace patterns of thought; indeed, raja yoga, which aims to control all thought processes, transmits the thoughts of the teacher into a blanked-out mind. These characteristics of irrationality and mind control made Eastern religious manifestations particularly attractive to totalitarian movements both of the left and of the right. As Nicholas Goodrick-Clarke has shown, Nazism fused German pagan mythology with Norse sagas and myths, while contemporary neo-Nazi cults have further fused Odinism (a form of German neopaganism) with Hindu Tantrism, Aryan mysticism, meditation and yoga.[46]

Such cults turn religion inside out. Take Madonna's "religion" of choice, "Kabbalah." This purports to be drawn from the Jewish mystical tradition of Kabbalah; but it is a travesty. The Kabbalah Centre where this fashionable cult is based doesn't merely trivialize Kabbalah but inverts it. The intention of traditional Kabbalistic meditation is to annihilate the ego in the quest for God. In the Centre's world, however, the spiritual quest is not about God but about the seeker. As Yossi Klein Halevi has pointed out, although the Centre does teach the need to give to others, it also teaches that the motive for such ostensible altruism is selfishness. According to one of the Centre's directors, Yehuda Berg, "We are a species of receivers, as in, 'What's in it for me?' And that's OK. That was the Creator's intent." Students at the Centre accordingly display self-regard dressed up in a simulacrum of moral purpose. "Kabbalah teaches us how to respect the human dignity of another. . . . But it has nothing to do with being a good person," said one student. "It's about not hurting myself. Not because God told me to be nice to others, but because my life becomes better. There's no motivation to be good for its own sake."[47]

This agenda of self-regard is the key to unlocking the mystery that has dogged us from the beginning of this book: how people who profess to be so rational they will have no truck with religion have nevertheless embraced beliefs and attitudes that defy reason. The self-centered happiness agenda links the pagans and occultists and nature-worshippers with their ostensible nemesis, the steely scientific materialists who thunder against *all* spiritual impulses as evidence that people have lost their minds. We have already noted that the sheer terror of allowing God to gain even "a foot in the door" is so overwhelming that it has caused those stern materialists of evolutionary biology to say irrational, unscientific and absurd things about the origins of life and matter. But just why are they so terrified of religion? Why should the apparently risible beliefs of credulous religious folk—those who are not inclined to blow up anyone else, at least—be such a terrible threat to *them*?

The answer was surely displayed on the side of a British bus. In a stunt in 2009 dreamed up by the British Humanist Association and the *Guardian* and backed by Richard Dawkins, eight hundred buses around the country sported for a time the advertising message: "There's probably no God. Now stop worrying and enjoy your life."[48]

What did this gnomic slogan mean? The suggestion that religious believers were miserable when they are often among the most joyous people alive was clearly absurd. And the idea that atheism is the automatic passport to the good life hardly squares with the terrible histories of Stalin, Mao or Pol Pot. No, the giveaway was surely the "stop worrying" part of the message. For what religion might cause people to be "worried" about is moral judgment—the constraints it places on individual behavior and self-gratification. What that bus message was effectively saying was "Do whatever you fancy, and to hell with the effect on anyone else because Biblical morality is a fairy story."

SOFT-CORE ATHEISM

The real threat that religion poses to our hyper-individualistic culture is the ethical constraints that interfere with the right to self-gratification and personal happiness. While the happiness agenda is all about the self, religious morality is about concern for the rest of humanity. It is the ethics of religion that have given us not merely constraints but also respect for life and liberty, which those constraints actually protect. Now, while the rejection of those constraints has led to the rejection of the religion and, at the extreme, to an antihuman agenda, the rights and freedoms that religion also bestows are detached from religion and jealously preserved.

As John Haught so cuttingly observed about "soft-core atheists" such as Richard Dawkins, they are not prepared to face up to the consequences of their own absence of belief. They want atheism to prevail at the least possible expense to the agreeable lives they lead—

which owe their freedoms and concept of human dignity to the very Biblical authority they reject and despise. Haught remarks:

> They would have the God religions—Judaism, Christianity and Islam—simply disappear, after which we should be able to go on enjoying the same lifestyle as before, only without the nuisance of suicide bombers and TV evangelists.... This approach to atheism, of course, is precisely the kind that nauseated Nietzsche and made Camus and Sartre cringe in their Left Bank cafes. Atheism at the least possible expense to the mediocrity of western culture is not atheism at all. It is nothing more than the persistence of life-numbing religiosity in a new guise.[49]

Nietzsche certainly understood that the death of God at the hands of man meant an end to the freedoms bestowed by Biblical "slave morality." Contemporary atheists who are not so "soft-core" but are more intellectually honest also acknowledge that with the destruction of religion inevitably comes the destruction of morality. The evolutionary biologist Daniel Dennett extolled Darwin's "dangerous idea" as a "universal acid," dissolving traditional ideas about both religion and morality.[50]

Peter Singer followed this thinking through to its inevitable and brutally reductionist conclusion. Since God had been killed, man himself could not be far behind. "It can no longer be maintained by anyone but a religious fanatic that man is the special darling of the universe, or that animals were created to provide us with food, or that we have divine authority over them, and divine permission to kill them," Singer wrote.[51] Far from creating a level playing field between species, however, Singer created a new, antihuman hierarchy. While animals should be treated like people, people could be treated worse than animals. In Singer's view, because a week-old baby was not a rational, self-conscious being, "the newborn baby is of less value than the life of a pig, a dog, or a chimpanzee."[52] While the idea that animals could be slaughtered when no longer useful was to be rejected, it appeared that man was not divinely prohibited from killing those fellow human beings whom he deemed to be worthless.

When challenged by this evidence of the potentially murderous consequences of destroying religious belief, Richard Dawkins declared: "Peter Singer is the most moral person I know, and that is an entirely rational point of view."[53]

If it was moral and rational to reject the innate right to life of every human being, then the religious precepts upholding that innate right were to be considered irrational. Such an argument was used by one of the high priests of secularism, the psychology professor Steven Pinker. In 1997, he came close to justifying infanticide by arguing that killing a baby on the day of its birth had been accepted practice in most cultures throughout history and was hard-wired into our genes through evolution. Although he hotly denied that he was justifying such a practice, he left a door open by saying that moral reasoning required people to act as if they had free will even though there was no free will in nature. In other words, we couldn't be blamed for infanticide because we were hard-wired to commit it, even if we pretended we were making moral choices. "A human being is simultaneously a machine and a sentient free agent depending on the purpose of the discussion," he wrote.[54] Thus, having provided a justification for nihilism he then created an opportunistic way of disavowing it.[55]

A decade later, Professor Pinker left himself no such escape route from his disdain for the concept of innate human value. Railing against the 2008 report by the President's Council on Bioethics, which opposed practices such as "therapeutic" cloning, Pinker furiously singled out the concept of human dignity as the barrier to enlightenment and progress. "Dignity," he raged, was a "squishy, subjective notion" with no meaning except as a physiological reaction to some environmental stimulus:

> Dignity is a phenomenon of human perception. Certain signals from the world trigger an attribution in the mind of a perceiver. Just as converging lines in a drawing are a cue for the perception of depth, and differences

in loudness between the two ears cue us to the position of a sound, certain features in another human being trigger ascriptions of worth. These features include signs of composure, cleanliness, maturity, attractiveness, and control of the body. The perception of dignity in turn elicits a response in the perceiver. Just as the smell of baking bread triggers a desire to eat it, and the sight of a baby's face triggers a desire to protect it, the appearance of dignity triggers a desire to esteem and respect the dignified person. This explains why dignity is morally significant: We should not ignore a phenomenon that causes one person to respect the rights and interests of another. But it also explains why dignity is relative, fungible, and often harmful.[56]

In this caricature of scientific reductionism Pinker made no attempt to explain the concept of "worth" and just why this should be triggered by certain features in other people. It was the very idea that human beings could be invested with any quality that was *not* reducible to "the absurd chatter of firing synapses," as the physicist and priest John Polkinghorne once memorably characterized reductionism, which so enraged Pinker.[57] And this transcendent aspect of the sacredness of Creation is the very essence of monotheistic religion.

THE CURIOUSLY SINGULAR TARGET OF UNIVERSALIST AGENDAS

At the very root of all the disparate secular ideologies under discussion throughout this book lies an attack on religion. But what is more remarkable is that, although the named religion that gets it in the neck is Christianity, the religion that surely constitutes the deepest target is Judaism.

It is Judaism, the mother-ship as it were of Christianity, that laid down the moral law that placed constraints on personal behavior in the interests of others, and which forms the very foundation of

Western morality. Although Christianity embedded that law into Western society, it is those tiresome Mosaic codes themselves that are the underlying target of the attack on sexual continence, duty and truth.

The account in Genesis of the world's formation is the target of the environmentalists, who wrongly interpret the "dominion" of mankind over the earth as an example of divine imperialism or colonialism—a hierarchy which must be destroyed by removing man from his position at the pinnacle of Creation and substituting the natural world itself in his place.

It is the Hebrew Bible that provokes Richard Dawkins to hysteria in *The God Delusion*, where he says:

> The God of the Old Testament is arguably the most unpleasant character in all fiction: jealous and proud of it; a petty, unjust, unforgiving, control-freak; a vindictive, bloodthirsty ethnic cleanser; a misogynistic, homophobic, racist, infanticidal, genocidal, filicidal, pestilential, megalomaniacal, sado-masochistic, capriciously malevolent bully.[58]

The untrammeled hatred in Dawkins's description is based on a wildly untrue and unjust reading of the Hebrew Bible as a handbook of genocide, enslavement, world domination and racial exclusivity. Among numerous other gross misrepresentations of both Hebrew scripture and the New Testament, Dawkins writes that "Christians seldom realise that much of the moral consideration for others which is apparently promoted by both the Old and New Testaments was originally intended to apply to a narrowly defined ingroup. 'Love thy neighbour' didn't mean what we now think it means. It meant only 'love another Jew.'"[59]

But this is not so at all. The Hebrew Bible explicitly commands the Jewish people to "love the alien as yourself for you were strangers in Egypt."[60] Dawkins appears to have drawn heavily for his analysis upon an article by one John Hartung, which he warmly commends. But Hartung's twisted hatred of Judaism emerged in another article in which he expressed the view that antisemitism was merely a form of "reactive racism" in response to the (as perceived by him) genocidal behavior of the Jews.[61] Yet Dawkins has treated Hartung, the justifier of Jew-hatred, as an authoritative source on the Bible.

It is also Jews who were the principal targets of the attacks by anti-Americans and anti-imperialists on the "neoconservatives," who were represented as mainly Jews who had formed a conspiracy to subvert American foreign policy in the interests of Israel. They were also accused of working hand in glove with Christian "fundamentalists," who are among the strongest defenders of Israel. The neoconservatives had previously also fallen foul of the left over their foundational attacks on moral and cultural relativism and the libertarian social agenda—a position which, despite the secular personal lifestyle of most of these thinkers, was clearly deeply influenced by the ethical codes of Judaism and found many echoes among scripture-faithful Christians.

What such Christians both implicitly and explicitly acknowledge is that if Judaism were ever to fall, Christianity would itself suffer a terminal blow. Christianity is under direct and unremitting cultural assault from those who want to destroy the bedrock values of Western civilization. The onslaught against Judaism thus also plays a tactical role in the attack on Christianity.

According to Professor Paul Merkley, a historian of religion, Judaism is more vulnerable than Christianity because Israel is vulnerable. Having won a significant part of the Christian world to the cause of defaming Zionism (in particular through the UN Durban Declaration of 2001), the enemies of both Judaism and Christianity need only establish the conviction that the sins of the Zionists follow from Judaism. These enemies are aware that the mainline churches are already well inside this fold. When Israel is no more, says Merkley, then it will be easy to focus on the sins of Christianity. The campaign to position the churches securely on the Arab side of the Middle East impasse, furthermore, leaves Christians hopelessly divided and an easy target for frontal attack.[62]

It is also no accident that the attack on religion by evolutionary atheists is closely bound up with the identification of "fundamentalist" Christians with the administration of President George W. Bush. The sundering of religion from science, with the resulting lurch into overweening "scientism," was in large measure brought about by the perception in the United States among those hostile to religion that Christianity was beginning to put up defenses to protect the body politic against the amoral acid of atheism. According to Merkley, the portrayal of Christians as obscurantist and illiberal has been used to delegitimize Christian activism whenever it appears on the American scene. During the 1970s, American commentators began noting that "out of nowhere" political activists had appeared who were motivated by the desire to bring back Judeo-Christian values. The most conspicuous among these were evangelicals and fundamentalist Christians, whose support helped bring Ronald Reagan to the White House in 1980. As these groups mobilized into a formidable political force, they sought to deepen their understanding of their own faith by studying Hebrew and the history of Israel and the Jews, and so their sympathetic interest in Israel and Judaism grew.[63]

There are many ironies in this situation—not least the fact that, since most American Jews are social liberals, there was hardly a political meeting of minds between these Christians and the American Jewish community, which mostly reacted against the "Christian Zionists" with unbridled hostility. Nevertheless, the rise of this Biblically based political force of social conservatism helps explain the panic among the evolutionary atheists in particular and the left in general about the risk of a challenge to secular individualism from resurgent religion. The battle against Judeo-Christian morality was the major factor in the "culture wars," with Christian evangelicals and

Biblical literalists marching alongside mainly Jewish neoconserva-tives, against the liberal Christian denominations and the massed ranks of the secular left.

The fact that there is a high proportion of Jews on the left, in both Britain and America (not to mention Israel), helps explain the very high representation of Jews in the forefront of the demoniza-tion of Israel *and* the attack on the normative moral values of West-ern civilization from within. The psychopathology at work is beyond the scope of this book; suffice it to say that most of these Jews are secular, deracinated or in some way deeply alienated from the faith of their forefathers. They embody perfectly the thinking of Karl Marx, himself of Jewish origin although brought up as a Lutheran, who declared: "In the final analysis, the emancipation of the Jews is the emancipation of mankind from Judaism."[64]

The division that matters is *not* between Jew and Christian; it is between atheist and religious, ideologues and pragmatists, left-wingers and social conservatives. And the pragmatic, social conser-vative agenda to defend the central values of Western Christian civilization is itself founded on the precepts of Mosaic morality.

This was all illustrated very clearly by Steven Pinker's venomous attack, in the article cited earlier, on a report by opponents of cloning and other biomedical developments. He ascribed this opposition to a "movement to impose a radical political agenda, fed by fervent reli-gious impulses"—and although his charge was mainly directed against Catholics, the arch-villain he singled out was an orthodox Jew, the bioethicist Leon Kass.

Pinker, an atheist who was born a Jew, inveighed against the reflections of Judeo-Christian doctrine in the essays:

> We read passages that assume the divine authorship of the Bible, that accept the literal truth of the miracles narrated in Genesis (such as the notion that the biblical patriarchs lived up to 900 years), that claim that divine revelation is a source of truth, that argue for the existence of an immaterial soul separate from the physiology of the brain, and that

assert that the Old Testament is the only grounds for morality (for example, the article by Kass claims that respect for human life is rooted in Genesis 9:6, in which God instructs the survivors of his Flood in the code of vendetta: "Whoso sheddeth man's blood, by man shall his blood be shed, for in the image of God was man made").

The Judeo-Christian—in some cases, explicitly biblical—arguments found in essay after essay in this volume are quite extraordinary. Yet, aside from two paragraphs in a commentary by Daniel Dennett, the volume contains no critical examination of any of its religious claims. How did the United States, the world's scientific powerhouse, reach a point at which it grapples with the ethical challenges of twenty-first-century biomedicine using Bible stories, Catholic doctrine, and woolly rabbinical allegory?[65]

From this dislike (and ignorant misrepresentation) of the Hebrew Bible and its ethical codes, Pinker seamlessly made the link with politics and the Christian "theocons" who were trying to foist the evils of "human dignity" upon America, along with the equally evil idea that in order to combat problems such as illegitimacy, pornography and abortion, society should "promote conformity to more rigorous moral standards, ones that could be applied to our behavior by an authority larger than ourselves"—a sinister program in which Catholics were joined by socially conservative Jewish and Protestant intellectuals.[66]

As George Steiner has observed, the concept of the Mosaic God is a unique development in human experience. There has been no genuinely comparable notion at any other place or time. It makes "unspeakable demands" of the mind: brain and conscience are demanded to invest belief, obedience and love in "an abstraction more inaccessible than mathematics." This God cannot even be imagined and yet demands that human beings transcend themselves to reach out to him. This, says Steiner, "tore up the human psyche by the roots"—and the break has never healed.[67]

The result has been a unique place for the Jews in the historical pantheon of global demonization. As Paul Berman has put it:

> The unstated assumption is always the same. To wit: the universal system for man's happiness has already arrived (namely, Christianity, or else Enlightenment anti-Christianity; the Westphalian state system, or else the post-modern system of international institutions; racial theory, or else the anti-racist doctrine in a certain interpretation). And the universal system for man's happiness would right now have achieved perfection—were it not for the Jews. The Jews are always standing in the way. The higher one's opinion of oneself, the more one detests the Jews.
>
> But the disdain takes another shape, too, which is cruder, though it follows more or less from the first version. In the cruder version, the Jews are not just regrettable for being retrograde. Much worse: the Jews have done something really terrible. By forming their state and standing by it, they have set out actively to oppose the principle of universal justice and happiness—the principle that decrees that a people like the Jews should not have a state. . . . Israel's struggle puts it at odds with the entire principle of universal justice and happiness, as people imagine it—no matter how they choose to define the principle. Other countries commit relative crimes, which can be measured and compared. But Israel commits an absolute crime. In the end, it is the grand accusation against the Jews, in ever newer versions: the Jews as cosmic enemy of the universal good.[68]

The attack on Western civilization at its most profound level is an attack on the creed that lies at the very foundation of that civilization.

15

REASON
AND THE BIBLE

E very era creates its heroes in its own image. With military prowess no longer viewed in the postnational West as a template of valor and with the defense of personal autonomy held up as the cause that trumps all others, an icon of the age is the lonely man of reason. Atheist crusaders against religion such as Richard Dawkins or Christopher Hitchens cast themselves as courageously confronting a pitiless universe armed with nothing but the sword of science and the shield of intellect, having scorned the religious superstitions that give shelter to the timorous multitudes.[1] These pioneers alone, they would have us believe, have the guts to face up to the bleak reality of our own existential pointlessness, unlike religious believers, who are as cosmically spineless as they are stupid.

What the crusaders for atheism present as an unchallengeable truth is the idea that science and religion repel each other. Reason cannot coexist with religious faith, which is superstitious and thus irrational; faith in turn repudiates science, whose truths it cannot reconcile with its dogma.

This is not, to put it mildly, a universal view. There have always been scientists who are religious believers; and with the exception of scriptural literalists, religion does not have a problem in accommodating science. For scientific atheists, however, religion is an evil that not

317

only cannot coexist with science but must be eradicated by science. In the view of the Nobel laureate and physicist Steven Weinberg, "The world needs to wake up to the long nightmare of religious belief.... [A]nything we scientists can do to weaken the hold of religion should be done, and may in fact be our greatest contribution to civilization."[2]

Scientific materialism is the ideology that seeks to destroy religion by claiming to be able to explain everything about the universe, leaving no role for any other kind of inquiry whatever, in an attempt to reconfigure how the world works. This utopian pretension has a long provenance—indeed, it goes back to the very birth of modern science itself.

Francis Bacon, a statesman-philosopher and one of the fathers of scientific enlightenment, perfectly described how ideology (meaning theology at the time) bends evidence to fit a prior idea. In *Novum Organum*, 1620, he complained that the medieval scientist "did not consult experience, as he should have done for the purpose of framing his decisions and axioms. But having first determined the question according to his will he then resorts to experience and bending her into conformity with his placets, leads her about like a captive in a procession."[3] The reason why Bacon venerated "experience," however, and lamented its manipulation by theology was not to advance knowledge but for "the relief of man's estate." As the philosopher Anthony O'Hear observes, Bacon's thinking embodied the utilitarian philosophy that the aim of science was the alleviation of pain and the pursuit of happiness. Thus, Bacon was proposing a kind of scientific reductionist utopia. In *The New Atlantis*, he envisaged a whole society run by scientists. Living in a kind of priestly community, they would study and interpret nature, using their discoveries to "produce great and marvellous works for the benefit of mankind." But the scientists alone would decide what discoveries should be communicated to the public and what should be done with them. They would define the direction of society and human life—in conscious rejection of ancient wisdom and ideals.[4]

This disturbing vision of a materialist dictatorship was developed into an actual movement in the nineteenth century when Auguste Comte propounded the doctrine of positivism, which purported to replace Christianity in Europe with science, in an attempt to free humanity from the "arbitrary" rule of an absolute sovereign Being. Humanity would be liberated by reason, using the truths uncovered by science to replace the doctrines of unknowable faith.[5] Comte openly presented positivism as a religion, with scientists becoming the new clergy. "I am confident that before the year 1860 I shall be preaching positivism at Notre Dame as the only real and complete religion," he wrote.[6] There was nothing to be feared from it, since it was "the normal regime" and "the final religion." In reality, it was a formula for tyranny: as the priesthood of humanity, positivists would decide what was to be thought, and there would be no deviation.

The positivists' claim to objectivity was also an illusion. Comte posited instead that knowledge had to be based on experience, but this led straight into a trap, since human experience is intrinsically subjective. As his thinking developed, he came to study human evolution more and more from the standpoint of subjective feelings and sentiment, from which he concluded that eventually the mind would free itself from science as well.

Thus "rational" positivism plunged headfirst into deepest irrationality, as Comte eulogized fetishism, or the worship of objects that were invested with spiritual qualities. He felt sympathy for "those primitive men who adored with naive tenderness the tree that gave them its fruit, the star that warmed them with its rays, the animal that provided them with its milk, its fleece and its flesh. I admire the obscure wisdom that is hidden in these childish acts." Accordingly, he envisaged a new kind of spirituality in which regenerate man "feels a need to show his constant gratitude to the unchangeable order on which his whole existence rests."[7]

The Comtean vision of science alone holding the keys to the explanation of all things has contributed to the hubristic claims of contemporary scientific materialists that anything that does not correspond to the rules of scientific explanation is irrational and worthless. But we can also see how it led to the pantheistic worship of natural objects and the attribution of spiritual qualities to nature: the antecedents of modern ecology's nature-fetish and all the pagan trimmings of environmentalism. So at one and the same time, scientific materialism spawned both the dogma of reason *and* the lurch into unreason. That helps explain the curious paradox of Richard Dawkins in one corner inveighing against irrational faith in anything not demonstrated by evidence, and James Lovelock in the other propounding his "Gaia hypothesis" that the earth itself is a living organism—both men nevertheless sharing the highest accolade of British science in being fellows of the Royal Society. Some may think this speaks to a refreshing pluralism in the scientific establishment; others may conclude that it merely displays an unhealthy intellectual hospitality to different varieties of dogma.

What both Darwinism and environmentalism also derive from the vision laid down by Comte and Bacon, who reduced everything to a materialist worldview, is their ruthless subordination of evidence to a prior unchallengeable idea. All are ideologies, and as such they block the path to true enlightenment. Environmentalism uses science to betray science, by putting forward bogus "research" that wrenches the facts about the natural world to support an idea for which there is scant persuasive evidence—that man's activities are altering the climate. Darwinism, meanwhile, is not so much science as materialism applied to biology. The belief that Creation was false did not derive from Darwinism. Darwinism derived from the belief that Creation was false. In trying to fit the natural world to a prior belief, and claiming to be the ultimate explanation of the origin of life, it overreaches and therefore fails to adhere to its own scientific principles.

The positivist thinking behind such over-reach caused the governing ideologies of the twentieth century to rest on ideas that were deemed to be irrefutable even though they were unproveable. As

Karl Popper has argued, Marxist theory of history and Freudian psychoanalysis are not science at all but pseudoscience. Despite their flaws, they all appeared able to explain virtually everything within their fields: once people were initiated into these purportedly verifiable "truths," they saw confirmation everywhere. People who refused to see these verifications were unbelievers.[8]

THE FALSE POLARITY BETWEEN RELIGION AND SCIENCE

The notion that the only rational beliefs are those that can be confirmed by scientific observation, experiment and measurement is yet another self-refuting proposition, since it is a statement that itself cannot be confirmed by scientific observation, experiment and measurement.[9] Although Popper's own "falsifiability" theory is open to serious criticism, his thinking is widely respected among scientists. Yet it was Popper who showed how rationality was undermined by the positivist idea that only verifiable scientific laws could be rational and so there could be no place for religious belief (not to mention concepts such as philosophy or morality, which are unproveable yet anything but irrational). He recognized that saying anything in the realm of metaphysics is meaningless displays a "naive and naturalistic" view of what meaninglessness is. It also makes science meaningless, because the laws of science are not verifiable; they go beyond what is observable and assert much more about the world than people can ever hope to "verify" or "confirm."[10]

This fact has been underpinned in particular by developments in physics, where the more discoveries were made, the more questions they provoked that could not be answered. So scientists have come to believe there are indeed limits to what they can ever hope to understand. The universe may be infinite, but scientific omniscience is not.

In 1927, the great atomic physicist Niels Bohr said in effect that atomic theory could not be a description of anything; it would be destroyed through its own internal contradictions unless it was viewed as a tool of knowledge rather than as knowledge itself.[11] Despite the fact that Bohr's philosophical statements about quantum mechanics were notoriously opaque, his theory has become accepted among scientists—leading to the curious fact that one of the most powerful scientific theories of the modern age is arguably also its least understood theory.

As this and other new theories took physicists into hitherto unimaginable territory, there was a legitimate concern they should be consistent with older and more established theories. Some of the new thinking that resulted genuinely expanded the scope of rigorous science. But it also led to a dangerous intellectual temptation. It is easy to be seduced by counterintuitive ideas just because the structures that result are consistent with each other. It is arguable, for example, that no physicist would ever have accepted the intellectual contortions needed to make quantum electrodynamics work had not consistency been a powerful consideration. Some resulting theories—such as the "multiverse" theory of many different universes, or the "anthropic principle," which seeks to explain the apparent fine-tuning of the universe to support life by means of "observer bias"—appear to be little more than imaginative and sometimes circular suppositions.

In any event, whether these theories were rigorous or fanciful, the fact was that, far from driving religion and science further apart, such insights arising within physics were bringing them closer together.

The "Big Bang" theory, for example, holds that this event was the beginning of "space-time" and that before it there had been neither space nor time. But how could anything have begun if there was no space or time to begin in? The suggestion that the universe was not infinite after all caused the physicist and Nobel laureate Arno Penzias to observe: "The best data we have concerning the Big Bang are exactly what I would have predicted had I nothing to go on but the five books of Moses, the Psalms, the Bible as a whole."[12]

But the problem didn't end there. Big Bang theory immediately came into question from scientists who argued that the universe was indeed infinite. At the University of Oregon, the astronomer James Schombert taught that the universe did not have a beginning at all:

> One thing is clear in our framing of questions such as "How did the Universe get started?" is that the Universe was self-creating. This is not a statement on a "cause" behind the origin of the Universe, nor is it a statement on a lack of purpose or destiny. It is simply a statement that the Universe was emergent, that the actual of the Universe probably derived from an indeterminate sea of potentiality that we call the quantum vacuum, whose properties may always remain beyond our current understanding.[13]

But how is this "clear"? Where is the evidence for it? On what basis is it being proposed other than blind guesswork? If the quantum can never be understood, how can anyone derive any theories from it? And why is this considered more rational than faith in God?

The mathematician David Berlinski has written amusingly and cuttingly about these confusions. He suggests that physicists were so alarmed by the theological implications of the Big Bang that they immediately tried to block off this dangerous line of thought altogether by suggesting that although the universe had a beginning, there was no beginner. Berlinski briskly concludes:

> Quantum cosmology is a branch of mathematical metaphysics. It provides no cause for the emergence of the universe and so does not answer the first cosmological question, and it offers no reason for the existence of the universe, and so does not address the second. If the mystification induced by its modest mathematics were removed from the subject, what remains would not appear appreciably different in kind from various creation myths in which the origin of the universe is attributed to sexual congress between primordial deities.[14]

A number of scientists, however, have accepted that the real lesson of quantum theory is that science alone cannot answer all the questions of the universe. Shahn Majid, a mathematics professor at London University, has written that scientists don't know whether the universe had a beginning or not because they still don't understand the basic notions of space and time—and don't even have a theory to test about this deepest layer of physics. Here, he suggests, science has to enlist the help of philosophy and theology, as well as art and life itself.[15]

Scientific discoveries are themselves leading some scientists to believe in a supernatural dimension. In particular, within the most fundamental building blocks of life, scientists have found information of previously unimagined complexity, and structures whose constituent parts work only because they are connected to other elements in precisely the way they are. These discoveries have led an increasing number of scientists and other thinkers to believe that matter could have arisen only through a governing intelligence.

Sir Roger Penrose, professor of mathematics at Oxford, says that the balance of nature's laws is so perfect and so unlikely to have occurred by chance that an intelligent Creator must have chosen them.[16] The philosopher Anthony Flew progressed from being Britain's most renowned atheist to a religious believer through a "pilgrimage of reason." Partly by rethinking philosophical concepts under the influence of the British philosopher David Conway, he found most crucially that recent discoveries of science made inescapable the conclusion that a divine intelligence was behind Creation. He simply followed where the argument led. What he found particularly compelling was evidence of the fine-tuning of the universe. From this he concluded that the laws governing the universe had been crafted to move it towards the sustenance of life, and that all the arguments seeking to explain this away were hopelessly flawed. He similarly dismissed the arguments seeking to explain away the cosmological discovery that the universe had a beginning, and concluded that where science thus stopped, divinity began.[17]

At a deeper level still, whether or not scientists admit it, there is an impulse within science that is akin to religious faith. It is the belief that there is always more to be known about the world. Stephen Barr, a theoretical particle physicist at the University of Delaware, observed that the search for this knowledge involves an element of faith:

> The scientist has confidence in the intelligibility of the world. He has questions about nature. And he expects—no, more than expects, he is absolutely convinced—that these questions have intelligible answers. The fact that he must seek those answers proves that they are not in sight. The fact that he continues to seek them in spite of all difficulties testifies to his unconquerable conviction that those answers, although not presently in sight, do in fact exist. Truly, the scientist too walks by faith and not by sight.[18]

The idea that religious belief and reason don't go together is contradicted by the innumerable scientists throughout history who have been staunch religious believers, and for whom science has actually served to confirm their faith. Rather than finding religion and science to be incompatible, such scientists believe they merely occupy different spheres of inquiry and reasoning—because these thinkers do not believe that all intellectual inquiry must fit one solitary paradigm.

WHY THE WEST PURSUED SCIENCE WHILE THE REST DID NOT

Far from being in opposition to religion, Western science actually depends on it—and, contrary to much popular assumption, specifically on the Hebrew Bible. There is a widespread belief that the roots of science lie in ancient Greece. For sure, Greek thinking played a significant role in the development of Western civilization, and important medieval Christian and Jewish thinkers sought to reconcile it with their own religious precepts. Yet in certain key respects, it was also inimical to a rational view of the universe. The Greeks—whose universe was an endless cycle of progress and decay, which transformed heavenly bodies into actual gods—explained the natural world by abstract general principles. Socrates thought empirical observation a waste of time, and Plato advised his students to "leave the starry heavens alone."[19]

For the development of science, monotheism was essential. As John Lennox puts it, "At the heart of all science lies the conviction that the universe is orderly."[20] This absolutely fundamental insight came not from the Greeks but thousands of years previously in the Hebrew Bible, with its proposition that the universe was governed by a single God rather than the whims of many gods.

Western science grew from the novel idea that the universe was rational; and that belief was given to us by Genesis, which set out the revolutionary proposition that the universe had a rational Creator. Without such a purposeful intelligence behind it, the universe could not have been rational; and so there would have been no place for reason in the world because there would have been no truths or natural laws for reason to uncover.

Atheism, by contrast, holds that the world comes from a random and therefore irrational source, so that reason is an accidental byproduct.[21] As Phillip Johnson has amusingly put it, to theists the concept of a supernatural mind in whose image we are created is the essential metaphysical basis for their confidence that the cosmos is rational. To a scientific naturalist, by contrast, the cosmos can be understood by a rational mind only if it was not created by a rational mind.[22]

It is *atheism*, therefore, that is innately hostile to reason. And it was religion, not secular thought, that propounded the view that nature was founded on deep rationality. The early Christian thinkers

Anselm of Canterbury and Thomas Aquinas believed that, since God created the universe through divine wisdom and endowed mankind with a reasoning mind, the universe must be supremely rational. Science was motivated from the start by the belief that there were comprehensible laws in nature—which could only have come from a rational Creator.

This is why many scientists from the earliest times onwards have been Christians and Jews. It is why Francis Bacon said that God had provided us with two books, the book of Nature and the Bible, and that to be properly educated one must study both. It is why Isaac Newton believed that the Biblical account of Creation had to be read and understood; why Descartes justified his search for natural laws on the grounds that they must exist because God was perfect and thus "acts in a manner as constant and immutable as possible" except for the rare cases of miracles; why the German astronomer Johannes Kepler believed that the goal of science was to discover within the natural world "the rational order which has been imposed on it by God"; and why Galileo Galilei said that "the laws of nature are written by the hand of God in the language of mathematics."

As C. S. Lewis wrote, "Men became scientific because they expected law in nature, and they expected law in nature because they believed in a lawgiver."[23] The philosopher John Haldane points out the similarities between the religious and scientific approaches:

> Thus science is faith-like in resting upon "creedal" presuppositions, and inasmuch as these relate to the order and intelligibility of the universe they also resemble the content of a theistic conception of the universe as an ordered creation. Furthermore, it seems that the theist carries the scientific impulse further by pressing on with the question of how perceived order is possible, seeking the most fundamental descriptions-cum-explanations of the existence and nature of the universe.[24]

The further point, however, is that it was not religion in general but the Hebrew Bible in particular that gave rise to Western science.

That is because of the revolutionary nature of its propositions about Creation. The Hungarian Benedictine priest Stanley Jaki has shown that in seven great cultures—the Chinese, Hindu, Mayan, Egyptian, Babylonian, Greek and Arabic—the development of science was truncated. All made discoveries that carried human understanding forward—India produced decimal notation, ancient Greece astronomy and geometry, for example—but none was able to keep its scientific discoveries going. Jaki attributes this failure to two critical features that these cultures had in common: a belief in pantheism and a cyclical concept of time. Science could proceed only on the basis that the universe was rational and coherent and thus nature behaved in accordance with unchanging laws. It was therefore impossible under pantheism, which ascribed natural events to the whims and caprices of the spirit world. The other vital factor for science was a linear concept of time, as found in the Bible. This meant history was progressive; every event was significant, and experience could be built upon. Progress was made possible by learning more about the laws of the universe.[25] As for the Eastern religions, these don't posit a creation at all. The universe is eternal and thus without purpose; it is a supreme mystery and therefore not to be understood, and so the path to wisdom is not through reason but through meditation and insight.[26]

Islam is a different matter again. Although it is the third great monotheistic and Abrahamic faith, its concept of reason departs radically from that of the Hebrew Bible and Christianity. It presents Allah not as the creator of a universe that runs according to its own natural laws, but as an active God who intrudes on the world as he deems appropriate. Natural laws are thus deemed blasphemous, for they deny Allah's freedom to act. So Islam does not teach that the universe runs along lines laid down by God at Creation but assumes that the world is sustained by his will on a continuing basis. And insofar as they subscribed to ancient Greek thought, Muslims historically accepted the Greek belief in a closed universe rather than investigating it and trying to prise its secrets open. As Rodney Stark has written, since medieval Islamic scholars progressed no further than Aristotle, they advanced only in certain areas that did not require any general theoretical basis, such as astronomy and medicine.[27]

Christianity embraced reason and logic as guides to religious truth because reason was a supreme gift from God and the means progressively to increase understanding of God and scripture. Augustine held that reason was indispensable to faith: while faith preceded reason "to purify the heart and make it fit to receive and endure the great light of reason," it was reason itself that persuaded us of this, and so reason must also precede faith.[28] Embodied in the great universities founded by the church, faith in the power of reason infused Western culture, stimulating the rise of science. Medieval thinkers believed in finding out what was not already known about God's will. In the thirteenth century, Thomas Aquinas set out logical "proofs" of Christian doctrine in the *Summa Theologica*, arguing that humans had to reason their way to knowledge step by step as they lacked the ability to see into the essence of things.[29]

THE MARRIAGE OF RELIGION AND REASON IN JUDAISM

Both Christianity and Judaism are vulnerable to the charge that reason does not sit easily with revelation. Although thinkers in both faiths have argued down through the centuries that a rational argument can be made for the existence of God, the core of religious belief lies beyond understanding. And without doubt, there have been deep conflicts between modernity and Jewish religious thinking just as there have been with Christianity. The principal difficulty here, however, has been reconciling Judaism to the key characteristic of modernity, the culture of individualism: personal choice over truth, autonomy over authority, self over society. As Britain's chief rabbi Lord Sacks has written, rabbis as various as Samson Raphael

Hirsch, Abraham Isaac Kook and Joseph Soloveitchik struggled to accommodate religion to modernity. Others such as Emanuel Rackman, Eliezer Berkovits and David Hartman sought to accommodate aspects of modernity within orthodox Judaism by emphasizing elements of the religion that promoted individual freedom and equality. Soloveitchik went further and attempted to construct a new philosophy of religion that was independent of science but parallel to it. Embracing modernity led to virtual civil war between different factions in the Jewish world; and some ultra-orthodox sects believed that the only way to preserve Judaism in the face of secularizing modernity was by isolating themselves as far as possible from its influence.[30]

Nevertheless, Christianity—particularly Protestantism—was rather more vulnerable to the attack mounted by secularism against revelation than was its parent religion of Judaism. And that was arguably because of the intrinsic differences between their respective claims to rationality.

Judaism, which underpinned Western rationalism through its assertion of an orderly universe, can lay reasonable claim to being the most rational of all religions. Unlike Christianity, Judaism is all about this world, not the next, and is firmly grounded in man's deeds, in historical memory and in the here and now. It is less concerned with proving God's existence than with asserting that he cares about mankind. As Berkovits has remarked, the foundation of Judaism is not that God *is*, but that he cares about the world. The Hebrew Bible is not a textbook of philosophy or metaphysics, but a record of man's encounter with God. Faith and collective experience are thus indissolubly linked.[31]

At Sinai, the children of Israel are described as *seeing* and *hearing* the revelation of God's commandments. The Biblical account does not purport to show or describe God, but describes a participatory event. So the big question is whether this encounter did actually happen. Those who don't believe God exists say it could not have happened; but Judaism always proceeds on the basis of what the evidence suggests is most likely to have occurred. Berkovits notes that according to the logic of Immanuel Kant himself the nonexistence of God cannot be proved any more than can his existence. And the encounter with God over time was witnessed by the prophets of Israel, men of unimpeachable integrity and courage; more important, the entire Jewish nation experienced this encounter through the Exodus, the revelation at Sinai and the journey through the wilderness. The experience of that sustained encounter was so seismic that it defined the existence of the Jewish people and caused it never to surrender to other cultures despite unparalleled attempts ever since to eradicate it.[32] From this point of view, therefore, the evidence can be said to support the idea that what was claimed to have happened was more likely than not actually to have happened.

In Christianity, as Rodney Stark observes, a commitment to the progressive reasoning of God's will requires believers to accept that the Bible is not only or always to be understood literally;[33] yet nevertheless the central beliefs of Christianity depend on the literal truth of supernatural events for which there is only fragile supporting evidence, if that. Within Judaism, many Biblical miracles are explained as either natural events or metaphorical allusions. In the twelfth century, the great Jewish sage Moses Maimonides wrote his seminal *Guide for the Perplexed* precisely to explain that there was no contradiction between rationalism and the Hebrew Bible. He argued, for example, that the Torah was full of similes that were not to be taken as the literal truth.[34]

Certainly, some miracles cannot be explained through such arguments but remain supernatural phenomena. But the idea that miracles are "against the laws of nature"—and that belief in them must be irrational—is itself undermined by arguments from philosophy and science. The laws of nature are said to be uniform and permit no deviation; but as John Lennox argues, only belief in a Creator provides a satisfactory basis for belief in the uniformity of Creation, since a random universe is a disorderly universe.[35] And if there is a Creator standing outside Creation, it follows that he can tear up his own laws from time to time. If he exists, he cannot be bound by the rules of the natural world since by definition he is outside that natural world. Moreover, the argument that a miracle is a phenomenon whose cause cannot be explained may now be applied to numerous discoveries in physics.[36] In other words, science and religion *both* rest on assumptions that properly belong to a domain beyond material evidence. Rationalism is not bounded by natural events. Science does not have an exclusive claim to reason; religion does not have an exclusive claim to metaphysics. The polarity is false.

This is not an attempt to assert the truths of religion. It is rather to suggest that there is nothing odd about the notion that religion underpins reason, and that certain religious beliefs are not in themselves unreasonable. Those who are resolutely skeptical of the existence of God or who subscribe to the dogma of atheism will remain unconvinced by such arguments. It is of course their privilege to disagree. The purpose of this exposition is not to make the case for the existence of God; it is to demonstrate that Judaism is not a fount of irrationality but stands in fact as the ultimate source of reason in the West.

Indeed, Talmudic exegesis takes reasoning to a highly advanced level in order to reconcile the Torah with the oral Jewish tradition. Moreover, the Bible's enigmatic and poetic text makes little sense if read literally; Genesis is filled with contradictions that defy such a reading. A sophisticated analysis that resolves these contradictions in a convincing way has existed within Jewish tradition since ancient times.

Maimonides was the classic exponent of the idea that metaphysical truths could be grasped only through the exercise of reason. He held that religion was the highest rung of metaphysical knowledge. Human perfection consisted in "the attainment of rational virtues ... the conception of ideas which lead to correct opinions of metaphysical matters."[37] So as Eliezer Berkovits has noted, for Maimonides only someone who had mastered all the disciplines of human knowledge such as logic, mathematics and natural science could attain the knowledge of God. Concentrating the intellect in this way was the highest form of spirituality. Even living according to the law was secondary to the intellectual service of God through contemplation.[38] That is why, even though loving your neighbor and promoting the "repair of the world" are stressed in Judaism as moral imperatives, the very highest calling in Judaism is learning, in order to act with understanding and knowledge.

Nor has there ever been a problem reconciling Judaism with science. As a nonbeliever, Professor Andrew Parker, a zoologist and lead researcher at London's Natural History Museum, was astounded by what he found when he studied the first page of Genesis in detail. For he realized that whoever had written it had set out with uncanny accuracy the precise order of events in the development of the universe, facts which those unknown authors thousands of years ago could not possibly have known. In his book *The Genesis Enigma*, he ponders how this might be explained:

> [T]he Bible has, in its opening page, correctly predicted the history of life on earth, with its series of macro-evolutionary steps, or fits and starts, from the origin of our solar system to the evolution of birds and mammals. We can be certain that the author of this Biblical account would have had no idea of these scientifically established events, covering billions of years—indeed, the final links in this chain have been forged only very recently. The possible explanations for this parallel between the Bible and modern science are clear-cut: either the writer of the creation account of Genesis 1 was directed by divine intervention, or he made a lucky guess.

Parker concludes that the "lucky guess" scenario is incredible; and therefore, "The true account of how we came to exist may have been handed to humans by God."[39]

This would not have surprised the Jewish thinkers of medieval times. Maimonides wrote that conflicts between science and the Bible arose from either a lack of scientific knowledge or a defective understanding of the Bible. Nor did those thinkers have a problem with reconciling evolution with God; the great thirtheenth-century Jewish philosopher Nahmanides wrote that "since the world came into existence, God's blessing did not create something new from nothing; instead the world functions according to its natural pattern."[40]

There was indeed a striking correspondence between these medieval Jewish sages and the conclusions being reached by the physicists, mathematicians and other scientists of today. Maimonides scorned the idea of an anthropomorphic God, and also demolished the argument that belief in God was irrational by stating that since God stood outside the natural world, his existence by definition could not be proved by means belonging *to* the natural world. The reality of our senses, he argued, was dependent upon the world beyond our senses—but the world beyond was not to be grasped by means of our thought processes. It was possible to demonstrate with certainty that the world had a first cause, but impossible to comprehend the nature of this first cause. This was not so much reconciling faith and reason as showing that philosophy and reason were part of faith itself.[41]

The sociologist Peter Berger, like Hegel and Max Weber before him, saw Judaism much more than Christianity as a victory of rationality *and* secularization over paganism. Far from seeing religion as hostile to secularization, Berger argued that the Western religious tradition carried within it the seeds of a secular accommodation with the everyday world. But this had played out differently in Christianity and Judaism. Protestantism divested itself, as much as possible, of the symbolic and mysterious trappings of religion and threw man back upon himself before God—not to break the link between man and religion, but to open man to God's grace. But with *only* this link remaining, once this personal relationship came to seem implausible there was dangerously little of the religion left.

The deepest connection with how people should conduct themselves in the everyday world, wrote Berger, was found in the religion of ancient Israel, which posited the radical idea of a God standing outside the cosmos, but who acted historically and was the author of radical ethical commands. This opened up a space for man as a unique individual responsible for his own actions, providing a religious framework for individual dignity and freedom of action. A rationalizing element was present in Judaism from the beginning in purging religion of all its magical and orgiastic elements, as well as imposing fundamental discipline on everyday life, translating itself into a body of laws that survived even the destruction of the Second Temple by the Romans. These aspects of Judaism promoted a rationalization of the modern West by way of Christianity—which in turn represented a step backwards from the worldly grounding of the Hebrew Bible and rabbinical Judaism because of the notions of the Incarnation and the Trinity.[42]

That regressive, antirational element within its foundational creed made Protestantism particularly vulnerable to the onslaught from atheism. The result, as detailed in the preceding pages, was the dislocation of science and reason from religion. But because religion underpins science and actually laid the ground for reason in the first place, the exile of religion from scientific and intellectual discourse has fatally undermined reason itself.

THE DEEP UNREASONABLENESS OF ABOLISHING GOD

The philosopher Anthony Flew, whose "pilgrimage of reason" through science took him from atheism to faith, says in effect that to hold that reason alone accounts for everything in the universe is profoundly unreasonable. The scientific atheists, he writes, overlook the most important aspect of all: the ineffable mysteriousness of self-consciousness, which is the "most obvious and unassailable and the most lethal" argument against the materialist worldview. [43]

The "self," writes Flew, cannot be explained in terms of physics or chemistry. These cannot explain phenomena in nature such as the code-processing systems of information in the cell; the fact that these have goals such as reproduction; or subjective awareness and conceptual thought. The only coherent explanation is that these are "supra-physical" phenomena—and these can only have originated in a "supra-physical" source, Flew concludes:

> It's simply inconceivable that any material matrix or field can generate agents who think and act. Matter cannot produce conceptions and perceptions. A force field does not plan or think. So at the level of reason and everyday experience, we become immediately aware that the world of living, conscious, thinking beings has to originate in a living Source, a Mind. [44]

But scientific materialism holds that religion can be given no quarter whatever and that matter somehow created itself. Far from upholding reason, science itself has therefore become unreasonable. And so, in the name of scientific reason, many scientists are now departing from their own rules. Detached from its conceptual anchorage, science effectively turned man into God and decided that truth was only what science declared it to be.

As a result, both the notion of truth and the West's moral codes were ripped up. It wasn't just the assault from crypto-Marxists and nihilists who set out to overthrow Western mores that did the damage. Even more fundamentally, the attack on Christianity struck a lethal blow at the very heart of Western morality. For in contrast to the vulgar notion that it is all about God delivering thunderbolts of vengeance and punishment, the Hebrew Bible is a quintessential text of reasoned self-criticism. Just about all its major players are flawed and behave badly, causing harm to others and usually reaping the consequences of their actions. Thus the reader takes an autonomous moral stance, drawing lessons from these stories on how best to behave. In short, the Hebrew Bible is a text for reasoned moral integrity; and with its willed decline, reasoned moral integrity in the West has declined as well.

According to Cardinal Henri de Lubac, the God of the Hebrew Bible liberated humanity from being the plaything of the gods or passive victims of fate, as they were in classical and Eastern antiquity, to become masters of their destiny and bend history in a humane direction. But what Biblical man perceived as liberation, proponents of atheistic humanism perceived as bondage. Human "greatness" required the rejection of God as a program to remake the world. De Lubac concluded, "It is not true, as it is sometimes said, that man cannot organize the world without God. What is true is that, without God, he can only organize it against man."[45]

The result has been the tyrannical ideologies of the modern age, which has forgotten that the reason upon which it prides itself and the science that flows from that reason owe their existence to religion. The result of this amnesia is the repudiation not just of reason but of humanity itself. As Pope Benedict XVI has written, "The radical detachment of the Enlightenment philosophy from its roots ultimately leads it to dispense with man."[46] Abolishing the Biblical God has abolished the rationality and freedom bestowed in his name. Four centuries after Francis Bacon complained that the Catholic Church was bending evidence into conformity with its precepts, it is now secular ideology that leads reason about "like a captive in a procession."

16

WHY BRITAIN IS IN
THE FOREFRONT

The picture is now becoming much more clear, if startling. The cause of the West's irrationality is the dislocation of reason from religion. The mistake was to believe that reason and religion were mutually exclusive, whereas reason was in fact underpinned by religion. More specifically, although in this war between materialism and religion the frontline casualty has been Western civilization's foundational creed of Christianity, the real target has been the faith and codes of the Hebrew Bible, from which Christianity derived the core precepts that are under attack.

This is no idle conceit. As has been detailed in these pages, the precepts of Judaism, the Hebrew Bible and the Jewish people are the underlying target in the uproar over social, cultural and moral issues, manmade global warming, Darwinism, the Iraq war, and of course Israel. This is not to say these issues constitute a willed conspiracy to "do down the Jews." But sometimes apparently quite disparate issues turn out to be rooted in the same fundamental assumptions, hidden or masked as these may be. And strange as it may at first seem, all these movements involve an attack on the bedrock values of Western civilization—and those values rest upon and are deeply intertwined with the teachings and fate of the Jewish people, a fact which is almost totally overlooked. Unless we understand this, we surely cannot make sense of these issues or acknowledge them for what they are.

But there are one or two more questions still to answer before we can finally join up all the dots. In particular, why does this all play differently in America from the way it plays in Britain and the rest of Europe? The trends that have been discussed in these pages now dominate progressive or left-wing thinking, where ideology rules with an iron grip. Environmentalism, anti-Zionism, anti-Americanism, Third Worldism, minority rights, victim culture, moral and cultural relativism, utilitarianism, transnationalism—these all define the Western progressive mind. But although steadily encroaching, they have not achieved the same reach and effects everywhere.

WHY ARE AMERICA, BRITAIN AND EUROPE ALL DIFFERENT?

America is very different from Europe. For sure, many of these issues are being fought out in America's "culture wars"; but at least there actually *is* a war over them, even though some would say it is being lost. Certainly, there are very high rates of teenage pregnancy, crime and drug use, and poor education standards with historical truth and objectivity being sacrificed to the ideologies of antiracism, feminism and other varieties of victimology. Nevertheless, there is also a fight-back mounted by conservatives and neoconservatives, the big think tanks, Fox News and talk radio, including an explosive battle between religious believers and scientific atheists. There is also still a defining pride in the nation, in the American flag and what it stands for—and still a consensus in support of Israel.

In Europe, the situation is different. Moral and cultural relativism and an explicit rejection of Christian ethics, along with the governing idea that the individual nation lacks the legitimacy of global institutions, are embedded in the European Union and in transnational institutions such as the European Court of Human Rights. These promote a universalist worldview that brooks no dissent and trumps the particulars of creed or culture. It is thus intrinsically antidemocratic, antiliberty and hostile to the precepts of

Christianity and Judaism. One might almost say that in its drive to equalize, homogenize and bureaucratize, and to treat any dissent as innately hostile to virtue and the brotherhood of man, the EU is the true heir to Robespierre.

Even so, family life in much of Europe remains anchored in households where mothers and fathers bring up their own children; there are still relatively high levels of social solidarity, education and cultural pride; and there are still general standards of courtesy, respect and orderliness. By contrast, these things are increasingly vanishing in Britain, which has become the brand leader in Western collapse—and with virtually no fight-back to speak of.

In Britain, whole communities have become social and moral deserts where there are no committed fathers, relationships are transient and children's lives are devastated. There are burgeoning numbers of unstable cohabitations, with corresponding increases in domestic violence and mental and physical fragility. Even middle-class households now form complex spidergrams of reconstituted relationships. The result is a rising tide of child distress, including depression and suicide, educational underachievement and the inability to form committed relationships. British teenagers today have some of the highest levels of antisocial behavior in Europe—binge drinking, drug use, teenage pregnancy and sexually transmitted diseases.

Educational standards are in freefall. Public space has been coarsened and degraded. There is a widespread breakdown in civility and respect. Obscenities have become commonplace in public discourse. Streets are filthy; carriages on London Tube trains are littered with empty food cartons and fruit peelings. In the early hours, girls stagger from nightclubs to collapse on the streets in a drunken stupor. On television, prime-time programs range from the foul-mouthed and scatological to the merely vulgar and puerile. Violent crime is high and rising, and the undercurrent of latent aggression from rowdy or drunken youths, or even drivers fighting for parking places, is just as great.

Why has Britain descended into such a state? During the past six decades, Britain has been systematically hollowing out its own culture, for two intimately related reasons: a loss of its national identity and purpose, and the crumbling of religious belief that underpinned its moral codes.

THE DEMORALIZATION OF BRITAIN

Britain's idea of itself as a nation rooted in a historic identity has simply collapsed. This is a different situation from mainland Europe. The transnationalism underlying the European Union grew from post–World War II trauma and the perceived need to constrain historically aggressive Germany forever. Moreover, countries in mainland Europe such as France and Germany had a history of permeable borders and accommodation to invasion, not to mention certain shared cultural assumptions in the fields of religion and law, which damped down opposition to shared sovereignty. Interestingly, this transnationalism is now being countered by the newer arrivals in the EU, the nations of Eastern Europe, which know from bitter experience what it is to live under a tyranny that destroys a nation's individual cultural and political identity.

Britain is very different. Unlike the countries of mainland Europe, Britain is an island that has not been invaded in the past one thousand years. With no permeable borders, Britain once had a very clear and proud idea of itself as a nation. It knew what it stood for and fought off its enemies across the seas. But this identity had become very much bound up with its place in the world; and when that place disappeared, Britain slowly fell apart.

Since the Norman invasion in the eleventh century, Britain had not been a society of immigrants. Such immigration as had taken place—the Huguenots in the eighteenth century, the Jews from Eastern Europe or Nazi Germany in the twentieth century—had been on a very small scale. With the postwar welfare state promising levels of provision for all that were beyond the country's own resources, however, Britain brought in immigrants from the West Indies and the Indian subcontinent to do the jobs that indigenous citizens were unable or unwilling to do, or to provide cheap labor in Britain's declining manufacturing industries. That in turn fueled the conviction that it was racist either to restrict immigration or to "impose" British culture on the new arrivals. The combination of large numbers of immigrants and the doctrine of multiculturalism turned Britain from a homogeneous society into one that no longer recognized its own face in the mirror.

But the problem went far deeper. With the loss of Britain's imperial role, together with its near bankruptcy after the Second World War and its reliance on American money to bail it out, the country's elite class was profoundly demoralized—a state of mind that culminated in the shattering humiliation of the Suez crisis of 1956, when America pulled the rug from underneath a covert plan by Britain, France and Israel to invade Egypt.

This demoralization left those elites vulnerable to ideas suggesting the emergence of a new kind of world altogether: the new Jerusalem. This was to be an utter repudiation of the old Jerusalem: a secular onslaught against Biblical morality and its replacement by the religion of the self. Many of these destructive ideas—"child-centered" education deriving from the work of the educationist John Dewey, quasi-Marxist "antiracism," the therapy culture and of course the sixties counterculture—came from America. Given the close transatlantic cultural ties, these therefore had a particularly sharp effect in Britain but were blunted in less America-centric Europe.

THE UNRAVELING OF BRITISH CULTURE

Antonio Gramsci, the Marxist thinker who became the guru of the former sixties radicals who are now entrenched among the elites, promoted the idea that Western society could be overturned by capturing the citadels of the culture—the universities, schools, churches, media, civil service, professions—and subverting its values. Enacting Gramsci's precepts to the letter, the British intelligentsia have ensured that morality and culture have indeed been turned upside down. Nowhere has this process been more deadly than in the crucible of knowledge itself, the schools and universities.

The shift away from reason is most clearly demonstrated by what has happened to the very place where individuals are taught to think—the British education system. For three decades and more, the Gramscian project has steadily been destroying the idea of education as the transmission of objective knowledge and values. In the universities, the intelligentsia bought heavily into subjective theories of education, ostensibly geared to the "child-centered" doctrine going back to Dewey and before him to Rousseau, holding that authority, rules and structure were an assault on children's autonomy and fettered the creativity that expressed their inner selves. Teachers stopped teaching and became mere "facilitators," as children were effectively expected to teach themselves. The resulting ignorance meant that children became less and less able to think for themselves. With objectivity junked by the academy, the way was open for propaganda to take hold—on issues such as global warming—and pupils no longer had the tools of intellectual inquiry with which to challenge it.

The overriding importance afforded to personal feelings and the corresponding doctrine that everyone's achievement must be valued identically meant that no one was allowed to fail and in effect everyone got a prize. From university downwards, standards were adjusted to enable this to happen—with the result that failure was relabeled success.

Thus as the pass rate on the "A-level" 18-plus exam (taken at age eighteen or higher) rose to almost 100 percent, examiners reported in 2005 that three-quarters of the brightest math students were unable to convert a fraction to a decimal. The official curriculum body proposed to "modernize" the teaching of English literature by effectively abolishing literacy. Films would be afforded the same status as books, while basic skills such as grammar, spelling and reading would be "re-evaluated." The knowledge content of subjects such as science was progressively emptied out in favor of "skills" and "relevance," so that instead of being taught how the world worked from scientific first principles, pupils were merely told about the uses of science in society. And meanwhile some half of all pupils left school at age sixteen functionally illiterate.

One of the most notable aspects of this new educational orthodoxy was the way it ditched all notions of linear progression. Structure in reading schemes, chronology in history, sequences in math or geography, the rules of syntax and grammar all gave way to the teaching of moments that bore no relation to each other: passages for study rather than whole books, random episodes in history that failed to tell a coherent story, nuggets of information, projects to assemble kaleidoscopes of information in a vacuum. The outcome was that children were left unequipped with the building blocks of rational thought processes.

The teaching of reading—the foundation stone of learning—fell victim to the "New Literacy" movement, which sought to redefine literacy into a social and political program. Regarding the child as an "autonomous meaning-maker," it junked systematic instruction in phonics and other reading schemes—the best way of teaching children to read by decoding words on a page—in favor of guesswork, memorizing the text and learning by osmosis. The result was mass illiteracy. Bizarre as this may appear, denying children the ability to read was regarded as a way of liberating them from capitalist oppression—the idea being that mass literacy had not resulted in the workers seizing political power. That is the argument that Peter Traves, an education adviser with Shropshire Council, made in 1991: "Public education has not produced an empowered people. Education has served the role of controlling and repressing the aspirations of the general population, and the teaching of reading has had a central part to play in this."[1]

Almost as devastatingly, the writing of essays was largely supplanted by "creative writing." As a result, subjectivity and fantasy replaced objectivity and reason. Instead of being taught to think, pupils were encouraged to imagine. The discipline of ordering one's thoughts, assessing evidence, marshalling an argument and arriving at a considered conclusion was replaced by storytelling and making things up—and eventually pupils could not tell the difference. They were no longer being taught to think, and did not realize what they couldn't do.

British schools similarly turned against the transmission of the nation's values. Children were no longer taught British political history as a coherent story that enabled them to understand the country and society in which they lived and to value its institutions. Instead, they were taught decontextualized episodes that made little overall sense, often through the ideological prism of "themes" such as gender or race, and similarly inadequate gobbets of other cultures. The teaching of Christianity gave way not just to other religions but to pagan cults, which were given equal status. In 2009, the government announced that pupils would learn about the rituals and teachings of Druids, Moonies and Rastafarians for a new "religious studies" 16-plus exam (taken at age sixteen), along with atheism and humanism. A draft outline of the new exam also included rap music, Stonehenge, human rights, gender equality, GM crops, multiculturalism in Britain, cloning and the effect of the internet on religion.[2]

This was all of a piece with the fact that Britain has become an increasingly post-Christian society. In 1964, 71 percent of those polled regularly attended religious services; by 2005, this number had declined to 31 percent.[3] Between 1979 and 2005, half of all Christians stopped going to church on Sunday, and between 1960 and 2000, membership of the Church of England halved.[4] Compare these figures with America, where church attendance among

Protestants has been increasing for six decades, reaching 45 percent between 2005 and 2008.[5] Polls in the mid 1990s showed that 95 percent of Americans believed in God, 82 percent identified themselves as Christian and 59 percent agreed that belief in Jesus Christ was the only assurance of eternal life.[6]

THE CRITICAL DESTABILIZATION OF THE CHURCH OF ENGLAND

So why has Christianity in Britain declined so much more precipitously than in Europe or America, where these trends exist but not on the same scale? In Europe, one might say that the Catholic Church was more resilient because it retained centralized authority while Protestantism was undone by fragmentation. But in America, although there are serious divisions between denominations, the Protestant churches form the principal bulwark *against* religious and moral collapse. And there lies the rub. In Britain, far from providing a bulwark, the established Church of England has been in the *forefront* of that collapse.

In the story of British de-moralization, the demoralization of the Church of England has been of critical significance. The story goes back once again to the German Romantic movement of the eighteenth century—a story about the pressures on Christianity in general, but to which the Church of England was particularly susceptible.

For more than two centuries, Christianity has struggled to deal with the profoundly destabilizing ideas unleashed by the Romantic movement. The "rationalist" eighteenth-century thinker Friedrich Schleiermacher de-emphasized all the supernatural elements of Christianity in favor of a "natural" religion that satisfied reason and the emotions, deferring to secular intellectuals—the "despisers of religion"—as the arbiters of acceptable thinking.[7] In the same century, the "Modernist" movement was started by the German theologian and dramatist Gotthold Lessing, who taught that reports of miracles were unreliable and that nothing could be demonstrated by means of historical truths.

Building upon these principles, Biblical criticism developed during the nineteenth century on the premise that the Bible had to be studied like any other book and in the light of growing knowledge of other cultures of the Near East. The realization of errors in translation leading to the production of the Revised Version of the Bible in the 1880s, and the arrival of Darwin's *Origin of Species* and the way this was seized upon by people with an anti-Christian agenda, all contributed to a growing sense of religious doubt and skepticism.[8]

The late nineteenth century saw the growth of secular agitation and a belief among intellectuals that religion was merely superstition and should be rejected. Modernists tried to cherry-pick Christianity and dispose of the elements that didn't appear to fit with reason. Although they believed in an inner spirituality, they were embarrassed by the idea of a God who was both transcendent and personal. R. J. Campbell, the minister at the influential City Temple in London from 1903 to 1915, acknowledged that Jesus was "divine," but defined this as being merely an exceptional man in tune with the evolving process of the universe. "We believe that there is no real distinction between humanity and Deity. Our being is the same as God's, though our consciousness of it is limited," Campbell wrote, setting aside ideas of sin and atonement as relics of man's animal nature.[9]

The First World War, however, was a terrible and indeed arguably terminal shock to this confidence in the primacy of reason. Thinking subsequently took a more traditional turn in response; but when optimism returned in Europe after World War II, liberal theology in Europe was in the ascendant once again. By locating religion within the consciousness of the believer, theology adapted itself to the emergent discipline of psychology. In the United States in particular, in the view of the sociologist Peter Berger, this had the effect of "legitimizing religious activities as some sort of psychotherapy."[10]

A SACRED FREE-FOR-ALL

As spirituality went inwards, so it opened the door in turn from Christianity to the New Age mélange of ecology, paganism and cults. As Christianity lost its appeal, increasing numbers found an alternative divinity in the natural world. In his book *The End of Nature*, Bill McKibben wrote that he had overcome his "crisis of belief" by "locating God in nature."[11] The church was urged to develop "bird liturgies which energise the human spirit" and recycling programs to tap into "the healing power of cardboard."[12] The Movement for Christian Democracy published a list of things that were badly wrong in Britain; in first place was the destruction of "97 percent of wildflower meadows and 190,000 miles of hedgerow." The fact that one pregnancy in five (at that time) was being terminated came fourth.[13]

Environmentalism was viewed explicitly as a renunciation of the Biblical importance placed on man and his elevation above animals and plant life. Instead, there was a call for returning to the ancient paganism in which humanity had revered nature, as the American historian Lynn White described it, speaking before the American Association for the Advancement of Science in 1966:

> In antiquity every tree, every spring, every stream, every hill had its own *genius loci*, its guardian spirit.... Before one cut a tree, mined a mountain or damned a brook, it was important to placate the spirit in charge of that particular situation.... By destroying pagan animism, Christianity made it possible to exploit nature in a mood of indifference to the feelings of natural objects.[14]

The belief that mankind had sinned against nature through science and technology, and that Christianity by promoting such "exploitation" was essentially destructive, seeped into the church itself. James Nash of the Churches Centre for Theology and Public Policy called on the churches to "eradicate the last vestiges of these ecologically ruinous myths."[15] In 1991, the American Jesuit priest Thomas Clarke wrote, "I do accept the scandal that the earth has suffered more from Christians than from any other religious group.... Has Christianity been a blessing or a curse to this earth? That is a very, very hard question for me."[16]

On the back of such environmental concerns, the church opened its doors to pantheism, paganism and occult practices. Self-hypnosis, transcendental meditation, "visualization" and yoga were all promoted by Christian bookshops and Christian parishes in Britain.[17] Off the wall as all this may seem—and indeed, totally antithetical to Christian teaching—it has nevertheless made inroads into respectable, even intellectual church thinking. For example, Rosemary Radford Ruether, a well-regarded and influential American Catholic professor of theology, has hailed a new spirit of ecumenism "in which all movements that seek a feminist earth-renewal spirituality in various traditions can see each other as partners," and called on progressive Christians to defend the civil liberties of pagans and Wiccans because all shared a commitment to the same "life-affirming values."[18]

In 2005, Ruether explained to an audience at Loyola Marymount University in Los Angeles her view that "Christianity is riddled by hierarchy and patriarchy." These sins, she had previously written, created a social order in which chaste "young women on their wedding night were, in effect, raped by husbands whose previous sexual experience came from exploitative relationships with servant women and prostitutes."[19] Given the ideological suspension of rationality involved in such thinking, it may not be surprising that Ruether is also a signatory to the "9/11 Truth Statement" that calls for an inquiry into evidence it says suggests high-level government officials may have deliberately allowed the September 11 attacks to occur.[20]

Perhaps the most prominent—and controversial—of these pagan "Christians" is Matthew Fox, the former Dominican friar and subsequently Episcopal priest. Fox, who has employed a witch on his staff and was thrown out of the Catholic Church, proposes a fusion of the world's religions. His "Creation Spirituality" is based on principles such as cosmology, feminism and free sexuality, and "truly honors the soil as a divine locus."[21] It also conveniently abolishes sin, or at least redefines it.

Saying he is "taking Eros back from the pornographers," Fox claims that the Christian concepts of the Fall and Redemption were created by the ruling class for political reasons. These concepts, he says, distract from the "original blessing" of nature. "In religion we have been operating under the model that humanity, and especially sinful humanity, was the centre of the spiritual universe. This is not so. . . . [T]he time has come to let anthropocentrism go, and with it to let the preoccupation with human sinfulness give way to attention to divine grace." Sin doesn't altogether disappear; it would consist of "injuring creation and doing harm to its balance and harmoniousness," with which religion was complicit during the centuries when "human/divine creativity was used to ... wipe out millions of species."[22]

Fox denounces the traditional church as worshipping a punitive and patriarchal Father, who links readily to fascist powers of control and demonizes women, the earth, other species, science, gays and lesbians. Instead, he reconfigures Christianity around the notion that humans have committed "matricide" against mother earth; the Resurrection takes the form of mysticism, and the "Cosmic Christ" will usher in "a global renaissance that can heal mother earth and save her by changing human hearts and ways."[23]

He also sacralizes the science of evolution, making life itself divine. This is potentially an antihuman creed, holding that humanity is "neither the end point of this evolutionary process, nor indispensable to the cosmos if we continue to prove unable to live in ecologically sustainable ways." Nevertheless, since human beings are themselves divine, whatever they do is therefore good; and that includes free sexuality, both heterosexual and homosexual. Indeed,

Fox's teachings place considerable stress on sexuality; sexual rituals and sexual mysticism are key to the new spirituality, with the erotic energy of the self supposedly drawing upon the erotic energy of the cosmos [sic].[24] He supports a "theology of pleasure," which would encourage lust as well as chastity. "Every time humans truly make love, truly express their love by the art of sexual lovemaking, the cosmic Christ is making love," he writes. Quoting the philosopher Rudolph Otto, he agrees that "sexuality is at bottom a religious issue, opening a door into the psyche which permits the god-image standing behind it an entrance into ego-awareness." The phallus has to be literally worshipped: the "sense of sacred phallus" should be gained by such means as "drumming, dancing and entering into the irrational processes that have been native ways of ritual and wisdom for tens of thousands of years."[25]

This can surely be described as a sacred free-for-all, or the sacrament of debauchery.

While Fox's influence should not be exaggerated, "progressive spirituality" has made inroads into the mainstream church in both America and Britain. In 2007, Fox preached at St. James's Church, Piccadilly, in the heart of London—which was so proud that it put up a photograph of this event on its website. And during the mid 1980s, Fox was considered by many theological students to be the most important theologian of the day.

Other irrational influences on the church have resulted in even more bizarre behavior. In the 1990s, more than a thousand British churches succumbed to an outbreak of mass hysteria inspired by charismatic church services in North America among groups such as the Kansas City Prophets and the Toronto Airport Vineyard Church. There were extraordinary scenes with worshippers clucking like chickens or barking like dogs, pogo-sticking, swooning and speaking in tongues. At the time of the Rwanda genocide, these churches were dissolving into spasms of uncontrollable laughter.

In America, Protestantism is riven between the evangelical, scriptural faithful on the one hand and the established but progressive, "inclusive" churches shading off into pagan cults on the other. In Britain, however, evangelicalism is a very small movement. Protestantism is dominated by the established Church of England—which has overwhelmingly succumbed to the Modernist scorn of supernatural belief and the embrace of victim culture and other progressive nostrums.

THE PARTICULAR VULNERABILITY OF THE CHURCH OF ENGLAND

The Church of England is susceptible to "progressive spirituality" because it was not founded on theological principle. It arose as a response to the turmoil following the break with Rome by Henry VIII, not over doctrinal issues but merely because the King wanted to be able to divorce his wives. The country, therefore, remained Catholic; Henry simply imposed Protestantism upon it. Terrible wars of religion followed. The settlement forged in the era of Elizabeth I centered on the one thing that could bring the country together and end the wars: worship according to the Book of Common Prayer. One could say that the Church of England was basically a prayer book with some ace cathedrals attached.

From the start, Anglicanism was therefore a religion of form; the question of what adherents actually believed in was much trickier. It stitched together Anglo-Catholics and evangelicals—the former looking to the bishops for authority and the latter to scripture. And all they had in common was the Prayer Book. As soon as any theological challenge came along, as it did from materialism and secularism, the edifice was too shallow to withstand it.

Moreover, since the Church of England was founded by royal fiat, it was ineluctably bound up with the idea of a Christian nation ruled by a Christian monarch.[26] While it is certainly to be argued that the decline of the church has contributed in great measure to the decline of Britain, it is also arguable that the decline of Britain—the erosion of its understanding of itself as a nation at all, let alone a Christian nation—has contributed in large measure to the decline of the church. The two are pulling each other under like drowning men locked together.

As the state changed, so the church itself mutated, in response to competing denominations and religions as well as secularism. After World War II, the New Jerusalem would be built to supersede the old. The welfare state not only displaced Christianity from the everyday lives of the people by nationalizing hospitals and schools, which previously had been run in large measure by churches and voluntary bodies, but more fundamentally it established a culture of hyper-individualism and entitlement based on wholly utilitarian calculations. The church retreated from the public sphere and became a voluntary organization with little sense of external compulsion: merely one denomination among many.[27] What delivered the *coup de grâce*, as Callum Brown argues, was first the profound change in the role of women, who had been the mainstay of the faith within the home, but who now looked outwards to the world of work, and second, the sexual revolution, where there was scant place for piety.[28]

It was in the 1960s that the rot really set in. Right after the Second World War, the church had been doing well: baptisms, confirmations and marriages were all going up. But in the Swinging Sixties, the fragile church swung with the prevailing wind and blew right over. The most lethal gust came from a bestseller by Bishop John Robinson titled *Honest to God: Objections to Christian Belief*, arguing that God was to be found not in Biblical transcendence but at some level within individuals themselves.

Robinson's book offered a fig leaf of religion to people who were attracted to spirituality but rejected supernatural Christianity. It thus helped deconstruct not just Christian belief but morality, and it gave Christian absolution to the permissive culture, which in turn was to validate recreational sex, drugs, divorce and cohabitation, pornography, abortion and homosexuality, thus destroying church and Biblical authority. David Holloway, vicar of Jesmond, Newcastle-on-Tyne, has written that the period 1970–1990 was a watershed during which time two churches appeared in Britain: one identified with the apostolic faith of the Bible and the Western reformed Catholic tradition, and the other heretical, gnostic and even pagan.[29]

Also in the sixties, extreme liberal theology started to be taught in the principal theological colleges at Cambridge and Southwark. In due course, moreover, church denominational colleges largely farmed out the teaching of theology to university departments of religion. As a result, the traditional disciplines of dogmatics and hermeneutics were diluted or abandoned. Comparative religion, essentially a branch of sociology or anthropology, was promoted to fill the vacuum. With the clergy and teachers in the church losing confidence in scripture, they became more open to contrarian theories about its sources. According to Professor Paul Merkley, even church publication houses now publish and sell the many Gnostic gospels, always regarded as false and heretical by the church, but which have the appeal of including syncretistic and "spiritualist" perspectives easily accommodated by New Age promoters.[30]

In Britain, with the supernaturalist framework largely put to one side as an embarrassment, the church lost faith in its own message. As the former archbishop of Canterbury, Lord Carey, put it, "Britain's unthinking secularism is the context for the Church's attitudes, shapeless form and its lack of any underpinning values."[31] And so the church embraced moral and cultural relativism. The prevailing view, as one bishop observed, came to be that "there is no one truth, and we all have to respect each other's truths."[32]

PAGANISM, ANGLICANISM AND THE NEW AGE

One of those "truths" that had to be respected was paganism. In his autobiographical book in 1996, Matthew Fox enthused about the "Nine O'Clock Service" in Sheffield, northern England. The NOS, a sect that developed out of the rave subculture, perfectly expressed his Creation Spirituality, Fox wrote.[33] Eventually it was exposed as a neopagan cult within the Church of England, with a domineering and manipulative leader, mind control and widespread sexual abuse.

Before these abuses were revealed, however, the Church of England was thrilled to be attracting hundreds of young people with the NOS. Robert Warren, who would become the church's national officer for evangelism, said, "It is integrating a whole number of strands of Christianity, not into a meaningless stew but into a rich whole which I firmly believe means that its significance is that of a prototype mass-culture church. Their impact is to bring into question what, and how, things are being done in the wider church."

Warren and the cult's leader, Chris Brain, wrote in the influential *Anglicans for Renewal* magazine in 1991 that God rejected fundamentalism and abusive power structures and a "repressive attitude to human sexuality." At a "techno-apocalyptic" service in 1992 at Greenbelt Arts Festival—a Christian music, art, politics and theology festival in Northamptonshire—an apocalyptic message about the Western world was projected onto a massive screen: a heavily made-up woman was shown reading from Deuteronomy, her words turning into groans, then screams and finally delirious laughter.

In 1993, after Brain was ordained as a priest, he started to introduce Matthew Fox's Creation Spirituality in order to fashion a "Planetary Mass," with Brain as a "techno-shaman." Following this event, he worked closely with Fox before the NOS was finally unmasked as an abusive cult in 1995. As the stories of abuse started to pour in and Brain was admitted to a psychiatric hospital, members of the cult experienced such trauma that some started throwing themselves against walls and mutilating themselves. The big question was how the Church of England could have been so blind to all this. Brain himself said, "It is the wishy-washiness of the Anglican church which has given us the freedom for these new things to come about."[34]

There have been a number of other examples of paganism within the church, sometimes at the heart of the establishment and usually associated with environmentalism. Martin Palmer is an Anglican lay reader, Chinese scholar and religious adviser to the World Wide Fund for Nature. He is also secretary-general of the Alliance of Religions and Conservation—which he cofounded with Prince Philip, Duke of Edinburgh, in 1995—as well as founder and director of the International Consultancy on Religion, Education and Culture, the world's largest interfaith consultancy, and a regular host of TV programs.

Palmer promotes a connection between religion and conservation, but goes much further. In 2000, he took part in a meeting of Christians and Druids in Salisbury to discuss the relationship between Christianity and paganism.[35] He has also endorsed *Kindred Spirit* magazine, which boasts of featuring articles on "New and progressive forms of complementary healthcare such as Zero Balancing and Holographic Re-patterning ... articles on angels and the latest explanation of the workings of Stonehenge ... ground-breaking stories such as the inner temple of Damanhur, the psychic surgery of John of God, and the link between our genetic conditioning and the I-Ching." Palmer praised as "even-handed" its "windows into the sheer diversity of alternative thinking and action in the country today."[36]

According to Palmer, the church had lost touch with the cosmic nature of Creation, in part because of the struggle against paganism and a fear of being too involved with ecology in case it smacked of pantheism. He ridiculed the fact that he had been called a pagan and a Satanist by fundamentalist Christians—but he then went on to condemn the special significance of humanity in Creation.[37]

Robert Whelan has charted the church's forays into syncretism under these New Age influences. Following its meeting in Assisi in 1986 to mark its twenty-fifth anniversary, the World Wide Fund for Nature (WWF) established a Network on Conservation and Religion. At a celebration in the basilica, a Muslim muezzin was called upon to praise Allah, followed by a Hindu dance, a prayer chanted by three Tibetan monks, readings from Hindu scriptures and the Qur'an, and a prayer to Shiva, the Hindu god of destruction and reproduction. In September 1989 the WWF took over Canterbury Cathedral, its precincts and other church property for a Celebration of Faith and the Environment, including contributions by Buddhists, Sikhs and other Eastern faiths—but with no mention of Jesus. One of the highlights was a Celebration of the Forest, which took place in the cathedral, with the choir from St. Augustine's Roman Catholic High School in Billington, Lancashire, performing an oratorio called *Yanamamo*, based on the beliefs of rainforest Indians, in which they sang: "The trees have power. We worship them. . . . We live because they give us life."[38]

Nature seemed to have become an alternative god, complete with powers of forgiveness. In 1987, the WWF organized a Harvest Festival, retitled Creation and Harvest, in Winchester Cathedral. After a symbolic act of atonement for environmental "sins" such as wheat and dairy overproduction, deforestation for financial gain and soil erosion, the dean of Winchester, Dean Beeson, said: "As a priest, I can offer absolution from God for those sins for which we ask his forgiveness. We shall not know if Nature has forgiven us for many years to come." Similarly, a Creation Festival liturgy held in Coventry Cathedral the following year, also organized by the WWF, included the prayer: "Our brothers and sisters of the creation, the mighty trees, the broad oceans, the air, the earth, the creatures of creation, forgive us and reconcile us to you."[39]

Even though belief in the Biblical God and the divinity of Jesus was waning within the church, it stuck firmly to its doctrinal paradigm of sin, guilt and redemption. It simply reconfigured this paradigm around the material world. Metaphysical guilt found secular expression not just in nature but also in social and political programs. The politics of Western expiation as expressed through victim culture met with a receptive audience among progressive Christians in both America and Britain.[40]

And just as in the secular world, once it was de-anchored from Biblical authority, progressive thinking inside the church pitched such Christians headlong against the bedrock values of Western civilization, including moral agency and sexual order. As Paul Gottfried has observed, whereas in earlier generations the battle had been between Christians who were either for or against scientific modernity, now modernizing liberals in seminaries and at conferences depicted St. Paul as a repressed homosexual, tried to purge theological language of its "sexism," and delivered invectives against the Christian West for offenses against the rest of humanity.[41]

SOCIAL WORK AT HOME AND
LIBERATION THEOLOGY ABROAD

The agenda now was to line up the church not with scientific progress but with the world's suffering victims and to reprogram the Western mind away from all types of "hate"—which, according to the Marxist calibration of victimhood, was always associated with power. So radical theology became fused with victim-centered feminism, as in the work of Rosemary Radford Ruether, who recast the narrative of the Fall, Christ's suffering and the promise of redemption in terms of feminist martyrology and linked it to the liberation of other oppressed groups "from status and hierarchical relations." Similarly, the theologian Chris Glaser represented Jesus as incipiently gay, suffering on the cross to dramatize the evil in a world not yet redeemed from insensitivity towards gay people.[42]

Abroad, victim culture was fueled by the "liberation theology" promoted by the World Council of Churches, which held that the problems of the poor peoples of the global South were social and economic, emanating from the capitalist West and America in particular. The WCC, which began life in 1948 with the aim of representing Christianity as the embodiment of civilized values, had turned into a body that used Christianity to beat up on civilized values.

As Professor Paul Merkley has written, from the very start there had been tension within the WCC between those who wanted to promote church unity—mainly the laity—and those who wanted to make Christian conscience an activist force in the life of nations—mainly the clergy and intellectuals. When church unity foundered under the pressure of the Cold War, the activist camp won and a theology of liberation was born. In 1968, the "Programme to Combat Racism" passed by the Uppsala Assembly adopted explicitly Third World rhetoric and Marxist-Leninist dogma on imperialism. The liberation theology that followed drew upon Marxist, Leninist, Maoist and neo-Marxist vocabulary from Franz Fanon and left-wing religious commentators. In the seventies and eighties, WCC declarations adhered to Soviet positions on world issues. After complaints from member congregations, however, the aggressive rhetoric was toned down and the WCC adopted instead the no less radical postmodernist deconstruction of the past—in 1990 denouncing Christopher Columbus, for example, for his contributions to "genocide, slavery and ecocide and the exploitation of the wealth of the land."[43]

Whereas in America there was a clear division between traditional scriptural Christians and the churches that took up these progressive or radical agendas, in Britain there was no obvious counterweight to the established church when, paralyzed by doctrinal doubt, it redirected itself towards relieving the "suffering just" associated with the supposed victim classes at home and the Third World abroad. Dismissing Scriptural believers as cretinous, deluded or "right-wing"—or all three—the Church of England stopped trying to save people's souls and instead tried to change society. Signing up to the doctrine that the world's problems were caused by poverty, oppression and discrimination rather than a spiritual void, it turned itself into a branch of social work at home and a liberation movement abroad.

Instead of holding the line for objectivity and reason, the church allowed itself to be drawn ever deeper into moral and cultural relativism. As secular society denounced the crimes of British cultural and political imperialism, so the Church of England abased itself for its own crime of religious imperialism—leading to such absurdities as the archbishop of Canterbury, Dr. Rowan Williams, apologizing to the Third World for the spread of Christianity. Addressing the Anglican conference in Cairo in 2005, Dr. Williams regretted that the church had taken "cultural captives" by exporting hymns and liturgies to remote parts of the world.[44] The fact that Christianity had brought civilization to remote parts, for the very good reason that it was superior to practices in those areas, was not acknowledged. The implicit assumption was that Christian values were trumped by the belief that everyone's culture is of equal value.

Something similar happened in the United States in 2007 when American Christians endorsed an outreach program to Muslims originating in Yale Divinity School, called "Loving God and Neighbor Together: A Christian Response to 'A Common Word Between Us and You.'" This was a response to an open letter from Islamic leaders to Christian leaders calling for peace between Muslims and Christians on the basis of common ground between the two faiths. The Yale manifesto regretted the West's sins towards Islam during the Crusades and the current war on terror, while minimizing differences between Christianity and Islam, and largely ignoring the problems of religious liberty under Islamist regimes and the history of Muslim attacks on Christians and Jews.[45]

In a similar vein, Dr. Williams responded to Islamist terrorism with repeated examples of moral equivalence and appeasement. In

Writing in the Dust, a meditation he wrote after 9/11 when he was still the archbishop of Wales, he said that we in the West "have something of the freedom to consider whether or not we turn to violence and so, in virtue of that very fact, are rather different from those who experience their world as leaving them no other option."[46] So according to Dr. Williams, Islamists were driven to mass murder because they had "no other option." He also commented that in the Palestinian/Israeli deadlock "both sides know what it is to be faced with regular terror" and that "the Muslim world is now experiencing—as it has for some time, but now with so much more intensity—that 'conscription' into someone else's story that once characterised the Church's attitude to Jews."[47]

Dr. Williams's prose style is famously opaque. But the future leader of the Anglican Communion appeared to be saying that Israeli self-defense against terror was morally equivalent to that terror, that attitudes to Muslims in the wake of 9/11 were morally equivalent to the church's persecution of the Jews, and that 9/11 had happened because its perpetrators couldn't help themselves.

In 2004, Dr. Williams chose the principal seat of Sunni Islamic learning, Al-Azhar University in Cairo, to mark the anniversary of 9/11 by saying that people should not take the action that might be necessary to prevent themselves and others from being murdered, characterizing such acts of self-defense as "revenge": "So whenever a Muslim, a Christian or a Jew refuses to act in violent revenge, creating terror and threatening or killing the innocent, that person bears witness to the true God. They have stepped outside the way the faithless world thinks."[48]

But of course, Christians and Jews do not use "indiscriminate violence and terror" against Muslims, as Dr. Williams suggested they did; it is certain Muslims who are indiscriminately murdering Christians and Jews. Condemning self-defense or the defense of others against murder as "revenge" or "indiscriminate violence and terror" condemns the innocent to death. It implies that if the Nazi

Holocaust were to happen again, the church would once again stand aside. In the current war being waged against the West, the head of the Anglican Communion was telling it to turn the other cheek.

In the face of the obscurantist and pagan onslaught against truth, reason and enlightenment, the most "progressive" forces within the church thus not only have failed to hold the line for the civilization to which Christianity had given rise, but have chosen to forsake its doctrines and join in the attack. In Britain, where the church continues to punch far above its weight in terms of cultural influence, the contribution this has made to the disintegration of national identity cannot be overstated. In the West generally, it has systematically eroded truth, reason and moral agency—and lined the church up alongside tyranny and bigotry in the most fundamental and morally significant global conflict of all.

17

THE REVIVAL OF CHRISTIAN JEW-HATRED

The Middle East impasse is the defining issue of our time. It is not an exaggeration to say that the position an individual takes on the conflict between Israel and the Arabs is a near-infallible guide to their general view of the world. Those who believe that Israel is the historic victim of the Arabs—and that its behavior, while not perfect, is generally as good as could be expected given that it is fighting for its existence against an enemy using the weapons of religious war—typically have a rational, nonideological approach to the world, arriving at conclusions on the basis of evidence. Those who believe that Israel is the regional bully hell-bent on oppressing the Palestinians, and who equate it with Nazism or apartheid, are generally moral and cultural relativists who invert truth and lies, right and wrong over a wide range of issues, and are incapable of seeing that their beliefs do not accord with reality.

Israel stands proxy for a rational and moral outlook because, of all the causes in the world, it alone has been singled out for systematic demonization built on fabrication, distortion and misrepresentation. If people stand truth and logic on their heads over Israel, it is very likely that they will do so elsewhere—not least because so much of the irrationality within the West rests at the most fundamental level on its denial or renunciation of Jewish moral precepts. It is therefore also no accident that for the Islamists who are determined to conquer Western civilization, the driving obsession is to eradicate Israel, subjugate the Jews and erase the precepts of Judaism that Islam believes it supersedes.

So where does Christianity stand on the pivotal issue of Israel? One might expect it to defend truth against lies and morality against relativism and nihilism, not least because it is founded on the religious precepts of Jesus the Jew. In fact, there is deep division among Christians over Israel. While successive popes have been cool or hostile towards Israel—and the Jews for their part have believed that the Vatican did not do what it could to counter the Nazi Holocaust—Catholic attitudes towards Israel have been warming over the years, and the Vatican entered into full diplomatic relations with it in 1993.[1] Within Protestantism, evangelicals are passionately supportive of Israel, while liberal, progressive churches are in general viscerally hostile and becoming more so.

In postreligious Britain, where hatred of Israel is positively unhinged, there is a common view that the church has become all but irrelevant in public life because so few people are now practicing, churchgoing Christians. Nothing could be further from the truth. The Church of England exercises a disproportionate influence on culture, because people assume that its spokesmen are motivated by conscience rather than any venal concerns and are people of integrity who always tell the truth. Accordingly, when bishops or Christian NGOs speak about the Middle East, they are believed to be providing a truthful account, and thus they play a crucial role in setting the moral tone of public discourse, establishing the benchmarks for decency, conscience and moral outrage.

Tragically, however, the established Church of England, which has succumbed in so many areas to the march of secularism and paganism, has sided with the forces of hatred, bigotry and unreason over Israel. Along with the Episcopalians and other liberal denominations in America, it lends its voice to the demonization of Israel and parrots the mendacious and hateful narrative propagated by the

Arab and Muslim world. In the face of suicide bomb and rocket attacks on Israeli civilians, the bishops and archbishops are silent. Instead they attack Israel for the measures it takes in self-defense. In sermons and speeches, through Christian charities and newspapers, in "God slots" on the BBC and in books and pamphlets, Christian clerics and thinkers systematically misrepresent Israel's history and libel its behavior, while sanitizing the murderous crimes against it by the Arabs.

ANGLICANS DIVEST THEMSELVES OF
THE TRUTH ABOUT THE MIDDLE EAST

Between 2005 and 2007, the leaders of several Protestant denominations in Britain and America put forward resolutions proposing divestment of any assets they held in companies perceived to be doing work in Israel contributing to its military and security programs. Although these initiatives were fought off, they had an enormous impact in helping create the impression that Israel was a pariah state to be shunned. And the churches did so using the language of bigotry and hatred.

In June 2005, a report by the Anglican Peace and Justice Network—which underpinned a short-lived move by the Anglican General Synod to disinvest from companies supporting Israel—compared Israel's security barrier to "the barbed-wire fence of the Buchenwald camp." Thus the Anglicans compared Jews to Nazis, on account of a measure aimed to prevent a second Jewish Holocaust.[2] This report and its recommendations were officially adopted in June 2005 by the Anglican Consultative Council (ACC), which in turn recommended to Anglican provinces worldwide a policy of disinvestment from companies "supporting the occupation" of Palestinian lands.[3] On February 6, 2006, the synod overwhelmingly backed a call from the Episcopal Church in Jerusalem and the Middle East to disinvest from "companies profiting from the illegal occupation" of

Palestinian territories.[4] Lord Carey, the former archbishop of Canterbury, had described the previous disinvestment plea by the ACC as "another knife in the back" for Israel.[5] Following the synod's decision, Lord Carey declared that he was "ashamed to be an Anglican."[6] The church's Ethical Investment Advisory Group later rejected the synod's decision.[7]

Helping to whip up the hysteria against Israel were the influential Christian NGOs. Christian Aid, for example, has for years presented a wholly one-sided and malevolently distorted account of Israel's history and actions. Israel's antiterror policies have been depicted as an attempt to ruin the Palestinian economy and destroy its infrastructure; the oppression of the Palestinians has never been a "claim" but an objective reality. Israeli security measures have repeatedly been condemned with scarcely any acknowledgment that they are a response to terrorist violence. Christian Aid has failed to examine Palestinian incitement to hate and murder Israelis, and failed to acknowledge the humanitarian aid that Israel brings the Palestinians. While dwelling obsessively on Israel, Christian Aid devotes infinitely less attention to the persecution of Christians by Muslims worldwide—which one might have thought would be a major preoccupation for a Christian charitable organization.

Its 2003 report, *Losing Ground*, was typical. Although in passing it condemned suicide bombings and human rights violations on both sides, the report represented Palestinian suffering as the result of a brutal occupation by Israel, in violation of international law— with no acknowledgment that hardships such as the security barrier were entirely the consequence of Palestinian violence. Worse still was the egregiously distorted history of Israel, omitting altogether the fact that the Arabs tried to destroy Israel at birth in 1948, saying instead: "In the war that followed, the Jewish armed forces made substantial territorial gains, establishing the state of Israel on 78 percent of the land area of Palestine." Christian Aid's report presented the Palestinians as constantly losing ground to Israel without mentioning that the original area of Palestine within which the Jews were promised the right to settle had been shrunk to a tiny fraction.[8]

The following year, Christian Aid's publication *Facts on the Ground* was anything but, as the NGO continued its propaganda. It accused Israel of preventing Palestinians from traveling on roads used by Israelis, without mentioning that this was *only* because of the security risk they posed. The separation barrier was presented not as a measure to prevent suicide bombings but as an attempt to ensure that settlements fell within the future borders of the state of Israel.[9] In April 2009, Christian Aid put on its website a "virtual pilgrimage" to the Holy Land, which presented the Israelis as insatiably hungry for Palestinian land. Heroic Palestinian "Davids" armed merely with video cameras were resisting the Israeli "Goliath," only resorting *in extremis* to weapons and suicide bombings. The "pilgrims" were shown Palestinian homes destroyed by Israel but told little about the destruction produced by the suicide bombers who had lived in them, and nothing at all about the thousands of dollars paid by Iran's agents Hamas and Hezbollah to the bombers' families in compensation for having a *shaheed* (martyr) in the family.[10]

Bishops and archbishops have repeatedly accused Israel of persecuting and dispossessing the Palestinians. In 2003 the archbishop of Wales, Dr. Barry Morgan, said in a lecture on the relationship between religion and violence: "Messianic Zionism came to the fore after the Six Day War in 1967 when 'Biblical territories were reconquered', and so began a policy of cleansing the Promised Land of all Arabs and non-Jews rather than co-existing with them."[11] But there has been no such Israeli "cleansing" at all in the disputed territories. The only attempt at "cleansing" has been the Palestinian effort to kill as many Israelis as possible; and the only people who subsequently were forcibly removed and resettled were the Israeli settlers in Gaza.

Dr. Morgan also eulogized Yasser Arafat upon his death, saying, "Yasser Arafat has given his life to the cause of the Palestinian people and will be remembered for his perseverance and resolve in the face of so many challenges and set-backs. When I heard the news of his death this morning, my initial reaction was to pray that in death Yasser Arafat will find that peace which only God can give and which was denied him in life."[12] But the only person who denied Yasser Arafat "peace" was Yasser Arafat, as a result of his terrorism against Israel.

Over and over again, the church scapegoats Israel for crimes it has not committed. Shortly before Christmas 2006, the archbishop of Canterbury, Dr. Rowan Williams, blamed the flight of Palestinian Christians from Bethlehem on Israeli policies and the security barrier, asking rhetorically, "I would like to know how much it matters to the Israeli Government to have Christian communities in the Holy Land. Are they an embarrassment or are they part of a solution? That's a question."[13]

Such thinking is simply absurd. Bethlehem has indeed been progressively emptied of its Christians, but that's because they have been fleeing the town's Muslim administration. Indeed, if Israel *were* the cause of flight by Bethlehem's Christians, why had Bethlehem's Muslims not similarly been driven out but actually increased in number? The fact is that Christians are being persecuted by Muslims all over the world. The *only* country in the Middle East where Christians have been thriving happens to be Israel.

In a 2006 article, "Who Harms Holy Land Christians?," the syndicated columnist Robert D. Novak, a longtime critic of Israel, paraphrased a letter from Michael H. Sellers, an Anglican priest in Jerusalem, to two U.S. congressmen, Michael McCaul and Joseph Crowley, who were circulating a draft resolution blaming the Christian decline on the discriminatory practices of the Palestinian Authority. Sellers insisted that "the real problem [behind the Christian Arab exodus] is the Israeli occupation—especially its new security wall." Yet two-thirds of the Christian Arabs had already departed between 1948 and 1967, when Jordan occupied the West Bank and Egypt the Gaza Strip, prior to the "occupation" and decades before construction began on the security barrier to protect Israel's population from waves of deadly suicide bombers. During the same period, hundreds of thousands of Christians were fleeing other Muslim-ruled countries in the Middle East, Asia, and North Africa. Every one of the more than twenty Muslim states in the Middle East has a declining Christian population. Israel is the only state in the region in which the Christian Arab population has actually *grown* in real terms—from approximately 34,000 in 1948 to nearly 130,000 in 2005.[14]

UPROOTING THE CHURCH FROM ITS JUDAIC HERITAGE

How could the archbishop of Canterbury have turned facts so upside down? While denouncing Israel, the Church of England maintains almost total silence on the persecution of Christians around the world at the hands of Muslims, with churches being burned and Christians killed, terrorized and converted under duress in many areas of Africa and elsewhere in the Third World. Instead of condemning all this, the church has sought to appease Islam by converging with it while distancing itself from Judaism. Remarkably, it is thus repudiating the religion from which it sprang while sucking up to the one that openly seeks to supersede it.

These developments have been charted by Margaret Brearley, a scholar of interfaith relations. In a paper in 2007, she wrote that Anglicanism as a whole seemed to be gradually uprooting itself from its Judaic heritage. It was no longer normative for Anglican clergy to know Hebrew, and if clergy studied another religion at theological college it was now likely to have been Islam rather than Judaism.

In 2006, the archbishop of Canterbury and the two chief rabbis of Israel signed a historic agreement in Lambeth Palace designed to facilitate a new joint dialogue process between Judaism and the Anglican Communion. Brearley noted disturbing omissions in this agreement. Although it affirmed the importance of the relationship between Christians and Jews, nowhere did it mention God's covenant with Moses, nor did it specifically affirm Judaism. This omission was all the more striking since, through a number of initiatives, the Anglican Church had taken major steps to affirm Islam as a fellow "Abrahamic faith." Indeed, wrote Brearley, "there is arguably a new realignment of Anglicanism with Islam, which may represent a seismic shift within the Anglican Church, reflecting a wider British preoccupation, even fascination, with Islam following 9/11."[15]

The most important of these initiatives was a high-powered Christian-Muslim seminar created by leading Anglicans titled "Building Bridges," convened by the archbishop of Canterbury in January 2002. The proceedings of the inaugural meeting stressed "the shared journey of Christians and Muslims" and "the importance of deepening our dialogue and understanding," especially following 9/11. Papers presented by Muslim and Christian scholars suggested at times equivalence, even unity, between Islam and Christianity. Bishop Kenneth Cragg, for example, stated that "*Magnificat* and *Allahu akbar* are the sure doxologies with which our two faiths begin" and that "In the mystery of our created human trust ... two faiths are one," while Professor David Kerr explained radical Islam "as a form of liberation theology."[16] Typical of this kowtowing to Islam was the willingness of the General Council of the United Church of Canada to consider a proposal to acknowledge formally the prophetic witness of Mohammed. Brearley wrote, "The rapprochement of Anglicanism and Islam has encouraged a process in which any critique of Islamic nationalism or Islamism is either extremely muted or completely absent."[17]

The appeasement of Islam and animosity towards Israel within the church were indeed intimately related to the repudiation of its Jewish theological roots. A letter to the prime minister in 2004 about the Iraq war, from the archbishops of Canterbury and York and backed by every bishop in the Church of England, showed how deeply the church's views about Iraq were dominated by the issue of

Israel, which they approached solely from the perspective of Arab and Muslim opinion. There was no mention in this letter of the rights of Israel or the Jews as the principal victims of annihilatory aggression and prejudice. Instead, the bishops wrote: "Within the wider Christian community we also have theological work to do to counter those interpretations of the Scriptures from outside the mainstream of the tradition which appear to have become increasingly influential in fostering an uncritical and one-sided approach to the future of the Holy Land."[18]

The target of the church hierarchy's attack was the Christian Zionists, and the "interpretations of the Scriptures from outside the mainstream of the tradition" referred to this movement's faithfulness to the Hebrew Bible.

THE ATTACK ON CHRISTIAN ZIONISTS

Christian Zionism is an umbrella term for those Christians whose support for Israel is based on theology. They believe that the restoration of modern Israel is the fulfillment of God's prophetic purpose that it would be restored to the Jews, its enemies destroyed and peace brought to the entire world. Within this broad definition there are different varieties of Christian Zionism, including the most controversial doctrine that the restoration of Israel will bring about the return of Christ to earth and a holocaust or mass conversion of the Jews, resulting in the end of days. But as Paul Merkley has written, this doctrine is not universal and does not form part of the Christian Zionism preached by the International Christian Embassy Jerusalem, which has more than eighty branches around the world and which was established in 1980 to represent all Christians who wanted to see their governments affirm the Jews' Biblical right to rule in Jerusalem.[19]

Christian Zionism derives from two historical periods of active philosemitism within the church: seventeenth-century Puritanism and nineteenth-century evangelicalism. What these two movements had in common was belief in and reverence for the Hebrew Bible and for God's "chosen people," the Jews.

English Puritans such as John Milton and Oliver Cromwell were members of a community that baptized their children with Hebrew names, went to the Hebrew prophets for precedents in conduct, and taught the desirability of the restoration of the Jews to their holy land. Just as today, these evangelical, scriptural Christians were highly protective of the Jews, in sharp distinction from the rest of English society.

The nineteenth and early twentieth century saw the rise of Christian Zionism among Anglican evangelicals, who by the mid nineteenth century constituted about half of all Anglican clergy. Such people were deeply sympathetic to the fact that in Judaism the religion, the people and the land were indissolubly linked. The great Victorian social reformer Lord Shaftesbury, who was chairman of the London Society for Promoting Christianity among the Jews, wore a ring engraved with the words "Oh, pray for the peace of Jerusalem," and throughout his life he repeated that Israel was "a country without a nation for a nation without a country."[20]

It was this Christian Zionism which led Lord Balfour to issue his famous declaration committing Britain to re-establish the Jewish national home in Palestine. "The position of the Jews is unique," he wrote in 1919. "For them race, religion and country are inter-related, as they are inter-related in the case of no other race, no other religion, and no other country on earth."[21]

Christian Zionism is no longer mainstream in Britain, and this fact furnishes the most significant contrast with the United States. For in America, while the liberal churches are losing membership, the conservative churches are gaining.[22] And those growing churches are overwhelmingly Christian Zionist. This is the real "Israel lobby"—a giant stretch of "Middle America," where elections are won and lost, that passionately endorses both the State of Israel and the Hebrew Bible.

In Britain, by contrast, mainstream Anglicanism regards Christian Zionism with as much horror as it regards the "Christian fundamentalists," who are faithful to Hebrew scripture and may believe in the literal truth of the Bible, and the "Christian Right," who it believes hijacked American foreign policy in the interests of Israel; indeed, these are all regarded as synonymous. Christians who support Israel take a variety of views about its policies, but mainstream Anglicans see Christian Zionists as invariably supporting an expansionist policy of "Greater Israel" that would colonize the disputed territories—which the Anglicans, with scant regard for history, view as "Palestinian"—on the basis of the Biblical promise of the land to the Jews. Indeed, for many Anglicans this expansionist form of Zionism *is* Zionism. They don't believe there is any other form.

What gives this animosity against Christian Zionism a particular edge is the church's drive to appease Islam—so powerful that it has now forced a wedge not just between evangelicals and liberals but into the evangelical movement itself. In July 2008, a group of influential Anglican evangelicals in the UK met discreetly to coordinate a new approach to Islam. The meeting was convened by Bryan Knell of the missionary organization Global Connections, and others from a group calling itself Christian Responses to Islam in Britain. The twenty-two participants, who met at All Nations Christian College in Ware, Hertfordshire, were sworn to secrecy. Their aim was to develop the "grace approach to Islam," which "tries to let Muslims interpret Islam rather than telling them what their religion teaches." The meeting had in its sights those "aggressive" Christians who were "increasing the level of fear" in many others by talking about the threat posed by radical Islam. The goal was thus to discredit and stifle prominent British Christians, such as the bishop of Rochester, Michael Nazir-Ali, the Africa specialist Baroness Cox and the Islam expert Dr. Patrick Sookhdeo, who warn against the Islamization of Britain and Islam's threat to the church.[23]

In January 2009, the website of Fulcrum, an evangelical group, carried a review by Ben White of Sookhdeo's book *Global Jihad: The*

Future in the Face of Militant Islam. The review trashed Sookhdeo's scholarship on the grounds that he had identified a theological problem with Islam when in White's view Islamic aggression was rooted instead in global grievances, particularly the existence and behavior of Israel. To cap a farrago of ignorance and historical illiteracy, White tried to damn Sookhdeo by association, citing "hard-line conservatives and pro-Israel right-wingers" who endorsed his work as proof that Sookhdeo was beyond the pale.[24]

A recurring thread of White's writing is his hatred of Israel and dubious attitude towards Jews. He justifies Palestinian terrorism against Israel as legitimate self-defense to bring about "decolonisation and liberation from occupation and Zionist apartheid."[25] He has said, "I do not consider myself an antisemite, yet I can also understand why some are" because of Israel's "ideology of racial supremacy and its subsequent crimes committed against the Palestinians" and also "the widespread bias and subservience to the Israeli cause in the Western media."[26] His book *Israeli Apartheid: A Beginner's Guide*, published in 2009, includes numerous distortions, omissions, errors and fabricated quotations in an attempt to portray Israel as an apartheid state.[27]

Such frenzied denunciations of Israel clearly amount to far more than mere ignorance, ideology or even prejudice. In their intensity and the representation of Israel as a demonic force of unparalleled aggression and vengeance, these attitudes have a distinctly metaphysical character. Indeed, for the anti-Zionist church, Israel crystallizes a complex combination of ancient theological prejudice against the Jews *and* a profound, civilizational guilt over the way Christianity has perpetrated that prejudice—a burden of guilt so unbearable that, led by the church itself, the Christian world *has to* turn the Jews into the architects of their own destruction.

THE ROLE OF THE WORLD COUNCIL OF CHURCHES

Almost immediately after 1948, as Paul Merkley has chronicled, attitudes within the church shifted to anti-Zionism, closing a tiny window of support in the years immediately following World War II. Christian attitudes were heavily influenced by the World Council of Churches, which as we have seen views the world through Marxist, anti-Western spectacles. Even in the early days of the WCC, its Middle East desk was composed of people from Arab countries and so Israel was never seen as an integral part of the region. An insider observed that in general "the critique of some Israeli sin would be severe, while Arab countries were spared any kind of condemnation in order not to jeopardize Christian missionary interests there."[28]

After the Six-Day War, hostility greatly intensified when the influential Protestant journal *Christianity and Crisis* switched from a pro-Israel position to the Palestinian camp on the grounds that nothing could "sanctify the right of conquest in the twentieth century." Arabs thence became the underdog and the WCC has marched ever since in lockstep with Arab rhetoric. It supported the PLO's need to train its "liberation armies," denounced the Camp David peace accords for shunting aside Palestinian autonomy, and reacted strongly against Israel's invasion of Lebanon in 1982 as "premeditated aggression" without even mentioning Syria's aggressive presence there, let alone its responsibility for the deaths of many thousands of Christian civilians.[29]

As Merkley writes, during the 1980s the WCC increasingly reflected the effects of bringing into its ranks the Middle East Council of Churches, an association formed in 1974 of seventeen Christian denominations belonging to Eastern Orthodox, Oriental Orthodox, Catholic and Protestant congregations—virtually all the 14 million Christians of the Middle East. Early in 1988, the MECC issued letters to Christian churches and organizations throughout the world warning them about Christian Zionism, which it called an ill-informed and biased corruption of Christianity. The MECC said that Christian Zionist ideas, such as those pronounced by the International Christian Embassy Jerusalem, were "dangerous distortions of the Christian faith," and that to "support Israel's policies from their understanding of the Bible will be anathema to the intent of Christian faith and will be detrimental to Christian presence and witness in our region."[30]

If one wonders how it could possibly be that both the liberal churches in particular and the West in general consistently blame Israel not just for crimes it has not committed but *of which it is often the victim,* one need look no further than the WCC. It consistently blames Israel for the failure of the "peace process" without mentioning the warmongering activities of the other side. It blames Israel for the decline of living conditions in the disputed territories throughout the fourteen years since the Palestinian Authority has been totally responsible for government there; Israel is to blame nonetheless for their economic failure, the growth of crime and violence and the failures of the educational system. It blames Israel exclusively for the rapid increase in harassment, intimidation and emigration of Christians from the West Bank and Gaza since 1994, when the Palestinians took control of their own government and despite the evidence of Muslim persecution of Christians in those areas. It blames Israel exclusively for the election of Hamas in 2006, for the ensuing struggle between Hamas and Fatah, and for the swift descent of Gaza into destitution and social chaos.[31] This is all routine Anglican rhetoric—repeated week in, week out by Britain's media and intelligentsia.

The WCC also played a major role in bringing about the anti-Israel and anti-Jewish hate-fest that took place in Durban, South Africa, a few days before 9/11, when WCC representatives attending the UN Conference on Racism, Racial Discrimination, Xenophobia and Related Intolerance demanded that the UN denounce

Israel for "systematic perpetration of racist crimes including war crimes, acts of genocide and ethnic cleansing."[32] Merkley observes:

> This Durban Declaration was achieved in large part by the active lobbying of the World Council of Churches serving as brokers between the Muslim states and western opinion in August 2001. Today, the Durban Declaration serves as the source of the mottos with which respectable people in our part of the world shape their campaigns to deprive Israel of her right-to-life. WCC statements on this theme are parroted by the official journals and newsletters of the major Protestant denominations in the United States and elsewhere around the world.[33]

"REPLACEMENT THEOLOGY" OR "SUPERSESSIONISM"

The real root of the extreme hostility within the church towards Israel lies in the resurrection of the previously discredited doctrine of "replacement theology," also known as "supersessionism," wrapped up in politics and ideology. Replacement theology goes back to the third century CE when Origen, regarded as the father of Christian doctrine, concluded that the Jews had lost their favored position with God and that Christians were now the "New Israel." The Jews' divine election was revoked and they were "destined to stand in perpetual opposition to God." This doctrine lay behind centuries of Christian anti-Jewish hatred until the Holocaust drove it underground. Now it's back, kick-started by Palestinian Christian liberation theology, which states falsely that the Palestinian Arabs were the original possessors of the land of Israel. Thus the former Anglican bishop of Jerusalem, Riah Abu El-Assal, claimed that Palestinian Christians "are the true Israel," adding, "no-one can deny me the right to inherit the promises, and after all the promises were first given to Abraham and Abraham is never spoken of in the Bible as a Jew.... He is the father of the faithful."[34]

This false claim that the Palestinians are the true people of the land combines with replacement theology to make the case against the State of Israel. To supersessionist Christians, Israel is an ungodly interloper and her defenders are the enemies of God—which is precisely the Muslim and Arab argument, a characterization which has tapped into unsavory echoes deep in church history.

Paul Merkley points out that the recurring claim within the church that Christian Zionism is a "heresy" comes from language used by the Middle East Council of Churches, which in turn reflects their historical experience. During the centuries in which they came under Muslim rule, the Eastern churches were treated as *dhimmi*—subjugated minorities—alongside the Jews. They wanted therefore to exaggerate the theological gulf between Christians and Jews to ensure that the Muslims would treat them better. The Eastern churches were deeply committed to supersessionism over the Jews, which helped them have more comfortable relations with Islam. They also turned to gnosticism, the elitist, esoteric and pagan teaching that lies outside scripture, and in particular to a form of gnosticism called Marcionism, a second-century Christian heresy that advocated a radical separation of the Christian faith from its origins in Judaism—and which provides yet another link between radical Christians and the pagan, New Age milieu.[35]

Canon Andrew White, formerly the archbishop of Canterbury's envoy to the Middle East and now the vicar of Baghdad, is a Christian Zionist who has attempted to sound a warning about the new eruption of Christianity's ancient prejudice against the Jews. According to White, replacement theology has now gone viral within the Church of England. He observes that the establishment of the State of Israel would probably have had more opposition from the church had it not been for the Holocaust. But now, with modern Israel being represented as behaving in an analogous fashion to the Nazis, that brake on the prejudice has been removed. The consistent interpretation has been that the Promised Land is where the church will be established, that Jerusalem is the heavenly city and that it will eventually be the home of all Christians. This view was reinforced by the development of a Palestinian "liberation theology," which found support among Western churches.[36] And that liberation theology was drawn in large measure from the radical ideas of the World Council of Churches.

The Palestinian church has faced a major theological crisis since Israel was established, says White, in large measure because of the perception that the Bible has been used as a Zionist text. Politics and theology have become inextricably intertwined. In liberation theology, the Biblical God is the God of those who are oppressed; the Palestinians are viewed as the oppressed. "Who is their oppressor?" White asks rhetorically. "The State of Israel. Who is Israel? The Jews. It is they therefore who must be put under pressure so that the oppressed may one day be set free to enter their 'Promised Land' which is being denied to them." This analysis, says White, has influenced whole denominations, as well as the majority of Christian pilgrimage companies and many of the major mission and aid organizations.[37]

The crucible of Palestinian Christian replacement theology is the Sabeel Ecumenical Liberation Theology Center in Jerusalem, run by Father Naim Ateek and used as a major resource by Anglican clergy, aid agencies and pilgrimage companies. Sabeel is thus a crucial source of systematic, theologically based lies and libels about Israel.

A close friend of many senior Anglican bishops, Ateek has written that because the Old Testament has been read as a Zionist text it has become "almost repugnant" to Palestinian Christians. His book *Justice and Only Justice* uses the Bible to delegitimize Israel by misrepresenting the Jews' relationship with God; it inverts history, defames the Jews and sanitizes Arab violence. Modern antisemitism gets precisely one paragraph, while Zionism is portrayed as an aggressive colonial adventure. Real antisemitism, says Ateek, is found within the Jewish community in its treatment of the Palestinians. Courageous Jews are those who confess to "moral suicide" and say that Judaism should survive without a state.[38]

Elsewhere, Ateek has recycled and redirected the ancient charge of deicide against the Jews. In December 2000, he wrote that Palestinian Christmas celebrations were "marred by the destructive powers of the modern-day 'Herods' in the Israeli government."[39] In his 2001 Easter message, he claimed that "the Israeli government crucifixion system is operating daily." In a direct reference to Calvary, or Golgotha, Palestine had become "the place of the skull."[40] And, in a sermon in February 2001, Ateek likened the Israeli occupation to the boulder sealing Christ's tomb.[41] With these three images, Ateek has figuratively blamed Israel for trying to kill the infant Jesus, crucifying him and blocking the Resurrection.

In 2005, the Sabeel Center issued a liturgy titled "The Contemporary Stations of the Cross," which equates Israel's founding with Jesus' death sentence and the construction of a security barrier with his death on the cross.[42] So it is hardly surprising that churches up and down Britain have replaced their traditional Christmas manger scenes with tableaux featuring the security barrier, making a specific analogy between the suffering Jesus and the suffering Palestinians.[43]

Sabeel's Palestinian supersessionism has brought Christian replacement theology out from the historical vault of shame in which it had supposedly been buried, and by playing into Western victim culture has given it a patina of high idealism. It has also made inroads into the church's evangelical wing, resulting in the conversion of a number of evangelicals from Christian Zionism to anti-Zionism. In his book *Who Are God's People in the Middle East?*, Gary Burge recounted how he converted from Christian Zionism after being told by Father George Makhlour of St. George's Greek Orthodox Church in Ramallah that "the church has inherited the promises of Israel. The church is actually the new Israel." Burge came to believe: "Followers of Jesus were the new people of God. And they would inherit the history and the promises known throughout the Old Testament.... Whatever the 'land' meant in the Old Testament, whatever the promise contained, this now belonged to Christians."[44]

At a meeting in London in 1986 hosted by the influential evangelical John Stott, the Lausanne Committee for World Evangelization set up a group called Evangelicals for Middle East Understanding to oppose the view that Israel was the fulfillment of Biblical prophecy. This organization subscribes to a movement that Paul Wilkinson has termed "Christian Palestinianism."[45]

One of this movement's key texts is *Whose Promised Land?*, in which the hugely influential Colin Chapman sets out the theological delegitimization of Israel. Although Chapman carefully condemns antisemitism and says the Christians have not superseded the Jews, he says nevertheless that the Jews' only salvation is through Christ. Christians now share the Jews' privileges; through Christ, the division between Jews and Christians broke down, and they have become as one "new man." And this "new man" therefore doesn't warrant a Jewish state. According to Chapman, "The coming of the kingdom of God through Jesus the messiah has transformed and reinterpreted all the promises and prophecies in the Old Testament." The delegitimization of Israel on theological grounds is thus made explicit.[46]

It also—despite Chapman's disavowals elsewhere of anti-Jewish prejudice—is indeed an exposition of precisely that bigotry, and thus leads unsurprisingly to Chapman's further view that the Jews are a force with a mysterious control over world events. Chapman wrote particularly of the supposed power of American Jews:

> Six million Jews in the USA have an influence that is out of all proportion to their numbers in the total population of 281 million. Through wealth, education, skill and single-mindedness over many years they have gained positions of power in government, business and the media. It is widely recognised, for example, that no one could ever win the presidential race without the votes and the financial support of substantial sections of the Jewish community.[47]

In the UK, "Christian Palestinianism" is spearheaded by Stephen Sizer, the vicar of Christ Church, Virginia Water in Surrey, who excoriates Israel and has endorsed the description of Christian Zionism by the Middle East Council of Churches as a "devious heresy" and an "erroneous interpretation of the Bible which is subservient to the political agenda of the modern State of Israel."48 Sizer believes that all God's promises to the Jews, including the land of Israel, have been inherited by Christianity. He has acknowledged that Israel has the right to exist, since it was established by a United Nations resolution. But he has also called it "fundamentally an apartheid state because it is based on race" and "even worse than South Africa" (despite the fact that Israeli Arabs have the vote, they are members of the Knesset and have even served in the Supreme Court). Asked whether Israel's existence could be justified, Sizer replied that South African apartheid had been "brought to an end internally by the rising up of the people." He said, "The covenant between Jews and God was conditional on their respect for human rights. The reason they were expelled from the land was that they were more interested in money and power and treated the poor and aliens with contempt." Today's Jews, it appeared, were no better. "In the United States, politicians dare not criticise Israel because half the funding for both the Democrats and the Republicans comes from Jewish sources."49

While Sizer, like many other "Christian Palestinianists," purports to disavow replacement theology, that is precisely what he preaches. Indeed, he has gone so far as to negate the essence of Judaism and the Jewish people altogether, writing, "Now we find that it is Gentiles (and Jews who believe in Jesus) who are declared to be the true children of Abraham and Sarah. Jews outside the new covenant of grace have, through the cross and because of their rejection of Jesus, become the children of Hagar."50 Having thus exiled the Jews from their own historical narrative, Sizer concludes elsewhere: "To suggest therefore that the Jewish people continue to have a special relationship with God, apart from faith in Jesus or have exclusive rights to land, a city and temple is, in the words of John Stott, 'biblically anathema.'"[51]

As Margaret Brearley has written, Sizer's book *Christian Zionism: Road-Map to Armageddon?* is endorsed by many leading British and American bishops and theologians.[52] Given that his church is a member of the Evangelical Alliance, says Paul Wilkinson, it is "disturbing" that Sizer is involved with such extreme Islamic organizations as Friends of Al-Aqsa, the Islamic Human Rights Commission, Crescent International and the Muslim Association of Britain.[53] But that's not all. Sizer has also given interviews to, endorsed or forwarded material from American white supremacists and Holocaust deniers. In 2008, he sent an article printed in the *Palestine Chronicle* about the alleged influence of "Israel in Washington" through "powerful overtly Jewish Washington organisations and, increasingly, through Christian Zionist organisations" to an appreciative Martin Webster, the former leader of the neo-Nazi National Front. Sizer claims that he has "never knowingly" given interviews, sent material from or endorsed such extremists.[54]

Wilkinson notes that "Christian Palestinianists" have successfully turned the minds of many against the Jewish people by using such emotive labels as "apartheid," "ethnic cleansing," "genocide," "massacre" and "occupation," and by comparing the Israelis to Nazis.[55] Rosemary Radford Ruether, the radical feminist whose sympathies also lie with paganism, has made an illusory connection between the Holocaust and "a special Israeli psychological need to batter Palestinians," while Marc Ellis describes the Palestinians as "the last victims of the Holocaust," suggesting it is time to bring "the era of Auschwitz" in the Israel-Palestinian conflict to an end.[56]

According to Canon Andrew White, replacement theology is dominant in the Church of England and present in almost every church, fueling the venom against Israel. The essential problem, said White, was the lack of will in the church to face the difference between Judaism and Islam. "They don't want to recognize that their faith comes from Judaism," he said. "They talk instead of the 'children of Abraham' as if we are all in it together. The reality is, however, that although Islam and Judaism have a lot in common in terms of customs, they are as far apart as Christianity is from heathenism."[57]

The former archbishop of Canterbury Lord Carey agrees that replacement theology is the most important driver behind the church's hatred of Israel.[58] The problem is particularly acute within Protestantism because, unlike the Catholic Church, it has never tried to make its peace with Judaism. Although the Catholic Church as late as the 1960s was teaching supersessionism, in the wake of the Holocaust it went in for much soul-searching over the historic Christian charge of deicide against the Jews. As result, in the seminal 1965 encyclical *Nostra Aetate* from the Second Vatican Council it explicitly affirmed the church's Jewish roots, condemned anti-semitism, absolved the Jews of collective guilt for the death of Jesus and stated explicitly that "the Jews should not be presented as rejected or accursed by God, as if this follows from the Holy Scriptures."[59]

As Paul Merkley records, the Muslim world reacted with horror to *Nostra Aetate*, regarding it as a theological retreat from the united front against Zionism. As a result of Muslim pressure, Pope Paul VI in 1970 preached that Christians had closer ties with Islam than with any other religion. Subsequently, papal relations with the Arab world improved over the years, while the Vatican refused to recognize Israel until the philosemitic Pope John Paul II finally did so in 1993.[60]

Although relations between the Vatican, Israel and the Jews have remained rocky, the significance of *Nostra Aetate* lay in the fact that the Catholic Church accepted that there was a problem in its attitude towards the Jews and tried to repair it. No such initiative has ever been forthcoming within the Protestant world, indicating that it cannot even accept there is a problem, let alone try to address it. This failure has allowed for the resurgence of replacement theology.

As a result, the church has lent its weight to the delegitimization of Israel, and the conflation of revisionist Christian theology with an Arab agenda has delivered a victory to the Islamists. A view that holds the enemies of civilization to be the Jews rather than the Islamists transfers righteous opposition from those who threaten the free world to their victims.

This visceral and ancient hostility within the church and the larger society helps explain why we are living through a hallucinatory level of anti-Israel and anti-Jewish animosity. The church is promoting once again a pre-Holocaust demonology of the Jewish people, expressed this time as hatred of Israel.

HOLOCAUST GUILT AND PATHOLOGICAL PROJECTION

It is conventional wisdom that opinion turned against Israel when it was transformed from "David" into "Goliath" after 1967. Not only is this a distorted perspective of the relative strength in the region, but it does not begin to explain the frenzied and irrational nature of this hatred. It doesn't explain, for example, why there is such an appetite for the monstrous portrayal of Israelis as Nazis, which effectively denies the reality of the Holocaust. It doesn't explain why, when hearts bleed for every "victim" group, Jewish victimization is airbrushed out of the picture altogether. It doesn't explain why, when the Second Intifada broke out in 2000 and Israelis were being blown to bits in cafes and on buses, opinion turned so savagely against the victims who were seeking to defend themselves.

The explanation may be that the deep and irrational bigotry displayed towards Israel in the West arises not just from a resurgence of a theologically based hatred of the Jews, but also from guilt over that hatred.

To try to unpick this, we need to set today's tumult in its historical context. Jew-hatred has very deep roots in Britain. From Chaucer to Shakespeare to Dickens to T. S. Eliot and beyond,

388 THE WORLD TURNED UPSIDE DOWN

English culture is responsible for some of the most enduring anti-Jewish stereotypes in the world. Central to the creation of these stereotypes was Christianity, its belief that the Jews were the killers of Christ, condemned in perpetuity and exiled as a result from the love of God to become the party of the devil. This belief lay behind sustained anti-Jewish prejudice in Britain over the centuries, with the medieval period punctuated by blood libels, massacres and pogroms before the Jews were expelled altogether in 1290.

There were two periods when a culture of Christian philo-semitism interrupted the otherwise dismal history of English Jew-hatred. The first was when the Jews were allowed back into England by Oliver Cromwell in 1656, when the prevailing Puritanism led to a veneration of the Hebrew Bible and a feeling of fellowship with the Jews. The second was the dominance of evangelicalism in the nineteenth century and the Christian Zionism to which it gave rise, which once again reconnected Christianity to Hebrew Scripture and led to the commitment by the British government, in the Balfour Declaration of 1917, to restore the Jewish national home in Palestine.

But from that high point, things rapidly went downhill again. The history of Britain in its colonial administration of Palestine is one of systematic betrayal. The belief in scripture and the veneration of the Jewish people that had led to the Balfour Declaration were on the wane, hammered by the trauma of World War I in combination with modernism and rising individualism. Britain's changing perception of its own national interest in the region led it to appease the Arabs by restricting the Jewish immigration it had promised to facilitate—thus swelling the death toll of the Holocaust—while turning a blind eye to illegal Arab immigration and kowtowing to terror by proposing to divide Palestine into a state for the Jews and a state for the Arabs. Eventually, Britain abstained in the 1947 United Nations vote to bring Israel into being; and the anger at Jewish terrorism, the perception that Britain had been humiliated in Palestine and the belief that it had been embroiled in an unnecessary and damaging project left deep public resentment—not at the Arabs who had terrorized both the British army and the Jews in Palestine to thwart the creation of Israel, but at the Jews for having caused the problem in the first place.

Anti-Jewish feeling persisted in Britain up to and into the Second World War; in the 1930s, anti-Jewish sentiment, along with a mood of appeasement towards Nazi Germany, was remarkably similar to what is happening today. When the enormity of the Holocaust was revealed, however, that prejudice went underground. One might say therefore that knowledge of the Holocaust provided a measure of protection from overt anti-Jewish feeling. But now, that protection has disappeared. So why has this happened?

On the surface, the story looks simple. In its early years, Israel basked in Britain's approval because it suited the spirit of the age. As Europe emerged from the horrors of the war, Israel was in effect hope reborn, a young idealistic country run on socialist principles and making the desert bloom. But when the skies darkened and Israel became embroiled in an apparently never-ending, messy new kind of warfare in which the Arabs could paint Israelis as brutal occupiers and themselves as victims, the mood sharply changed. Pictures of Palestinian women weeping over the rubble of houses destroyed by the Israeli army turned the militarized Jews into oppressors. The resentful memory of the Palestine Mandate and the belief formed during that time that a Jewish state would only bring trouble were given new and virulent life.

But there is arguably a still deeper and darker explanation. The cause of this pathology is surely guilt over the Holocaust and centuries of Christian persecution, along with a desire to expiate that guilt. It is a collective guilt, since those who manifest it did not in the main play any part in those atrocities. They have no personal moral responsibility. Moreover, many of them harbor nothing but benign feelings towards Jews as people and find all forms of racial prejudice repugnant. Their guilt is thus a pathological cultural projection, which might help explain both its intensity and its irrationality.

The warmth expressed towards Israel in its early years was surely due at least in part to the fact that it effectively redeemed the Holocaust. Not only had it risen from the ashes of the Jews of Europe, but it seemed to create a new kind of Jew altogether. The black-garbed moneylenders of stereotype had been replaced by fresh-faced young people in shorts growing tomatoes and peppers from rock and sand.

With the old Jews of Europe firmly fixed in its mind as dead victims, Britain now saw instead plucky new Jews bravely fighting off the Arab Goliath. They were under attack, for sure, but they weren't victims. Their feats of military prowess, from the Six-Day War to the rescue of Israeli hostages at Entebbe, involved an apparently miraculous ability to achieve victory over impossible odds. These tall bronzed young people planting orange groves meant that Britain didn't have to feel guilty about Jewish suffering anymore. The centuries-old British and European "Jewish problem" appeared to be finally over. The Christian West had achieved its absolution.

Even after Israel occupied the disputed territories in 1967, opinion did not significantly change overnight. It was only when systematic Palestinian terror started and Israel had to move in to contain it that the mood dramatically altered.

This was surely because the sight of Jews in battledress and tanks putting down the wretched of the earth has aroused in Christian Europe two overwhelming and visceral feelings. It has revived the deep belief that the very existence of the Jews is an insult and a reproach to the essence of Christianity, which wishes deep down that the Jews would simply disappear off the face of the earth. But second, *because* Christian Europe has done its best over the centuries to make that happen and is responsible for anti-Jewish bloodbaths through the ages, culminating in the Nazi Holocaust, liberal Christians—who are particularly sensitive to the evils of racial prejudice—cannot accept that the Jews are locked in battle to prevent the same from happening all over again. To acknowledge this would remind them too painfully of their own historic behavior. So they turn the Jews into the attackers, and thereby release themselves from the guilt they feel over the Holocaust.

That's why liberal Christian Europe calls the Israelis "Nazis." Relieved of its self-denying ordinance to suppress its anti-Jewish feelings, it can now use the image it creates of the Nazi Jew to slough off its own guilt. That's why the hatred explodes whenever Israel is attacked. Western liberals ignore the attack and focus instead, instantly and obsessively, on the fact that the Israelis will undoubtedly kill Palestinians in response. Such killings are invariably called "vengeance" and "punishment"; the idea that they might be appropriate and necessary is denied, because to acknowledge as much would be to admit that the Jews are once again victims. So the more Israel and its supporters protest that the Jews are the victims of another attempted genocide—indeed, the more Israelis are attacked—the more hostile Western liberals become.

This is all a source of immense pain for the many decent Christians who are horrified by their church's attitude and understand very well where it is leading. Dexter van Zile, a Christian researcher for the American Campaign for Accuracy in Middle East Reporting, observes:

> Since extremist movements typically attack Jews first, they evoke feelings of guilt at precisely those moments in history when Western intellectuals and religious leaders need to think clearly. We saw this with Nazism and now we see it in response to Islamist extremism targeting Israel and the West. Progressive Christians cannot respond reasonably to the threats facing Western civilization because it reminds them of their own historical sins, which makes them think that their civilization is not worthy of a robust defense.[61]

Israel was the ultimate millenarian dream, but it went bad for the dreamers, both Christian *and* secular. At the beginning it was Eden restored, an orange-grove utopia that was to create a new Jew and a new world where guns were beaten into greenhouses. It was going to redeem Christian guilt over the historical persecution of the Jews by solving the "Jewish problem" once and for all. When utopia failed to arrive and the Jews found themselves yet again facing an exterminatory onslaught, the Christian and post-Christian West turned on the people whose crime was to have thwarted redemption by failing to efface their own history.

18

THE DISENCHANTMENT
OF REASON

The Enlightenment is consuming its own progeny. In the West, the culture of reason is dying, brought down by a loss of faith in progress and in the rationality that underpinned it. The replacement of objective truth by subjective experience has turned some strands of science into a branch of unreason, as evidence is hijacked by ideology. The perceptive Anglican bishop Lesslie Newbigin grasped this fact back in the 1980s. In his essay *The Other Side of 1984*, he wrote, "I have started from the perception, which I believe to be valid and widely shared, that we are nearing the end of the period of 250 years during which our modern European culture has been confidently offering itself to the rest of the world as the torchbearer for human progress."[1]

The Western world's exhilaration that what was previously obscure could now be explained has given way to the realization that "explanation" does not meet all human need—not least because explanation hits a wall or turns in on itself. As Newbigin put it, "To speak of an 'explanation' is to speak of the ultimate framework of axioms and assumptions by means of which one 'makes sense of things'. 'Explanations' only operate within an accepted framework which does not itself require explanation."[2] In other words, religion. The Enlightenment deemed one framework inadequate and so another took its place. Religious dogma was replaced by reason. Now that one has been shown to be inadequate too.

The age of reason was supposed to end all the ills in the world. Since these problems were held to derive from religion's suppression of the defining characteristic of the human race, the intellect, it was assumed that once exposed to the full power of the mind they would fade away. But just like every other millenarian fantasy, this brave new world failed to materialize. War, bigotry and tyranny did not come to an end. Materialism and science were heavily implicated in the two greatest tyrannies of the twentieth century. Modernity lost its shine. Technology created anomie. Progress threatened the planet. Mankind was viewed as a pollutant. The Enlightenment project was yet another utopia that had failed.

Yet at the same time, any perspective that was not scientific was regarded as illegitimate. Religion and reason were held to be intrinsically incompatible. But this was a fundamental and fatal error. It was religion that gave the world the concepts of progress and reason in the first place. When Nietzsche declared that God was dead, reason was killed off alongside him, as Nietzsche knew only too well. Those who wanted science to destroy religion didn't realize that destroying religion would in turn destroy science. Thus modernity is in danger of disappearing up its own fundament.

In 1958, the philosopher of science Michael Polanyi wrote that the past four or five centuries had resulted in unrivaled moral and cultural enrichment. "But its incandescence has fed on the combustion of the Christian heritage in the oxygen of Greek rationalism," he said, "and when the fuel was exhausted the critical framework itself burnt away."[3]

For sure, terrible things have been done in the name of religion, which has itself given rise over the centuries to both irrationality and oppression. But the fact remains that religion was the wellspring of reason, order, progress, human dignity and liberty. Without it, these would not have existed; and as religion has been progressively edged out of Western life, so truth and morality have crumbled, leading to irrationality, prejudice and disorder. And it was not just any religion that created reason and progress but very specifically Christianity, and the Hebrew Bible from which it sprang.

THE WARPED IMPULSES OF DERACINATED SPIRITUALITY

What has also become very clear is that disposing of religion has not meant disposing of the religious impulse. The drive to connect with something beyond the self is fundamental and ineradicable. Dislocated from the religious source of reason, however, it becomes irrational and embraces animism, magic and the occult. The environmental campaigner Al Gore perfectly expressed this warped spirituality when he wrote in 2000 that the "froth and frenzy of industrial civilization mask our deep loneliness for that communion with the world that can lift our spirits and fill our senses with the richness and immediacy of life itself."[4] The way he dealt with that deep spiritual yearning was not to connect with the religion that explained the orderliness and wonder of the natural world, but to commune with the earth itself.

As deracinated spirituality turned to pantheism and paganism, it left both rationality *and* religion far behind. But remarkably, these postreligious forms of spirituality still embodied assumptions specific to Christianity and even its most egregious historical extremes. They all reproduced the specifically Christian motifs of sin, guilt and redemption—whether they involved the sins of capitalism or colonialism, greed or ignorance, which would be redeemed by campaigning for the environment or against America, for the Palestinians or against creationists.

More remarkably still, these ideologies were secular variations on millenarian fantasies, positing the utopias of a healed planet, a world without war, a society populated by a New Man (insofar as he was allowed to exist at all without consuming any natural resources) free of prejudice of any kind, and an age of perfect reason. And just like the millenarian movements of medieval times, these secular ideologies have come fully equipped with priesthoods of the elect who guard access to truth, and with savage tactics for dealing with heretics and stifling dissent.

It was in mainland Europe, rather than in more moderate Britain, that the Enlightenment turned into a wholesale attack on religion. Today's European Union is engaged in repudiating the Christian heritage that gave rise to Europe's civilization. After an acrimonious debate, the EU Constitution was drafted without any acknowledgment of Christianity as a source of European civilization and of contemporary Europe's commitments to human rights and democracy.[5] And in 2004, the Catholic Italian politician Rocco Buttiglione was turned down for a post as EU justice commissioner because he had said that homosexuality was a sin.[6]

The Jacobins who created the Committee of Public Safety would doubtless have approved of the European Commission. The EU project claims higher legitimacy than individual member democracies because it embodies "universal" values that cannot be gainsaid. Christian codes of moral order are illegitimate; the "universal" and unchallengeable moral, social and ideological foundations of the EU include gay rights, feminism and multiculturalism.[7] The EU came into being principally to constrain Germany and prevent fascism from ever again coming to power in Europe. Ironically, a project to redeem Europe from the crime of breeding a tyranny based on the pagan repudiation of religion and reason—albeit fed by prejudices of medieval Christianity—is itself repudiating the Christianity that underpinned reason and stood against paganism.

Moreover, as we have seen, the idea that getting rid of religion gets rid of intolerance is the opposite of the case. Secularism breeds its own intolerance against dissenters. Just as with medieval Christianity, it represents a perfectly closed thought system that is believed to embody virtue. Heretics must therefore be punished and suppressed. Hence the medieval-style witch-hunts against global warming skeptics, intelligent design theorists, "homophobes" and the State of Israel, through which persecution the most high-minded of the Western intelligentsia believe they are exercising their progressive consciences.

That is because, just as with the medieval millenarian movements, these are attempts to redeem collective guilt in order to arrive at utopia. Paul Edward Gottfried observes that the desperate efforts being made by Western countries—particularly Protestant ones—to elevate themselves morally by receiving large immigrant populations entirely distinct from themselves represent an ostentatious guilt over their historical past. Gottfried notes that, with sin redefined as insensitive behavior, continuity with religion has not been totally broken. "Contemporary liberal Christianity combines rituals of western self-rejection with established Protestant attitudes about individuality and equality, the radically fallen state of the sinner and the simultaneous self-debasement and self-elevation of the saint," he writes.[8]

Gottfried cites the Italian historian Augusto del Noce, who in 1977 detected totalitarianism in the "scientific" management of society, the discrediting of traditional authority and the progress of a secular managerialism that attempted to recode human nature. Behind this managerial project lay a "war against all forms of knowing that are not deemed as scientific." Science and reason were thereby turned into instruments of ideology. Science was reduced to superstition or a "certification wrapped in a mystery" and attached to a group of privileged power-bearers. And this, writes Gottfried, was part of the natural course in mass democracy, "a process that begins with the loss of the Greek discovery of morality and ends with the negation of philosophic reason and the persecution of dissidents."[9]

THE TOTALITARIANISM OF VIRTUE

Gottfried says that scientific totalitarianism has been superseded by a new "soft totalitarianism" of social guilt and victimhood, grounded at least partly in religious sentiment. Hurtful thoughts and insensitive communications are brought relentlessly under surveillance, but such strong-arm tactics are masked as effusive caring or as resistance to prejudice. "Thus the muzzling of dissent becomes a proactive step in combating bigotry," Gottfried observes, "while in Europe the jailing of those who present the past inappropriately is justified as an attempt to curb 'hate'. Inconvenient facts are suppressed or wilfully and proudly distorted as acts of inclusiveness, while those who provide empirical verification for 'hurtful' opinions in Canada and Europe suffer grave legal consequences as part of their 'resocialisation.'"[10]

It might be described as the totalitarianism of virtue—or, in yet another tribute to Rousseau, as "forcing people to be free." Meanwhile, modernity itself appears in certain respects to have been put into reverse. Family life is now deeply disordered. In Britain, the protection for young girls against sexual abuse enshrined in the legal age of consent to sexual intercourse—a measure which was considered a progressive and humane act when introduced by the Victorians—is now viewed as an affront to the right of children under sixteen to have sex. Similarly, while the huge reduction in rates of illegitimacy was considered a triumph of enlightened progress in the late nineteenth century, the very concept of illegitimacy has now been abolished in the interests of the "right" of every girl and woman to bring a fatherless child into the world.

Respect for the innate value of every human life has been abolished and replaced by the calculus of utility, robbing of their elementary protection both those who have yet to begin life and those who are approaching its end. Education leaves young people in ignorance, unable to distinguish between fact and propaganda and with their capacity for reasoning dulled by repeated spoon-feeding and a tickbox approach that rewards mediocrity and conformity.

FAILING TO HOLD THE LINE FOR WESTERN VALUES

Not only is the West loosening its own grip on reason and modernity, but it is also failing to hold the line against those who are waging an explicit war against them from without. Instead of fighting off the encroachment of Islamic obscurantism—part of a campaign to conquer the free world for Islam—the West is embracing that obscurantism as if it had a cultural death wish. In part, this is the misguided *realpolitik* of appeasement; but more deeply, it is once again the result of a complete loss of moral and cultural bearings through multiculturalism and victim culture, along with the acting out of collective Western guilt as an act of expiation to bring about peace on earth—with the result that truth and justice are turned on their heads.

President Obama's speech of conciliation to the Muslim world in Cairo in June 2009 was a startling example of this genuflection to the forces of irrationality and antimodernity. Not only did he parrot Arab and Muslim claims that the Palestinians had "suffered in pursuit of a homeland," thus ignoring their six decades of aggression against Israel. Not only did he state that the Jews' aspiration for their homeland was rooted in the Holocaust—the Arab and Muslim claim that negates the Jews' historic and unique dominion over Israel and its centrality to the Jewish religion. The president also sanitized Islam and its history. He selectively and misleadingly quoted the Qur'an to present a passage that is a prescription for violence and murder against Jews and "unbelievers" as instead a precept affirming the value of preserving human life; and he also claimed that Islam played a major role in the European Enlightenment:

> As a student of history, I also know civilization's debt to Islam. It was Islam—at places like Al-Azhar University—that carried the light of learning through so many centuries, paving the way for Europe's Renaissance and Enlightenment. It was innovation in Muslim communities

that developed the order of algebra; our magnetic compass and tools of navigation; our mastery of pens and printing; our understanding of how disease spreads and how it can be healed. Islamic culture has given us majestic arches and soaring spires; timeless poetry and cherished music; elegant calligraphy and places of peaceful contemplation. And throughout history, Islam has demonstrated through words and deeds the possibilities of religious tolerance and racial equality.[11]

But these claims were absurd, as the Islam scholar Robert Spencer noted in some detail:

> The astrolabe was developed, if not perfected, long before Muhammad was born. The zero, which is often attributed to Muslims, and what we know today as "Arabic numerals" did not originate in Arabia, but in pre-Islamic India. Aristotle's work was preserved in Arabic not initially by Muslims at all, but by Christians such as the fifth century priest Probus of Antioch, who introduced Aristotle to the Arabic-speaking world. . . . The first Arabic-language medical treatise was written by a Christian priest and translated into Arabic by a Jewish doctor in 683. The first hospital was founded in Baghdad during the Abbasid caliphate—not by a Muslim, but a Nestorian Christian. . . . In sum, there was a time when it was indeed true that Islamic culture was more advanced than that of Europeans, but that superiority corresponds exactly to the period when Muslims were able to draw on and advance the achievements of Byzantine and other civilizations. But when the Muslim overlords had taken what they could from their subject peoples, and the Jewish and Christian communities had been stripped of their material and intellectual wealth and thoroughly subdued, Islam went into a period of intellectual decline from which it has not yet recovered.[12]

Not only is the West increasingly absorbing the Arab and Muslim narrative about both the Middle East and Islamic achievement, but it is also, under Islamic pressure, progressively negating core Enlightenment values of free speech and equality. For example, the principle of one law for all is axiomatic in a democracy. So is equality for women under the law and other basic human rights. Yet astoundingly, the British legal and clerical establishment is sanguine about embracing Islamic Sharia law, which denies these principles, within the English system.

In 2008, the archbishop of Canterbury argued for an end to the "legal monopoly" of English law and called for an accommodation that would allow people to choose between Islamic and English law for the resolution of disputes and the administration of marriage, divorce, inheritance and other matters.[13] Later that year, Britain's most senior judge, Lord Phillips, also gave a green light to the growth of Sharia in family matters and the arbitration of disputes.[14] Evidence emerged that Sharia courts were being used by British Muslims not just to arbitrate civil disputes but in some cases as an alternative to English criminal law; at least one case of stabbing was dealt with not by the police but by a Somali court in south London.[15] In 2009, it was revealed that at least eighty-five Sharia courts were operating in Britain, and some were said to be advising actions that were illegal under English law,[16] while up to 5 percent of cases heard by the Muslim Arbitration Tribunal involved non-Muslims.[17]

Yet Sharia law embodies principles that run contrary to fundamental Western values, such as equality for women and tolerance of apostates. Accepting the growth of what is effectively a parallel legal system not only destroys the principle of one law for all, but effectively consigns Muslim British citizens to have their lives ruled by medieval concepts that negate modern rights and freedoms. There could hardly be a more graphic or troubling demonstration of the indifference or worse towards modernity than this willingness by the British establishment for part of British society, in effect, to remain imprisoned in the seventh century.

Under pressure from Islamists, the West is also tearing up the basic Enlightenment principle of free speech. The French academic Robert Redeker has had to live in hiding ever since his article "*Face aux intimidations islamistes, que doit faire le monde libre?"* (How should the free world confront Islamist intimidation?) appeared in *Le Figaro* in 2006, two days after Pope Benedict XVI's speech on the relationship between Islam and violence at Regensburg. The outrage provoked by the pope's observations, wrote Redeker, was an attempt by this same Islam to stifle freedom of thought and expression, the most precious Western value, which did not exist in any Muslim country. Islam was trying to impose its rules on Europe, he said, citing prohibition of caricatures, pressure to allow girls to wear the hijab to school, and accusations of Islamophobia. Immediately after the publication of this article, Redeker received death threats from Muslims and was forced into hiding—thus proving his point that Europe was indeed reneging on its own fundamental values.[18]

This fact was further underlined by the way the United Nations and the European Union threatened to suppress free speech about Islam. In June 2008, the UN Human Rights Council announced that it would not tolerate criticism of Sharia law, following complaints and pressure by Islamist delegates.[19] In 2009, a nonbinding UN resolution banned any perceived offense to Islamic sensitivities as a "serious affront to human dignity" and a violation of religious freedom, and threatened to pressure UN member states at all levels to erode free speech guarantees in their "legal and constitutional systems."[20]

Such appeasement of Islamic sensibilities has turned reason and logic inside out. In February 2009, Geert Wilders, the Dutch member of parliament who has made an uncompromising stand against the Qur'anic sources of Islamist extremism and violence, was due to give a screening of his film *Fitna* to the British House of Lords. *Fitna* called upon Muslims to end the Islamization of Europe and to reform their faith by revising the Qur'an. The British home secretary banned Wilders from entering Britain on the grounds that his presence would "threaten community harmony and therefore public security in the UK."[21]

Wilders threatened no one. *Fitna* did not advocate violence; it condemned violence. Yet it was Wilders who was considered a "serious threat to one of the fundamental interests of society," because the result of his stand for life and liberty against those who would destroy them might be an attack by those who really *did* threaten "the fundamental interests of society." Wilders's crime was apparently to incite Islamists to hatred and violence by saying that they practiced hatred and violence. To put it another way, they were saying in effect: "If you insult my faith by saying it's violent, I'll kill you"—and Britain's home secretary endorsed this logic. Eventually, the ban was reversed and Wilders was allowed into the country.

In a similar vein, on pro-Hamas marches in 2009 during the Gaza war, British police confiscated the Israeli flag on the grounds that it would provoke violence, while those screaming genocidal incitement against the Jews were allowed to continue doing so.[22] The reasoning was that the Israeli flag might provoke thuggery while the genocidal incitement would not. So those actually promoting aggression were allowed to do so because they were aggressive, while those who threatened no one at all but represented the receiving end of the aggression were repressed. Thus the British state has stood justice on its head.

THE APPEASEMENT OF TERRORISM

Such appeasement of terror by effectively endorsing the narrative that underpins it is arguably one of the main reasons why the free world is currently being held for ransom. The West did not merely rewrite history over Iraq. More fundamentally, it has long connived at the Big Lie about the Middle East put out by the Arab and Muslim world, which after 1967 recast the existential Arab war against Israel as a war between Israel and the Palestinians over territory. Then, in talking up a "two-state solution" to the impasse, America and Britain proceeded to validate the spurious cause of Israel's would-be exterminators and, treating them as legitimate potential statesmen, attempted through the "peace process" to force Israel to accept a boundary settlement that would deliver it to its enemies.

In January 2008, President George W. Bush declared, "The establishment of the state of Palestine is long overdue. The Palestinian people deserve it."[23] This was surely the first time in history that people who had been waging a war of extermination for almost a century had been said to "deserve" a state of their own in reward. But when terror is rewarded, it is encouraged to press for ever greater prizes. When truth and justice are stood on their heads in the global theater, the result is tyranny and war. That is surely why the Middle East impasse has endured for so long: from the 1920s onwards, the response of the Western world to Arab and Muslim terror has been to appease it and validate its cause as having legitimacy. The conflict between the Arabs and Israel will be solved only if the free world starts to treat Israel as the historic victim of aggression, injustice and a six-decade violation of international law, and correspondingly treats its Arab and Muslim aggressors as international, diplomatic and economic pariahs.

The same process of Western denial—and over the same issue— lies behind the regard in which the United Nations is held and the way this has turned international relations upside down. For Western progressives, the United Nations is the arbiter of acceptable behavior. No wars can be waged without its imprimatur, and it is supposedly the body that will end global conflict and injustice. But this view is the equivalent of putting the foxes in charge of the henhouse.

A few days before 9/11, the UN put on a World Conference against Racism, Racial Discrimination, Xenophobia and Related Intolerance in Durban, South Africa. The title was a grotesque misnomer. The conference turned into a frenzied hate-fest demonizing Israel as a Nazi and apartheid state, promoting Holocaust denial and using images of anti-Jewish hatred straight out of the Nazi lexicon.

Shocking as this was, it was hardly surprising since the UN is institutionally programmed against Israel. In 1975 it supported the infamous "Zionism is racism" resolution. It repeatedly singles out Israel for condemnation for defending itself against attack, while ignoring the true human rights violations of its accusers and other despotic member states. For example, it has made no comment about such abuses in China or Syria while over a thirty-five-year period it has targeted almost 30 percent of its hostile resolutions against Israel. Shortly after a Palestinian suicide bomber killed thirty Israelis at a Passover Seder in 2002, the UN Commission on Human Rights affirmed "the legitimate right of the Palestinian people to resist Israeli occupation."[24]

Such support for killing the innocent is endorsed by the UN "human rights" envoy to the Palestinian Territories, John Dugard, who equates Palestinian terrorism with the French resistance against fascism.[25] The Human Rights Council's special rapporteur on the Palestinian territories, Richard Falk, has compared Israelis to Nazis.[26] Yet this is the body that the world regards as its policeman to guard against abuses of human rights and to safeguard peace and justice.

One has to ask how the West can possibly believe that the UN acts in the interests of peace and freedom. How can it be rational to believe that a body so much in thrall to the world's most murderous tyrannies and jihadists can end conflict and injustice in the Middle East or anywhere else?

Part of the answer lies in the fact that, for Western progressives, the UN is an important element in the utopian fantasy of a brotherhood of man in which war is replaced by law and all conflict is solved by the application of rational self-interest. As with all such fantasies, cold reality—such as the religious fanaticism of a death cult—is not allowed to obtrude into the enlightened mind. But this is only part of the explanation.

THE SOFT BIGOTRY OF THE ENLIGHTENED

In the Islamist onslaught upon the free world, the West is confronting an ideology that hijacks evidence and distorts and falsifies it for its own ends. The disconcerting fact, as we have seen in the preceding pages, is that the West has been doing precisely the same thing. From manmade global warming to Israel, from Iraq to the origin of the universe, the West has replaced truth with ideology. Faced with an enemy that has declared war upon reason, the West has left the citadel undefended.

The correspondences between Western progressives and Islamists are really quite remarkable. Both are attempting to create utopias in order to redeem past sins; both permit no dissent from the one revealed truth; both demonize and seek to suppress their opponents; both project their own bad behavior onto others; both are consumed by paranoid conspiracy theories. Both are giving expression to a totalitarian instinct that involves a wholesale repudiation of reason. The West has gone down this road in order to allow the full and unimpeded flowering of the autonomous individual and the fulfillment of his needs and desires. The Islamists have gone down this road to subjugate the individual and snuff out his needs and desires. Both have ended up suppressing freedom and imposing a tyranny of the mind.

What they also have in common is hostility to Judaism, Israel and the Jewish people. The genocidal hatred of Israel and the Jews that drives the Islamic jihad against the West is not acknowledged or countered by the West because its most high-minded citizens share at least some of that prejudice. Both Western liberals and Islamists believe in utopias to which the Jews are an obstacle. The State of

Israel is an obstacle to both the rule of Islam over the earth *and* a world where there are no divisions based on religion or creed. The Jews are an obstacle to the unconstrained individualism of Western libertines *and* to the Islamist attack on individual human dignity and freedom. Both the liberal utopias of a world without prejudice, divisions or war and the Islamist utopia of a world without unbelievers are universalist ideologies. The people who are *always* in the way of universalizing utopias are the Jews.

The great Victorian novelist and passionate Christian Zionist George Eliot understood this very well. In 1879, she wrote that while liberal progressives were free of the kind of antisemitism that held Jews guilty of the Crucifixion, these rationalists who had won full citizenship for Jews, Dissenters and Catholics nevertheless condemned the Jews for not having discarded their Jewishness and become completely assimilated. Such liberals, she wrote, had reverted to "medieval types of thinking," complaining of the Jewish spirit of "universal alienism" and "cosmopolitanism" because the Jews were "holding the world's money bag."[27]

How contemporary she sounds. Christian Europe despised the Jews because they were an obstacle to the universalizing doctrine of the redemption of mankind by Jesus. Now the progressives who are intent upon destroying the Christian West despise those Jews who do not subscribe to the universalizing dogma of the brotherhood of man but obdurately insist on asserting their particular claim to heritage and history. If universalism is the dogma, Zionists and Israelis are the contemporary heretics to be burned.

As George Eliot understood only too well, it is those who claim to be the very acme of enlightened opinion who are often among the most prejudiced. The power of reason offers no protection against bigotry: quite the reverse. And today it is once again among the most progressive and enlightened people in Britain, Europe and America, the secular rationalists and the most liberal Christians, who march behind the banners of human rights and high-minded conscience, that one finds the most virulent hatred of Israel and medieval prejudice against the Jews.

One wonders, though, whether the pathology is yet deeper and more devastating. As has been noted, all the utopias of the West involve at some level a repudiation of Jewish precepts. But it was the Jews who gave the world the concepts of an orderly universe, reason and progress—the keys to science and our modern age. And the State of Israel is the front line of the defense of the free world against the Islamist assault on modernity.

In repudiating Jewish teaching and its moral codes, the West has turned upon the modern world itself. In turning upon the State of Israel, the West is undermining its defense against the enemies of modernity and the Western civilization that produced it. The great question is whether it actually wants to defend reason and modernity anymore, or whether Western civilization has now reached a point where it has stopped trying to survive.

NOTES

Chapter 1: Cults and Conspiracies from Diana to Obama

1 Yossi Klein Halevi, "Like a Prayer: Kabbalah Goes Hollywood," *New Republic*, May 10, 2004.

2 Laura Coventry, *Daily Record*, April 7, 2008.

3 Paul Scott, "And What She Forgot to Mention," *Daily Mail*, May 17, 2008.

4 Chris Partridge, *The Re-Enchantment of the West: Alternative Spiritualities, Sacralization, Popular Culture and Occulture*, vol. 1 (Continuum, 2004), p. 67.

5 *Sunday Times*, October 31, 1999.

6 *Express*, July 2, 2007.

7 *Times*, London, October 17, 2005.

8 *Daily Telegraph*, July 16, 2009.

9 Scripps Howard/Ohio University poll, January 8, 2006, http://www.scrippsnews.com/911poll

10 David Icke, *The Robots' Rebellion: The Story of the Spiritual Renaissance*, cited in Nicholas Goodrick-Clarke, *Black Sun: Aryan Cults, Esoteric Nazism and the Politics of Identity* (New York University Press, 2003), pp. 29–92.

11 Text of Barack Obama's victory speech, June 3, 2008, Associated Press, http://www.breitbart.com/article.php?id=D912VD200&show_article=1

12 *New York Daily News*, December 10, 2007.

13 *New York Times*, December 9, 2007.

14 *Christianity Today*, February 22, 2009.

15 *The Hill*, January 21, 2009, http://thehill.com/leading-the-news/stars-heap-praise-on-obama-2009-01-21.html

16 MSNBC, April 3, 2007, http://www.msnbc.msn.com/id/17927102/

[17] *Newsbusters*, June 5, 2009, http://www.newsbusters.org/blogs/kyle-drennen/2009/06/05/newsweek-s-evan-thomas-obama-sort-god

[18] Norwegian Nobel Committee, citation for Nobel Peace Prize 2009, http://nobelprize.org/nobel_prizes/peace/laureates/2009/press.html

Chapter 2: The Myth of Environmental Armageddon

[1] Matthew Moore, "Climate Change Scientists Face Calls for Public Inquiry over Data Manipulation Claims," *Daily Telegraph*, November 24, 2009.

[2] See for example Christopher Booker, "Climategate Reveals 'the most influential tree in the world,'" *Sunday Telegraph*, December 5, 2009; also David Rose, "Special Investigation: Climate Change Emails Row Deepens as Russians Admit They Did Come from Their Siberian Server," *Mail on Sunday*, December 13, 2009.

[3] See in particular "The Smoking Gun at Darwin Zero," http://wattsupwiththat.com/2009/12/08/the-smoking-gun-at-darwin-zero/ as well as the extended analysis of the CRU emails on *Watts Up with That*, http://wattsupwiththat.com/climategate/; also Steve McIntyre, "IPCC and the 'trick,'" *Climate Audit*, http://climateaudit.org/2009/12/10/ipcc-and-the-trick/#more-9483 and other analysis on *Climate Audit*, http://climateaudit.org/

[4] Interview with Sir David King on *Today*, BBC Radio 4, December 15, 2009; interview with Ed Miliband on *Today*, BBC Radio 4, December 7, 2009.

[5] *Independent*, January 9, 2004.

[6] Sir David King, "The Science of Climate Change: Adapt, Mitigate or Ignore?" Ninth Annual Zuckerman Lecture, Foundation for Science and Technology, October 31, 2002.

[7] *Daily Telegraph*, December 15, 2009.

[8] *Guardian*, December 18, 2009.

[9] *Observer*, December 21, 2008.

[10] BBC News Online, September 27, 2006.

[11] Christopher Booker, *Sunday Telegraph*, May 24, 2009.

[12] *Financial Post*, Canada, June 20, 2007.

[13] Ian Plimer, *Heaven and Earth: Global Warming, The Missing Science* (Quartet Books, 2009), p. 438.

[14] Walter Cunningham, "In Science, Ignorance Is Not Bliss," *Launch Magazine,* July–August 2008, http://launchmagonline.com/walt-cunninghams-viewpoint/64-in-science-ignorance-is-not-bliss

[15] Roy Spencer, *Climate Confusion: How Global Warming Hysteria Leads to Bad Science, Pandering Politicians and Misguided Policies That Hurt the Poor* (Encounter Books, 2008), p. 64.

[16] Nils-Axel Mörner, *The Greatest Lie Ever Told,* booklet available at morner@pog.nu

[17] Reuters, September 15, 2006.

[18] Reuters, March 19, 2009, http://www.news.com.au/story/0,23599,25210705-2,00.html

[19] *Wall Street Journal,* January 3, 2007.

[20] Dr. Mitchell Taylor, Department of the Environment, Nunavut, Canada, http://meteo.lcd.lu/globalwarming/Taylor/last_stand_of_our_wild_polar_bears.html

[21] Plimer, *Heaven and Earth,* p. 259.

[22] P. T. Doran et al., "Antarctic Climate Cooling and Terrestrial Ecosystem Response," *Nature,* vol. 415, pp. 517–20.

[23] Duncan Wingham et al., "Mass Balance in the Antarctic Ice Sheet," *Philosophical Transactions of the Royal Society A,* 364, pp. 1627–35.

[24] Arctic Research Center, University of Illinois; cited on DailyTech blog: http://www.dailytech.com/Article.aspx?newsid=13834

[25] John McLean, *Prejudiced Authors, Prejudiced Findings* (Science and Public Policy Institute, 2008).

[26] *More Than 700 International Scientists Dissent over Man-Made Global Warming Claims,* U.S. Senate Committee on Environment and Public Works, Minority Staff Report, December 11, 2008, updated March 16, 2009, http://epw.senate.gov/public/index.cfm?FuseAction=Files.View&FileStore_id=83947f5d-d84a-4a84-ad5d-6e2d71db52d9

[27] *Daily Telegraph,* December 12, 2008.

[28] Richard Wood, "Climate Change: Natural Ups and Downs," *Nature* 453 (May 1, 2008), pp. 43–45.

[29] *Observer,* January 18, 2009.

[30] *Times,* London, May 27, 2009.

[31] Louise Gray, *Daily Telegraph,* May 20, 2009.

[32] Reuters, May 22, 2009, http://www.reuters.com/article/mnCarbon Emissions/idUS148975034620090522

[33] Michael McCarthy, *Independent*, March 11, 2009.

[34] Richard A. Kerr, "Galloping Glaciers of Greenland Have Reined Themselves In," Fall Meeting of the American Geophysical Union, *Science*, vol. 323, no. 5913 (January 23, 2009).

[35] Reuters, February 14, 2009.

[36] David Adam, *Guardian*, March 11, 2009.

[37] David Adam, *Guardian*, March 10, 2009.

[38] David Adam, *Guardian*, March 11, 2009.

[39] McLean, *Prejudiced Authors, Prejudiced Findings*.

[40] Spencer, *Climate Confusion*, p. 91.

[41] Plimer, *Heaven and Earth*, pp. 15, 444.

[42] James Lovelock, *The Vanishing Face of Gaia: A Final Warning* (Allen Lane, 2009).

[43] Lord May of Oxford, 2004 Anniversary Address, Royal Society, November 30, 2004.

[44] William McLean, "UN Expert: Climate Change Skeptics a Tiny Minority," Reuters, April 5, 2001.

[45] *Washington Post*, May 28, 2006.

[46] Bill Blakemore, ABC News, August 30, 2006, http://abcnews.go.com/US/print?id=2374968

[47] *National Post*, Canada, April 6, 2006.

[48] *More Than 700 International Scientists Dissent over Man-Made Global Warming Claims*, U.S. Senate Committee on Environment and Public Works, Minority Staff Report, December 11, 2008, updated March 16, 2009.

[49] Lawrence Solomon, *The Deniers: The World-Renowned Scientists Who Stood Up Against Global Warming Hysteria, Political Persecution, and Fraud* (Richard Vigilante Books, 2008).

[50] Gerhard Gerlich and Ralf D. Tscheuschner, "Falsification of the Atmospheric CO_2 Greenhouse Effects within the Frame of Physics," *International Journal of Modern Physics B*, vol. 23, no. 3 (January 30, 2009), pp. 275–364, http://arxiv.org/PS_cache/arxiv/pdf/0707/0707.1161v4.pdf

51 Associated Content Network, August 14, 2007.

52 Alanna Mitchell, "Scientists Raise Alarm of Climate Catastrophe," *Globe and Mail*, Canada, January 22, 2001.

53 David Deming, "Global Warming, the Politicization of Science, and Michael Crichton's *State of Fear*," *Journal of Scientific Exploration*, v. 19, no. 2 (2005), pp. 247–56.

54 Edward J. Wegman, David W. Scott and Yasmin H. Said, *Ad Hoc Committee Report on the "Hockey Stick" Global Climate Reconstruction*, U.S. Senate Committee on Energy and Commerce, 2006.

55 Ross McKitrick, "Defects in Key Climate Data Are Uncovered," FPComment, *Financial Post*, Canada, October 1, 2009, http://network.nationalpost.com/np/blogs/fpcomment/archive/2009/10/01/ross-mckitrick-defects-in-key-climate-data-are-uncovered.aspx

56 Eric J. Steig, David P. Schneider, Scott D. Rutherford, Michael E. Mann, Josefino C. Comiso, Drew T. Shindell, "Warming of the Antarctic Ice-Sheet Surface since the 1957 International Geophysical Year," *Nature*, vol. 457 (January 22, 2009), pp. 459–62.

57 Steve McIntyre, *Climate Audit*, February 1–2, 2009, http://www.climateaudit.org/?p=5044; http://www.climateaudit.org/?p=5054

58 Nils-Axel Mörner interview, *Executive Intelligence Review*, June 22, 2007, http://www.climatechangefacts.info/ClimateChangeDocuments/NilsAxelMornerinterview.pdf

59 Christopher Booker, *The Real Global Warming Disaster* (Continuum, 2009), pp. 144–50.

60 Stephen Schneider, *Discover*, October 1989.

61 Quoted by Dixy Lee Ray, *Environmental Overkill: Whatever Happened to Common Sense?* (Regnery Gateway, 1993).

62 Gill Ereaut and Nat Segnit, *Warm Words: How Are We Telling the Climate Story and Can We Tell It Better?* Institute for Public Policy Research, 2006.

63 Plimer, *Heaven and Earth*.

64 Walter Cunningham, "In Science, Ignorance Is Not Bliss," *Launch Magazine*, July–August 2008, http://launchmagonline.com/walt-cunninghams-viewpoint/64-in-science-ignorance-is-not-bliss

Chapter 3: The Iraq War

[1] Max Hastings, *Guardian*, September 20, 2004.

[2] Ken Macdonald, "Addicted to Secrecy, Inured to Public Hostility," *Times*, London, June 17, 2009.

[3] See for example the text of the motion for war debated by the House of Commons and Prime Minister Tony Blair's speech, *Hansard*, March 18, 2003; President George W. Bush speech, October 8, 2002, CNN transcript, http://archives.cnn.com/2002/ALLPOLITICS/10/07/bush. transcript/; also Tony Blair's Sedgefield speech, March 5, 2004, http://www.guardian.co.uk/politics/2004/mar/05/iraq.iraq

[4] Remarks by George J. Tenet, Director of Central Intelligence, at Georgetown University, February 5, 2004.

[5] Ibid.

[6] Joint Intelligence Committee, March 15, 2002, in *Review of Intelligence on Weapons of Mass Destruction: Report of a Committee of Privy Counsellors, chaired by the Rt Hon Lord Butler of Brockwell* (Butler Report), House of Commons, HC 898, July 14, 2004.

[7] Statement by David Kay on the *Interim Progress Report on the Activities of the Iraq Survey Group (ISG)* before the U.S. House Permanent Select Committee on Intelligence, the House Committee on Appropriations, Subcommittee on Defense, and the Senate Select Committee on Intelligence, October 2, 2003.

[8] *New York Times*, October 3, 2003.

[9] *Washington Post*, October 3, 2003.

[10] *Los Angeles Times*, October 3, 2003.

[11] David Kay interview, Fox News, October 5, 2003, transcription at *FrontPage Magazine*, http://www.frontpagemag.com/readArticle.aspx? ARTID=16061

[12] *Daily Telegraph*, January 24, 2004.

[13] *Independent*, January 24, 2004.

[14] Ibid.

[15] Testimony of David Kay before the U.S. Senate Committee on Armed Services, January 28, 2004.

[16] David Kay interview, Fox News, February 1, 2004, http://www.foxnews.com/story/0,2933,110091,00.html?referer=www.clickfind.com.au

[17] Sir John Scarlett, the chairman of the UK Joint Intelligence Committee at the time of the war and subsequently head of MI6, gave evidence to the inquiry into the Iraq war led by Sir John Chilcot that "dismantling" or "dispersal," of which there was evidence at the time, is recognized as a way of concealing such material; http://www.iraqinquiry.org.uk/media/39390/091208scarlett.pdf

[18] Testimony before the U.S. Congress by Charles Duelfer, Director of Central Intelligence Special Advisor for Strategy Regarding Iraqi Weapons of Mass Destruction (WMD) Programs, March 30, 2004.

[19] George J. Tenet, Director of Central Intelligence, remarks at Georgetown University, February 5, 2004.

[20] Testimony of David Kay before the U.S. Senate Committee on Armed Services, January 28, 2004.

[21] Ben Johnson, *FrontPage Magazine*, May 21, 2004; first reported in *NewsMax*, April 17, 2004.

[22] *Sunday Telegraph*, January 25, 2004.

[23] Bill Gertz, *Washington Times*, October 29, 2003.

[24] Georges Sada, *Saddam's Secrets: How an Iraqi General Defied and Survived Saddam Hussein* (Integrity Publishers, 2006).

[25] Georges Sada, conversation with author, November 4, 2006.

[26] *Times*, London, May 14, 2003.

[27] *Washington Post*, October 16, 2003.

[28] *Weekly Standard*, April 3, 2006.

[29] Lawrence F. Kaplan and William Kristol, *The War over Iraq* (Encounter Books, 2003).

[30] *Wall Street Journal*, March 24, 2008.

[31] *New York Times*, June 17, 2004.

[32] *Washington Post*, June 18, 2004.

[33] Stephen Hayes, *Weekly Standard*, August 2, 2004.

[34] George Tenet, *At the Center of the Storm: My Years at the CIA* (HarperCollins, 2007).

[35] *Review of Intelligence on Weapons of Mass Destruction: Report of a Committee of Privy Councillors, chaired by the Rt Hon Lord Butler of Brockwell* (Butler Report), House of Commons, HC 898, July 14, 2004.

[36] NBC News, June 29, 2004.

[37] Stephen Hayes, *Weekly Standard*, June 30, 2005.

[38] Andrew Sullivan, *Sunday Times*, April 26, 2009.

[39] President George W. Bush speech, October 8, 2002, CNN transcript, http://archives.cnn.com/2002/ALLPOLITICS/10/07/bush.transcript/

[40] Jonathan Foreman, *National Review Online*, March 6, 2007.

[41] *Times*, London, November 9, 2004.

[42] Simon Jenkins, "Nothing to Fear but Fear Itself," *Spectator*, March 13, 2004.

[43] Simon Jenkins, *Times*, London, October 20, 2004.

[44] Simon Jenkins, *Times*, London, July 2, 2004.

Chapter 4: The Misrepresentation of Israel

[1] President Obama speech, Al-Azhar University, Cairo, June 4, 2009, http://www.whitehouse.gov/the_press_office/Remarks-by-the-President-at-Cairo-University-6-04-09/

[2] Josephine Bacon and Martin Gilbert, *The Illustrated Atlas of Jewish Civilisation* (Quarto, 1990).

[3] Palestine Mandate, July 24, 1922.

[4] Churchill White Paper, June 3, 1922.

[5] *Justice for Jews from Arab Countries*, http://www.justiceforjews.com

[6] *Independent*, April 28, 2008.

[7] William Blackstone, *Palestine for the Jews* (Oak Park, Ill.: self-published, 1891), reprinted in *Christian Protagonists for Jewish Restoration* (Arno, 1977), p. 17; also Alexander Keith, *The Land of Israel According to the Covenant with Abraham, with Isaac, and with Jacob* (William Whyte & Co., 1843), p. 43; Israel Zangwill, *New Liberal Review*, December 1901.

[8] James Finn to the Earl of Clarendon, September 15, 1857, F.O. 78/1294.

[9] Benjamin Netanyahu, *A Place Among the Nations* (Bantam, 1993).

[10] Report of the Palestine Royal Commission (Peel Report), 1937.

[11] *Al-Qibla*, March 23, 1918, quoted in Samuel Katz, *Battleground: Fact and Fantasy in Palestine* (Bantam, 1977).

[12] Richard Hartmann, *Palestina unter den Araben, 632–1516* (Leipzig, 1915); Jacob de Haas, *History of Palestine: The Last Two Thousand Years* (Macmillan, 1934), p. 147.

[13] F. Eugene Roger, *La Terre Sainte* (Paris, 1637), cited by de Haas, *History of Palestine*, p. 342.

[14] James Parkes, *Whose Land? History of the Peoples of Palestine* (Pelican, 1970).

[15] *Encyclopaedia Britannica*, 11th ed., vol. 20, p. 604.

[16] *Syria and Palestine*, Foreign Office, Historical Section, handbook no. 60 (London, HMSO, 1920), p. 56.

[17] Howard M. Sachar, *A History of Israel from the Rise of Zionism to Our Time* (Knopf, 2003).

[18] Netanyahu, *A Place Among the Nations.*

[19] Report of the Palestine Royal Commission (Peel Report), 1937.

[20] Avner Yaniv, Israel Universities Study Group for Middle Eastern Affairs, August 1974.

[21] Quoted in Moshe Ma'oz, *Assad: The Sphinx of Damascus* (Weidenfeld & Nicholson, 1988).

[22] *Trouw*, Netherlands, March 1977.

[23] *Guardian*, May 15, 2008.

[24] Robert Fisk, *Independent*, January 24, 2009.

[25] King Abdallah, *My Memoirs Completed* (Longman Group, 1978).

[26] *Economist*, October 2, 1948.

[27] *The Memoirs of Haled al Azm* (Beirut, 1973).

[28] *Al-Hayat al-Jadida*, December 13, 2006.

[29] Reuters, March 12, 2002.

[30] Eugene Rostow, *New Republic*, April 23, 1990.

[31] David Miliband, Associated Press, November 4, 2008.

[32] Eugene Rostow, *New Republic*, April 23, 1990.

[33] Foreign Office, conversation with author, November 17, 2008.

[34] David Solway, *FrontPage Magazine*, July 30, 2008, http://www.frontpagemag.com/readArticle.aspx?ARTID=31808

[35] Al-Jazeera, January 14, 2009.

[36] *Anderson Independent Mail*, South Carolina, May 25, 2008.

[37] Ilan Pappe, *Electronic Intifada*, September 2006.

[38] Media Monitors Network, December 2, 2000.

[39] Gunnar Heinsohn, *Financial Times*, June 14, 2007.

[40] Steven Stotsky, "Professor Accuses Israel of Slow-Motion Genocide," CAMERA, July 15, 2008, http://www.camera.org/index.asp?x_context=7&x_issue=22&x_article=1506

[41] Joshua Teitelbaum, *What Iranian Leaders Really Say about Doing Away*

with Israel, Jerusalem Center for Public Affairs, http://www.jcpa.org/text/ahmadinejad2-words.pdf

⁴² Hamas Charter (1988), published with commentary by the Intelligence and Terrorism Information Center, http://www.terrorism-info.org.il/malam_multimedia/English/eng_n/pdf/hamas_charter.pdf

⁴³ Jon Pilger, "Illegal Occupation: the tragedy of an epic injustice that is at the root of Bush's and Blair's threats of war," Peace Movement Aotearoa, Action Alerts, September 16, 2002, http://www.converge.org.nz/pma/cra0887.htm

⁴⁴ "Egypt Bans Marriage to Israelis," *Jewish Journal,* June 3, 2009, http://www.jewishjournal.com/world/article/egypt_bans_marriage_to_israelis_20090603/

⁴⁵ *Guardian,* April 17, 2002.

⁴⁶ UN figures reported by the BBC, August 1, 2002, http://news.bbc.co.uk/1/hi/world/middle_east/2165272.stm

⁴⁷ Compilation of journalistic fabrications and staged events in *The Corruption of the Media,* EU Referendum, August 15, 2006, http://eureferendum.blogspot.com/2006/08/corruption-of-media.html

⁴⁸ *Guardian,* March 24, 2009.

⁴⁹ Author's account of court hearing, http://www.spectator.co.uk/melaniephillips/354621/the-al-durah-blood-libel.thtml

Chapter 5: Scientific Triumphalism

¹ Debate between Richard Dawkins and John Lennox, Natural History Museum, Oxford, October 21, 2008.

² Francis Crick and Leslie E. Orgel, "Directed Panspermia," *Icarus,* vol. 19 (1973), pp. 341–46.

³ Francis Crick, *Life Itself: Its Origin and Nature* (Futura, 1982), pp. 15–16.

⁴ Ibid., p. 153.

⁵ Leslie E. Orgel and Francis H. C. Crick, "Anticipating an RNA World: Some Past Speculations on the Origin of Life: Where Are They Today?" *FASEB Journal,* vol. 7, no. 1 (January 1993), pp. 238–39.

⁶ Albert Einstein, *Science, Philosophy and Religion: A Symposium,* 1941.

⁷ Peter Atkins, "Will Science Ever Fail?" *New Scientist,* August 8, 1992, pp. 32–35.

[8] Quoted in John Lennox, *God's Undertaker: Has Science Buried God?* (Lion Hudson, 2007), p. 29.

[9] Peter Medawar, *Advice to a Young Scientist* (Harper & Row, 1979); *The Limits of Science* (Oxford University Press, 1984).

[10] Richard Dawkins, "Thoughts for the Millennium," *Microsoft Encarta Encyclopedia 2000*; W. Sellars, *Science, Perception and Reality* (Routledge & Kegan Paul, 1963), quoted in M. R. Bennett and P. M. S. Hacker, *Philosophical Foundations of Neuroscience* (Blackwell, 2003).

[11] Bennett and Hacker, *Philosophical Foundations of Neuroscience.*

[12] David Berlinski, *The Devil's Delusion: Atheism and Its Scientific Pretensions* (Crown Forum, 2008), pp. 50–51.

[13] Stephen M. Barr, "Retelling the Story of Science," Sixteenth Annual Erasmus Lecture, Institute on Religion and Public Life, New York, November 15, 2002, http://www.leaderu.com/science/storyofscience.html

[14] Lennox, *God's Undertaker*, p. 42.

[15] *BBC Christmas Lectures Study Guide*, BBC, 1991, quoted in Lennox, p. 55.

[16] John C. Polkinghorne, *One World: Interaction of Science and Theology* (SCPK Publishing, 1986), p. 92.

[17] Roger Scruton, *An Intelligent Person's Guide to Philosophy* (Duckworth, 1996).

[18] Eliezer Berkovits, *God, Man and History*, ed. David Hazony, 4th ed. (Shalem Press, 2004), p. 70.

[19] Richard Dawkins, *The Blind Watchmaker: Why the Evidence of Evolution Reveals a Universe Without Design* (Longmans, 1986).

[20] Richard Dawkins, *Climbing Mount Improbable* (Penguin, 1996).

[21] Richard Dawkins, *The God Delusion* (Transworld, 2007), p. 52.

[22] Peter W. Atkins, *Creation Revisited: The Origin of Space, Time and the Universe* (Penguin, 1994).

[23] Quoted in Lennox, *God's Undertaker*, p. 63.

[24] Sir Fredrick Hoyle and Chandra Wickramasinghe, *Evolution from Space* (Simon & Schuster, 1984), p. 148.

[25] Harold Morowitz, *Energy Flow in Biology* (Academic Press, 1968).

[26] Robert Shapiro, *Origins: A Skeptic's Guide to the Creation of Life on Earth* (Simon & Schuster, 1986).

27 Dawkins, *The God Delusion*, p. 147.

28 Lennox, *God's Undertaker*, p. 158.

29 Leo Strauss, "Why We Remain Jews: Can Jewish Faith and History Still Speak to Us?" in *Jewish Philosophy and the Crisis of Modernity: Essays and Lectures in Modern Thought* (State University of New York Press, 1997).

30 George C. Williams, *The Third Culture: Beyond the Scientific Revolution* (Simon & Schuster, 1995), pp. 42–43.

31 Werner Gitt, *In the Beginning Was Information* (Master Books, 2006).

32 Richard Lewontin, review of Carl Sagan, *The Demon-Haunted World*, in *New York Review of Books*, January 9, 1997.

33 George Wald, "The Origin of Life," *Scientific American*, vol. 191, no. 48 (May 1954).

34 Gerald L. Schroeder, *The Science of God: The Convergence of Science and Biblical Wisdom* (Broadway Books, 1997), p. 84.

35 Anthony Flew, *There Is a God: How the World's Most Notorious Atheist Changed His Mind* (HarperOne, 2007);

36 Paul Davies, "Universes Galore: Where Will It All End?" in *Universe or Multiverse?* ed. Bernard Carr (Cambridge University Press, 2007), and at http://cosmos.asu.edu/publications/chapters/Universes%20galore.pdf

37 Richard Swinburne, "Design Defended," *Think*, Spring 2004.

38 Lewontin, review of *The Demon-Haunted World*.

39 Phillip E. Johnson, *Darwin on Trial*, 2nd ed. (InterVarsity Press, 1993), pp. 152–55.

40 Richard Dawkins, "The Alabama Insert: A Study in Ignorance and Dishonesty," *Journal of the Alabama Academy of Science*, vol. 68, no. 1 (January 1997).

41 David Stove, "Darwinism's Dilemma," in *Darwinian Fairytales: Selfish Genes, Errors of Heredity, and Other Fables of Evolution* (Encounter Books, 2007).

42 Charles Darwin, *The Descent of Man, and Selection in Relation to Sex*, 2nd ed. (1874), quoted in Stove, "Darwinism's Dilemma," p. 15.

43 Stove, "Darwinism's Dilemma," passim.

[44] Stephen Jay Gould, "Is a New and General Theory of Evolution Evolving?" *Paleobiology*, vol. 6, no. 1, reprinted in *Evolution Now: A Century after Darwin*, ed. Maynard Smith (W. H. Freeman, 1982).

[45] Brian Goodwin, *How the Leopard Changed Its Spots: The Evolution of Complexity* (Scribner, 1996), preface.

[46] Harry Whittington, *The Burgess Shale* (Yale University Press, 1985), p. 13, quoted in Jonathan Wells, *The Politically Incorrect Guide to Darwinism and Intelligent Design* (Regnery, 2006).

[47] Eugene Koonin, "The Biological Big Bang Model for the Major Transitions in Evolution," *Biology Direct*, vol. 2, no. 21 (August 20, 2007).

[48] Niles Eldredge, *Time Frames: The Evolution of Punctuated Equilibria* (Princeton University Press, 1985), pp. 144–45.

[49] Michael Behe, *The Edge of Evolution: The Search for the Limits of Darwinism* (Free Press, 2008).

[50] Michael Behe, "Conservatives, Darwin and Design: An Exchange," *First Things*, November 2000.

[51] Alexander Rosenberg, *The Structure of Biological Science* (Cambridge University Press, 1984).

[52] Karl Popper, *Unended Quest: An Intellectual Biography* (Routledge, 1992).

[53] Stove, *Darwinian Fairytales*, p. 175.

[54] Richard Dawkins, *The Selfish Gene* (Oxford University Press, 1976).

[55] Stove, *Darwinian Fairytales*, p. 193.

[56] Alister McGrath, *The Dawkins Delusion? Atheist Fundamentalism and the Denial of the Divine* (SPCK Publishing, 2007).

[57] Keith Thomson, "Huxley, Wilberforce and the Oxford Museum," *American Scientist*, vol. 88, no. 3 (May–June 2000), http://www.americanscientist.org/issues/id.3371,y.0,no.,content.true,page.1,css.print/issue.aspx

[58] "Physics Nobelist Takes Stand on Evolution," Inside Science News Service, June 2006.

Chapter 6: The Secular Inquisition

[1] J. L. Talmon, *The Origins of Totalitarian Democracy* (Secker & Warburg, 1952).

[2] Roger Scruton, *Culture Counts: Faith and Feeling in a World Besieged* (Encounter Books, 2007).

[3] Karl Popper, *The Open Society and Its Enemies* (1945; Routledge, 2003, repr. 2008).

[4] *Daily Mail*, December 16, 2009.

[5] *Times*, London, January 14, 2006.

[6] *Daily Mail*, June 3, 2009.

[7] *Sunday Times*, February 1, 2009.

[8] *Daily Telegraph*, May 14, 2009.

[9] *Daily Mail*, September 6, 2006.

[10] Christian Institute, June 13, 2009, http://www.anglican-mainstream. net/?p=11860#more-11860

[11] *Express*, April 27, 2009.

[12] Robert A. J. Gagnon, "Why a Sexual Orientation and Gender Identity 'Hate Crimes' Law Is Bad for You," June 18, 2009, http://www. robgagnon.net/articles/homosexHateCrimePart3.pdf

[13] *Times*, London, October 21, 2004.

[14] "A Shameless Conspiracy to Convict More Men of Rape," *Daily Mail*, July 2, 2004.

[15] See for example Michelle Carrado et al., "Aggression in British Heterosexual Relationships," *Aggressive Behaviour*, vol. 22 (1995); M. A. Straus and R. G. Gelles, "Societal Change and Change in Family Violence from 1975 to 1985 as Revealed by Two National Surveys," *Journal of Marriage and the Family*, vol. 48 (1986); Straus and Gelles, *Physical Violence in American Families* (Transaction Publishers, 1990).

[16] Quoted in Norman Dennis, George Erdos and Ahmed Al-Shahi, *Racist Murder and Pressure Group Politics: The Macpherson Report and the Police* (Institute for the Study of Civil Society, 2000).

[17] Stuart Taylor and K. C. Johnson, *Until Proven Innocent: Political Correctness and the Shameful Injustices of the Duke Lacrosse Rape Case* (St. Martin's, 2007).

[18] Mary Lefkowitz, *History Lesson: A Race Odyssey* (Yale University Press, 2008).

[19] Steven Pinker, "The Stupidity of Dignity," *New Republic*, September 8, 2008, http://www.tnr.com/story_print.html?id=d8731cf4-e87b-4d88-b7e7-f5059cd0bfbd

[20] Gary Hurd, "Review of Proposed Changes to Kansas State Science Standards," Kansas State Department of Education, http://www.ksde.org/outcomes/sciencereviewhurd.pdf

[21] *Evening Standard*, London, August 13, 1999.

[22] Phillip E. Johnson, *The Wedge of Truth: Splitting the Foundations of Naturalism* (InterVarsity Press, 2000), pp. 127–28.

[23] Francis Collins, *The Language of God: A Scientist Presents Evidence for Belief* (Pocket Books, 2007).

[24] David Klinghoffer, "The Branding of a Heretic," *Wall Street Journal*, January 28, 2005, http://www.opinionjournal.com/taste/?id=110006220

[25] David Klinghoffer "Unintelligent Design: Hostility toward Religious Believers at the Nation's Museum," *National Review Online*, August 16, 2005, http://www.nationalreview.com/comment/klinghoffer200508160826.asp; and at http://www.discovery.org/a/2790

[26] Fred Heeren, "The Deed Is Done," *American Spectator*, December 2000/January 2001.

[27] Jim Brown and Ed Vitagliano, "Professor Dumped over Evolution Beliefs," *Agape Press*, March 11, 2003, http://www.headlines.agapepress.org/archive/3/112003a.asp

[28] Barbara Bradley Haggerty, "Profile: Intelligent Design and Academic Freedom (Transcript)," *NPR*, November 10, 2005, http://www.discovery.org/a/3083

[29] *Expelled: No Intelligence Allowed*, film by Ben Stein, 2008.

[30] Jonathan Wells, *The Politically Incorrect Guide to Darwinism and Intelligent Design* (Regnery, 2006).

[31] Gro Harlem Brundtland, *UPI*, May 10, 2007.

[32] *From Seesaw to Wagon Wheel: Safeguarding Impartiality in the 21st Century*, BBC Trust, June 2007.

[33] Richard Lindzen, comments at the Heartland Institute's Second International Conference on Climate Change, March 9, 2009, reported in *Quadrant Online*, http://www.quadrant.org.au/blogs/doomed-planet/2009/03/heartland-2-session-one

[34] *Guardian*, September 20, 2006.

[35] Testimony of Richard S. Lindzen before the U.S. Senate Committee on Environment and Public Works, May 2, 2001, http://wwweaps.mit.edu/faculty/lindzen/Testimony/Senate2001.pdf

[36] Richard Lindzen, *Wall Street Journal*, April 12, 2006.

[37] Christopher C. Horner, *Red Hot Lies: How Global Warming Alarmists Use Threats, Fraud, and Deception to Keep You Misinformed* (Regnery, 2008), p. 76.

[38] U.S. Senate Committee on Environment and Public Works, Minority Staff Report, December 11, 2008.

[39] U.S. Senate Committee on Environment and Public Works, press blog, March 6, 2008.

[40] U.S. Senate Committee on Environment and Public Works, press blog, July 27, 2007, http://epw.senate.gov/public/index.cfm?FuseAction= Minority.Blogs&ContentRecord_id=04373015-802A-23AD-4BF9-C3F02278F4CF

[41] U.S. Senate Committee on Environment and Public Works, press blog, January 17, 2007.

[42] *Daily Express*, November 5, 2008.

[43] *The Great Global Warming Swindle*, Channel 4 TV, March 2007, http://www.channel4.com/science/microsites/G/great_global_ warming_swindle/

[44] *Ofcom Broadcast Bulletin*, no. 114, July 21, 2008.

[45] Martin Durkin, *Independent on Sunday*, August 10, 2008.

[46] *Guardian*, September 21, 2006.

[47] U.S. Senate Committee on Environment and Public Works, press blog, January 17, 2007.

[48] David Roberts, "The Denial Industry," *Grist*, September 19, 2006, http://www.grist.org/article/the-denial-industry/

[49] *National Post*, Canada, February 7, 2008.

[50] Stuart Blackman and Ben Pile, "Battle in Print: Climate science," *Battle of Ideas*, October 2007, http://www.battleofideas.org.uk/index.php/ site/battles/957/

[51] Horner, *Red Hot Lies*, p. 69.

[52] George Monbiot, *Guardian*, September 5, 2006.

[53] Nigel Lawson, "The Economics and Politics of Climate Change: An Appeal to Reason," lecture at the Centre for Policy Studies, November 1, 2006.

[54] Letter to *Daily Telegraph*, November 2, 2006.

55 Lawrence Solomon, "Bitten by the IPCC," *National Post*, Canada, March 23, 2007.

56 Letter to *Daily Telegraph*, November 2, 2006.

57 William A. Dembski, *The Design Revolution: Answering the Toughest Questions about Intelligent Design* (InterVarsity Press, 2004).

58 Vaclav Klaus, comments at the Heartland Institute's Second International Conference on Climate Change, March 9, 2009, reported in *Quadrant Online*, http://www.quadrant.org.au/blogs/doomed-planet/2009/03/heartland-2-session-one

Chapter 7: The Middle East Witch-Hunt

1 Tom Zeller, *New York Times*, May 4, 2003.

2 Michael Lind, "How Neoconservatives Conquered Washington—and Launched a War," *Salon*, April 9, 2003, http://dir.salon.com/story/opinion/feature/2003/04/09/neocons/index.html

3 Thomas Powers, "Tomorrow the World," *New York Review of Books*, March 11, 2004.

4 Naomi Klein, "Pillaging Iraq in Pursuit of a Neocon Utopia," *Harper's Magazine*, September 2004.

5 David Brooks, "The Neocon Cabal and Other Fantasies," in *Neoconservatism*, ed. Irwin Stelzer (Atlantic Books, 2004).

6 Douglas Murray, *Neoconservatism: Why We Need It* (Social Affairs Unit, 2005), pp. 54–55.

7 John Walsh, "The Philosophy of Mendacity," *Counterpunch*, November 2, 2005, http://www.counterpunch.org/walsh11022005.html

8 Shadia B. Drury, *Leo Strauss and the American Right*, 1997, cited in Murray, *Neoconservatism*.

9 Will Hutton, "A Dark Week for Democracy," *Observer*, November 10, 2002, cited in Murray, *Neoconservatism*.

10 Lyndon LaRouche, interview on the *Jack Stockwell Show*, Salt Lake City, March 3, 2003; also Murray, *Neoconservatism*.

11 Lyndon LaRouche, *Children of Satan*, http://www.scribd.com/doc/4025294/Children-of-Satan

12 Jeffrey Steinberg, "LaRouche Exposé of Straussian 'Children of Satan' Draws Blood," *Executive Intelligence Review*, May 16, 2003.

13 Lind, "How Neoconservatives Conquered Washington—and Launched a War."

14 "The War Party," *Panorama*, BBC One, May 18, 2003.

15 Adam Curtis, *The Power of Nightmares*, BBC Two, October 2004.

16 Robin Shepherd, "A Barrage against Israel," *Times*, London, January 31, 2008.

17 Robin Shepherd, conversation with author, June 11, 2009.

18 Keith Burnet, letter to *Jerusalem Post*, September 5, 2009, http://www.jpost.com/servlet/Satellite?cid=1251804495980&pagename=JPost%2FJPArticle%2FPrinter

19 Manfred Gerstenfeld, ed., *Academics Against Israel and the Jews* (Jerusalem Center for Public Affairs, 2007).

20 Elizabeth Redden, "Israel Boycott Movement Comes to U.S.," *Global Research*, Centre for Research on Globalization, http://www.globalresearch.ca/index.php?context=va&aid=12072

21 David Horowitz, *Indoctrination U: The Left's War Against Academic Freedom* (Encounter Books, 2007).

22 *Engage* website, June 3, 2007, http://www.engageonline.org.uk/blog/article.php?id=1071

23 Shalom Lappin, "Responding to the Boycott," *Normblog*, June 3, 2007, http://normblog.typepad.com/normblog/2007/06/responding_to_t.html

24 Steven Rose, "Why Pick on Israel? Because Its Actions Are Wrong," *Independent*, June 4, 2007.

25 Michael Beloff and Pushpinder Saini, University and College Union Joint Opinion, May 13, 2008, http://www.stoptheboycott.org/files/ucu%20opinion_%20Final.PDF

26 Eve Garrard, letter to Sally Hunt, General Secretary, University and College Union, July 1, 2008, http://normblog.typepad.com/normblog/2008/07/resignation-letter-by-eve-garrard.html

27 Polly Curtis, *Guardian*, May 12, 2005.

28 *Report of the All-Party Parliamentary Inquiry into Antisemitism*, HMSO, September 2006.

29 *Guardian*, July 8, 2002.

30 *Times*, London, October 28, 2003.

31 *Ynet*, December 11, 2006.

[32] Letter to *Guardian*, February 16, 2009.

[33] Editorial, *Times*, London, March 4, 2009.

[34] *Jerusalem Post*, April 21, 2009.

[35] Jacqueline Rose et al., letter to *Guardian*, June 15, 2007.

[36] Derek Summerfield, "Palestine: The Assault on Health and Other War Crimes," *British Medical Journal*, October 16, 2004.

[37] Karl Sabbagh, "Perils of Criticising Israel," *British Medical Journal*, February 24, 2009.

Chapter 8: The Jihad against Western Freedom

[1] Osama bin Laden, transcript of interview, CNN, February 5, 2002, http://archives.cnn.com/2002/WORLD/asiapcf/south/02/05/bin-laden.transcript/index.html

[2] Raymond Ibrahim, *The Al Qaeda Reader* (Broadway Books, 2007), p. 26.

[3] Suleiman Abu Gheith, Centre for Islamic Research and Studies, http://www.memri.org/bin/articles.cgi?Page=archives&Area=sd&ID=SP38802

[4] Osama bin Laden transcript, MEMRI Special Dispatch no. 838, December 30, 2004, http://memri.org/bin/articles.cgi?Page=subjects&Area=jihad&ID=SP83804

[5] Quoted in Daniel Benjamin and Steven Simon, *The Age of Sacred Terror: Radical Islam's War Against America* (Random House, 2003), pp. 16–17.

[6] Richard Bonney, *Jihad: From Qur'an to bin Laden* (Palgrave Macmillan, 2004), pp. 113–21.

[7] Benjamin and Simon, *The Age of Sacred Terror*, p. 52.

[8] Ibid., pp. 56–57.

[9] Sayid Abul ala Maududi, *Jihad fi Sabillah: Jihad in Islam*, trans. Kurshid Ahmad, ed. Huda Khattab (UK Islamic Mission Dawah Centre, Birmingham, 1995); also International Islamic Federation of Student Organisations (Damascus, 1977).

[10] Osama bin Laden, "Letter to the American People," *Observer*, November 24, 2002.

[11] Nazi N. Ayubi, *Political Islam: Religion and Politics in the Arab World* (Routledge, 1991).

[12] Syed Qutb, "The America I Have Seen," 1951, in *America in an Arab Mirror: Images of America in Arabic Travel Literature* (Kashf ul Shubuhat Publications); also John Calvert, "Sayyid Qutb in America," *Newsletter of the International Institute for the Study of Islam in the Modern World*, no. 7 (March 2001), p. 8, http://www.isim.nl/files/newsl_7.pdf

[13] Syed Qutb, *Milestones* (Islamic Book Service, 2001, repr. 2007), pp. 510–11.

[14] Qutb, "The America I Have Seen."

[15] David Zeidan, "The Islamic Fundamentalist View of Life as a Perennial Battle," *Middle East Review of International Affairs*, vol. 5, no. 4 (December 2001).

[16] Jacques Jomier, *Esprit et Vie*, February 17, 2000, cited in Caroline Fourest, *Brother Tariq: The Doublespeak of Tariq Ramadan* (Social Affairs Unit, 2008).

[17] Fourest, *Brother Tariq*, pp. 231–34.

[18] Tariq Ramadan lecture, "Islam et Occident: références et valeurs," quoted in Fourest, *Brother Tariq*.

[19] Tariq Ramadan, *L'identité musulmane: construire notre discours*, quoted in Fourest, *Brother Tariq*.

[20] Sayed Qutb, *In the Shade of the Koran*, trans. and ed. Adil Salahi (Islamic Foundation, Leicester, 2004).

[21] Syed Qutb, *The Religion of Islam* (Al-Manar Press, 1967), quoted in Efraim Karsh, *Islamic Imperialism: A History* (Yale University Press, 2006), p. 211.

[22] Ali A. Allawi, *The Crisis of Islamic Civilization* (Yale University Press, 2009), pp. 104–7.

[23] Matthias Küntzel, *Jihad and Jew-Hatred: Islamism, Nazism and the Roots of 9/11*, trans. Colin Meade (Telos Press, 2008), p. 76.

[24] Syed M. N. al-Attas, quoted in Küntzel, *Jihad and Jew-Hatred*, p. 77.

[25] Küntzel, *Jihad and Jew-Hatred*.

[26] Allawi, *The Crisis of Islamic Civilization*, pp. 10–12.

[27] Douglas Murray, "Why We Must Debate the Extremists," *Guardian*, June 19, 2009, http://www.guardian.co.uk/commentisfree/belief/2009/jun/19/religion-islam-muhajiroun-choudary/print

28 Qutb, *Milestones,* p. 94.

29 Ibid., p. 62.

30 Ibid., p. 63.

31 Raphael Israeli, *Muslim Antisemitism in Christian Europe* (Transaction Books, 2009).

32 Ibid.

33 Ibid.

34 Jason Lewis, *Mail on Sunday,* September 11, 2005.

35 NOP poll, August 7, 2006.

36 The lower number is based on a study of victims whose religion was known, while the higher number is based on the last names of victims; http://en.wikipedia.org/wiki/9/11_conspiracy_theories#cite_note-sfgateTruthAbout911ConspiracyTheories-101

37 *Al-Raya* (Qatar), September 20, 2004, MEMRI Special Dispatch no. 792, October 2, 2004, http://memri.org/bin/articles.cgi?Page= archives&Area=sd&ID=SP79204

38 *Al-Hayat* (London), October 7, 2008, MEMRI Special Dispatch no. 2091, October 22, 2008.

39 *Al-Liwa* (Lebanon), October 3, 2008, and *Al-Yawm* (Saudi Arabia), October 5, 2008, MEMRI Special Dispatch no. 2091, October 22, 2008.

40 David Zeidan, "The Islamic Fundamentalist View of Life as a Perennial Battle," *Middle East Review of International Affairs,* vol. 5, no. 4 (December 2001).

41 *Al-Raya* (Qatar), September 20, 2004, MEMRI Special Dispatch no. 792.

Chapter 9: Islamic Jew-Hatred

1 Dean Nelson, *Daily Telegraph,* February 24, 2009.

2 P. Krishnakumar and Vicky Nanjappa, *Rediff India Abroad,* November 30, 2008, http://www.rediff.com/news/2008/nov/30mumterror-doctors-shocked-at-hostagess-torture.htm

3 *Daily News and Analysis,* January 5, 2009, http://www.dnaindia.com/report.asp?newsid=1218869&pageid=0

[4] B. Raman, "Lashkar-e-Toiba: Spreading the Jehad," *Business Line*, January 5, 2001, http://www.hinduonnet.com/businessline/2001/01/05/stories/040555ra.htm

[5] *Jerusalem Post*, March 6, 2008.

[6] *New Yorker*, October 14, 2002.

[7] *Jerusalem Post*, April 3, 2008.

[8] "Palestinian Authority Sermons 2000–2003," MEMRI Special Report no. 24, December 26, 2003, http://www.memri.org/bin/articles.cgi?Area=sr&ID=SR2403

[9] MEMRI TV, clip 2042, January 17, 2009.

[10] Osama bin Laden, interview on *Frontline*, PBS, May 1998.

[11] Christian Eggers, "Die Juden werden brennen," quoted in Matthias Küntzel, *Jihad and Jew-Hatred: Islamism, Nazism and the Roots of 9/11*, trans. Colin Meade (Telos Press, 2007).

[12] Jane Gerber, "Towards an Understanding of the Term 'The Golden Age' as an Historical Reality," in *The Heritage of the Jews in Spain*, ed. Aviva Doron, cited in Andrew Bostom, *The Legacy of Islamic Antisemitism* (Prometheus, 2008); Richard Fletcher, *Moorish Spain* (University of California Press, 1993), cited in Bostom.

[13] Bat Ye'or, *The Dhimmi* (Associated University Presses, 1985); Bostom, *The Legacy of Islamic Antisemitism*.

[14] Bostom, *The Legacy of Islamic Antisemitism*.

[15] *Moses Maimonides' Epistle to Yemen: The Arabic Original and the Three Hebrew Versions*, ed. Abraham S. Halkin, trans. Boaz Cohen (American Academy for Jewish Research, 1952), cited by Ibn Warraq in foreword to Bostom, *The Legacy of Islamic Antisemitism*.

[16] Raphael Israeli, *Muslim Antisemitism in Christian Europe* (Transaction Books, 2009).

[17] Ibid.

[18] Qur'an, 5:60; Haggai ben Shammai, *Jew-Hatred in the Islamic Tradition and Qur'anic Exegesis*, in Shmuel Almog, *Antisemitism Through the Ages*, quoted in Bostom, *The Legacy of Islamic Antisemitism*.

[19] *Moses Maimonides' Epistle to Yemen*, in Bostom, *The Legacy of Islamic Antisemitism*.

[20] Abu'l A'la Maududi, *Islam, An Historical Perspective* (London, 1980), quoted in Bat Ye'or, *Islam and Dhimmitude: Where Civilizations Collide* (Associated University Presses, 2002), p. 309.

[21] Paul Charles Merkley, *Christian Attitudes towards the State of Israel* (McGill-Queen's University Press, 2001), pp. 103–5.

[22] Talmud Yerushalmi 23a; another Talmudic reference in Sanhedrin 37a refers specifically to Jews: "Man was created alone to teach you that anyone who destroys a single soul of Israel—scripture considers it as though he has destroyed the whole world; anyone who preserves a single soul of Israel—scripture considers it as though he has preserved the entire world."

[23] Osama bin Laden, "Letter to the American People," *Observer*, November 24, 2002.

[24] Osama bin Laden, "Sermon on the Feast of the Sacrifice," MEMRI Special Dispatch no. 476, March 6, 2003, http://www.memri.org/bin/articles.cgi?Page=subjects&Area=jihad&ID=SP47603

[25] Osama bin Laden, transcript of interview, CNN, February 5, 2002, http://archives.cnn.com/2002/WORLD/asiapcf/south/02/05/binladen.transcript/index.html

[26] Syed Qutb, *Our Struggle with the Jews*, reproduced in Ronald L. Nettler, *Past Trials and Present Tribulations: A Muslim Fundamentalist's View of the Jews* (Pergamon Press, 1987), quoted in Küntzel, *Jihad and Jew-Hatred*.

[27] Syed Qutb, *Milestones* (Islamic Book Service, 2001, repr. 2007).

[28] Küntzel, *Jihad and Jew-Hatred*, p. 84.

[29] Robert Wistrich, *Antisemitism: The Longest Hatred* (Methuen, 1991).

[30] Paul Berman, *Terror and Liberalism* (Norton, 2003), p. 68.

[31] Wistrich, *Antisemitism: The Longest Hatred*.

[32] Hamas Charter (1988), "The Charter of Allah: The Platform of the Islamic Resistance Movement," http://www.thejerusalemfund.org/www.thejerusalemfund.org/carryover/documents/charter.html

[33] Osama bin Laden, interview on *Frontline*, PBS, May 1998.

[34] *Time*, January 11, 1999, http://www.time.com/time/world/article/0,8599,174550-2,00.html

[35] Israeli, *Muslim Antisemitism in Christian Europe*.

[36] Wistrich, *Antisemitism: The Longest Hatred.*

[37] "Hate Industry: Anti-Semitic, anti-Zionist and anti-Jewish Literature in the Arab and Muslim World," Intelligence and Terrorism Information Center at the Center for Special Studies, Information Bulletin no. 4 (September 2002).

[38] "Incitement and Propaganda against Israel, the Jewish People and the Western World, conducted in the Palestinian Authority, the Arab World and Iran," Intelligence and Terrorism Information Center, Information Bulletin no. 1 (January 2002).

[39] Mas'ud Sabri, "The Wars of the Prophet: The Wars against Bani Qainuqa," Intelligence and Terrorism Information Center, Information Bulletin no. 4.

[40] Abdallah Nasih Alwan, in Intelligence and Terrorism Information Center, Information Bulletin no. 4.

[41] Itamar Marcus and Barbara Crook, "Kill a Jew—Go to Heaven: The Perception of the Jew in Palestinian Society," *Jewish Political Studies Review*, vol. 17, nos. 3–4 (Fall 2005).

[42] Ibid.

[43] Esther Webman, *Antisemitic Motifs in the Ideology of Hizbullah and Hamas*, Project for the Study of Antisemitism, Tel Aviv University, 1998.

[44] Ibid.

[45] *Al-Thawra*, April 20, 2009, and *Teshreen*, April 21, 2009, quoted in MEMRI Special Dispatch no. 2351, May 11, 2009, http://www.memri.org/bin/articles.cgi?Page=archives&Area=sd&ID=SP235109

Chapter 10: Western Jew-Hatred

[1] Harold Evans, "We Are All Hezbollah Now. Really?" *Guardian*, August 8, 2006, http://www.guardian.co.uk/commentisfree/2006/aug/08/weareallhizbullahnowreall

[2] Jeff Jacoby, *Boston Globe*, January 7, 2009; video of demonstration in Fort Lauderdale, Florida, http://www.youtube.com/watch?v=j3Xl68kP4wo

[3] Aron Heller, Associated Press, January 19, 2009.

[4] *Jerusalem Post*, January 28, 2009.

[5] Leon Symons, "Schoolgirl Terrorised by Mob," *Jewish Chronicle*, February 5, 2009.

[6] Community Security Trust, *Antisemitic Incidents Report 2008.*

[7] *Report of the All-Party Parliamentary Inquiry into Antisemitism*, HMSO, September 2006.

[8] Anti-Defamation League, *Attitudes Towards Jews and the Middle East in Six European Countries*, July 2007.

[9] Community Security Trust, *Antisemitic Incidents January–June 2009.*

[10] Johnny Paul, *Jerusalem Post*, March 17, 2009.

[11] Howard Jacobson, "Pox Brittanica," *New Republic*, April 15, 2009.

[12] Manfred Gerstenfeld, ed., *Behind the Humanitarian Mask: The Nordic Countries, Israel and the Jews* (Jerusalem Center for Public Affairs/ Friends of Simon Wiesenthal Center for Holocaust Studies, 2008).

[13] "Americans and Europeans Differ Widely on Foreign Policy Issues," Pew Research Center for the People and the Press, April 17, 2002, cited in Robin Shepherd, *Israel: A State Beyond the Pale* (Orion, 2009).

[14] Edward Said, *The Question of Palestine* (Vintage, 1980), quoted in Ibn Warraq, *Defending the West: A Critique of Edward Said's "Orientalism"* (Prometheus, 2007).

[15] Ibn Warraq, *Defending the West.*

[16] Ibn Warraq, "Islam and Intellectual Terrorism," *New Humanist*, vol. 116, no. 4 (Winter 2001), http://newhumanist.org.uk/473

[17] UN figures, cited in Natan Sharansky and Ron Dermer, *The Case for Democracy* (Perseus, 2004). The UN claimed that only 26 of the 52 Palestinian casualties were armed; Israel claimed that only three were unarmed.

[18] Dr. Aaron Lerner, "Hamas Placed Children on Rooftops as Human Shields Preventing Israeli Attack on Qassam Workshops and Warehouses," *Independent Media Review Analysis*, March 4, 2008, http://www.imra.org.il/story.php3?id=38440

[19] Tovah Lazaroff and Yaakov Katz, "UN: IDF Did Not Shell UNRWA School," *Jerusalem Post*, February 4, 2009.

[20] Israel Defense Forces, "Majority of Palestinians Killed in Operation Cast Lead: Terror Operatives," March 26, 2009, http://dover.idf.il/ IDF/English/News/today/09/03/2602.htm

[21] *Guardian*, September 6, 2004.

22 Jeremy Bowen, "How 1967 Defined the Middle East," BBC News Online, June 4, 2007, http://news.bbc.co.uk/1/hi/world/middle_east/6709173.stm

23 See Michael Oren, *Six Days of War: June 1967 and the Making of the Modern Middle East* (Presidio Press, 2003, repr.).

24 BBC Trust, *Editorial Standards Findings*, March 3, 2009, http://www.bbc.co.uk/bbctrust/assets/files/pdf/appeals/esc_bulletins/2009/mar.pdf

25 Jonathan Dimbleby, *Index on Censorship*, May 13, 2009.

26 *Independent*, April 25, 2009.

27 *Observer*, July 13, 2003.

28 *Independent*, April 16, 2009.

29 Johann Hari, *Independent*, April 28, 2008.

30 Zafrir Rinat, "West Bank Pollution Threatening Israeli Groundwater," *Ha'aretz*, December 16, 2007.

31 Martin Rosenberg, "Side by Side, Arabs and Israelis Repair a Wreck of a River," *New York Times*, March 16, 2004.

32 Benny Morris, letter to *Independent*, November 21, 2006.

33 Jimmy Carter, *Palestine: Peace not Apartheid* (Simon & Schuster, 2007); also comments in *Ha'aretz*, January 4, 2009.

34 Chris McGreal, "Worlds Apart," *Guardian*, February 6–7, 2006.

35 War on Want, "Israeli Apartheid: A Beginner's Guide," http://www.waronwant.org/news/events/events/latest-events/16575-israeli-apartheid-a-beginners-guide

36 NGO Monitor, February 2009 *Digest* (vol. 7, no. 6), http://www.ngo-monitor.org/digest_info.php?id=2331

37 *Up Front: Sixty Years*, War on Want, May–June 2008.

38 *Third Sector* magazine, July 30, 2008.

39 Oxfam press release, December 28, 2008.

40 NGO Monitor, "HRW's Gaza Campaign: Advocacy not Accuracy," March 25, 2009.

41 CARE International et al., *The Gaza Strip: A Humanitarian Implosion*, 2008, http://www.oxfam.org.uk/resources/downloads/oxfam_gaza_lowres.pdf

42 *Times*, London, January 26, 2009.

[43] "BMJ's Bad Medicine," *HonestReporting*, Media Critiques, March 3, 2009, http://www.honestreporting.com/articles/45884734/critiques/new/BMJs_Bad_Medicine.asp

[44] *Lancet*, March 2, 2009.

[45] *Lancet*, February 10, 2009 (subsequently removed).

[46] Mohamed Abdel Ghani El Ganasy, *The October War: The Memoirs of Field Marshal El Ganasy of Egypt* (American University in Cairo Press, 1973), p. 79.

[47] Correspondence in the *Lancet*, February 18, 2009, http://www.thelancetglobalhealthnetwork.com/archives/611

[48] Correspondence in the *Lancet*, March 2, 2009, http://www.thelancetglobalhealthnetwork.com/archives/608

[49] Robin Shepherd, *Israel: A State Beyond the Pale* (Orion, 2009).

[50] Dave Brown cartoon published in the *Independent*, January 27, 2003.

[51] Caryl Churchill, *Seven Jewish Children*, performed at the Royal Court Theatre, London, February 6–24, 2009.

52 Michael Billington, "Royal Court Theatre Gets Behind the Gaza Headlines," *Guardian*, Theatre Blog, February 11, 2009, http://www.guardian.co.uk/stage/theatreblog/2009/feb/11/royal-court-theatre-gaza

[53] Efraim Karsh, "What's Behind Western Condemnation of Israel's War against Hamas?" Jerusalem Center for Public Affairs, vol. 8, no. 17 (January 11, 2009).

[54] Colin Brown, *Sunday Telegraph*, May 4, 2003.

[55] Press Association, October 13, 2006.

[56] Geoffrey Wheatcroft, *Guardian*, March 22, 2007.

[57] Brian Reade, *Daily Mirror*, March 5, 2009.

[58] "John Pilger on Terror in Palestine," *New Statesman*, March 22, 2004, and in *Morning Star*, March 20, 2004.

[59] "Inside Britain's Israel Lobby," *Dispatches*, Channel 4, November 16, 2009.

[60] *Guardian*, October 1, 2007.

[61] John J. Mearsheimer and Stephen M. Walt, "The Israel Lobby and U.S. Foreign Policy," John F. Kennedy School of Government, Faculty Research Working Paper Series, March 2006, accessible at http://

ksgnotes1.harvard.edu/Research/wpaper.nsf/rwp/RWP06-011/
$File/rwp_06_011_walt.pdf

[62] John J. Mearsheimer and Stephen M. Walt, *The Israel Lobby and U.S. Foreign Policy* (Penguin, 2007).

[63] Alan Dershowitz, "Debunking the Newest—and Oldest—Jewish Conspiracy: A Reply to the Mearsheimer-Walt 'Working Paper,'" *Harvard Law School*, April 2006.

[64] Gabriel Schoenfeld, "Dual Loyalty and the 'Israel Lobby,'" *Commentary*, November 2006, http://www.commentarymagazine.com/viewarticle.cfm/dual-loyalty-and-the—israel-lobby—10136

[65] Benny Morris, "About Mearsheimer and Walt's 'The Israel Lobby,'" *New Republic*, April 28, 2006.

[66] Martin Kramer, *Sandbox* blog, December 10, 2007, http://sandbox.blog-city.com/mearsheimer_walt_and_cold_feet.htm

[67] Richard Littlejohn, *Daily Mail*, July 7, 2007.

[68] Nick Cohen, *What's Left? How Liberals Lost Their Way* (Fourth Estate, 2007).

[69] Nick Cohen, "Hatred Is Turning Me into a Jew," *Jewish Chronicle*, February 12, 2009.

[70] *Observer*, February 18, 2001.

[71] *Al-Ahram Weekly*, April 4–10, 2002.

[72] *Independent*, July 26, 2006.

[73] Tom Gross, "Media Missiles: Working for the Enemy," *National Review Online*, August 2, 2006, http://article.nationalreview.com/print/?q=YjVlMmRjNDllNzhkZmE1OWM3NmE1OGQ4OGQxMDA1YjQ=

[74] *Independent*, July 23, 2005.

[75] *Jerusalem Post*, January 21, 2009.

[76] Leo McKinstry, *Daily Express*, May 31, 2007.

[77] Associated Press, March 26, 2002.

[78] Quoted by Paul Berman, "Bigotry in Print: Crowds Chant Murder," *Forward*, May 24, 2002.

[79] Readers' thread below "Israelis React with Fury to British Boycott Call" by Donald Macintyre, *Independent*, March 4, 2009, http://www.independent.co.uk/news/uk/home-news/israelis-react-with-fury-to-british-boycott-call-1636842.html

[80] *Daily Telegraph*, September 24, 2009.

81 John Podhoretz, "Hatefest by the Bay," *New York Post*, May 14, 2002.

82 Jonathan Hoffman, *Harry's Place* blog, June 19, 2009, http://www. hurryupharry.org/2009/06/19/a-work-of-fiction/

83 On *Lenin's Tomb* blog, http://leninology.blogspot.com/2009/01/ extremist-minority-who-should-be.html

84 Dave Rich, "Holocaust Resonance," *Harry's Place* blog, February 26, 2009, http://www.hurryupharry.org/2009/02/26/holocaust-resonance/ #comments. Story about SOAS report and repercussions in *Jewish Chronicle*, February 19, 2009, http://www.thejc.com/articles/ boycott-targets-kosher-shops

85 Nick Cohen, "Hatred Is Turning Me into a Jew."

Chapter 11: The Red-Black-Green-Islamic Axis

1 Nick Cohen, *What's Left? How Liberals Lost Their Way* (Fourth Estate, 2007).

2 Noam Chomsky, "War on Terror," Amnesty International Annual Lecture, January 18, 2006, http://www.chomsky.info/talks/20060118.pdf; also MEMRI Special Dispatch no. 165, http://memri.org/bin/articles. cgi?Page=archives&Area=sd&ID=SP116506

3 George Galloway speech at the University of Damascus, televised on Al-Jazeera TV on November 13, 2005.

4 David Horowitz, *Unholy Alliance: Radical Islam and the American Left* (Regnery, 2004).

5 "Against the War, For Our Troops," BNP website, March 19, 2003, http://www.bnp.org.uk/news/2003_march/news_mar15.htm, cited in Dave Rich, "The Barriers Come Down: Antisemitism and Coalitions of Extremes," Community Security Trust.

6 Julian Borger, "The Spies Who Pushed for War," *Guardian*, July 17, 2003; John Pilger, *New Statesman*, March 22, 2004, and *Morning Star*, March 20, 2004, cited in Rich, "The Barriers Come Down."

7 David Rose, "Iraqi Defectors Tricked Us with WMD Lies, but We Must Not Be Fooled Again," *Observer*, May 30, 2004, cited in Rich, "The Barriers Come Down."

8 *Baghdad Message* special issue, May 2002, published by the Permanent Secretariat of Baghdad Conference, http://www.uruklink.net/ iraqnews/emessage.htm, cited in Rich, "The Barriers Come Down."

[9] "Programma ASEFI 13/2002," http://www.asefi.it/ProgrammaASEFI/documenti/archivio/2002/200213.htm. For details on Wyssa and Van den Eynde, see http://votants.free.fr/ra/01/Owyssa.htm, and http://www.vlaamsblok.be/vbkamer/fractie. asp?id=6, cited in Rich, "The Barriers Come Down."

[10] Postings and quotations from internet guestbooks at http://www.skrewdriver.net; http://www.wnpuk.org; http://www. natfront.com, all in Rich, "The Barriers Come Down."

[11] Jeremy Reynalds, *American Daily*, September 3, 2005, http://www.americandaily.com/article/7040

[12] Daveed Gartenstein-Ross, "The Peculiar Alliance: Islamists and Neo-Nazis Find Common Ground by Hating the Jews," *Weekly Standard*, January 9, 2005, http://www.weeklystandard.com/Content/Public/Articles/000/000/006/012qltyo.asp?pg=2

[13] Robin Hahnel, "Change How the World Works? Yes We Can," *Times*, London, April 1, 2009; also Patrick Barkham, "G20 Protests: Carnival of the Rainbow Coalition Turns Nasty," *Guardian*, April 2, 2009.

[14] *Le Monde*, January 27, 2003.

[15] Anti-Defamation League, "Purported 'Anti-Globalisation' Web Site Fronts for Neo-Nazi Group," July 12, 2002.

[16] Imam Muhammad Imam, "Qatar: Speakers at Islamic Conference Discuss Globalization Effects on Islam," *Al-Sharq al-Awsat*, January 17, 2003, translated by FBIS, cited in Rich, "The Barriers Come Down."

[17] Eric Hoffer, *The True Believer: Thoughts on the Nature of Mass Movements* (1951; HarperCollins Perennial Classics, 2002).

[18] Jamie Glazov, *United in Hate: The Left's Romance with Tyranny and Terror* (WND Books, 2009).

[19] Lord Tebbit, letter to *Daily Telegraph*, April 21, 2006.

[20] Zeev Sternhell, with Mario Sznajder and Maia Asheri, *The Birth of Fascist Ideology*, trans. David Maisel (Princeton University Press, 1994), pp. 1–7.

[21] Zeev Sternhell, *Neither Right nor Left: Fascist Ideology in France*, trans. David Maisel (Princeton University Press, 1986), pp. 270–71.

[22] *New York Times*, December 6, 1979.

[23] Karl Marx, *On the Jewish Question*, 1844, http://www.marxists.org/archive/marx/works/1844/jewish-question/

24 Isaiah Berlin, *The Life and Opinions of Moses Hess* (W. Heffer, 1959).

25 Mussolini, *Opere*, III, 55, cited in Richard Wolin, *The Seduction of Unreason: The Intellectual Romance with Fascism from Nietzsche to Postmodernism* (Princeton University Press, 2004), pp. 60–62.

26 Marx to Engels, December 19, 1860, in Richard Weikart, *From Darwin to Hitler: Evolutionary Ethics, Eugenics, and Racism in Germany* (Palgrave, 2004).

27 Thomas Malthus, *Essay on the Principle of Population* (1798).

28 Weikart, *From Darwin to Hitler*, p. 78.

29 Diane Paul, "Eugenics and the Left," *Journal of the History of Ideas*, vol. 45, no. 4 (October–December 1984).

30 Jonah Goldberg, *Liberal Fascism: The Secret History of the American Left, from Mussolini to the Politics of Meaning* (Doubleday, 2007), p. 295.

31 Weikart, *From Darwin to Hitler*, pp. 186–87.

32 Ibid.

33 Anna Bramwell, *Ecology in the 20th Century: A History* (Yale University Press, 1989), p. 39.

34 Peter Staudenmaier, "Fascist Ecology: The 'Green Wing' of the Nazi Party and Its Historical Antecedents," in *Ecofascism: Lessons from the German Experience*, by Janet Biehl and Peter Staudenmaier (AK Press, 1995), http://www.spunk.org/texts/places/germany/sp001630/peter.html

35 Ibid.

36 Ibid.

37 Oswald Spengler, *Man and Technics* (Allen & Unwin, 1932).

38 Staudenmaier, "Fascist Ecology."

39 Goldberg, *Liberal Fascism*, pp. 385–87.

40 Bramwell, *Ecology in the 20th Century*, p. 204.

41 Ibid., p. 213.

42 Robert A. McDermott, "Rudolf Steiner and Anthroposophy," in *Modern Esoteric Spirituality*, ed. Antoine Faivre and Jacob Needleman (Crossroad Publishing, 1995).

43 Bramwell, *Ecology in the 20th Century*, p. 218.

44 Ibid., pp. 219–25.

45 Ibid., p. 232.

46 Ibid., p. 232.

[47] Nicholas Goodrick-Clarke, *Black Sun: Aryan Cults, Esoteric Nazism and the Politics of Identity* (New York University Press, 2003), pp. 5–6.

[48] Ibid., p. 54.

[49] Ibid., pp. 4–5.

[50] Ibid., p. 292.

[51] Ibid., p. 300.

[52] Laurent Murawiec, *The Mind of Jihad* (Cambridge University Press, 2008).

[53] Alexander A. Benningsen and S. Enders Wimbush, *Muslim National Communism*, quoted in Murawiec, *The Mind of Jihad*.

[54] Murawiec, *The Mind of Jihad*.

[55] Ibid., p. 312.

[56] Ibid., p. 271.

[57] Matthias Küntzel, *Jihad and Jew-Hatred: Islamism, Nazism and the Roots of 9/11*, trans. Colin Meade (Telos Press, 2007).

[58] Howard M. Sachar, *A History of Israel from the Rise of Zionism to Our Time* (Alfred Knopf, 2003); *The Arab Higher Committee: Its Origins, Personnel and Purposes*, documentary record submitted to the United Nations, May 1947.

[59] Murawiec, *The Mind of Jihad*, p. 238.

[60] Albert Speer, *Spandauer Tagebücher* (Frankfurt/M, 1975), entry for November 18, 1947, quoted in Küntzel, *Jihad and Jew-Hatred*, p. xix.

[61] Joseph Goebbels, April 1943: "One can really describe the USA as a Jewish state," in Jeffrey Herf, *The Jewish Enemy: Nazi Propaganda During World War II and the Holocaust*, p. 203, quoted in Küntzel, *Jihad and Jew-Hatred*, p. xx.

[62] Küntzel, *Jihad and Jew-Hatred*, p. xx.

[63] Ian Buruma and Avishai Margalit, *Occidentalism: The West in the Eyes of Its Enemies* (Atlantic Books, 2004).

[64] "Benjamin Franklin: 'The Jewish Threat on the American Society,'" *The New Dawn*, monthly newsletter of the MAB, no. 2, October–November 2000; also "Prophecy of Benjamin Franklin in Regard of the Jewish Race," leaflet distributed at Manchester University, March 2002, in Rich, "The Barriers Come Down."

[65] "Two Jewish Authors Underscore Israeli Holocaust against Palestinians," *Palestine Times*, November 2002, in Rich, "The Barriers Come Down."

66 Abu ala al-Maududi, *War in the Cause of Allah* (1939), quoted in Richard Bonney, *Jihad from Qur'an to bin Laden* (Palgrave, 2004).

Chapter 12: The Quest for Redemption

1 Norman Cohn, *The Pursuit of the Millennium: Revolutionary Millenarians and Mystical Anarchists of the Middle Ages* (Oxford University Press, 1961).

2 Ibid.

3 Jan-Olaf Blichfeldt, *Early Mahdism: Politics and Religion in the Formative Period of Islam*, cited in Laurent Murawiec, *The Mind of Jihad* (Cambridge University Press, 2008).

4 Murawiec, *The Mind of Jihad*.

5 Abu ala Maududi, *Moral Foundations of the Islamic Government*.

6 Syed Qutb, *Milestones* (Islamic Book Service, 2001, repr. 2007).

7 Paul Berman, *Terror and Liberalism* (Norton, 2003).

8 David Horowitz, *Unholy Alliance: Radical Islam and the American Left* (Regnery, 2004).

9 Quoted in Franklin L. Baumer, *Religion and the Rise of Scepticism* (Harbinger, 1959).

10 Quoted in Alec R. Vidler, *Essays in Liberality* (SCM Press, 1957).

11 Richard Landes, *Heaven on Earth: The Varieties of the Millennial Experience* (Oxford University Press, forthcoming).

12 Ibid.

13 J. L. Talmon, *Origins of Totalitarian Democracy* (Secker & Warburg, 1952).

14 Karl Marx, *Poverty of Philosophy* (International Publishers, 1951), cited in Landes, *Heaven on Earth*.

15 Peter S. Fischer, *Fantasy and Politics: Visions of the Future in the Weimar Republic* (University of Wisconsin Press, 1991), cited in Landes, *Heaven on Earth*.

16 Ludwell Denny, "France and the German Counter Revolution," *Nation*, March 14, 1923, cited in Landes, *Heaven and Earth*.

17 Landes, *Heaven and Earth*.

18 Cohn, *Pursuit of the Millennium*.

19 Eric Hoffer, *The True Believer: Thoughts on the Nature of Mass Movements* (1951; HarperCollins Perennial Classics, 2002).

[20] George Monbiot, *Guardian*, September 21, 2006.

[21] Richard Dawkins, *The God Delusion* (Black Swan, 2007).

[22] Landes, *Heaven and Earth*.

[23] Diane Ravitch, *The Language Police: How Pressure Groups Restrict What Children Learn* (Vintage, 2004).

[24] Hoffer, *The True Believer*.

[25] Phillip E. Johnson, *Darwin on Trial*, 2nd ed. (InterVarsity Press, 1993), p. 118.

[26] Dawkins, *The God Delusion*.

[27] Stephen Jay Gould, *Rocks of Ages: Science and Religion in the Fullness of Life* (Vintage, 2002); Dawkins, *The God Delusion*.

[28] Cited in Dawkins, *The God Delusion*, p. 67.

[29] Richard Dawkins, *New York Times*, April 9, 1989.

[30] Ian Buruma and Avishai Margalit, *Occidentalism: The West in the Eyes of Its Enemies* (Atlantic Books, 2004).

Chapter 13: How Enlightenment Unraveled

[1] Iain Hampsher-Monk, *A History of Modern Political Thought: Major Political Thinkers from Hobbes to Marx* (Blackwell, 1992).

[2] Martin Fitzpatrick, "Heretical Religion and Radical Political Ideas in Late Eighteenth-Century England," in *The Transformation of Political Culture: England and Germany in the Late Eighteenth Century*, ed. Eckhart Hellmuth (Oxford University Press, 1990) pp. 341–42.

[3] Lesslie Newbigin, *The Other Side of 1984: Questions for the Churches* (World Council of Churches, 1983).

[4] Gertrude Himmelfarb, *The Roads to Modernity* (Alfred A. Knopf, 2004), pp. 18–19.

[5] Roy Porter, "The Enlightenment in England," in *The Enlightenment in National Context*, ed. Roy Porter and Mikulas Teich (Cambridge University Press, 1981).

[6] Himmelfarb, *The Roads to Modernity*, p. 152.

[7] Isaiah Berlin, *The Crooked Timber of Humanity* (Princeton University Press, 1990), p. 240.

[8] Himmelfarb, *The Roads to Modernity*, pp. 167–68.

[9] Jean-Jacques Rousseau, *The Social Contract*, 1762.

[10] Himmelfarb, *The Roads to Modernity*, p. 185.

[11] J. L. Talmon, *The Origins of Totalitarian Democracy* (Secker & Warburg, 1952), pp. 3–7.

[12] Keith Ward, *Is Religion Dangerous?* (Lion Hudson, 2006), p. 143.

[13] Isaiah Berlin, *The Roots of Romanticism* (Chatto & Windus, 1999), p. 44.

[14] Bertrand Russell, *History of Western Philosophy* (Allen & Unwin, 1961), p. 704.

[15] Berlin, *The Crooked Timber of Humanity*, p 242.

[16] J. W. Burrow, *The Crisis of Reason: European Thought, 1848–1914* (Yale University Press, 2000) pp. 218–19.

[17] Ibid., pp. 226–29.

[18] Rabbi Joseph B. Soloveitchik, *The Halakhic Mind* (Seth Press, 1986).

[19] Burrow, *The Crisis of Reason*, pp. 62–69.

[20] Anthony O'Hear, *After Progress: Why We Should Change Our Thinking* (Bloomsbury, 1999), pp. 60–74.

[21] Alain Finkielkraut, *The Undoing of Thought*, trans. Dennis O'Keeffe (Claridge Press, 1988), pp. 16–29.

[22] Soloveitchik, *The Halakhic Mind*.

[23] Georg Lukács, *The Destruction of Reason* (Merlin Press, 1980).

[24] Robert Paul Wolff, *A Critique of Pure Tolerance* (Beacon Press, 1965).

[25] T. W. Adorno, Else Frenkel-Brunswik, Daniel J. Levinson and R. Nevitt Sanford, *The Authoritarian Personality* (Harper & Row, 1950).

[26] Christopher Lasch, *The True and Only Heaven* (Norton, 1991).

[27] Theodor Adorno and Max Horkheimer, *Dialectic of Enlightenment* (1944; Verso, 1979).

[28] George Bataille, "The Sacred Conspiracy," in *Visions of Excess: Selected Writings 1927–29* (University of Minnesota Press, 1986), cited in Richard Wolin, *The Seduction of Unreason: The Intellectual Romance with Fascism from Nietzsche to Postmodernism* (Princeton University Press, 2004), p. 159.

[29] Wolin, *The Seduction of Unreason*, pp. 7–8.

[30] Hans-Georg Gadamer, *Philosophical Hermeneutics*, trans. D Linge (University of California Press, 1976).

[31] Claude Levi-Strauss, *The Savage Mind* (University of Chicago Press, 1962), cited in Michael E. Zimmerman, *Contesting Earth's Future: Radical Ecology and Postmodernity* (University of California Press, 1994).

[32] Wolin, *The Seduction of Unreason*, p. 6.

[33] Ibid., p. 41.

[34] Michel Foucault, "Nietzsche, Genealogy, History," in *The Foucault Reader*, ed. Paul Rabinow (Pantheon, 1987), p. 95.

[35] Mike Hulme, "The Appliance of Science," *Guardian*, March 14, 2007.

[36] Silvio Funtowicz and Jerry Ravetz, *The Encyclopedia of Earth*, http://www.eoearth.org/article/Post-Normal_Science

[37] Efraim Karsh and Rory Miller, "Did Edward Said Really Speak Truth to Power?" *Middle East Quarterly*, vol. 15, no. 1 (Winter 2008), pp. 13–21, http://www.meforum.org/1811/did-edward-said-really-speak-truth-to-power

[38] Quoted in Robin Shepherd, *Israel: A State Beyond the Pale* (Orion, 2009).

[39] Isaiah Berlin, "The Romantic Revolution," in *The Sense of Reality* (Chatto & Windus, 1996).

Chapter 14: The Attack on Western Civilization

[1] This attitude in fact stretches back into the preceding Conservative administration, when the chancellor of the exchequer, Kenneth Clarke, abolished the married couples' tax allowance.

[2] D. J. Nutt, "Equasy—An Overlooked Addiction with Implications for the Current Debate on Drug Harms," *Journal of Psychopharmacology*, vol. 23, no. 1 (2009), pp. 3–5.

[3] Andy Parrott, "The Psychobiological Dangers of Recreational Ecstasy or MDMA," presentation to the Advisory Council on the Misuse of Drugs, November 2008.

[4] *Times*, London, April 25, 2002.

[5] Gender Recognition Act 2004, http://www.opsi.gov.uk/acts/acts2004/ukpga_20040007_en_1

[6] Daniel Patrick Moynihan, "Defining Deviancy Down," *American Scholar*, Winter 1993, pp. 17–30.

[7] Kate Millett, *Sexual Politics* (Virago, 1977).

[8] Quoted in M. Green, D. Holloway and D. Watson, *The Church and Homosexuality* (Hodder & Stoughton, 1980).

9 Claire Chambers, "The SIECUS Circle: A Humanist Revolution, 1977," cited in Valerie Riches: *Sex Education or Indoctrination? How Ideology Has Triumphed over Facts* (Family and Youth Concern, 2004).

10 Brock Chisholm, "The Psychiatry of Enduring Peace and Social Progress," *Psychiatry*, vol. 9 (1946), cited in Riches, *Sex Education or Indoctrination?* Dr. Chisholm was wedded to the idea of world government and believed that those who opposed him were neurotic, selfish or mentally ill.

11 *Daily Telegraph*, December 19, 2004.

12 Alain Finkielkraut, *The Undoing of Thought*, trans. Dennis O'Keeffe (Claridge Press, 1988).

13 Bronislaw Malinowski, *Sex, Culture and Myth* (Hart-Davis, 1930).

14 Anna Bramwell, *The Fading of the Greens* (Yale University Press, 1994).

15 Michael E. Zimmerman, *Contesting Earth's Future: Radical Ecology and Postmodernity* (University of California Press, 1994).

16 T. J. Burnham, "Greenpeace Co-founder Moore Shuns Ag Conflict," *Western Farmer-Stockman*, November 2006, http://magissues.farmprogress.com/WFS/WS11Nov06/wfs07.pdf

17 *Nature Religion Today: Paganism in the Modern World*, ed. Joanne Pearson, Richard H. Roberts and Geoffrey Samuel (Edinburgh University Press, 1998), p. 59.

18 Ibid., pp. 101, 106, 176.

19 Zimmerman, *Contesting Earth's Future*.

20 Mark Satin, *New Age Politics* (Dell Publishing, 1979), cited in Zimmerman, *Contesting Earth's Future*.

21 Fritjof Capra, *The Tao of Physics: An Exploration of the Parallels Between Physics and Eastern Mysticism* (Flamingo, 1975), cited in Zimmerman, *Contesting Earth's Future*.

22 Edward Goldsmith, *The Way: An Ecological World View* (Rider, 1992).

23 Christopher Manes, *Green Rage: Radical Environmentalism and the Unmaking of Civilisation* (Little Brown, 1990), p. 232.

24 In ibid., p. 141.

25 Rupert Sheldrake, *The Rebirth of Nature: The Greening of Science and God* (Bantam Books, 1991).

[26] Carl Sagan, *Pale Blue Dot: A Vision of the Human Future in Space* (Ballantyne, 1997).

[27] Andrew Ferguson, "How Steven Pinker's Mind Works," *Human Life Review*, Spring 1998, http://findarticles.com/p/articles/mi_qa3798/is_199804/ai_n8787548/pg_2/?tag=content;col1

[28] Deutsche Presse-Agentur, August 1988.

[29] Prince Philip, foreword to *If I Were an Animal* (Robin Clark Ltd., 1986).

[30] "Caring for Creation," North American Conference on Religion and Ecology, National Press Club, Washington D.C., May 18, 1990.

[31] Paul Ehrlich, *The Population Bomb*, 1968.

[32] Alexander King and Bertrand Schneider, *The First Global Revolution* (The Club of Rome, 1993).

[33] *Sunday Times*, March 22, 2009.

[34] T. Hesketh, Li Lu and Zhu Wei Xing, "The Effect of China's One-Child Family Policy after 25 Years," *New England Journal of Medicine*, vol. 353 (2005), pp. 1171–76.

[35] Frank Barnaby, *The Gaia Peace Atlas* (Pan, 1988).

[36] Norman Myers, *The Gaia Atlas of Planet Management* (Pan, 1985).

[37] Paul Watson, quoted in Troy Mader, "The Enemy Within," *Abundant Wildlife*, September 1992.

[38] BBC News, August 20, 2003.

[39] *Sunday Express*, December 16, 1990.

[40] Ingrid Newkirk, quoted in Charles Oliver, "Liberation Zoology," *Reason*, June 1990.

[41] Chip Brown, *Washington Post*, November 13, 1983.

[42] Katie McCabe, "Who Will Live, Who Will Die," *Washingtonian*, vol. 21, no. 11 (August 1986).

[43] Peter Singer, "Sanctity of Life or Quality of Life," *Pediatrics*, July 1983, pp. 128–29.

[44] Richard Dawkins, *The Selfish Gene* (Oxford University Press, 1976).

[45] Charles Darwin, *The Descent of Man* (Penguin, 2004).

[46] Nicholas Goodrick-Clarke, *Black Sun: Aryan Cults, Esoteric Nazism and the Politics of Identity* (New York University Press, 2003), pp. 3–5.

[47] Yossi Klein Halevi, *New Republic*, May 10, 2004.

[48] *Times*, London, January 7, 2009.

[49] John F. Haught, *God and the New Atheism: A Critical Response to Dawkins, Harris and Hitchens* (John Knox Press, 2008).

[50] Daniel C. Dennett, *Darwin's Dangerous Idea* (Penguin, 1995).

[51] Peter Singer, *Animal Liberation* (Avon Books, 1975).

[52] Peter Singer, "Taking Life: Abortion," in *Practical Ethics* (Cambridge University Press, 1981), p. 118.

[53] Richard Dawkins in debate with John Lennox, Natural History Museum, Oxford, October 21, 2008.

[54] Steven Pinker, *How the Mind Works* (Norton, 1997).

[55] Andrew Ferguson, *Weekly Standard*, January 12, 1998, quoted in Phillip E. Johnson, *The Wedge of Truth: Splitting the Foundations of Naturalism* (InterVarsity Press, 2000).

[56] Steven Pinker, "The Stupidity of Dignity," *New Republic*, May 28, 2008.

[57] John C. Polkinghorne, *One World: Interaction of Science and Theology* (SCPK Publishing, 1986).

[58] Richard Dawkins, *The God Delusion* (Bantam, 2006).

[59] Ibid., pp. 288–89.

[60] Bible, Leviticus 19:34.

[61] John Hartung, 1995 review of Kevin MacDonald, *A People That Shall Dwell Alone: Judaism as a Group Evolutionary Strategy* (1994), http://www.lrainc.com/swtaboo/taboos/aptsda01.html; discussed in John Cornwell, *Darwin's Angel* (Profile, 2007).

[62] Professor Paul Merkley, correspondence with author.

[63] Paul Charles Merkley, *Christian Attitudes towards the State of Israel* (McGill-Queen's University Press, 2001) ch. 8. Merkley develops the story further in *American Presidents, Religion, and Israel: The Heirs of Cyrus* (Praeger, 2004), passim.

[64] Karl Marx, *On the Jewish Question*, 1844, http://www.marxists.org/archive/marx/works/1844/jewish-question/

[65] Pinker, "The Stupidity of Dignity."

[66] Ibid.

[67] George Steiner, *In Bluebeard's Castle* (Yale University Press, 1971).

[68] Michelle Sieff, "Gaza and After: An Interview with Paul Berman," *Z Word*, March 2009, http://www.z-word.com/z-word-essays/gaza-and-after%253A-an-interview-with-paul-berman.html?print

Chapter 15: Reason and the Bible

1 Richard Dawkins, *The God Delusion* (Black Swan, 2007); Christopher Hitchens, *God Is Not Great* (Atlantic Books, 2007).

2 *New York Times*, November 21, 2006.

3 Anthony O'Hear, *After Progress* (Bloomsbury, 1999).

4 Ibid.

5 Henri de Lubac, *The Drama of Atheist Humanism* (Ignatius Press, 1985).

6 Ibid.

7 Auguste Comte, *Synthèse Subjective*, 1856, cited in de Lubac.

8 Karl Popper, *Conjectures and Refutations* (1963; Routledge, 2002, repr. 2008).

9 Keith Ward, *Is Religion Dangerous?* (Lion Hudson, 2006).

10 Popper, *Conjectures and Refutations*, pp. 349, 379.

11 Ibid.

12 *New York Times*, March 12, 1978.

13 James Schombert, "Early Universe," Astronomy 123, Lecture 17, Department of Astronomy, University of Oregon, http://abyss.uoregon.edu/ ~js/ast123/lectures/lec17.html

14 David Berlinski, *The Devil's Delusion: Atheism and Its Scientific Pretensions* (Crown Forum, 2008), pp. 107–8.

15 Preface by Shahn Majid in Alain Connes, Michael Heller et al., *On Space and Time* (Cambridge University Press, 2008).

16 Roger Penrose, *The Emperor's New Mind: Concerning Computers, Minds, and the Laws of Physics* (Penguin, 1991).

17 Anthony Flew, with Roy Abraham Varghese, *There Is a God: How the World's Most Notorious Atheist Changed His Mind* (HarperOne, 2007).

18 Stephen M. Barr, "Retelling the Story of Science," Sixteenth Annual Erasmus Lecture, Institute on Religion and Public Life, New York, November 15, 2002, http://www.leaderu.com/science/storyofscience.html

19 Rodney Stark, *The Victory of Reason: How Christianity Led to Freedom, Capitalism and Western Success* (Random House, 2006), p. 7.

20 John Lennox, *God's Undertaker: Has Science Buried God?* (Lion Hudson, 2007), p. 19.

[21] Joseph Ratzinger, *Christianity and the Crisis of Cultures* (Ignatius Press, 2006).

[22] Phillip E. Johnson, *Darwin on Trial*, 2nd ed. (InterVarsity Press, 1993), p. 164.

[23] Quoted in Lennox, *God's Undertaker*, p. 20.

[24] John Haldane in J. J. C. Smart and J. J. Haldane, *Atheism and Theism* (Blackwell, 1996).

[25] Stanley L. Jaki, "The Last Century of Science: Progress, Problems and Prospects," *Proceedings of the Second International Humanistic Symposium*, Hellenistic Society for Humanistic Studies, 1973, cited in Robert Whelan, Joseph Kirwan and Paul Haffner, *The Cross and the Rain Forest: A Critique of Radical Green Spirituality* (Acton Institute, 1996).

[26] Stark, *The Victory of Reason*.

[27] Ibid., p. 21.

[28] Ibid., p. 7.

[29] Ibid., p. 10.

[30] Jonathan Sacks, *Tradition in an Untraditional Age* (Valentine Mitchell, 1990), p. 98.

[31] Eliezer Berkovits, *God, Man and History*, ed. David Hazony (Shalem Press, 2004), p, 15.

[32] Ibid., pp. 27–31.

[33] Stark, *The Victory of Reason*, pp. 9–10.

[34] Moses Maimonides, *The Guide for the Perplexed*, 3:54 (bnpublishing.com, 2007).

[35] Lennox, *God's Undertaker*, p. 205.

[36] Gerald L. Schroeder, *The Science of God: The Convergence of Science and Biblical Wisdom* (Broadway Books, 1997), p. 74.

[37] Maimonides, *The Guide for the Perplexed*.

[38] Berkovits, *God, Man and History*, p. 4; Maimonides, *The Guide for the Perplexed*, introduction, also 1:34, 3:51, 3:52.

[39] Andrew Parker, *The Genesis Enigma: Why the Bible Is Scientifically Accurate* (Doubleday, 2009), pp. 201–2.

[40] Nahmanides, *Commentary on Exodus* 25:24 (1250 CE), quoted in Shroeder, *The Science of God*, p. 5.

[41] Maimonides, *The Guide for the Perplexed*.

[42] Peter L. Berger, *The Sacred Canopy: Elements of a Sociological Theory of Religion*, 3rd ed. (Anchor Books, 1990).

[43] Flew, *There Is a God*.

[44] Ibid.

[45] Henri de Lubac, *The Drama of Atheist Humanism* (Ignatius Press, 1985).

[46] Joseph Ratzinger, *Christianity and the Crisis of Cultures* (Ignatius Press, 2006).

Chapter 16: Why Britain Is in the Forefront

[1] Peter Traves, conference at Ruskin College, Oxford, 1991, cited in Melanie Phillips, *All Must Have Prizes* (Little, Brown, 1996).

[2] *Daily Mail*, April 4, 2009.

[3] *British Social Attitudes*, 23rd Report, 2007, cited in *Families in Britain: An Evidence Paper*, Cabinet Office, December 2008.

[4] Mark Chapman, *Anglicanism: A Very Short Introduction* (Oxford University Press, 2006).

[5] UPI, April 9, 2009.

[6] *Gallup Poll Monthly*, May 4, 1995, and March 1, 1995.

[7] Peter L. Berger, *The Sacred Canopy: Elements of a Sociological Theory of Religion*, 3rd ed. (Anchor Books, 1990).

[8] B. G. Worrall, *The Making of the Modern Church*, rev. ed. (SPCK, 1993).

[9] Ibid.

[10] Berger, *The Sacred Canopy*.

[11] Bill McKibben, *The End of Nature* (Random House, 1989).

[12] Sean McDonagh, *The Greening of the Church* (Geoffrey Chapman, 1990).

[13] "A Christian Initiative in British Politics," membership leaflet for Movement for Christian Democracy, undated, cited in Robert Whelan, Joseph Kirwan and Paul Haffner, *The Cross and the Rain Forest: A Critique of Radical Green Spirituality* (Acton Institute, 1996).

[14] Lynn White Jr., "The Historic Roots of Our Ecologic Crisis," *Science*, vol. 155, no. 3767 (March 10, 1967), quoted in *The Cross and the Rain Forest*.

[15] James Nash, *Loving Nature: Ecological Integrity and Christian Responsibility* (Abingdon Press, 1991), quoted in *The Cross and the Rain Forest*.

16 Thomas Berry and Thomas Clarke, *Befriending the Earth: A Theology of Reconciliation between Humans and the Earth* (Twenty-Third Publications, 1991), quoted in *The Cross and the Rain Forest*.

17 Randy England, *The Unicorn in the Sanctuary: The Impact of the New Age on the Catholic Church* (Tan Books, 1991), cited in *The Cross and the Rain Forest*.

18 Rosemary Radford Ruether, *Goddesses and the Divine Feminine* (University of California Press, 2005).

19 *California Catholic Daily*, July 9, 2008, http://www.calcatholic.com/news/newsArticle.aspx?id=ed9c4908-9296-4bb6-a517-4108b7e2bc68

20 9/11 Truth Statement, http://www.911truth.org/article.php?story=20041026093059633

21 Matthew Fox, *Creation Spirituality: Liberating Gifts for the Peoples of the Earth* (HarperCollins, 1991).

22 Matthew Fox, *Original Blessing: A Primer in Creation Spirituality* (Bear & Co., 1983).

23 Matthew Fox, *The Coming of the Cosmic Christ* (HarperOne, 1988).

24 Gordon Lynch, *The New Spirituality: An Introduction to Belief beyond Religion* (I. B. Tauris, 2007).

25 Fox, *The Coming of the Cosmic Christ*.

26 Chapman, *Anglicanism: A Very Short Introduction*.

27 Ibid.

28 Callum G. Brown, *The Death of Christian Britain* (Routledge, 2001).

29 David Holloway, *Church and State in the New Millennium* (HarperCollins, 2000).

30 Professor Paul Merkley, conversation with author.

31 Lord Carey, interview with author.

32 Interview of bishop by author.

33 Matthew Fox, *Confessions: The Making of a Post-Denominational Priest* (HarperCollins, 1996).

34 Roland Howard, *The Rise and Fall of the Nine O'Clock Service* (Mowbray, 1996).

35 *Times*, London, July 1, 2000.

36 *Kindred Spirit* website: http://www.holisticlocal.co.uk/expo/view/kindred_spirit

37 Martin Palmer, *Expository Times*, vol. 106 (1995).

[38] Whelan et al., *The Cross and the Rain Forest*.

[39] Ibid.

[40] Paul Edward Gottfried, *Multiculturalism and the Politics of Guilt: Toward a Secular Theocracy* (University of Missouri Press, 2002).

[41] Ibid.

[42] Rosemary Radford Ruether, *To Change the World: Christology and Cultural Criticism* (Crossroad Publishing, 1989); Chris Glaser, *Come Home: Reclaiming Spirituality and Community as Gay Men and Lesbians* (Harper & Row, 1990), cited in Gottfried, *Multiculturalism and the Politics of Guilt*.

[43] Paul Charles Merkley, *Christian Attitudes towards the State of Israel* (McGill-Queen's University Press, 2001).

[44] *Times*, London, November 1, 2005.

[45] The letter from Muslim leaders to Christians was titled "A Common Word Between Us and You." The reply can be found at the Yale Center for Faith and Culture, "A Christian Response to 'A Common Word Between Us and You,'" http://www.yale.edu/faith/acw/acw.htm

[46] Rowan Williams, *Writing in the Dust: Reflections on 11th September and Its Aftermath* (Hodder & Stoughton, 2002).

[47] Ibid.

[48] Archbishop of Canterbury's address at Al-Azhar al-Sharif, Cairo, September 11, 2004.

Chapter 17: The Revival of Christian Jew-Hatred

[1] Paul Charles Merkley, *Christian Attitudes towards the State of Israel* (McGill-Queen's University Press, 2001).

[2] Anglican Peace and Justice Network 1985–2005: A Report of Its Deliberations in Jerusalem, September 14–22, 2004.

[3] Matthew Davies, "Israeli-Palestinian Peacemaking Central in Anglican Network Report," Episcopal News Service, June 24, 2005, http://www.ecusa.anglican.org/3577_63218_ENG_HTM.htm

[4] Ruth Gledhill, *Times*, London, February 7, 2006.

[5] Ibid.

[6] Stephen Bates, *Guardian*, April 24, 2000.

[7] Matthew Davies, "Israeli-Palestinian Peacemaking Central in Anglican Network Report," Episcopal News Service, June 24, 2005, http://www.cofe.anglican.org/news/pr29cat06.html

[8] Christian Aid, *Losing Ground: Israel, Poverty and the Palestinians*, 2003.

[9] Christian Aid, *Facts on the Ground: The End of the Two-State Solution*, 2004.

[10] "Journey to Jerusalem," Christian Aid, 2009, http://lentpilgrimage.christianaid.org.uk/

[11] Archbishop of Wales, UNA lecture, November 20, 2003.

[12] Church in Wales, press release, November 11, 2004.

[13] *Tablet*, December 9, 2006.

[14] Justus Reid Weiner, "Christians Flee Growing Islamic Fundamentalism in the Holy Land," Jerusalem Issue Briefs, vol. 6, no. 14 (December 6, 2006), Jerusalem Center for Public Affairs.

[15] Margaret Brearley, "The Anglican Church, Jews and British Multiculturalism," Posen Papers in Contemporary Antisemitism, no. 6 (2007), Vidal Sassoon International Center for the Study of Antisemitism, http://sicsa.huji.ac.il/ppbrearley.pdf

[16] Remarks by Kenneth Cragg and David Kerr in *The Road Ahead: A Christian-Muslim Dialogue*, ed. Michael Ipgrave (Church House Publishing, 2002), cited in Brearley, "The Anglican Church, Jews and British Multiculturalism."

[17] Brearley, "The Anglican Church, Jews and British Multiculturalism."

[18] Stephen Bates, *Guardian*, July 1, 2004.

[19] Merkley, *Christian Attitudes towards the State of Israel*.

[20] Donald Wagner, *Anxious for Armageddon* (Herald Press, 1995).

[21] Nahum Sokolow, *History of Zionism, 1600–1918*, with introduction by Lord Balfour (Longmans, Green & Co., 1919).

[22] "Trends in Large U.S. Church Membership from 1960," *Demographia*, http://www.demographia.com/db-religlarge.htm

[23] Barnabas Fund, February 9, 2009, http://www.barnabasfund.org/News/archives/text.php?ID_news_items=439

[24] Ben White, review of Patrick Sookhdeo, *Global Jihad: The Future in the Face of Militant Islam* (2007), on Fulcrum website, http://www.fulcrum-anglican.org.uk/page.cfm?ID=380

25 Ben White, "Non-violent Resistance: A Means, Not the End," *Electronic Intifada*, October 12, 2007, http://electronicintifada.net/v2/article9036.shtml

26 Ben White, "Is It Possible to 'Understand' the Rise in 'Antisemitism'?" *Counterpunch*, June 18, 2002.

27 Jonathan Hoffman, "Lies, Damn Lies and the Apartheid Analogy," *Z Word*, July 8, 2009, http://blog.z-word.com/2009/07/lies-damn-lies-and-the-apartheid-analogy/

28 Merkley, *Christian Attitudes towards the State of Israel.*

29 Ibid.

30 Paul C. Merkley, "What Part Are the Churches Playing in the Present Renewal of Antisemitism?" expanded version of a presentation made to the Global Forum for Combating Antisemitism, Jerusalem, February 24–25, 2008.

31 Presentation to the Global Forum for Combating Antisemitism.

32 Paul Charles Merkley, *American Presidents, Religion, and Israel* (Praeger, 2004), pp. 220–22.

33 Paul Merkley, correspondence with author.

34 Bishop Riah Abu El-Assal, interview by Julia Fisher, January 26, 2002, St. George's Cathedral, Jerusalem.

35 Paul Merkley, personal exchange with author.

36 Andrew White, "Israel and Christian Theology," *The Future of Israel in Jewish-Christian Relations.*

37 Canon Andrew White, Terence Prittie Lecture, 2001.

38 Naim Ateek, *Justice and Only Justice: A Palestinian Theology of Liberation* (Orbis, 1989).

39 Naim Ateek, "The Massacre of the Innocents—A Christmas Reflection," *Cornerstone*, Christmas 2000, http://www.sabeel.org/old/news/newslt20/ateek.htm

40 Naim Ateek, "An Easter Message from Sabeel," Sabeel Center, April 6, 2001, http://www.sabeel.org/old/reports/easter01.htm

41 Naim Ateek, "Who Will Roll Away the Stone," Sabeel Center, February 24, 2001, http://www.sabeel.org/old/conf2001/ateekser.htm

42 Robert Everett and Dexter Van Zile, *Jerusalem Post*, June 24, 2005.

43 Simon Caldwell, Catholic News Service, December 12, 2006.

44 Gary M. Burge, *Who Are God's People in the Middle East? What Christians Are Being Told about Israel and the Palestinians* (Zondervan, 1993).

45 Paul Richard Wilkinson, *For Zion's Sake: Christian Zionism and the Role of John Nelson Darby* (Paternoster, 2007).

46 Colin Chapman, *Whose Promised Land? The Continuing Crisis over Israel and Palestine* (Lion Hudson, 2002).

47 Ibid.

48 Stephen Sizer, "Christian Zionism: Justifying Apartheid in the Name of God," *Churchman*, Summer 2001; also quoted in Wilkinson, *For Zion's Sake*.

49 Stephen Sizer, conversation with author, 2002; see Melanie Phillips, "Christians Who Hate the Jews," *Spectator*, February 16, 2002.

50 "Christian Zionism: Justifying Apartheid in the Name of God."

51 Stephen Sizer, *Christian Zionism: Road-map to Armageddon?* (InterVarsity Press, 2004).

52 Margaret Brearley, "The Anglican Church, Jews and British Multiculturalism," Posen Papers in Contemporary Antisemitism, no. 6 (2007), Vidal Sassoon International Center for the Study of Antisemitism, http://sicsa.huji.ac.il/ppbrearley.pdf

53 Wilkinson, *For Zion's Sake*.

54 References to these links on the *Seismic Shock* blog, http://seismic-shock.blogspot.com/2008/11/christ-church-virginia-waters-stephen.html; reference to Sizer's communication with Martin Webster on Webster's website, http://northwestnationalists.blogspot.com/2008/06/power-of-labour-friends-of-israel.html

55 Wilkinson, *For Zion's Sake*.

56 Cited in ibid., pp. 58–59.

57 Canon Andrew White, interview with author.

58 Lord Carey, interview with author.

59 Text of *Nostra Aetate* in Helga Croner, *Stepping Stones to Further Christian-Jewish Relations: An Unabridged Collection of Christian Documents* (Stimulus Books, 1977).

60 Merkley, *Christian Attitudes towards the State of Israel*.

61 Dexter van Zile, correspondence with author.

Chapter 18: The Disenchantment of Reason

1 Lesslie Newbigin, *The Other Side of 1984* (World Council of Churches, 1984).

2 Ibid.

3 Michael Polanyi, *Personal Knowledge: Towards a Post-Critical Philosophy* (Routledge, 1958).

4 Albert Gore, *Earth in the Balance: Ecology and the Human Spirit* (Houghton Mifflin, 2000).

5 George Weigel, "Is Europe Dying? Notes on a Crisis of Civilizational Morale," History News Network, George Mason University, August 15, 2005, http://hnn.us/articles/12295.html

6 Rocco Buttiglione, "Of God and Men," *Wall Street Journal*, November 10, 2004.

7 Paul Edward Gottfried, *Multiculturalism and the Politics of Guilt: Toward a Secular Theocracy* (University of Missouri Press, 2002).

8 Ibid.

9 Cited in Ibid.

10 Ibid.

11 President Obama's speech at Al-Azhar University, Cairo, June 4, 2009, http://www.nytimes.com/2009/06/04/us/politics/04obama.text.html?_r=2&pagewanted=all

12 Robert Spencer, *Jihad Watch*, June 4, 2009, http://www.jihadwatch.org/archives/026426.php

13 Jonathan Petre, "Uproar over Archbishop's Sharia Law Stance," *Daily Telegraph*, February 8, 2008.

14 Lord Phillips, "Equality Before the Law," speech at the East London Muslim Centre, July 3, 2008, http://www.judiciary.gov.uk/docs/speeches/lcj_equality_before_the_law_030708.pdf

15 Joshua Rozenberg, "Sharia Law Is Spreading as Authority Wanes," *Daily Telegraph*, November 29, 2006.

16 *Guardian*, June 29, 2009.

17 *Times*, London, July 21, 2009.

18 Nidra Poller, "Refugee in His Own Country," *Jerusalem Post*, February 6, 2009.

19 *Pakistan Daily Times*, July 19, 2008.

[20] *UN Watch,* March 11, 2009, http://www.unwatch.org/site/ c.bdKKISNqEmG/b.1289203/apps/s/content.asp?ct=6831061&tr=y &auid=4613715

[21] *Daily Telegraph,* February 12, 2009.

[22] David S. on *Harry's Place* blog, January 8, 2009, 10:58 a.m., http://www.hurryupharry.org/2009/01/08/at-the-israeli-embassy-last-night/#comments

[23] President George W. Bush, press statement, January 10, 2008, http://news.bbc.co.uk/1/hi/world/middle_east/7182041.stm

[24] Dore Gold, *Tower of Babel: How the United Nations Has Fueled Global Chaos* (Crown Forum, 2004).

[25] BBC News, October 15, 2007, http://news.bbc.co.uk/1/hi/world/ middle_east/7044069.stm

[26] Richard Falk, "Slouching Toward a Palestinian Holocaust," *JewishConscience.org,* July 2007, http://www.jewishconscience.org/11.html

[27] George Eliot, *Impressions of Theofrastus Such* (1879), quoted in Bernard Semmel, *George Eliot and the Politics of National Inheritance* (Oxford University Press, 1994).

INDEX